Robert Steele is as consistently fascinating as he is consistently right; his insights on intelligence have always been at least a decade ahead of the establishment.

Ralph Peters, author of
Fighting for the Future: Will America Triumph?

Over a broad canvas reflecting the changing nature of information and information technologies, Robert Steele lays the foundation for the future of e-intelligence.

Commodore Patrick Tyrrell, OBE, Royal Navy

Bosnia, Rwanda, Kosovo, East Timor—genocide has become a feature of the post-Cold War world. Robert Steele's book shows how genocide and other global problems can be effectively monitored without shortchanging traditional national security. This book is invaluable to both humanitarians and national security experts.

John G. Heidenrich, author on genocide prevention

All intelligence services—as well as non-governmental organizations and non-state actors—will benefit from a study of this book. Robert Steele goes well beyond the original visions of the best of the former Directors of Central Intelligence, and has crafted a brilliant, sensible, and honorable future for the intelligence profession.

Major General Oleg Kalugin, KGB (Retired)
Former Elected Deputy to the Russian Parliament

Robert Steele storms into the core of intelligence issues without fear. The scope of his work is impressive and whether you agree with him or not, you cannot ignore what he says. The book is an important addition to the literature on intelligence.

The Honorable Richard Kerr
Former Deputy Director of Central Intelligence

Peter Drucker told us in 1998 that the next information revolution for business will be in the exploitation of *external* information. This book is an essential reference because it defines how government, business, and the academy can finally share intelligence without being tainted by espionage or handicapped by secrecy.

The Honorable John A. Bohn
Former CEO, Moody's Investors Service
Former President, Export-Import Bank

As NATO, its Partnership for Peace and the European Defense and Security Initiative devise new models for meeting their future intelligence needs, this book ought to be considered and discussed. Robert Steele's vision for the future of intelligence is clearly "internationalist" in nature. It focuses on regional partnerships between governmental and non-governmental organizations and on the value of open source intelligence collection. European Institutions should seize the opportunity to be the first to succeed in implementing this new model.

Rear Admiral Dr. Sigurd Hess, German Navy (Retired)
Former Chief of Staff,
Allied Command Baltic Approaches

ON INTELLIGENCE

Spies and Secrecy in an Open World

Robert David Steele

MA, MPA, NWC, CIA, USMC, OSS

OSS International Press
Oakton, Virginia

This book and the others in the series are available at quantity discounts for group or class distribution. Please communicate with the publisher.

OSS International Press is the book publishing arm of Open Source Solutions Inc., publisher of *OSS NOTICES* (occasional series) and *Proceedings of the Global Information Forum* (annual).

Published by OSS International Press (OSS)   October 2001
Post Office Box 369
Oakton, Virginia 22124-0369 USA
(703) 242-1700 Facsimile (703) 242-1711

Printed and bound in the United States of America.

Cover graphic: The view of Africa, Antarctica, the Indian and Atlantic Oceans from 23,000 miles out in space as the last Apollo flight coasted to the moon, December 1972. Original photo credit NASA 1989. Available in sticker form as item Apollo 17(E). Correspond with EarthSeals, Post Office Box 8000, Berkeley, CA 94707 USA..

9 8 7 6 5 4 3 2

LIBRARY OF CONGRESS CATALOGING-IN-PUBLICATION DATA

Steele, Robert D., 1952-
  ON INTELLIGENCE: Spies and Secrecy in an Open World/by Robert David Steele
     p.   cm.
  Includes bibliographical references and index.
  ISBN 0-9715661-0-0 (alk. paper)
  1.   Intelligence service—United States. 2. Intelligence service. 3. Military Intelligence. 4. Law enforcement intelligence. 5. Business intelligence. 6.   Internet. 7.   Organizational change. 8.   Strategic planning. 9. Leadership. 10. Information Technology. 11. Economic forecasting. 12. Business forecasting. 13. Knowledge, theory of. 14. Power (Social sciences). 15. Information science—social aspects. 16. Competition. 17. National security—management of. 18. Political planning.
I.   Title
JK468.I6S74 2000
327.1273—dc21   00-029284

Publisher's Foreword

The attack on the World Trade Center and the Pentagon—as well as the failed attacks on the Capitol and others that were thwarted by the grounding of the entire U.S. aviation fleet—have not yet led to needed intelligence reform. There were six specific failures in intelligence and counterintelligence, and all of them could have been avoided had the political and intelligence leadership of this Nation been willing to listen to the many internal and external advocates for dramatic legislatively-mandated intelligence reform.

1. The clandestine service of the Central Intelligence Agency (CIA) is a decrepit dysfunctional organization that is incapable of penetrating foreign bureaucracies without being caught, and is largely ineffective against terrorist groups. The President is being mis-led about this reality.
2. The field offices of the Federal Bureau of Investigation (FBI) failed to properly enter (to automate) their on-going investigations into flight training and other activities of suspected individuals, and failed to act on French intelligence information the week prior to the attack with respect to the French Algerian terrorist arrested in Boston with Boeing flight manuals and aircraft construction manuals.
3. The leadership of the FBI, both in Washington and in New York, is guilty of gross dereliction of duty in failing to translate all Arabic documents captured in the aftermath of the first bombing attack on the World Trade Center, as well as documents captured elsewhere around the world.
4. The continued fragmentation of the information available to the various agencies is inexcusable. America urgently needs an "all-source" processing center where foreign intelligence, law enforcement intelligence, and other relevant data can be fully integrated. The President must act on this!
5. The Department of State must be held accountable, together with the CIA and the FBI, for issuing visas without proper investigation and validation. We must not issue visas to individuals without a *host country* records check, and we must dramatically improve our ability to track potentially hostile individuals within our own borders.
6. Lastly, we must recognize that all other nations, including those knowingly hosting and funding terrorists, failed to penetrate these groups or to share their knowledge with us. This was an *international* intelligence failure.

Legislatively-mandated reform is vital—without intelligence and counterintelligence reform, America will continue to suffer terrible surprises. See more at <www.oss.net> and <www.council-on-intelligence.org>. *St.*

Foreword

In 1992 I introduced Senate bill 2198, legislation proposed to revitalize and reinforce our national intelligence community—a community that we at the time routinely defined as being *limited* to those specific U.S. Government organizations devoted to *secrets*. This legislation was set aside pending the results of the Aspin/Brown Commission on Intelligence.

Today, after noting that few if any of the major recommendations of the bi-partisan Commission on Intelligence have been implemented, I believe that we must return to a mandated legislative reform initiative for national security. This book is clearly relevant to the national debate that needs to take place on this important topic before such legislation can be developed.

I have always had a special appreciation for "big ideas" that can make a difference. There are a number of such ideas in this book. Whether one agrees with all of them or not is beside the point—America is a great nation because it can absorb many ideas, and from a thoughtful democratic debate, one can hope for progress and reform over time.

The chapter on Presidential Intelligence is especially timely. This is an election year. In January of 2001 a new President will take office. Whether Democrat or Republican, our new President will have an opportunity to take initiatives, in partnership with Congress, to substantially enhance both the capabilities of our existing classified intelligence community, and the emergence of the unclassified "virtual intelligence community" that is defined in this book.

I personally believe that "open source" intelligence will play a far greater role in the years ahead. We are entering a period in which an understanding of broad cultural trends and the movement of public opinion is becoming as essential if not more essential for policy makers than the kinds of military doctrines or codewords that can best be acquired by secret and clandestine methods.

This means that the community must restructure itself in a way that makes it easier to take advantage of the important work done by scholars who do not want to become employees of traditional intelligence agencies. Employees of those agencies themselves urgently need refreshment and stimulation from the outside. As long as there are potential military adversaries and terrorist threats, it is doubtful that *"open source" intelligence* can ever totally replace *secret intelligence*. However, the role of each and the way that they must interact in the future is an extremely important area for thought and discussion. This book advances that discussion, which urgently needs to take place.

I note with appreciation that the author is a graduate of the University of Oklahoma, and an elected member of *Pi Alpha Alpha*, the national honor society for public administration.

President
University of Oklahoma
(Former U.S. Senator and Chairman,
U.S. Senate Select Committee on Intelligence)

Table of Contents

List of Figures

Publications Review Board

CIA's Publications Review Board has reviewed the manuscript for this book to assist the author in eliminating classified information, and poses no security objection to its publication. This review, however, should not be construed as an official release of information, confirmation of accuracy, or an endorsement of the author's views.[1]

---

[1] The Publications Review Board completed its review in less than two weeks, and its recommended changes to the book were entirely reasonable and promptly accepted. The process works and I am very glad to have been able to avail myself of this professional means of ensuring that intelligence reform manuscripts are not inadvertently harmful to national security.

Acknowledgments

There are literally thousands of individuals, from over forty countries, that have enabled me to press forward with the open source revolution in the face of enormous resistance. The five hundred or so speakers at the fifteen conferences I have managed personally, as well as all those attending both my conferences and the several national strategic information conferences organized by various countries, together comprise the open source network that meets at www.oss.net.

A few people merit special mention because of their role in helping me move forward at specific junctures in time, and I am probably forgetful—with apologies—of several others. I list them alphabetically: Mr. Stephen Aftergood; Mr. John Perry Barlow; The Honorable John Bohn; Col Walter J. Breede, III; Madame Judge Danielle Cailloux; Col Alan Campen; Dr. David Charters; Maj Mark Coffin; The Honorable William Colby; Mr. Jack Davis; Dr. Douglas Dearth; Mr. Stevan Dedijer; Mr. Jack Devine; Mr. Arnie Donahue; Mr. William Donnelly; Ms. Mary Eisenhart; Mr. John Fisher; Mr. John Guenther; Mr. Chris Haakon; Ms. Zhi Hamby; Mr. Jan Herring; MajGen Barry Horton; Dr. Loch Johnson; Mr. Roy Jonkers; Dr. Mich Kabay; Mr. Kevin Kelly; The Honorable Dick Kerr; Dr. Michael Leavitt; Mr. Vernon Loeb; Dr. Mark Lowenthal; Col Forest Lucy; Col Earl Madison III; Mr. Winston Maike; Dr. Joseph Markowitz; MajGen John Morrison, Jr.; Ms. Phyllis Provost-McNeil; Mr. Arnie Nachmanoff; Dr. Gary Nelson; Mr. Joseph Paska; Mr. John Pike; Col Nick Pratt; Mr. Howard Rheingold; Mr. Winn Schwartau; Mr. Larry Shand; Mr. Paul Strassmann; Adm William Studeman; Mr. Bruce Sterling; Mr. Boyd Sutton; Mr. Glenn Tenney; Mr. Alvin Toffler; Commodore Patrick Tyrrell; Mr. Michael Valerius; Mr. Paul Wallner; Mr. Tom Will; LtCol Ian Wing; and LtGen C. Norman Wood.

I also wish to express my special thanks to the leadership of the eighteen intelligence communities around the world that brought me in to lecture to significant numbers of their personnel—including their own spies—and to the 5,000 or so folks that chose to join the "virtual intelligence community" at an OSS conference. Finally, I would salute each of the Golden Candle Award winners from 1992 to date. Their individual and organizational efforts are what kept the flame going, both in myself and in the open source movement. They are all listed at the end of this book and are the "behind the lines" heroes of this story.

Preface

All that follows in this book emerged from my experience over a quarter-century as a national intelligence and defense professional, and my subsequent ten-year campaign to help intelligence professionals around the world understand the power of open sources of information. I'm not a librarian touting the library—I am a former spy, someone who has done it all the hard way, stealing secrets hither and yon, who has come late to the realization that both governments and corporations are incredibly ignorant about how to collect and exploit open sources of information to create unclassified intelligence.

My catalytic experience—from 1988 to 1993—involved the expenditure of over $20 million of the taxpayer's funds on the USMC Intelligence Center. Having been a clandestine service officer and having served in three of the four Directorates at the Central Intelligence Agency, I had been accustomed to thinking of myself as a "god"—national intelligence could do no wrong. For the first time in my career, as the senior civilian and *de facto* director of research for our Nation's newest national intelligence production facility, I actually had to respond to the real needs of real customers and I was stunned to discover that most of what they needed was not classified, not available from the Central Intelligence Agency, and not funded by the government: they needed hard facts from open sources of information. From this finding emerged the first international conference on "National Security & National Competitiveness: Open Source Solutions. Fifteen conferences later, ten years and forty countries later, I would say we still have a long way to go. The focus of effort must now be on corporate America and the regular citizen, for only the financial contributors and voters can motivate the next President—and Congress—to do the right thing in this little understood arena.

I dedicate this book to my wife Kathy, who has nurtured our growing family during rough times, over twelve years, so that I might pursue this Holy Grail from a strong home front; and to the international civilian and military professionals (and the very few business intelligence professionals) who practice intelligence and counterintelligence every day in every clime and place. I think of them as very good people trapped in a very bad system. It is a system we can fix. This book outlines how we might create a "virtual intelligence community" that better serves every citizen, our Nation, and ultimately the Whole Earth.

xi

Part I:
From Secrecy to Openness

The secrecy paradigm has lost, the openness paradigm has won! It is (my) position that trying to embargo (knowledge) is a little bit like trying to embargo wind. And this is a fact you are going to have to come to grips with. Digitized information, when you don't have those cubbies and you don't have those bottles to stamp "classified", and to encode, and to file. This stuff (knowledge) is incredibly leaky, it's very volatile, it's almost a living form in the sense that it is self-propagating. I think you have to accept the idea that we are moving into an environment where information—if it is interesting to people— is going to get out. And there is nothing you can do about it. This is not necessarily a bad thing!

John Perry Barlow[1]

Part I contains five chapters and covers the period 1990-1994 during which it became obvious to Congress that our existing national intelligence structure and capabilities were not as effective as the U.S. taxpayer had a right to expect from a $30 billion a year endeavor. The five chapters taken together seek to take both the intelligence professional as well as the external business, academic or media reader along a gradual slope that begins with some high-level criticisms and proposed solutions, peaks with a detailed critical evaluation of the U.S. intelligence community and very specific testimony on the costs of secrecy, and then gently comes down the other slope with emerging concepts and doctrine for a more open intelligence community—one that is fully connected to a larger national information community as well as to a global architecture for more deliberate information-sharing between governmental and non-governmental organizations across national and cultural boundaries.

---

[1] John Perry Barlow, co-founder of the Electronic Frontier Foundation and lyricist to the *Grateful Dead*, speaking at OSS '92, the inaugural open source intelligence conference, to 629 intelligence professionals from over 30 countries.

Chapter 1, "Recasting National Security in a Changing World" introduces the concept of a changed threat environment and the need to study our environment in a multi-dimensional way (i.e. not just the political or military dimensions) and then in this light discusses in detail six general areas where we need substantive improvements in natonal intelligence: 1) meeting the needs of public programs; 2) indications & warning methods for revolutionary change; 3) theory & methods for counterintelligence & operational security; 4) information technology strategy; 5) a requirements system; and 6) resource realignments.

Chapter 2, "Avoiding Strategic Intelligence Failures", expands on the first chapter by discussing in detail the six modern sins of national intelligence: 1) excessive technical collection; 2) inadequate clandestine collection and severely limited open source collection; 3) severe inadequacies in community-wide resource management; 4) mind-set inertia compounded by organizational inertia; 5) lack of acquisition manager accountability for being uninformed about technologies and countermeasures; and 6) no commitment to our people.

Chapter 3, "A Critical Evaluation of U.S. National Intelligence Capabilities" introduces a simple but powerful framework for evaluating the entire national intelligence endeavor based on a three-dimensional matrix that combines the levels of analysis (strategic, operational, technical, tactical) with the four major elements of the intelligence cycle (direction, collection, analysis, and dissemination) with the individual organizations being served—and then grades our performance both in relation to the traditional threats, and in relation to the emerging threats. Detailed comments are provided. Chapter 3 then goes on to discuss some basic definitions, the fundamental differences between intelligence producers and intelligence consumers, and several barriers to useful analysis, none of which are addressed by official or unofficial reform proposals.

Chapter 4, "Testimony on the Need to Reduce & Eliminate Secrecy" both predates and supports the findings of the Commission on Protecting and Reducing Government Secrecy. Detailed insights not available in the public record are provided for the first time.

Chapter 5, "E3I: Ethics, Ecology, Evolution, and Intelligence", is something of a manifesto for the future. It describes an alternative paradigm for national intelligence, one that emphasizes people and openness. Above all, it redefines national security so as to embrace the power of the people to *think*.

Recasting National Security
In a Changing World

I am constantly being asked for a bottom-line defense number. I don't know of any logical way to arrive at such a figure without analyzing the threat; without determining what changes in our strategy should be made in light of the changes in the threat; and then determining what force structure and weapons programs we need to carry out this revised strategy.

Senator Sam Nunn

This chapter will discuss the changing threat in terms of six challenges critical to our over-all national security posture in the early years of the 21st Century. To adapt intelligence to our new threat and fiscal environments, we must make radical and comprehensive changes in how we manage and conceptualize national intelligence.

Our Environment

We find ourselves in a multi-polar and multi-dimensional environment in which a critical distinction must be drawn between the conventional threat and the emerging threat.

This distinction, first articulated by General Alfred M. Gray, then Commandant of the Marine Corps,[1] is straight-forward: the conventional threat is generally associated with a government, conventional or nuclear in nature, represented by static orders of battle, linear in the development and deployment of its capabilities, employed in accordance with well-understood rules of

---

[1] General Alfred M. Gray, Commandant of the Marine Corps, "Global Intelligence Challenges in the 1990's", *American Intelligence Journal* (Winter 1989-1990).

engagement and doctrine, relatively easy to detect in its mobilization, and supported by generally recognizable intelligence assets.

The emerging threat, by contrast, is non-governmental, non-conventional, dynamic or random, non-linear, with no constraints or predictable doctrine, almost impossible to detect in advance, and supported by an unlimited 5th column of criminals and drug addicts.

The conventional threat lends itself very well to conventional intelligence collection capabilities that include a strong ability at stand-off technical collection and a fairly methodical, repetitious and largely bureaucratized way of doing "analysis"; the emerging threats, in sharp contrast, simply cannot be spotted, assessed, fixed, and neutralized by our existing capabilities.

The "war on drugs" and our concern over arms control (not just verification of Russian reductions but also control of nuclear and bio-chemical weapons proliferation in the Third World) are both representative of these new threats.

Narcotics, in both the intelligence and the operational worlds, must be seen as representative of a "type" threat, not as an odious and undesirable distraction from the "real" threat.

The multi-dimensional nature of change in our multi-polar world must also be considered as we evaluate how best to meet these threats.

Political-Legal
Socio-Economic
Ideo-Cultural
Techno-Demographic
Natural-Geographic

Figure 1: Dimensions of Change

Intelligence must be much more than simply political reporting or military Order of Battle "bean counting". Intelligence must be able to identify emerging sources of power and emerging sources of instability in each dimension, and forecast their rate of change.

Our emphasis on the need to modify our "world view" and our definition of what merits attention from our intelligence community in no way reduces the importance of continued attention to the former Soviet Union.

Three areas in particular must be acknowledged:

First, we must continue to monitor the strategic nuclear threat.

Second, intelligence must be capable of monitoring "plans and intentions" of the Russians and other major powers. We must be prepared to identify regression and deception, i.e. selected "overtures" may actually be a *strategic deception*, a means by which a competing great power might enhance its technological depth and gain a competitive edge.

Third and finally, the emerging democracies in Eastern Europe and on-going schisms between the Russians and the largely Islamic states on the periphery of Russia call for much more intelligence on the ground inside of Russia and the adjacent countries, and a much greater sensitivity to the socio-economic, psychological, and cultural factors that were previously overshadowed by the military threat from the Warsaw Pact.

Having established in this way the environment within which intelligence must operate in the 21st Century we can now outline each of the six challenges and what it means for our intelligence structure and the allocation of resources in future years.

Meeting the Needs of Public Programs
Indications & Warning Methods of Revolutionary Change
Theory & Methods for Counterintelligence and Operational Security
Information Technology Strategy
Requirements System
Resource Alignments

Figure 2: Six Areas of Challenge

5

Challenge Number One:
Meeting the Needs of Public Programs

Today there is insufficient emphasis on defining and meeting the intelligence needs of overt civilian agencies, law enforcement activities, and contingency military forces.

This point has major fiscal implications well beyond those of concern to defense force structure managers.

There are two major fiscal strategies that intelligence must support:

First, the strategy of "spending smart" and investing in cheaper peaceful nation-building capabilities as early as possible, rather than waiting for situations to deteriorate to the point that military intervention is required; and

Second, the strategy of fighting a truly "total war" in which we recognize that a failure on our part to be competitive in the international trade and financial markets is tantamount to losing a "real" war.

Selected public programs not necessarily associated with "national security" in fact offer an exceptional return on investment in terms of enhancing our strategic depth at home and our operational positions overseas.

General Alfred M. Gray, former Commandant of the Marine Corps, has emphasized the need for "more and better Third World intelligence...(so) corresponding resource allocations can be appropriately balanced". He has also said, with the emphasis in the original statement:

*If threat is a factor in determining national investments in security assistance and foreign aid, then a more aggressive program of Third World intelligence analysis and forecasting is needed if we are to justify long overdue and underfunded **peaceful preventive measures** in this vital area of concern and potential.*

Warriors pray for peace. General MacArthur made this point with unusual eloquence, and it remains true today. The task of the warrior is made more difficult and costs the nation much more in the lost lives of its sons and daughters as well as simple economic cost if pre-revolutionary conditions are not identified and dealt with through "peaceful preventive measures".

Monitoring corruption associated with our military assistance programs, identifying popular foreign misconceptions about our Nation that should be corrected, and understanding the true and often unarticulated needs of Third World countries are extremely important tasks that intelligence can undertake in defense of our over-all national security.

Intelligence must help us make investment decisions and evaluate our programs, with special emphasis on overt and covert programs focused on "nation-building" and/or the furtherance of our interests.

Challenge Number Two:
Indications & Warning of Revolutionary Change

Our intelligence and foreign affairs communities have demonstrated only a limited understanding of revolutionary change, no methodology for studying the preconditions, precipitants, and actualization of such change, no framework for ensuring that collection and analysis priorities respect the importance of all the dimensions (e.g. religion) within which revolutions can be spawned, and no indications & warning (I&W) capability suitable to this challenge. There are several contributing factors:

Firstly, we have never been comfortable with intangibles, and are even less comfortable with abstract concepts and ideo-cultural meaning. It is far easier to count tanks and compare things that it is to try to understand people, especially people whose entire psycho-social fabric is alien to our own.

Secondly, our planning, programming, and budgeting system (PPBS) perpetuates this tendency. Only very large, obvious, "tangible" threats have in the past been acceptable justifications for major planned investments. All other investments, for instance in the Third World, have generally been *ad hoc* responses to crises, and therefore poorly conceived, coordinated, and effected.

Thirdly, our national skills lean to the technical, and away from the human factor. We have become so enamored of our overhead technical capabilities that we have failed to balance our tremendous signals and imagery intelligence (SIGINT/IMINT) *collection* with a commensurate *processing* ability and have exacerbated that deficiency with a comparative abdication in the arena of human intelligence (HUMINT).

Heavy reliance on foreign intelligence and security services, and officers under official cover, does not constitute a serious clandestine HUMINT capability. Such a capability takes years to develop, and patience, a trait for which we are not noted. Our lack of commitment to strong language programs, longer tours, and non-official cover mechanisms facilitating access to every level and dimension of foreign societies and non-governmental groups will continue to frustrate policy-makers attempting to improve our national capabilities for "low intensity conflict" or countering attacks—including anonymous electronic sabotage or bio-chemical terrorism—from non-state actors.

Lastly, we have paid insufficient attention to open source intelligence (OSINT), and the development of an infrastructure for capturing and exploiting the vast outpouring of print and voice information about the Third World as well as more developed and technically competitive nations such as Germany, Japan, Singapore, and Brazil.

The community has done well in developing a capability for strategic warning of attack by a major governmental nuclear and/or conventional force, largely because of the relatively static and linear manner in which these capabilities are developed, deployed, and prepared for employment.

These facilitating conditions do not hold for the emerging threat. The threat today and onward into the 21st Century is often not clearly associated with a government, it may not come in conventional forms, its bearers are not constrained in any way, and their actions may be dynamic or even random as the frenzy of the moment moves them to action. Their capabilities do not develop in a necessarily linear fashion because they draw their weapons from all sources, including commercial enterprises, and their motivations are not well enough understood to permit any kind of reliable forecasting.

A great deal of work needs to be done in this arena, in terms of both substantive research, and designs as well as methods. Among the approaches that appear to offer some merit are those of cognitive mapping, social network theory, psycho-linguistics, and good old-fashioned listening by experienced

8

diplomats, official representatives, business and academic personnel, and selective agents (in the spy sense) in place.

Even more fundamental is the desperately needed commitment to realign existing and future intelligence resources toward basic analysis (not necessarily production) outside the standard political and military spheres, and in relation to the Third World.

We must take initiatives, not simply defend ourselves. Our methods of I&W should lend themselves to identifying opportunities for advantage as well as opportunities for dealing legal active blows to our present and future opponents. Failure in either area will cost billions over time and will hamper our ability to correct our own vulnerabilities at home.

Challenge Number Three:
New Theory & Methods of Counterintelligence

Closely related to our severely deficient clandestine HUMINT capabilities and our lack of understanding of foreign entities is our virtually complete vulnerability to penetration by representatives of non-governmental groups posing a non-conventional threat to our national security.

We must, quickly and comprehensively, begin addressing the threat posed by individuals seeking our technical secrets for economic warfare; by good individuals involuntarily suborned by criminal organizations, terrorist groups, and religious cults; and by individuals whose motivations we may never fathom, but whose reliability cannot be determined with any assurance by our present system of background investigation.

We need an entirely new theory and practice of counterintelligence (CI) capable of dealing with both the expanded access of representatives of foreign governments, and the more pervasive and subtle threat from a virtually unlimited "5th column" of criminals, narco-terrorists, and cult zealots.

This will require an unprecedented degree of cooperation between national agencies (including financial and economic agencies), private industry (including especially high-tech firms and financial institutions), and law enforcement.

It will require a totally new and comprehensive approach to the management of information about people, an approach that must integrate legal safeguards through the development of artificially intelligent "expert systems" and the partial automation of Inspector General functions.

We must also completely reevaluate what we want to protect, and what we mean by "confidential", "secret", "top secret", and "sensitive compartmented information" (SCI). The system we have today is so fragmented and inconsistent that even the most loyal individuals have difficulty taking it seriously.

Although efforts have been made to address these issues, we simply cannot resolve the contradictions of counterintelligence without an overarching strategy that includes personnel compensation and quality of life issues as well as a comprehensive approach to the management and secure administration of both electronic and hard-copy information across agency boundaries.

We must move quickly to develop an effective means of organizing and "tagging" our electronic records—both within the government and in the private sector where intellectual property now comprises the true heart of national power—with essential information about their source, classification, and control parameters. We must also develop inter-agency methods of electronic sharing that maximize our exploitation of information while affording us much greater automated auditing and alert capabilities essential to the identification of unauthorized or inappropriate diversions of knowledge.

We must carefully redefine both the intellectual and physical properties that we wish to protect, with special reference to both private sector technology and our own national infrastructure (water, power grids, lines of communications, automated financial systems). We should pay particular attention to critical nodes in our infrastructure that if sabotaged or penetrated would render irreparable harm to our gross national production and general security as well as public welfare.

We should be less concerned about the "illegal" export of technology. Advanced information technology applications and capabilities, for instance, are developing so fast that they have usually left the country years before they can be added to the "dual use" list of controlled items. More to the point, information technology (to take one example) evolves so fast that whatever is stolen is out-dated with 6-18 months and off the market within 36 months. We are better off concentrating on staying ahead than on keeping other folks behind.

We must recast our domestic as well as our international security resources to better blend the efforts of those responsible for law enforcement, physical security, background investigations, offensive counterintelligence, and operations. Counter-intelligence cannot be treated as a separate discipline in isolation; it must permeate all aspects of national operations in the same way that "administration" crosses all boundaries, and be migrated to the private sector as well. Our corporations must learn to protect their intellectual property upon which depends the stockholder value and hence our national economy.

"Operational security" (OPSEC) requires much greater emphasis, especially in the counternarcotics arena and particularly in the execution of interdiction operations. We have given the narcotics criminals decades in which to build up billion-dollar war chests and capabilities that in many cases exceed our own at the tactical and operational levels where the confrontations take place. We must be much smarter about how we plan and conduct operations in this environment.

As with I&W, CI must protect the Nation against the massive costs associated with treason and compromise, or with terrorism unleashed on our population and infrastructure. Financial and economic counterintelligence should become a recognized sub-discipline. For the latter to be successful, there must be a closer working relationship between government and the private sector, a willingness on the part of the private sector to identify and correct its areas of vulnerability, and a national recognition that international finance and trade competition is the "second front" of the 21st Century, with drugs and terrorism, the latter with access to weapons of mass destruction, comprising the first front.

Challenge Number Four: Developing a National Information Technology Strategy

We need a national information technology architecture and management infrastructure that integrates telecommunications, computing, and

11

analysis, and consequently enables the full exploitation and integration of data from human, signals, imagery, and open sources.

Our current situation is of our own making. Military service and civilian agency fragmentation has been allowed to continue within a resource-rich environment where inter-operability and inter-changeability of information technologies (and related multi-discipline databases) were not required. The infrastructure within the Department of Defense has at least a modicum of cohesion; the same is not true of the array of law enforcement, civilian government agencies, and private enterprises (including universities), that have had little occasion in the past to require direct electronic connectivity. Now we are discovering that knowledge is indeed power, and that the shorter the loop in exploiting knowledge, the more secure and competitive our Nation.

We must get serious about cybernetics, and exploiting knowledge *in relation* rather than in isolation. This requires the development of a national electronic information and records management architecture that goes far beyond the existing plethora of database management applications and isolated proprietary or domain/agency specific databases. Every traditional function of "hardcopy" records management must be automated and integrated into every organization's knowledge management architecture.

Reliable and tested multi-level security operating systems are critical to our national knowledge management strategy and must be fielded before a serious program of cross-agency and federal to private data sharing and exploitation can be considered. Much greater emphasis at the policy level is required on this topic, for without this capability four of the six challenges cannot be fully addressed. It bears comment that multi-level security may finally enable us to link operators directly to analysts, and break down the "green door" that has isolated intelligence for so long from its consumers.

In addition, it is critical that the Services, agencies, and private industry work closely together to avoid at all costs incompatible interfaces and applications that have in the past restricted the transfer of data between applications and between users. A total commitment by all information vendors to "open systems" is vital to national productivity and competitiveness in the 21st Century.

An important element of this information technology or knowledge management strategy must be a commitment to fund a global program to capture and make available to both government and private industry those essential open source print and voice records necessary to compete in all dimensions of international life. This will enhance private sector competitiveness overall while avoiding the dangers inherent in attempting to provide classified information to selected enterprises.

A basic program to help both government and industry in the open source arena would include measures to digitize newspapers and journals from the Third World countries (and should include technical journals from such countries as Germany and Japan and China); the establishment of a central repository of government-owned open source data bases such as those developed by the Foreign Broadcast Information Service (FBIS); a national program to digitize hard-copy records pertinent to our national interests in the Third World; and the expansion of the Defense Gateway Information System (DGIS) to include management of the latter initiatives.

U.S business overseas can make a significant contribution by assuming responsibility for digitizing open sources in specific countries or technical areas. The data entry problem is so large, only private assumption of this responsibility will permit the national strategy to succeed.

Our demographic trends make an investment in multi-lingual knowledge management tools imperative. The primary way we will be able to improve our national productivity in the 21st Century is with a major national investment strategy focusing on advanced information technologies and automated knowledge exploitation *in relation to real-world content.*

Challenge Number Five:
Establishing a Responsive Requirements System

We need a national intelligence requirements system that is useful in the management of resources (financial, personnel); is cross-disciplinary, automated and "zero-sum"; and is responsive to individual customers by allowing the customer to track the satisfaction of their requirements by country, topic, discipline, and timeframe.

13

There are a number of contributing factors to our continued incapacity in this area, a few of which are being addressed, most of which will take another decade or so to work out.

The greatest problem lies in the complete fragmentation of intelligence management over-all; between disciplines, between major management areas, and between levels and types of organizations, each committed to doing business "its way".

<u>Disciplines</u>
Imagery Intelligence
Signals Intelligence
Human Intelligence
Open Source Intelligence

<u>Decision Areas</u>
Design & Methods
Funding
Collection Management
Production Management
Counterintelligence & Security

<u>Levels of Effort</u>
National
Theater
Departmental
Country Team (Embassies)

Figure 3: Fragmentation of Intelligence Management

We have absolutely no way of evaluating our "return on investment" (ROI) by intelligence discipline or by element of the intelligence cycle or even by agency.

The continued fragmentation of the intelligence community into disciplines with their own "pipelines" for the tasking of subordinate units and the reporting back of information to their headquarters will make serious all-source fusion a virtual impossibility unless, as General Gray has noted elsewhere:

> *Capabilities must be integrated both vertically and horizontally—inter-agency policies and practices must be developed which permit the fusion of information at every hierarchical level, beginning with the Country Team. At the same time, we should avoid the redundant processing of the same information by every agency and service.*

It is vital that the existing requirements system, which includes means of specifying topics of immediate interest to policy-makers as well as priorities for topics of mid-range and longer-term interest, be automated and structured so that all capabilities are working in consonance with one another. While some disciplines are undeniably more effective than others at obtaining particular types of information, they should be managed in unison and at the lowest possible level.

The second greatest difficulty is the absence of a clear consensus within the intelligence community over the purposes of our various requirements documents and processes. Although a document exists to forecast future intelligence requirements and is intended to guide investments in new designs and methods, in fact it is both moribund and nothing more—at this point—than a rehash of the imagery requirements document from which it was born two decades ago.

There is no over-all management of funding trade-offs between disciplines or between elements of the collection cycle. The new Assistant Director of Central Intelligence for Collection simply does not have the programmatic authority—nor even the staff expertise in hand—to make a difference across the disciplines. We still spend too much on technical collection and not enough on clandestine HUMINT or the processing of imagery, signals, and human intelligence. We spend virtually nothing on the single most valuable (and cheapest) source of intelligence, foreign public print and voice media.

Collection and production management continues to be dominated by the owners of the respective disciplinary collection resources, or the owners of the analysts. This is a major reason why we have redundant or unprocessable collection, and redundant production. The community has made some strides in eliminating redundant production but it will not meet with full success until there is a cross-agency, cross-service mechanism for balancing collection versus production and for balancing the needs of the Theater Commanders-in-Chief (CINC) and each Country Team led by an Ambassador, with the needs of national policy-makers and other consumers.

There is another subtle mis-cue built into the system. There is no provision for weighting first-time collection and production requirements over those requirements that may have a higher over-all priority but against which voluminous efforts have been made in the past. As we seek to address ever-changing issues and make our intelligence process more responsive to our needs for new data, this feature must be established.

Lastly, we come to the problem of distinguishing between timeframes for the management of intelligence resources (i.e. one-year, five-year, twenty-year). This is important in each of the decision areas. Although the national policy-makers can certainly impose "emphasis" on the individual disciplines, and get what they want if it is collectable with existing resources, they cannot expect to receive the kind of information for which years are required to develop agents in place, or sophisticated tailored technical devices, or special softwares, without a balanced priorities process that respects the "build-up" period required to collect plans and intentions intelligence as well as strategic and tactical readiness information.

We simply cannot have topics of current interest driving what should be the five-year priorities plan, and no serious twenty-year plan. What should be happening is that current requirements should drive collection and production by existing resources; the five-year plan should drive the reassignment of existing resources and the development of mid-term new capabilities; and the twenty-year plan should be driving the development of completely new designs and methods unconstrained by existing technical collection preconceptions, and without regard to existing "standard operating procedures" including the now clearly misplaced obsession with doing everything *secretly* and only inside government-owned facilities.

It has been my experience that for all the lip-service being paid to the need for a "revolution in intelligence affairs", every agency, and especially the National Reconnaissance Office (NRO) and the National Security Agency (NSA) are bogged down with incremental changes on the margin.

Challenge Number Six:
Realigning Resources in an Era of Change

There is limited experience within our present-day intelligence community in managing declining resources. We also have very little experience at identifying emerging threats. In combination, this leads us to do badly at realigning limited resources to address threats we really do not understand very well. Perhaps of even greater concern, we appear reluctant to establish a flexible process for fulfilling this fundamental requirement. The bitter resistance of both the mainstream military and the intelligence community to such concepts as "low intensity conflict", "special operations" or even the most basic aspects of exploiting "open sources" or providing support to law enforcement, all call into question the suitability of our present intelligence bureaucracy, and portend an era of bureaucratic helplessness and inertia at precisely the time when innovative, flexible, and cooperative efforts are going to be critical to our Nation's security in the 21st Century.

On the positive side, Congress has shown an inclination to direct innovative solutions where it must and where it has not been able to get constructive proposals from the beneficiaries themselves. The negative side of this is that appropriated funds are meaningless if not properly and rapidly obligated, and the budget executed. With the best of intentions, and no resort to such historic gambits as impoundment, the lead agencies can fail to expend funds for lack of strategic planning or programming talent, and for lack of responsive and flexible procurement and accounting capabilities. The 21st Century will be characterized by extremely short resource management cycles in which some initiatives will move from conception to obligation to expenditure in under a year. The "war on drugs" is an ideal opportunity to develop, test, and refine a new process for allocating resources and restructuring capabilities under revolutionary conditions, with special reference to developing new intelligence capabilities for tracking digital financial transactions that occur in massive number every nano-second.

In order for the shortened PPBS cycle to be effective, top-level managers *must* be willing to delegate authority down to the project and program management levels. The execution requirements of manning, training, procurement, facilities and maintenance as well as operations are simply too complex and time consuming to permit top-down micro-management.

17

We must introduce the same "mission type order" to our PPBS process as we expect on the battlefield. We must eliminate as much of the paperwork and documentation as possible, and drastically reduce requirements for top-level approval of lower-level adjustments in organization, equipment, tasks, and production, where these are consistent with the strategic guidance.

In the computer field, the "rapid prototyping" approach has much to offer us as an example, in sharp contrast to the system acquisition and life cycle planning approach that is so detailed and lengthy that the system is obsolete before it gets to the production line.

We urgently need a streamlined budget execution process in which the individual responsible for the mission has full obligational authority over funds earmarked for that mission, e.g. the director of a new intelligence center or a joint task force should be able to establish the grade and skill mix, hire people, buy equipment, contract for external assistance, and make structural changes to assigned facilities without being bound by inappropriate regulations and entrenched preferences of the parent organization's civilian personnel, automated data processing, and other established staff elements whose processes have grown too complex and time-consuming while contributing little of substance. One must stress that this in no way exempts the obligating official from oversight and accountability.

Put another way: if Congress authorizes and appropriates ceiling spaces and funds for a particular activity, the activity director should not then have to fight on a "second front" with his or her own bureaucracy, slugging out each personnel and procurement action through the budget execution....nor should the activity director have to fight on yet a "third front" against departmental and service financial administrators bent on taxing, redirecting, and restricting earmarked funds.

Conclusion

The six challenges facing national intelligence as we enter the 21st Century are all linked together—success in one will serve as a catalyst for success in another, failure in any will stymie success in all. These six challenges together have a direct bearing on the fiscal health of the Nation as well as the soundness of its national security structure as we begin the new millennium.

We must recognize that "warfare" has once again gone through a major redefinition. We must now compete with other nations in the context of a "total peace" in which the tools for peaceful competition are every bit as important to national security as the tools of war. If intelligence does not meet the needs of our "front line", the civilian agencies implementing peaceful preventive measures and enforcing the law, then our defenses will continue to erode, and no amount of investment in "strategic deterrence" and conventional military forces will suffice to keep our Nation safe in the 21st Century.

We must place a great deal more emphasis on understanding all the dimensions of power and change, and especially conditions in the increasingly lethal and volatile Third World.[2] Without an entirely new methodology that affords us indications & warning of revolution change in every dimension, we will continue to be vulnerable to both worst-case bio-chemical and technical terrorism and also less threatening but ultimately more costly losses of initiative in various non-military arenas of competition.

"Intelligence" cannot limit itself to stereotypical perceptions of what is and is not a threat. Intelligence must inform decision-makers about every aspect of human endeavor upon which good order and the prospects for a prosperous future depend. Intelligence must identify emerging sources of power and opportunities for advantage as well as emerging threats.

The other side of this coin is counterintelligence and operational security. An entirely new theory and entirely new methods of counterintelligence are required. We must reassess what it is we want to protect and we must reassess the threat at all levels, to include special emphasis on both domestic and foreign non-governmental actors. We must institute comprehensive new means of coordinating and controlling our law enforcement, intelligence and counterintelligence resources, to include oversight mechanisms and the firm protection of the rights of our citizens. If

---

[2] Despite the number of political, military, economic, and human disasters occurring in the Third World in the closing decade of the 20th Century, as of the first spring of the new century the applicable Presidential Directive continues to relegate all these nations to "lower tier" status for which classified collection and production are without priority.

we do not design and implement this new and comprehensive program, then we will leave at risk our most precious strategic assets: our population, our infrastructure, and our scientific and technical leads.

None of the above three challenges can be met without developing an information technology strategy that is national in scope, comprehensive (integrating telecommunications, computing, and production across government and private industry as well as academic lines), and visionary. We simply cannot afford to perpetuate the continued fragmentation of systems development and continued investments in labor-intensive computer systems that do not optimize the integration of available applications, databases, and human capabilities. We must aggressively pursue means of exploiting all available sources of data, both classified and unclassified.

The establishment of a responsive requirements system within our government, one that acknowledges the importance of open sources and also focuses resources on gaps rather than repetitive collection against the same static interests, is critical to the development of informed national acquisition strategies and the articulation of national interests. If we cannot "shorten our loop" in the acquisition and exploitation of knowledge, we simply will not be able to identify multiple challenges and opportunities within our multi-polar and multidimensional world in time to be effective, in time to prosper as we should.

Lastly, if we are to meet the first five of these challenges, we must develop a process for realigning resources in an era of radical change. We cannot be content with simply "cutting back" across the board or even selectively eliminating specific vertical slices of our national intelligence community. We require a dramatic paradigm shift, one that recognizes that the real "national" intelligence community includes all of the expertise and unclassified information in the private sector. Recognizing new needs, developing new initiatives, and funding research and development beneath the umbrella of this much more powerful perspective, will be critical to our strategic longevity.

Realignments must occur, and occur quickly. We in the national intelligence community should plan on giving up any increase over base, and taking from base a full forty percent—twenty percent to fund new initiatives tailored to emerging threats, and twenty percent for *basic* research and development in critical areas such as artificial intelligence, cognitive mapping, and the general theory of cybernetics. We must also protect the mission and program managers responding to strategic direction from Congress and the President, and buffer them from intermediate authorities seeking to undermine if not destroy new initiatives.

The complexity and lethality of the emerging threats, and the severely constrained fiscal environment within which we must plan for national security in the 21st Century, require vision, energy, a commitment to cross-agency and cross-service cooperation, and an understanding of Third World multi-cultural perspectives, such as we have never been willing or able to muster.

Avoiding Strategic Intelligence Failures

If there is one thing we have learned from this long [Congressional Church Committee] study, it is that we must be very concerned about how human nature works when we clothe people with secret power, particularly with great secret power. If we are not careful, it will almost certainly lead to abuse.

Senator Walter Mondale as cited by Dr. Loch Johnson[1]

I have three concerns that I consider central to ensuring that the restructuring of our intelligence community will be meaningful and successful.

First, we must ask ourselves, what "sins" of strategic intelligence persist in the face of restructuring? As we will see in more depth in chapter twelve, where we draw on a Congressionally-directed summary of past Commission findings, our most important sins appear to have persisted through every single Congressional and Presidential review carried out from the 1940's to date.

Second, how must the nature of the individual intelligence analyst, their working conditions, and their relationship to policy-makers change if we are to avoid strategic intelligence failures in the future?

Third, how must we relate intelligence restructuring within government to a broader national effort to establish a truly *national* knowledge management and information technology strategy, a strategy to empower our enterprises and schools while enabling our government to make informed policy decisions in all areas?

---

[1] *A Season of Inquiry* (University of Kentucky, 1985), page 241.

Six Sins of National Intelligence Today

Here are the major sins I believe we are committing today:[2]

(1) Excessive collection of technical intelligence (including much too much emphasis on repetitive collection against higher priorities instead of baseline collection against lower, e.g. Third World, priorities);

(2) Cursory attention to both open source collection, and the need for a modest and redirected expansion of our clandestine human intelligence collection capability;

(3) Severe shortcomings in control over intelligence resources—those responsible for billions of dollars in each year's budget have no capability to evaluate relative returns on investment across programs or elements of the intelligence cycle, and no adequate mechanisms for ensuring government-owned capabilities are shared and not duplicated.

(4) Mindset inertia—we still have very senior bureaucrats and appointees insisting that we maintain our traditional priorities against Russia and China and a few major economic powers. To be clear on this problem:

(a) It will continue to be difficult for our policy-makers and senior intelligence managers to focus on the need for changed priorities because our intelligence and foreign affairs communities are at least two generations away from fully understanding the Third World and dimensions of change outside the political-military and transnational economic environment (and even in those traditional areas we make huge mistakes of perception and judgment). We do not have an adequate methodology for studying the preconditions and precipitants of revolutionary change, and no indications & warning capability suited to this challenge.

(b) Our entire intelligence structure, our designs and methods, do not lend themselves to being restructured and reconstituted. It is as if, after decades of learning how to build Cadillacs, our single very fine Cadillac, accustomed to traveling the same super-highway back and forth between Moscow and Washington, must suddenly be taken apart and put back together as an off-road

---

[2] This chapter was inspired by Dr. Loch Johnson's seminal work "Seven Sins of Strategic Intelligence", *World Affairs* (Fall 1983). Virtually nothing has changed!

vehicle able to deal with the treacherous terrain and back roads of the Third World. Worse, we don't need just one off-road vehicle, we need several, and a multitude of motorcycles and bicycles as well. We can't get where we need to go with this one relatively "fixed" investment. It is obvious that we not only need to pay much more attention to different designs and methods, but that the fastest way to create our multitude of new vehicles, given our lack of resources, is by melting down and recasting some portions of the existing community in their entirety.

(5) There is a lack of accountability among acquisition managers and the intelligence professionals who support them. We spend billions on complex weapons systems that cannot be supported by existing or planned communications, computer, or intelligence capabilities. This sin also merits elaboration.

(a) Many of our acquisition managers and action officers want nothing to do with classified information—their offices are not cleared to hold what would want to hold; they tend to assume that once the Required Operational Capability (ROC) is approved that the threat ticket has been punched; they don't understand the intelligence community or how to make it work; no one has sponsored them for the appropriate clearances; and they have no process for prioritizing their needs for ongoing threat support to their respective life cycles.

(b) Our concept for providing intelligence support to acquisition is flawed. We tend to focus on the technical lethality aspect of the threat, while ignoring the equally if not more important aspects of tactical reliability, operational availability (and mobility), and strategic sustainability. It makes sense to have capabilities able to deal with worst-case scenarios—it does not make sense to burden expeditionary forces with mainstream conventional weapons systems if cheaper, more mobile, and more easily sustainable alternatives are available.

(6) Finally, our worst sin, a lack of commitment to people. Our grade structure, working conditions, and turnover rates (both job reassignments and resignations) leave us with a largely "un-expert" population whose historical memory is both conventional (what little is in the files) and of short duration. We are not growing the kind of analyst so immersed in their topic that they can *sense* change and underlying analytical trends and anomalies. When someone says "protect the people in the budget" what they really mean is "keep as many low-rent serfs on board as possible". They do *not* mean "nurture our best, give

25

them time and money for travel, training and reflection, protect them from day-to-day 'gotta have an update' calls." Our personnel strategies, some of which seek to keep personnel costs down by having a bulge in the most junior analytical ranks, do not provide the career opportunities needed to keep the best and the brightest focused on analysis for an entire career. We literally drive people away from analysis and toward management or administrative positions for which they are generally not well suited by temperament or training. We compound this sin by failing to provide the analysts we do manage to keep on board with the tools they need to manage the multiple incoming firehose streams of multi-media data and to carry out higher-level analysis tasks including pattern analysis and modeling. In combination, our existing lack of tools, lack of training, and undisciplined production requirements perpetuate the "cut and paste" syndrome. This is all part of a broader national failure, my most fundamental and over-arching concern.

The six sins discussed above come together in our failure to develop a national knowledge management strategy and a related national information technology strategy. We spend too much on classified collection that we cannot process, and not enough on open source information, including foreign scientific and technical literature, that is vital to both our national security and our national economic competitiveness. We have done well at linking a vast array of classified computer databases and capabilities, but at a huge cost in terms of people and maintenance dollars and without significantly improving the individual analyst's access to data. We have failed completely at developing a standard advanced analyst's toolkit (a workstation with integrated applications), and we are therefore wasting tens if not hundreds of millions of dollars *per year* building hundreds of different workstations and local area networks that provide slightly different implementations of the same generic functionality at thousands of sites throughout the world.

In short, we have done nothing to improve the quality of life for our individual analysts, and little to improve their intellectual reach. In a broader context, outside the intelligence arena, we have failed to use federal funds in the knowledge management arena to support, direct, and synergize private outlays in the commercial and academic sectors. Our Nation is significantly behind its potential in exploiting the available knowledge of the world, and the available information technologies. This is a "grand strategy" failure of enormous proportions. Within intelligence, we will continue to have strategic failures so long as we continue to intellectually shackle and starve our diminishing population of analysts by failing to act in the two areas offering very significant

26

returns on investment: the integration of now-operational advanced information processing technologies into a single analysis "toolkit" exportable to any enterprise; and the development of a multi-level and multi-media database architecture that seamlessly merges classified and unclassified data, and extends the analyst's reach to every corner of the globe.

As an aside, let me note my continued support for those initiatives sponsored by the Federal Coordinating Council for Science, Engineering, and Technology ("Grand Challenges: High Performance Computing and Communications") as well as the related "computer superhighway" concepts coming from Congress. Both reflect our national tendency to focus on big problems and technical solutions. Where my emphasis differs from these initiatives, in a complementary way, is in focusing on enabling tools that give large numbers of people access to enormous quantities of unclassified information that can be exploited online—I do not wish to see Congress focus on putting great computer power in the hands of an elite few, while overlooking the very real and often more important intelligence and computing requirements of the average corporate and individual citizen.

What Is To Be Done?

(1) We should adopt David Abshire's idea of an Advisor to the President for Long-Term Planning, but adapt it to encompass both a White House advisor on global strategy and a White House based Director-General of National Intelligence. Working in tandem, these two individuals will devise and champion on behalf of the President a national knowledge management strategy explicitly confirmed by Congress through legislation. I discuss this in more detail in Part III of this book.

(2) We should establish a Senior Inter-Agency Group (SIG) tasked with directing resources toward a global communications and computing architecture that provides multi-level security access (to include foreign nationals with no clearances), integrates multi-media databases worldwide, and establishes a standard advanced analysis "toolkit" that is generic and available to all governments, corporations, and individuals world-wide. This "extranet" will displace the majority of our legacy systems within the U.S. government and eventually other governments. Put more bluntly, we need to recapitalize our national government software capabilities by investing in largely out-sourced solutions that can be shared with corporations and other governments.

(3) We should use the Corporate Information Management (CIM) initiative established within the Department of Defense by Paul Strassmann to begin exploring inter-agency solutions and mechanisms for fully integrating open source and unclassified databases into a global architecture. In particular, we should strive to end the isolation of intelligence information and intelligence analysts from all other government and private sector databases.

(4) We should establish some means of integrating the National Technical Information Service (NTIS), the Defense Technical Information Center (DTIC), the Foreign Broadcast Information Service (FBIS), the restored Joint Publications Research Service (JPRS), and the Federal Research Division (FRD) of the Library of Congress, while creating a new joint government-business Center for the Exploitation of Open Sources (CEOS). I address this in more detail in Part III. Such a national investment could be fruitfully directed to:

(a) Engage in "competitive analysis", using only open sources, as a means of challenging the assumptions of the remainder of the intelligence community regarding the value of extremely expensive and fragmentary classified sources;

(b) Emphasize direct support to national and private sector research endeavors, with a view to stimulating and reinforcing business and academic research and development in all domains, with a special expertise in finding and putting online key foreign language and foreign area information;

(5) We should establish an Open Source Committee, under the Assistant Director of Central Intelligence for Collection, to serve as a focal point for intelligence community collection and processing of open source information (including commercial multi-spectral imagery, public signals, unclassified documentation, and open debriefings and interviews). We can utilize military personnel and capabilities in peacetime to "jump start" the open source process—this will help the military because many of the Third World intelligence gaps stemming from our obsession with the former Soviet Union can be filled relatively quickly through systematic legal and overt access to foreign information, and it is the military that most often must execute unplanned contingencies in Third World countries for which we do not have adequate classified information or even the most basic maps.

(6) We should reorganize the U.S. Intelligence Community to provide our Nation with four distinct capabilities:

(a) a national intelligence analysis capability with numerous inter-agency collection management and analysis centers organized along the lines of the existing centers focused on special topics;

(b) a clandestine operations capability with its own communications and computing capabilities but integrating tactical SIGINT, necessary technical support, and a new separate Office for Military Contingencies manned jointly by military and civilian personnel;

(c) a national technical intelligence capability to manage overhead technical collection systems; and finally

(d) a national intelligence research & development capability under a new Director-General for Research & Development based in the White House, with an Assistant Director of Central Intelligence for Research & Development responsible for consolidating and managing the now fragmented intelligence R&D efforts scattered among the different services and agencies.

Conclusion

Knowledge is power. Technology has broken down the walls that previously required vast technical and human endeavors to isolate nationally vital information about plans, intentions, and capabilities. At the same time, the vast outpouring of multi-media multi-lingual knowledge has presented us with an enormous technical and intellectual challenge, one worthy of the same kind of national attention occasioned by the Sputnik launch, or past energy crises.

There is still a role for clandestine human collection and covert technical collection, but it must be more tightly focused. Our emphasis must shift: from collection to analysis; from indiscriminate collection to integrated processing; from analysts as assembly-line producers chained to their desks to analysts as observers and partners in the national decision-making process—not making policy, but informing policy.

Finally, we must shift away from a strategy of producing highly classified compendiums of information for a few select customers, and toward maximizing public access to basic knowledge in all areas of endeavor.

The sins of intelligence will always be with us in one form or another; restructuring will cure some ills and bring on others. Our greatest challenge continues to be one of strategic vision—if we can change the way we view analysts and their role in the daily decision-making process; if we can adopt a national knowledge management strategy that accelerates our integration of national communications and computing systems; and if we can address the open source challenge, then we will have accomplished a far more fundamental and constructive restructuring of our community. We will have applied a new paradigm.

A Critical Evaluation of U.S. National Intelligence Capabilities

Adversarial relationships exist between CIA, the Department of State, and the military. First Hoover Commission, 1949

There is a general failure in communication, coordination, and overall planning. Taylor Commission, 1961

There has been a rise in ... size and cost [with the] apparent inability to achieve a commensurate improvement in the scope and overall quality... Schlesinger Commission, 1971

State must improve overt collection of economic and political data. Church Committee, 1976

Over 85 percent of the intelligence budget is executed by agencies not under the DCI's control. He exercises no line authority over ... agencies other than the CIA and has little recourse when these agencies choose to ignore [him]. Aspin/Brown Commission, 1996

From their inception, the intelligence capabilities created by the *National Security Act of 1947* have been subject to on-going criticism.

Today, at the beginning of the 21st Century, United States national and defense intelligence capabilities, while strong in many respects, are unbalanced because of their excessive emphasis on technical collection combined with inadequate human and open source collection. They are completely unsuited for and constrained in analysis and dissemination. Also unbalanced are their direction and responsiveness to the full gamut of consumers of intelligence across all the departments of government and at all levels: strategic, theater, tactical, and technical.

As the same time, how the U.S. "does" intelligence is fundamentally flawed. One the one hand, intelligence professionals keep their consumers at arm's length. In fact, the intelligence community itself long ago decided which consumers would have the "privilege" of being supported. On the other hand, the intelligence community has completely ignored the flood of unclassified information reaching the consumer, arrogantly assuming that the consumer would pay greater heed to its classified "nuggets". This aloof attitude has led consumers to rely far more on the 90 percent of their information that is unclassified and unanalyzed.

Part I: Getting It Right—"A Bird's Eye View"

Some restructuring has been is underway (beginning in 1993), responding to both the lessons learned from the Gulf War and to mandates from Congress inspired by severe fiscal constraints. There has also been a sense that all is not well with national intelligence support to military operations and with certain aspects of defense intelligence. The immediate future offers a unique opportunity for reflection, revitalization, and *serious intelligence reform*.

In evaluating the degree to which the intelligence community as a whole may need realignments and redirection, the focus here is on the four levels of executive action: strategic, operational, tactical, and technical. Four major areas of intelligence endeavor may be distinguished irrespective of discipline: direction, collection, analysis, and dissemination. This matrix may be applied to every executive department and its relationship to the intelligence community, in this way creating a Rubic's Cube of green, yellow, and red performance indicators, or "best guess" grades.

The intelligence community is not doing well at all in relation to six non-traditional consumers of intelligence at the federal level, the departments of Agriculture, Commerce, Education, Energy, Interior, and Justice. Treasury is in transition. We are barely adequate for the obvious needs of Defense and State. Even though the intelligence community is guided by Presidential priorities, a deepening of the consumer base would now appear warranted, and this chapter strives to address shortcomings in a manner that will highlight needed improvements.

Figure 4 illustrates a gross evaluation of how the United States is doing now against the old threat and (in parenthesis) the emerging Third World non-conventional threats including non-military threats and circumstances. Naturally these grades could be argued by anyone, but I feel that these crude evaluations are both useful and informed, and serve as a foundation for reflection.

	Direction	Collection	Analysis	Dissemination
Strategic Level	C (D)	B (C)	C (F)	D (F)
Operational Level	C (D)	D (F)	B (C)	B (C)
Tactical Level	D (F)	C (D)	D (F)	D (F)
Technical Level	B (C)	B (C)	C (D)	B (D)

Figure 4: Intelligence Performance Evaluation Matrix

The top mark in each box is the grade for how the U.S. is doing against conventional (e.g. Russian) targets of interest to the traditional consumers of intelligence. The lower mark, in parenthesis, is the grade for how the U.S. is doing and is likely to do in the absence of major reform, against non-traditional targets (e.g. global environmental and energy targets, non-proliferation, potential epidemic disease, demographic trends) of concern both to the President in this much more complex global environment, and to the non-traditional consumers of intelligence including law enforcement and commerce.

At the strategic level, we need to be most concerned with the analysis of unconventional threats and opportunities.

At the operational level, the concern should be with the United States' lack of an effective system for monitoring stability in close coordination with the Country Teams and with an eye for non-military problems. This is particularly important because the multitude of influences causing regional instability are generally non-military and often cloaked in cultural intangibles that U.S. intelligence analysts are simply incapable of "computing".

At the tactical level, the United States is unprepared to effectively collect information on and understand three of the four warrior classes that it is facing today. The four warrior classes are:

(1) The High-Tech Brutes similar to the United States—those relying on expensive technical capabilities and huge logistics trains.

(2) The Low-Tech Brutes such as narcotics traffickers and terrorists—those presenting the "needle in the haystack" problem.

(3) The Low-Tech Seers, such as the Islamic Fundamentalists or cults that rely on cultural and religious power that is difficult for a Western analyst to understand.

(4) The High-Tech Seers, such as highly-skilled computer engineers or criminal "hackers" who are able to penetrate the most advanced communications, computing, financial, and power systems with any of several motives: economic espionage, individual theft, information warfare attack, or terrorism, or simple electronic vandalism.

The United States has spent forty years building command, control, communications, computer and intelligence (C4I) systems designed to wage battle with the High-Tech Brutes. These largely static capabilities (the theater headquarters and the North Atlantic Treaty Organization's C4I architectures come to mind) are relatively useless in confronting the other three warrior classes, or environmental disasters requiring close collaboration and the sharing of "intelligence" with coalition military partners that do not have classified information clearances or even equipment, and non-governmental organizations that eschew any suggestion that they are privy to secrets or spying.

At the technical level, the United States still does not offer the policymaker responsible for acquisition decisions a basis for evaluating the true utility, sustainability costs, and return on investment for major systems. Most major systems are not only geared to fighting the high-tech warrior class and are completely unsuited for fighting the other three warrior classes, but most systems have also been designed without regard to strategic generalizations bearing on their value: seventy-ton tanks that cannot be off-loaded in half the countries we expect to go to, and then even if off-loaded, exceed the average bridge loading capability of thirty tons by a full forty tons again!

Most intelligence products are limited to specific topics, weapons systems, and countries, and are couched in terms of the target, not in terms of the decision requiring support. In one instance, as the senior civilian at the Marine Corps Intelligence Center, I was unable to persuade my uniformed colleagues that we should be producing annual unclassified reports for each mission area (e.g. artillery). These would have informed the General Officer responsible for each respective mission area of the regional averages (gun size, prime mover weight, special ammunition, general ranges as achieved in exercises rather than as claimed by the manufacturers) as well as environmental constraints such as cross-country mobility and bridge loading data. With such reports, received on an annual basis, these General Officers would have been far better equipped to consider (and often reject) proposals from the arms industry for "bigger and better bangs" that are neither affordable in the long run, nor supportable in the expeditionary environment—a real world context almost always absent from both U.S. intelligence products, and U.S. defense acquisition decision-making.

The United States is also not ready to provide near-real-time technical intelligence support and *ad hoc* countermeasures in a computer warfare environment. Its scientific and technical intelligence capabilities are static, based in large centers within the United States, and organized for long-term analysis of conventional weapons systems that develop linearly over time, can be stolen, and can be studied through "hands-on" examination in a laboratory. The U.S. is completely incapable of routinely providing rapid tactical assessments of a technical threat buried in cyberspace, and of quickly developing tactical countermeasures.

As the U.S. Intelligence Community evaluates foreign threats, four major and quite distinct consumer groups for intelligence must be kept in mind—distinctions that do not exist today in intelligence community production planning:

(1) Departmental planners and programmers, who require both strategic generalizations (rather than a flood of detailed reports about tiny parts

35

of many problems), and political-military information heavily laden with informed judgments about future plans and intentions.

(2) Regional theater planners and programmers, who require regionally-applicable generalizations, and very detailed mobility information. The U.S. Country Teams (the Embassies) are not well integrated into the regional planning process. Civilian disasters and disorder, which could have been anticipated and addressed with civilian programs, often are allowed to emerge unchecked for lack of "action-inducing" intelligence, to the point that military action is required. Since the military did not budget for these unplanned contingency operations, the military budget is routinely turned inside out as the various services are then "taxed" to pay for operations that could have been avoided.

(3) Tactical commanders require both "vanilla" orders of battle that can be shared with troops that do not have clearances, and in-depth understanding of the sustainability, availability, reliability, and lethality of specific weapons systems. Tactical commanders, and the theater commanders that give them direction, also require maps with contour lines. This may well be the single greatest intelligence deficiency impacting on U.S. policymaking and operational readiness. Of the 67 countries and two island groups of interest to the Marine Corps in 1988, there were no (zero) 1:50,000 tactical maps for 22 of the countries; and very *old* maps for the cities and ports *only* for an additional 37 (i.e. not reflecting roads and airfields built in the last two decades, and not covering the maneuver areas from the sea to the capitals). For the 10 countries that were comprehensively covered, such as North Korea and Cuba, the maps were very out-dated.[1] The smartest thing I ever heard a Marine Corps intelligence officer say to a senior group was: "I don't care how much order of battle data you give me, if I cannot plot it on a map it is useless to me."[2]

---

[1] As documented in Marine Corps Intelligence Center, *Overview of Planning and Programming Factors for Expeditionary Operations in the Third World* (Marine Corps Combat Development Command, March 1990).

[2] Col Bruce Brunn, USMC, then Director of the Marine Corps Intelligence Center, speaking to the Council of Defense Intelligence Producers at their 1992 meeting. There has been no significant reduction in our tactical mapping shortfalls since then because the National Imagery and Mapping Agency (NIMA) and its "big brother" the National Reconnaissance Office (NRO) have refused for a decade to acknowledge the value of commercial imagery from foreign providers.

(4)   Acquisition program managers and their system designers are required to have some variation of a System Technical Assessment Report (STAR) but three concerns remain unanswered today:

(a)   No intelligence process exists to support policy-level decisions about whether a system is really needed in terms of cost-benefit analysis (including likelihood of utilization), existing (often foreign built) alternatives, or sustainability and supportability in relation to amphibious shipping or logistics.

(b)   No process exists to assure that expensive and technically complex systems are supportable by command and control, communications, computing, and intelligence systems. For instance, fast-moving aircraft with limited loiter times and precision missiles do not have the "sensor to shooter" framework (or the digital mapping baseline) to be effective in 90% of the world.

(c)   Severe deficiencies exist in the United States's ability to introduce updated information into the systems design and acquisition process.

Evaluation of Strategic Intelligence Capabilities

A persistent problem at the strategic level, illustrated in Figure 5, is the overemphasis on the "top 100" policymakers in the traditional national security arena, and a consequent lack of attention to the needs of the action officers who actually formulate the strategic plans, recommend programmatic actions, and identify opportunities for advantage. Also, because of a focus on the "inside the beltway" group, American doctrinal, architectural, and technical capabilities for secondary dissemination of multi-media intelligence have not been satisfactory. Even today, as the World-Wide-Web explodes around us, the U.S. intelligence community persists in spending billions on a variety of internal Top Secret and Codeword (beyond Top Secret several times over) "intranets" while ignoring the enormous opportunities and needs represented by the combination of the Web and the need to exchange information with coalition partners and non-governmental organizations that will *never, ever* join a U.S. owned classified information architecture.

37

STRATEGIC LEVEL

Direction.   No tracking system for consumer satisfaction, no automated integrated multi-discipline requirements database, non-traditional consumers not well represented.

Collection.   Superb but ossified capability with limited utility against emerging threats.

Analysis.   Cut-and-paste community consisting of the "green and the gray"—the new and the old with the middle having quit long ago—most with no idea of life overseas and no foreign area or foreign language skills.

Dissemination.   Cumbersome compendiums of limited utility to day-to-day decisions, laboriously created over time and very very classified, a bore to read and often too much (security) trouble to bother getting.

Figure 5: Strategic Level Intelligence Deficiencies

Evaluation of Operational Intelligence Capabilities

U.S. operational deficiencies, shown in Figure 6, have existed for so long under the premise that the Soviet Union was *the* main enemy that, even in theaters far removed from the Soviet Union and focused instead on the Third World, the United States has paid little attention to developing encyclopedic intelligence for campaigns and contingencies.

Many of these Third World nations have glaring disaster problems—environmental, medical and demographic—as well as problems of their own making such as genocidal and mass atrocity programs and massive corruption—that require much more deliberate intelligence collection and analysis than is now the case.

OPERATIONAL LEVEL

Direction. Self-imposed over-emphasis on "worst case" threats continues, with a complete lack of focus on such basics as Third World mapping or Third World communications intelligence.

Collection. Virtually no support for human contingency requirements, limited low intensity conflict indications & warning capability. No real access to indigenous foreign-language open source information.

Analysis. Highly motivated and responsive analysts in the joint intelligence centers.

Dissemination. Excellent dissemination from national to theater headquarters level, very poor capability to support theater (forward), Joint Task Force commanders, or Country Team members.

Figure 6: Operational Level Intelligence Deficiencies

In addition to a lack of encyclopedic intelligence (most of which should be unclassified) there is a very limited capability to deal with these pressing issues, in part because of a severe shortage of analysts who are fluent in Third World languages. The likelihood that U.S. analysts might actually have *lived* in the country they puport to understand is very remote.

Finally, the United States is severely deficient in the day-to-day communications, computing, connectivity, conferencing, and intelligence sharing—in relation to unclassified as well as the classified topics—among theaters, country teams, parent agencies and services at home, coalition partners abroad, and non-governmental organizations. The United States never learns from the recurring experiences it has every time it does a humanitarian relief mission. In Bangladesh LtGen Harry Stackpole, commander of the Joint Task Force responsible for the Sea Angel relief effort, found that his C4I system, designed for tactical military communications in a combat situation, was not at all suited to interagency coordination requirements including, of all things, interactive unclassified voice communications (the telephone!). He could not communicate well with foreign military, foreign government, and international relief organizations.[3] Finally, when LtGen Stackpole asked his intelligence officer for information about disaster conditions, the officer (from another service, this being a joint task force) said, as recounted within Headquarters U.S. Marine Corps circles, "General, we only do threat intelligence." A new J-2 was soon found but the problem persists today.

Evaluation of Tactical Intelligence Capabilities

During the war in Southwest Asia (the "Gulf War") the U.S. service intelligence centers, notably the Army's Intelligence and Threat Analysis Center (now folded into the National Ground Intelligence Center) performed heroically.

However, although improvements have been underway since the Gulf War concluded, including a transition to digital backbones, the U.S. is not yet ready for global joint interoperable intelligence nor for combined and humanitarian operations. At the tactical level our personnel are simply not trained, equipped, or organized for coalition operations or operations other than war (OOTW). This is particularly true with respect to the communication and computing of tactical intelligence.

Figure 7 summarizes our deficiencies in tactical intelligence capabilities.

---

[3] US. theater commands have either a regional focus (such as the Pacific or Central Commands) or a functional focus (such as the Transportation or Special Operations Commands). Country Teams are the Embassy principals representing the major functional agencies (State, Defense, Commerce, Customs, others) in each country where an official U.S. presence is maintained. Parent agencies, themselves fragmented into smaller fiefdoms, constitute the third part of the U.S. coordination triangle. If we add to this C4I tar pit the regional coalition partners, international relief organizations, and the host country government and private sector parties with whom coordination is necessary "from the sea", the inadequacies of our highly structured and narrowly focused communications and computing environment become easily apparent.

TACTICAL LEVEL

Direction. From whom? How? At the mercy of national capabilities not designed to support the tactical commander, with a theater staff between the tactical units and the national organizations.

Collection. Adequate organic capabilities with the exception of wide-area imagery surveillance; ground reconnaissance skills (basic patrolling, adequate numbers of remote ground sensors) appear to very weak; completely inadequate prisoner handling and interrogation capabilities.

Analysis. Mixed bag, with personnel generally consumed by volumes of traffic and additional duties—they are overloaded with raw *classified* data and have very mediocre hardware and software.

Dissemination. Secondary imagery dissemination problems will be fixed eventually but the lack of a realistic communications architecture to support multi-media intelligence broadcasts as well as digital mapping data suggest this will be a showstopper for some time to come. Vulnerability to high energy radio frequency and other information warfare techniques will persist.

Figure 7: Tactical Level Intelligence Deficiencies

Evaluation of Technical Intelligence Capabilities

The 21st Century will require that our policymakers and commanders pay much greater attention to two major fundamental deficiencies in technical intelligence: sources and methods.

TECHNICAL LEVEL

Direction. The mechanisms are well-established and the scientific and technical analysts know how to get what they want but they do not always ask the right question.

Collection. Very good against denied areas, less so against emerging technical powers, our present-day allies, and non-governmental groups.

Analysis. Too much emphasis on technical countermeasures and single system threat assessments. Virtually no strategic generalizations to support cost savings in major acquisition areas.

Dissemination. Adequate because consumers today occupy fixed sites within the U.S. Not ready for "tactical technical" intelligence.

Figure 8: Technical Level Intelligence Deficiencies

Open sources, although somewhat more available to the technical analysts than to any other group of intelligence producers, remain a virtually untapped resource of enormous potential, while also being extremely cheap.[4] Perhaps of greater concern to us, however, should be the fact that our unconventional opponents, including terrorists and criminals, have learned how to use open sources against us.

As various Third World nations and present-day allies choose in the future to confront the U.S. over selected issues, the U.S. deficiency in open source exploitation will be recognized—a decade too late—as critical. This

---

[4] As this book goes to press I am informed that funding for open source collection, already judged by the Aspin/Brown Commission to be "severely deficient", is being actively reduced in both the science & technology collection arena sponsored by elements of the Department of Defense, and in media monitoring as sponsored by the Central Intelligence Agency. There are some good initiatives within the CIA, for Global Coverage and other experiments, but on balance OSINT has yet to find a home.

deficiency cannot be corrected without a broad partnership between the government and the private sector. Once corrected, significant dividends will be reaped in terms of elevating our national science & technology baseline with a consequent enhancement of our national competitiveness.

Current U.S. technical intelligence methods, in contrast to our naïve and shallow approach to open source collection, emphasize highly sophisticated modeling and simulation techniques, and pay very heavy attention to technical countermeasures issues. They have almost completely excluded intelligence about operational geography and civil properties (road networks, hospitals, airfields) of the utmost importance in determining the general utility, reliability, mobility, and sustainability of U.S. systems across a range of countries, not just a single country (such as Germany where the "worst case" threat and benign terrain are assumed).

In a declining fiscal environment, when the external threat itself is changing rapidly, there is no finer or more important means of responsibly reducing acquisition costs than by modifying technical analysis methods. The goal is to develop intelligence supportive of more meaningful selective procurement, and the surgical employment of U.S. capabilities.

Conclusion to the Bird's Eye View

Radically altering the relationship between the analyst and the consumer by substituting the concept of distributed analysis for that of distributed production is important, as is including the analyst as a member of the policy team—not to make policy, but to inform policy at every turn of the policy discussion leading to a decision.

Restructuring attempts, from the Hoover Commissions in the 1940's to the Schlesinger Commission in 1971 to the Aspin/Brown Commission in 1996 have all been abysmal failures—despite their brilliant and correct findings—for two simple reasons:

(1) Only the President has the programmatic authority to make substantive reform in a community where the Director of Central Intelligence controls less than 15% of the resources and the Secretary of Defense does not care about the 85% of the resources controlled by his office but actually left

"out of control". Unfortunately, only four Presidents in our *history* have understood intelligence—Washington, Eisenhower, Kennedy, and Bush—and no President has ever confronted the combination of circumstances that face us as we enter the 21ˢᵗ Century. Both President Clinton and Vice President Gore have studiously avoided any oversight of the intelligence community and any discussion of the role of a revitalized community in nurturing a "smart Nation" that is able to apply the *distributed* intelligence of all sectors. This has been a serious mistake spanning eight years, and it has seriously undermined our readiness for understanding 21ˢᵗ Century challenges.

(2) The elements of the U.S. Intelligence Community do not want to change. They have been bureacraticized to the point that they are literally unable to comprehend the external world—especially the world of open sources and methods—and they are so locked into legacy programs and legacy investments in expensive but now inappropriate collection systems—that they must, like someone suffering from a very debilitating disease, be subject to externally-guided remedies. Only Congress has the power to pass legislation, a *National Security Act of 2001*, and only the next President has the power to make this a priority for his Administration. The intelligence community has never come to grips with the fundamental question about its purpose: is it in the business of producing "secrets"? Or is it in the business of informing policy? In my view, the intelligence community is a vital part of a larger national information continuum that runs "from school house to White House" and includes universities, libraries, businesses, non-profit centers, and individual citizen experts, "intelligence minutemen".[5]

The next Vice President should be tasked by the President with being the Chief Information Officer (CIO) of the Nation, and should be charged with the task of fully implementing a variety of intelligence and information reforms, many outlined in this book, and others worthy of consideration in the books by my reformist colleagues.[6]

---

[5] Alessandro Politi, today advisor to the Minister of Defense of Italy, is one for Europe's foremost strategists on intelligence reform, and coined this phrase— "intelligence minuteman"—when attending the first international conference on open source intelligence in 1992.

[6] The following three books are recommended: Greg Treverton, *Reshaping Intelligence for an Age of Information* (Cambridge University Press, 2000); Bruce Berkowitz and Allen E. Goodman, *Best Truth: Intelligence in the Information Age* (Yale University

I said this in 1993 and I have continued to document the case since then: we need a minimum of $1 billion a year in taxpayer funds to be earmarked for a national open source collection and exploitation program that will have three immediate dividends:

(1) It will overcome the "severe deficiencies" in open source access that the Aspin/Brown Commission highlighted in its report as being detrimental to the competency of the U.S. Intelligence Community. This is especially important because history, context, tip-off, and much of what we need in the way of current intelligence about foreign events is not classified and must be fully integrated into the intelligence process.

(2) It will revitalize the ability of the departments of government to collect and analyze their own open sources. As the Aspin/Brown Commission was careful to note, those intelligence requirements that can be answered predominantly by open sources of information should *not* be referred to nor accepted by the U.S. Intelligence Community for action.

(3) Finally, but in the long-run most importantly, such an investment will be the foundation for creating and nurturing a new national intelligence community that truly is able to harness, not only the distributed intelligence of the Nation, but the distributed intelligence of the Whole Earth. It will be the catalyst for finally moving toward Tielhard de Chardin's vision, toward H.G. Well's vision, toward my own vision of an integrated world brain that helps avoid and resolve conflict while also optimizing global resource management and global prosperity.[7]

Press, 2000); and Craig Eisendrath (Ed.), *National Insecurity: U.S. Intelligence After the Cold War* (Temple University Press, 2000). Earlier official reformist studies whose ideas merit continued consideration are summarized in the first chapter of Part III, my bottom-up review of intelligence and counterintelligence that proposes detailed financial realignments.

[7] There are a number of reference materials that touch on this vision. Four merit mention here: Teilhard de Chardin, *The Phenomenon of Man* (Harper, 1959); H. G. Wells, *World Brain* (Adamantine, 1994); Hans Swegen, *The Global Mind: The Ultimate Information Process* (Minerva, 1995); and Edward O. Wilson, *Consilience: The Unity of Knowledge* (Alfred A. Knopf, 1998).

Part II: How the U.S. "Does" Intelligence

Any executive or legislative action to improve national and defense intelligence must address not only authority and organization, but also *perspectives* and *objectives*. Only then will the United States be able to accommodate the changed nature of the threat, the changed fiscal environment, and the changed external information environment.

The Basics of Intelligence Analysis

Before considering "intelligence" and its purposes in some greater detail, it is helpful to absorb some basic definitions developed by Jack Davis, one of the grand masters of analysis.

INTELLIGENCE ANALYSIS: The process of producing written and oral assessments designed to improve the policymaking process by helping officials better understand and deal more effectively with current and prospective national security issues, including opportunities as well as threats to U.S. interests.

ESTIMATING: The means by which intelligence professionals address aspects of national security issues that cannot be known with full confidence and thus require conditional judgments, interpretation of evidence, and inference.

INTELLIGENCE SUCCESS: Support to the policymaking process that has the potential to assist policy officials to avoid or mitigate the damage of threat to U.S. interests and to enhance the gain from opportunities: that is, assessments that are timely, insightful, relevant, and attention-demanding.

INTELLIGENCE FAILURE: The inadequate preparation of policymakers for an important threat to or opportunity for U.S. interests, because of the absence of timely and attention-demanding assessments or the presentation of flawed assessments.

Figure 9: Basic Intelligence Terminology

Davis, a recently retired member of the Senior Intelligence Service (SIS) within the Central Intelligence Agency, created both the "Intelligence Successes and Failures" course at CIA, and also the forerunner of the Harvard Executive Program's "Intelligence Policy Seminar". His capstone document, *A Compendium of Analytic Tradecraft Notes* (CIA, February 1997), stands alone.

What is remarkable about these definitions, apart from their common sense, is the fact that they are not well understood nor often honored by the vast majority of all U.S. intelligence collection and production managers and working-level personnel.

Davis is unusual for his emphasis on opportunities as well as threats, on the importance of timeliness not just accuracy, and on the vital aspects of relevancy and compelling presentation. Despite his decades of teaching within the CIA, these concepts are not established within the CIA or the defense intelligence community, in part because there is so much personnel turn-over, in part because we emphasize voluminous production over competent reflection, and in part because—the dirty little secret of the U.S. intelligence community—most policymakers and action officers really don't care whether or not they get classified intelligence because it is not focused on their real needs.

I preferred the Early Bird with its compendium of newspaper stories [to the President's Daily Brief, CIA's capstone daily product].[8]

Colin Powell

Figure 10: Colin Powell's Preference for the *Early Bird*

Different Mental Maps, Different Objectives

Apart from internal issues of definition and purpose, we have learned from generations over time that intelligence frequently fails to impact on

---

[8] Colin Powell, *My American Journey* (Random House, 1995), page 293. At the time he was serving as the principal military assistant to then Secretary of Defense Casper Weinberger.

policymakers—even products tailored for the individual policymaker—because there are profound differences between the analysts and the policy makers.

We are providing here two different "looks" at the dramatic differences in outlook between producers and consumers of intelligence. Greg Treverton, then with the Council on Foreign Relations and subsequently Vice Chairman of the National Intelligence Council staff, provided the first of these looks while teaching the Harvard Executive Program's "Intelligence Policy Seminar" in the late 1980's. The second was provided by Sumner Benson, a former CIA senior analyst who was absorbed into the defense policy staffing structure some years earlier but returned to lecture each of Jack Davis' classes.

Each look has its own unique contributions to make to our understanding of this very deep and very fundamental obstacle to how we go about providing intelligence support to policymakers, commanders, and acquisition managers.

ANALYSTS	POLICYMAKERS
• Facts/Disengaged	• Beliefs/Accountable
• Objective	• Intuitive
• "Balanced" View	• Agenda-Driven
• Long-Term View	• Short-Term View
• Descriptive	• Action-Oriented
• Employer-Driven	• Constituency-Driven
• Protect Information	• Use Information
• International Focus	• Domestic Focus
• Perfection/Accuracy	• "Good Enough"/Utility
• Written Compendiums	• Oral Shorthand
• Facts/Things	• People/Personalities
• Tenure/Continuity	• Short Tours
• Generic Audience	• Specific Audiences
• Single Output	• Multiple Inputs

Figure 11: Producer versus Consumer Outlooks, Version I

When evaluating the intent and utility of any future legislative action or administrative restructuring, we must be very careful to consider how we can increase the intellectual and political authority of the individual intelligence analyst in relation to their consumers and their credibility with the consumers' organizations. As Andy Shepard, a senior analyst manager now serving on the Intelligence Community Staff, has noted elsewhere, such authority must rest in part on the analyst's direct access on a day-to-day basis to the consumer, and also on a corresponding familiarity and understanding by the analyst with the consumers everyday as well as longer term concerns.

- The analyst focuses on all-source INTERNATIONAL DATA while the policymaker focuses on DOMESTIC POLITICAL ISSUES as the primary criteria for decisionmaking.

- The analyst focuses on (and is driven by community managers in) producing "PERFECT" products over a lengthier timeframe while the policymaker requires "GOOD ENOUGH" products immediately. *Analysts continually run the risk of having ZERO IMPACT because their review process delays their product to the point that it is overtaken by events.*

- The analyst is accustomed to INTEGRATING all-source information at the CODEWORD level, while most policymaker staffs, and especially those actually implementing operational decisions, have at best a SECRET clearance. "A secret paragraph is better than a codeword page."

- The analyst and community management focus on SUBSTANCE and ACCURACY while the policymaker focuses on POLITICS and PROCESS, an arena where disagreement can be viewed as insubordination. Even if new information is received, POLITICAL considerations may weigh against policy decisions.

Figure 12: Producer versus Consumer Outlooks, Version II

Changing the organization, funding, and authority of the DCI will not impact on this *fundamental* deficiency in the U.S. national intelligence community.

Barriers to Useful Intelligence Analysis

The barriers to analysis being useful to policymakers can also be looked at in relation to larger generic obstacles to effective intelligence analysis. These are *institutionalized* barriers that lead to distorted and erroneous perceptions by both intelligence producers and intelligence consumers. Below we present four kinds of barriers as taught by Jack Davis.

International Barriers	Barrier Impact
• Complexity of world affairs; multiple interests and actors; national cultural differences; impact of U.S. actions.	• Ambiguity of information; noise; deception; paradigm bias; domestic collection confusion or gaps in understanding.

Figure 13: International Barriers to Useful Analysis

Potential measures to overcome these international barriers include a mandated inter-agency sharing of information at multiple levels of security; required overseas assignments for most analysts; and radically expanded collection of both clandestine human intelligence and open sources of information.

Policy Barriers	Barrier Impact
• Misperception of foreign actors (policy mirroring); wishful thinking; policy momentum	• Threat distortion; distrust of analysts; hoarding and manipulating of information

Figure 14: Policy Barriers to Useful Analysis

Policy barriers require Congressional action. For example, each Department of government should be required to include in its annual report to congress its own intelligence analysis of the "state of the world" in terms that clearly identify both threats and opportunities as they are perceived by the Departmental leadership. At the same time, there is a need to fully integrate all-source intelligence professionals as well as open source intelligence support staffs into each of the Departments.

Organizational Barriers	Barrier Impact
• Resource limitations; emphasis on authoritative publications and predefined missions and roles; fragmentation of missions, functions, knowledge, and data	• Mixed management signals if not active subversion; resistance to alternative views; information choke points (both internal and external)

Figure 15: Organizational Barriers to Useful Analysis

To overcome organizational barriers, it would be helpful to have both Congressional and Executive "ombudsmen" that are easily reachable by individuals. There also needs to be increased emphasis on cross-program oversight by functional area, and a formalized program evaluation process that evaluates intelligence capabilities, including especially the very expensive technical collection capabilities, in relation to the return on investment as perceived by the policy-makers and the analysts.

Analysis Barriers	Barrier Impact
• Substantive biases and cognitive traps; parochialism; monasticism; lack of exposure to the real world	• Arrogance or overconfidence if not naivete; tunnel vision; resistance to outside views and priorities

Figure 16: Analysis Barriers to Useful Analysis

Analysis barriers can be addressed with mandated inter-agency training and substantial foreign travel and study for all analysts. Better yet, we should only hire analysts who have *already* established themselves as world-class authorities on their respective areas of interest, and have proven themselves as masters of the language and the foreign area knowledge needed to fully exploit classified information. We must do much better at exploiting both foreign and U.S. experts, both to feed into the classified analysis process, and to provide competing analyses that draw solely on open sources of information. Consumers must have regular direct contact with the analysts supporting them, or risk losing that support. Finally, at some point in the oversight process there needs to be a very firm and regular evaluation of specific analytical product lines to determine their utility and relevance to their clients, to include critiques of format, medium, timeliness, and depth.

Each of these barriers has doctrinal, architectural, and technical remedies of one sort or another. In all cases the two key ingredients for improving the prospects for intelligence success lie in personal relationships—the relationships between the individual analysts and individual intelligence consumers on the one hand, and the relationships between the individual analysts and their intelligence managers on the other.

Policy Constituencies and Policy Failure

Figure 17, with credit to Jack Davis, illustrates a fact of life that most intelligence managers and analysts fail to fully appreciate: the intelligence community is but one small element in a much larger spectrum of constituencies, all of whom offer the policymaker attractive incentives for listening: votes, money, power, and sex. In the marketplace for influence, the U.S. Intelligence Community runs a poor third behind these tangible offerings, and the ideas put forth by think tanks that know how to use the media to publicize their concerns.

Beyond the fragmentation shown in Figure 17, is the reality that no organization is monolithic—each has its own fragmented culture to worry about. It is not uncommon for members of one Directorate or Bureau or Service to carry entirely contradictory messages to individual policymakers.

There is one other very important reality illustrated in Figure 17 and that is the reality that roughly 90% of the "input" to the policymakers mind is both *unclassified* and *unanalyzed*. As good as the policymaker might be, the lack of true intelligence staffs in all but two departments (State and Defense, and even then they rarely do day-to-day decision support) drives home the point that the people who do "all-source analysis" for a living are "out of the loop" 90% of the time.

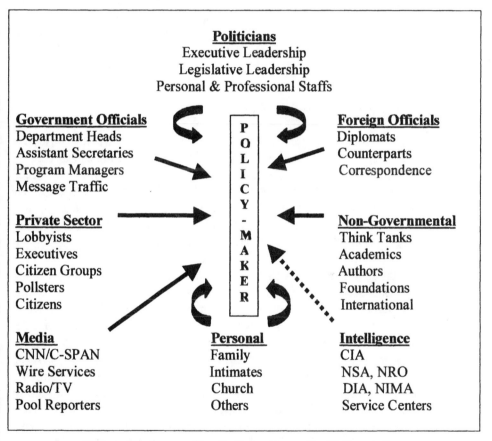

Figure 17: Competing Influences on the Policymaker

In brief then, national and defense intelligence managers are in charge of a vast conglomeration of fragmented resources, created in a piecemeal fashion over time to serve an even more fragmented array of consumers, most of whom do not really care one way or the other if intelligence is at their table. Only after a failure is the refrain, "Where was intelligence?" heard.

There is one final reality: no matter how good the intelligence might be, it cannot make up for deliberate policy choices that discount the intelligence to the point that it becomes irrelevant. Intelligence failures can often be attributed to the policy process, whether in the definition of the problem or the rejection of the product. Since there is no short-term or personal cost to the policymaker for ignoring intelligence, the Intelligence Community has little recourse but to plug along and hope its offerings can "fit in" to the larger picture.

Conclusion to the "How" of Intelligence

Who is the customer? What do they need? Most individual contemplating improvements to U.S. national and defense capabilities appear to be focusing mostly on organizational charts and funding authority, when in fact the root issues are more fundamental. "How" we do business must change radically, both in relation to externally available unclassified information, and in relation to how we empower the individual intelligence analyst with serious information processing tools and external expert adjunct analysts.

A great deal is "right" with U.S. intelligence, and many unsung heroes have proven themselves adept at developing "work arounds" to the existing cumbersome bureaucratic approach to intelligence. Unfortunately, the reality is that the intelligence community today has isolated itself, both from its consumers, and from the real world of cultural complexity, fast-moving events, and changing priorities. The current discussions about restructuring and reform have not yet embraced two aspects of the future of intelligence: the full integration of the expertise and capabilities represented by the private sector; and the need to substantially alter our methods so as to be able to provide intelligence support—and share both the costs and results of intelligence—with an infinite variety of ever-changing allies. If the next President, and the next Congress, do not come to grips with these basics, then nothing now planned by in the way of "improvements" is going to make a real difference in our national security or our national competitiveness in the 21st Century.

Testimony on the Need to Significantly Reduce Secrecy

March 3, 1997

Dear Mr. President:

We hereby transmit the report of the Commission on Protecting and Reducing Government Secrecy.

The Commission's report is unanimous. It contains recommendations for actions by the Executive Branch and the Legislative Branch, with the object of protecting and reducing secrecy in an era when open sources make a plenitude of information available as never before in history.

Respectfully submitted,
Daniel Patrick Moynihan
Chairman

On 9 June 1993, four years before the brilliant Daniel Patrick Moynihan reported out on the matter, it was my privilege to testify to the Committee on Excessive Classification, one of several elements of a Presidential Task Force on National Security Information. Later, when the more august Commission on Secrecy met, it was my great privilege to not only provide staff testimony, but also to be invited to sit down with Senator Moynihan one evening. This chapter summarizes what I told him, based on my own experience. The official report does not go into this level of detail, and I believe these views need to be published now and for the public.

We can eliminate 75% of our security issues, and save billions of dollars each year, by eliminating excessive classification and unnecessary secrecy. Savings will be seen not only within the U.S. intelligence community, but also—through improved dissemination of more information—in the rest of the government and in the private sector. There are three kinds of waste caused by excessive classification:

System Costs of Excessive Secrecy

First, there is system cost, the waste of billions of dollars to create Sensitive Compartmented Information (SCI) information collection and information handling systems, with all of their emission controls, restricted access areas, employee clearance costs, and so on, only to find that at least 75% of the information processed is either not secret at all (the vast majority), or of a lesser classification such as Secret or Top Secret and therefore not warranting such expensive measures.

There is also a "reverse" cost associated with these vast SCI-high bureaucracies that are in effect "bunkers" where all those working within this compartmented arena are "locked up". What this really means is that they are restricted in their insights and direct knowledge to only that information that can be entered into the SCI-high system, and they are literally "cut off" from all available unclassified information in the private sector, prevented from traveling overseas to see for themselves because of "risk of capture", or even prevented from doing something so simple as consulting an "uncleared" scholar or foreign expert. We are handicapping our best collectors and analysts— including those on contract in the private sector—and preventing them from being effective.

We have created a security bureaucracy that has lost sight of its purpose, and has no idea how to deal with the changed circumstances of a world in which the U.S. intelligence community no longer controls the bulk of the information. Worse, we have an entire community of intelligence professionals—good people trapped in a bad system—who have been trained by rote to stay inside their little box, and literally have no understanding of the vast wealth of information available to them outside the bunker, often for no more than the price of a telephone call.

Policy Costs of Excessive Secrecy

Second, there is policy cost, the waste of billions of dollars in lost opportunities for executive action, and the cost of misinformed or uninformed policy, that is a direct result of over-classification that results in vital useful intelligence being too time-consuming and burdensome for the policymaker to access and absorb its contents.

It has been my experience that national intelligence accesses less than 10% of the available information, and spills 80% of that information by not processing it or over-classifying what it does process, with the result that the policymaker is receiving less than 2% of the available foreign intelligence through our normal intelligence process.

At the same time, policymakers are inundated with unclassified information for a vast array of foreign and private sector parties, each with their own agenda. The fact that this information comprises 90% of what the policymaker reads and acts upon, the fact that this external information is not properly analyzed or integrated with our classified knowledge, should be of concern.

One of the greatest myths of intelligence is that it is actually useful to policymakers. In my experience, most policymakers do not have the time to read their intelligence reports, and very little of what we produce actually lends itself to strategic decisionmaking.

There is an even more important policy cost, and it impacts on all those good citizens outside of Washington, D.C. who in fact comprise the "front line troops" in the age of information warfare. By obsessing on over-classified information we have in effect deprived the larger national policy community—the private sector—of valuable knowledge from our Embassies and our general collection resources. We are therefore not contributing to the "information commons" and not helping our private sector compete effectively in the global economy.

The President should be focusing on excessive classification as a first step in substantially re-inventing our intelligence community so that it is in the service of the Nation as a whole, not some intelligence bureaucrat's arbitrary classification of the "top 100" policymakers.

Functional Cost: The Cement Overcoat of the Bureaucrat

Finally, there is functional cost, the waste of billions of dollars used to create massive classified collection systems whose collection we cannot process and whose product we cannot disseminate as widely as actually necessary to influence policy at the working level. There are two major costs in this area.

The first results from erroneous or excessive classification. I am certain, and others more senior than I, including members of the National Security Council, have spoken publicly on this point, that no less than 75% and perhaps as much as 90% of our classification is motivated by a desire to protect bureaucratic turf, not by any genuine need to protect national security.

Erroneous classification also results from tens of thousands of poorly trained employees who routinely classify information by rote, adopting the most conservative route because the bureaucratic penalties for under-classification are severe, while there are no penalties for all those—thousands of people every year—guilty of excessive classification.

The second cost, more easily corrected, results from embedded classification, where as much as 75% of the information in a document might be unclassified or of a lower classification, but is classified at the highest level of any paragraph in the total document. This effectively removes all of the unclassified or less classified information from the broader government library of information accessible to most government and private sector individuals. This is the "cement overcoat" of the intelligence bureaucracy, successfully burying its perceived competitor—useful unclassified information—deep within highly classified documents that cannot be widely disseminated.

Astonishing as this may seem to any person with common sense, the U.S. Intelligence Community then goes on to note that once classified, such information cannot be unclassified even if it appears in its unclassified form in a private sector publication.

Intelligence Microscopes, Like Mainframes, Are Relics

The reality is that we have built an enormous classified microscope in outer space that is good only for looking at the strategic nuclear threat in the former Soviet Union, and is relatively useless against economic or other targets, even economic targets in the former Soviet Union and China. The failure of the intelligence community to predict the fall of the Berlin Wall and the implosion of the Soviet empire, is a direct result of our over-reliance on very expensive narrowly focused classified systems whose validity and utility are not subject to sufficient scrutiny and oversight.

We have lost touch with the traditional art of scholarship. Our intelligence community, secure with an arrogance born of privilege—the privilege of being able to decide for itself which policy-makers "qualified" for their secrets, has virtually no capability for rapidly collecting, processing, and disseminating unclassified public information, what we call "open source" or open source intelligence (OSINT). Excessive classification has created an ossified intelligence community that is now in grid-lock, unable to cope with fleeting and rapidly changing threats and opportunities.

Three Real-World Examples

I offer you now three real-world examples of failure, each based on my direct personal experience.

(1) In 1988 I was selected to be the founding Special Assistant and Deputy Director of the Marine Corps Intelligence Center. We were given twenty million dollars to spend over five years, ten million of which we spent on precisely the kind of excessively classified system you are concerned with: an SCI-high communications and computing architecture that was, with some effort, approved to receive just about anything disseminated by the CIA or NSA or the ground processing elements of the NRO. Imagine our shock when we turned that wonderful system on and started doing real work, only to discover that the national intelligence community does not have any significant information about the Third World, nor about factors of extreme importance to the Marine Corps, such as bridge loading data, port and airhead usability, and so on. Imagine our chagrin when we learned that most of what we needed *was*

59

available from commercial information services, but that because of the existing funding structure of the U.S. intelligence community, we had no monies available with which to buy this very inexpensive but immediately useful open source information. My bottom line: if I were to do it over again, I would have limited my SCI-high equipment to one terminal and one secure phone line, and spent the extra ten million buying better analysts and a wealth of commercial open source information support from around the world.

(2) In 1990 I was afforded an opportunity to reflect on national intelligence policy issues at Harvard, and refined some insights I had developed while completing my second graduate thesis, an examination of the information flow from three Embassies back to Washington. There are two straight-forward findings:

(a) We collect less than 10% of the overtly available information. As one who has served three tours overseas, and also three Washington-based tours, I must stress to you my concern about the current situation overseas. Among U.S. officials overseas, the only people who have the funds with which to buy information locally are the spies, who demand treason and secrecy as a condition of employment, and then classify anything they collect, whether it is secret in the first place or not. The overt collectors, the diplomats and the attaches, have no funds with which to engage local experts in legal and ethical information production tasks, at the same time that manpower has been cut and secretarial staff largely eliminated. As there is no way around the physics of the 24-hour day, I am confident that my thesis findings are accurate, and that our Embassies are far less productive than they could be if we adopted a different view of how to collect and process national security information.

(b) We spill 80% of what we do collect from the Embassies, resulting in a 2% (80% of 10%) final outcome for foreign intelligence. The reality of Embassy coordination is such that it is much easier to send information back to one's corresponding "desk" in Washington through the diplomatic pouch or the regular mail, than to send it by electronic message, for the simple reason that the first does not have to be coordinated with the Ambassador and others in the Embassy, while the latter does. In brief, the bulk of what we collect overtly goes into shoeboxes in single offices in Washington, and not into some larger digital library that can be accessed across the government and even by the private sector.[1]

(3) I am personally familiar with a situation in the late 1980's, when both Congress and the White House were pushing for the procurement of very large, expensive, and highly classified space reconnaissance systems, while consistently refusing to provide funds for ground-based processing and exploitation. This situation got so bad that at one point a very senior intelligence community official actually had to decline, in writing, any more satellite systems, pointing out that we could not process what we were collecting with the existing systems. It is my understanding, from very senior authoritative sources, that we process less than 6% of our most important signals (probably less than 3% of our total signals collected) and that we process less than 10% of the classified images we collect from outer space.

No Strategy, No Understanding

In my years of service, and especially from 1987 to 1993 when I was either the CIA or Marine Corps representative to the Foreign Intelligence Priorities Committee, the Future Intelligence Requirements Working Group, the Council of Defense Intelligence Producers, and other key forums for establishing strategic direction, I have been appalled by how we do business. We literally go through the motions. We do not have a strategic plan for intelligence collection designs and methods in relation to one another and our needs, and there is little likelihood that such a plan will be produced in the future unless the President of the United States—the only person with the necessary authority over *all* intelligence resources—chooses to get personally involved. This is important to note because excessive classification is inherent in the way we do business now, and is likely to continue unchecked unless the next President pursues substantive recommendations to drastically reduce funding for classified systems while increasing funding for unclassified

---

[1] These observations are based, apart from real experience in three overseas tours and a decade in Washington, on my second graduate thesis, "Strategic and Tactical Information Management for National Security (MPA, University of Oklahoma, 1987), in which I reviewed what was available to Embassies, what and how they took it in, what they did with it, and where it went from there.

collection, all-source processing, and multi-level secure dissemination to include dissemination to non-governmental organizations.

Concluding Observations

I would conclude my testimony on secrecy with two observations.

First, fiscal decline can be a most refreshing tonic, to adapt one of Winston Churchill's sayings. It brings out new perspectives and forces objective reevaluations. When Robert Koehler, a senior TRW officer and former head of the CIA office responsible for building satellites, stands up and says he thinks we can declassify most of what we do in imagery; when William Schneider, former Undersecretary of State, says we should eliminate export controls on our intelligence technologies; when Ken Bass, first Council for Intelligence Policy in the Department of Justice states publicly that most of what he has reviewed for the courts is over-classified, then indeed, a fresh breeze is stirring. It will not be easy, changing the way we do business. It will require Congressional legislation *and Presidential commitment*.

Second, and here I want to paraphrase a warfighter who spoke at a Navy information technology meeting in 1991 where new concepts were being tested—I believe he was the commander of the lead wing going into Baghdad during the war in Southwest Asia—he said something along the lines of: "If it is 85% accurate, on time, and I can *share* it, then that is a lot more useful to me than an SCI compendium that is too much, too late, and needs a safe and three security officers to move it around the battlefield." There are unquestionably some things that will always need to be done using sensitive classified sources and methods, but on balance I believe that between 75% and 90% of what our national policymakers need to know to keep America safe, as well as the needs of the broader consumer community responsible for national competitiveness, can be satisfied with unclassified intelligence that is faster, cheaper, and has two extraordinary additional advantages: it is risk-free, and it can be shared with Congress, the press, and the public.

Until the U.S. Intelligence Community is forced to use open sources of information as the "source of first resort", and until the intelligence community is forced to produce unclassified intelligence products to the maximum extent possible, then we will continue to waste billions of dollars while depriving most government officials, our private sector corporate partners, and individual citizens of the fruits of our intelligence effort because we wish to blindly pursue secrets for secrets' sake, rather than working to inform policy.

Alvin Toffler, Stevan Dedijer, Harlan Cleveland, Robert Carkhuff, Howard Rheingold, and Peter Drucker—these are but a few of the many smart individuals addressing how we must change our ways in the age of information, the age of the knowledge executive, the age of the "gold collar" worker, *the age of the privatization of intelligence.* The fact is that much of what we need in the way of intelligence support to government can and should be done by the private sector—this includes much of what is needed in the way of overhead imagery and broadcast signals collection. It is time for our intelligence community managers to demonstrate effective returns on the taxpayers' investment in national intelligence, or retire and let the next generation, under a new President, bring fresh ideas into government. It is time for them to give up the erroneous belief that they are in the business of collecting secrets alone, and accept the more challenging role of being in the business of informing policy. We can help them make that adjustment by redefining what constitutes a secret, and indeed, what constitutes national security.

Observations on the Executive Regulation Itself

The following additional observations are made a matter of record with respect to Executive Order 12356, "National Security Information".

(1) National Security Information should *not* be classified "by definition". The most fundamental flaw in this Presidential directive over time has been its equation of national security information with classified information. In a quarter century as an intelligence and defense professional I have never ever seen any documentation or demonstration that information of importance to national security must of necessity be classified. Indeed, in resigning from the government in 1993, I have dedicated myself to demonstrating that the opposite case is true, that the wealth and health of the Nation depend much more on a public intelligence capability, a capability to collect, process, and disseminate unclassified information.

(2) The existing definitions of "Top Secret", "Secret", and "Confidential" are adequate in theory, but are rendered irrelevant because of the

complete lack of Presidential direction as to how one should define "national security", "exceptionally grave damage", "serious damage", or "damage". The fact of the matter is that the agencies considered to be part of the national security apparatus have taken it upon themselves to define everything they do, everything about them, to "be" be vital to national security, and they have taken it upon themselves to classify everything about themselves, their operations, their budgets, and their products, without regard to the definitions established by the President in this Executive Order.

(3) In my experience, at least 50% of what the intelligence community does is unclassified—unclassified sources, unclassified methods, unclassified products, all erroneously classified, that is to say, over-classified. Unfortunately, because of the total discretion allowed to the community, all that is unclassified is buried, literally, inside of tightly controlled documents bearing the classification of the most sensitive piece of information.

(4) Employees have not been trained to exercise discrimination in classification. It has been my experience that employees of the various intelligence community organizations routinely classify *everything* they collect, everything they write. This is in part because there are severe penalties for under-classifying information, and *there are no penalties at all for over-classification, even if the over-classification is erroneous or against the public interest.*

(5) Firm limits on the duration of classification are urgently needed: two years from Confidential, five years for Secret, and ten years for Top Secret. This is the age of information and the laws of cybernetics rather than the laws of physics should now be paramount. The "half-life" of information, including classified information, gets shorter every year. In my judgment, a new Executive Order should, in addition to providing much firmer direction on what constitutes "national security" and "damage", must also specify that with certain very strictly limited and supervised exceptions, all classified information is to be automatically declassified when it reaches ten years of age. Confidential should be declassified after two years, Secret after five, and Top Secret after seven to ten years depending on the topic and the country. This does not apply to clandestine human intelligence sources and methods, which must be protected indefinitely.

(6)   The prohibition on the use of classification to conceal impropriety or questionable activities appears routine and suffers no sanction.   The prohibition properly contained in the Executive Order is routinely violated with frequency.   The following quotation from a former member of the National Security Council is instructive:

> *Everybody who's a real practitioner, and I'm sure you're not all naïve in this regard, realizes that there are two uses to which security classification is put: the legitimate desire to protect secrets, and the protection of bureaucratic turf. As a practitioner of the real world, it's about 90 bureaucratic turf; 10 legitimate protection of secrets as far as I am concerned.*[2]

(7)   I would recommend that the Executive Order be revised to including the following three elements:

(a)   First, a requirement for the integration of training on the revised Executive Order and the intent of the President regarding classification, into the training programs of all government employees and their private sector counterparts.   The training model used in relation to Executive Order 12333 stands as proof that reaching individual employees can make a difference.

(b)   Second, elimination of "delegated" classification authority.   In my experience, employees at the very lowest levels of the intelligence community routinely classify documents using the identification number of the agency head or senior officer that *does* have the authority to classify documents Instead, in conjunction with the training program, we need to make the actual collector or originator of any document, fully accountable for its classification.

(c)   Third, a much stronger program of oversight, beginning with a complete review of all intelligence production including the daily current intelligence products provided to the President and his senior staff.   Measures should be adopted that require all intelligence producers to follow the military model of classifying paragraphs individually, and sanctions should be imposed on organizations and individuals that fail to comply with this better practice.

---

[2] Rodley B. McDaniel, then Executive Secretary of the National Security Council, to a Harvard University seminar. He was quoted in Thomas P. Croakley (ed.), *C3I: Issues of Command and Control* (National Defense University, 1991), page 68.

(8) Routine declassification simply does not happen. Although the existing Executive Order calls for the declassification or downgrading of information as soon as national security considerations permit, this provision is, in my experience, ignored in its entirety within the national intelligence community. All documents are classified for the maximum period possible, and all documents that can be exempted from automatic declassification are exempted. This is not done for malicious reasons—it is done for bureaucratic convenience, for it is far easier to "play safe" and have one (maximum) standard than to train and oversee employees in the application of discretionary judgment.

(9) I have never, in the eighteen years when I was dealing regularly with classified materials, encountered a representative of the Intelligence Security Oversight Office, or even seen any written reference to this office. Although the order provides this Office with the authority to conduct on-sight inspections, this does not appear to be a common practice. In my experience, the Intelligence Security Oversight Office has been irrelevant and ineffective. It needs teeth—a staff, the authority to spot check, and the authority to issue sanctions that cause pain and discomfort at the most senior levels of the offending agency. It should pay particular attention to the over-classification of information that was unclassified to begin with.

(10) I strongly recommend an across the board evaluation of intelligence community collection, external research and analysis, and production, with a view to determining the percentage of sources, contracts, and products that are inherently unclassified, but whose value is being lost because of excessive classification. In my view, any document that is comprised of 50% or more of unclassified information, should be split into an unclassified primary document with a classified appendix.

(11) There should not be any exemptions to the regulations pertaining to access to classified information. I find the exemption of the President and his staff to be contrary to democratic principals. They should have the same authority to classify information as do the national security agencies, but they should not be exempted from declassification review.

(12) I am troubled by the laxity with which departing political appointees are treated such that they can literally cart out all of the classified

66

documents they wish when they leave, and/or return at will to examine classified documents for their private purposes, generally (one assumes) associated with the writing of their memoirs. Former Presidential appointees should be held to the same standards as former government employees, and not granted privileged access once having departed office.

(13) Special Access Programs (SAP) are abused and lead to enormous waste. These programs are especially abusive as means of protecting bureaucratic interests rather than genuine national security interests, and they impose on the taxpayer hundreds of millions of dollars in unnecessary government and contractor expense. We should revise this authority to allow agency heads to recommend the establishment of special access programs, but only a single office responsive to the President should actually have the approval authority. There also needs to be a uniform standard for the administration of these special access programs. It has been my experience that individual programs are administered capriciously, often ignorantly, and impose unwarranted expense and inconvenience on contractors that are required to maintain parallel infrastructures for a variety of programs that could all be reasonably groups at Top Secret/Codeword.

(14) The fundamental premise of this Presidential directive is flawed. Any future Presidential direction on national security information absolutely must begin with the understanding and stated premise that information, including intelligence, is most valuable when widely disseminated, and that information must be considered unclassified until a solid case for its classification can be established. That is not the practice today.

Congressional Oversight of "Sources & Methods"

The most common error that Congressional oversight authorities fall prey to in contemplating the value of "sources and methods", is to permit those who would avoid scrutiny to use the specter of betrayed human assets to avoid Congressional oversight.

"Sources and methods" *per se* are indeed worth protecting from discovery, in that selected techniques, such as secret writing (a capability eliminated by revelation in the memoirs of a U.S. prisoner of war in Viet-Nam), lose most of their value once their existence is known. Much of the success of "sources and methods" stems from obscurity rather than undetectability. Once identified or even suspected, the thin veneer of secrecy is soon stripped away.

There are, however, severe flaws in the current argument that anything having to do with "sources and methods" must be exempt from Congressional or any other kind of scrutiny.

"Sources and Methods" must be evaluated and understood in relation to five different aspects of intelligence operations:

1) The *source or method*, that is, the specific identity or technique that, in isolation, is precious. Examples include the real identities of specific human sources, the fact of a technical capability such as the ability to eavesdrop on Politburo mobile telephones (a capability eliminated by a U.S. President's open mention) and the existence of techniques, largely in support of surreptitious entry or clandestine communications, that if known to exist would be readily detected when employed.

2) The *process* within which that source or method is utilized. Giving a secret camera to an agent who is easily identified by the local counterintelligence service because the agent's case officer is a young person operating out of a U.S. installation and not taking the time to exercise good counter-surveillance techniques, makes a mockery of our professed reverence for "sources and methods". As Mr. Richard Haver, a former Director of the Intelligence Community Staff (a position now confirmed by the Senate) has observed, "We have to stop lying to ourselves." Until we have a clandestine service that is truly clandestine and not easily identified because of its lax approach to daily operational tradecraft, then it is the clandestine service itself that is betraying "sources and methods", and this of itself should be cause for both exercising Congressional oversight and for public outrage.

3) The *context* within which "sources and methods" are employed. Too often, the clandestine service employs classified "sources and methods" because they are the only tools they understand or have available to them, when in fact the risk of exposure is such that the operation, if discovered, would be far more destructive than the value of the information obtained—especially when the information could be easily obtained through open "sources & methods". Clandestine operations against Canada would fall into this

68

contextual category. All of our Embassy operations in all foreign countries have the same contextual issue, in that the clandestine service is the only organ of government readily able to pay for information, but it requires its informants to betray their employers or their country and agree to a secret relationship as part of the bargain. At the same time, vast quantities of solid open source information—expert local knowledge that is legally and ethically available—cannot be obtained by the Embassy for lack of time and funding.

4) The *objective*. As the Commission on Intelligence has noted, many intelligence questions can be answered by the consumers themselves, using predominantly open sources, and it is the Commission's judgment that under such circumstances, the Intelligence Community should not be tasked for collection or analysis—the consumer should be the primary party responsible for obtaining and analyzing the openly available information needed to answer their intelligence requirement. *We should not send a spy where a schoolboy can go*, and consequently Congress should consider a fundamental reassessment of how each element of our government is or is not trained, equipped, and organized to collect open sources and analyze open sources.

5) The *return on investment* integrates all of the above issues, and ultimately informs the responsible policy maker, acquisition manager, or commander—the consumer of intelligence—as to the risk, the cost, and the value of applying specific "sources and methods" to specific national intelligence topics. Unfortunately, the entire system breaks down because *the problem with spies is they only know secrets* and they are unable to understand what is available through open sources, or to advise the intelligence consumer of the relative trade-offs between classified and unclassified approaches to a specific intelligence question. When a national intelligence community is properly managed, ninety percent of the necessary information will be obtained legally and ethically, at low cost, for a fraction of what the classified intelligence community costs to maintain, and the redirected classified intelligence community will be better able to collect and exploit the ten percent of the information that is absolutely vital to national security and must be obtained "by other means."

In conclusion, I would observe that the break-down of objective oversight regarding "sources and methods" is not limited to clandestine espionage alone, but in fact applies even more strongly to technical collection and especially to the significant disconnects between very expensive classified national imagery capabilities that are not well-suited for wide-area surveillance, and the very cheap and responsive commercial imagery capabilities that are—Congressional oversight should demand that the two be properly integrated. This issue of "sources and methods" also applies to intelligence analysis, where a heavy reliance on cheap and largely inexperienced community analysts, to the exclusion of the broad community of world-class experts in the private sector, levies severe opportunity costs and political costs, upon badly informed policymakers, acquisition managers, and commanders.

The fastest way to redress these imbalances and dramatically improve the fiscal return as well as the political return and the intellectual return on our national intelligence investments is to establish an honest and open method of appraising the *transaction costs*[3] of classified versus unclassified "sources and methods", and to ensure that Congressional oversight is not stone-walled by those who would deny the flaws in process, context, objective, or return on investment. We will always need spies and satellites, but by improving our Congressional oversight, we can quickly move toward "just enough" secrecy (at substantially lower cost to the tax-payer) while simultaneously improving—by an order of magnitude—the amount of unclassified "intelligence" available to both our government and our non-government participants in national security and national competitiveness decision-making.

---

[3] The concept of *transaction costs* as a means of comparing classified versus unclassified intelligence sources and methods is one I attribute to Senator Daniel Patrick Moynihan (D-NY). The bi-partisan nature of the Commission on Secrecy precluded his integration of this brilliant idea for substantive reform into the investigative direction of the Commission. Separately, Robert J. Hermann, a distinguished member of the expanded U.S. Intelligence Community, has conceptualized a voucher system that empowers the consumers of intelligence without placing the funds for intelligence at risk of realignment to non-intelligence activities. I would utilize such a voucher system to permit consumers to select between classified and unclassified intelligence collection and analysis alternatives, with the bulk of the latter being out-sourced to the private sector.

E³i: Ethics, Ecology, Evolution, and Intelligence

Government is not built to perceive great truths; only people can perceive great truths. Governments specialize in small and intermediate truths. They have to be instructed by their people in great truths. And the particular truth in which they need instruction today is that new means for meeting the largest problems on earth have to be created.

Norman Cousins[1]

The era of national intelligence, with its unsung heroes and occasional rogue elephants in the war against communism, socialism, and other perceived evils, has come to an end. The Department of Defense and the national intelligence community are pretending to restructure, desperately seeking to preserve a semblance of their once massive organizations. Both are pretending to redefine their roles and missions in order to remain competitive in the budget battles of the future, but they explicitly reject the view that "reform" is required.

The brain and heart of the national security "firm" have always been command and control, communications, computers, and intelligence, known by the acronym C³I. I propose an alternative paradigm for the intelligence community of the 21ˢᵗ century, one that focuses on objectives and outcomes rather than sources and methods. My approach, which integrates ethics, ecology, evolution, and *unclassified* intelligence (E³i) represents a radical change in perspective on what we should be emphasizing as we adapt to our changed circumstances and prepare for future challenges. Such a paradigm could be described as an "open books" equivalent to the "open skies" concept being applied to arms control: the true value of "intelligence" lies in its informative value, a value which increases with dissemination. The emphasis

---

[1] *The Pathology of Power* (Norton, 1987)

within our national intelligence community should be on open sources, free exchanges between government and private sector analysts, and unclassified production.

We have an opportunity to recast our national intelligence apparatus, and truly put it in the national service—that is, the service of the public—rather than repeat its history of servitude and sublimation in the shadow of a restricted, myopic group of policy-makers whose circumstances have frequently precluded long-range planning and rational (as opposed to political) decision-making. I propose to link national intelligence with national competitiveness in a very tangible way, making intelligence the apex of the knowledge infrastructure, and the catalyst for a dramatic improvement in our ability to recognize change and opportunities for advantage. Only in this way can we quickly retrain our people, retool our plants, and revise our product line so as to maintain a prosperous and profitable nation.

There are three questions with which we must grapple if we are to manage our national security, and the intelligence community, in a responsible fashion.

First, how do we define national security? Do we limit ourselves to "megaprotection"—strategic nuclear and conventional deterrence—while ignoring domestic crime, the loss of economic competitiveness, and the degradation of our external environment and our internal competence (a combination of character and education)? If "national security" is defined as the preservation of our national culture, of our way of life, of the conditions which permit the pursuit of happiness and prosperity, then something is seriously wrong with both our defense structure (including law enforcement) and our "national" intelligence capabilities.

Second, who is the customer for national intelligence? Is it the president, who has little time to digest the distilled product of a multibillion-dollar global network of human and technical capabilities? Is it the top one hundred government officials? Is it Congress? Is it a combination of congressional staffers and executive-branch action officers? Or could "the customer" include the media, the academy, and the private sector?

Third, given a sense of national security (however defined) and an adequate definition of the customer base that national intelligence is meant to serve, the final question must be "What is our objective?" To what *end* do we wish to maintain a national intelligence capability? Is it to warn us of threats (unprovoked nuclear attack, biochemical terrorism, computer "hit-and-run" assaults)? Is it to inform us of systematic campaigns to undermine our economy, our sociology, or even our biology? Or is it part of a "commonwealth" sensor system, intended to monitor our internal and external stability, to educate our officials, our citizens, and our foreign partners regarding emerging conditions, organizations, and personalities inimical to "steady-state" evolution? If the nation is defined as the citizenry and its commonweal, rather than as the political apex of the government bureaucracy, then a radical new interpretation of the mission, sources, and methods of the national intelligence apparat is required.

Such an interpretation is intended to make national intelligence more relevant to what should be two top national priorities: the preservation of our culture and a strong ethical foundation for that culture; and the preservation (indeed, the restoration) of our environment. Intelligence can play a very significant part in the recasting of our national government and its relationship with the private sector; intelligence can be teacher, mentor, lifeguard, and coach. National intelligence is an essential element of our national competence, vision, purpose, and cohesion. Only a small fraction of national intelligence should be "classified"; while some classified information is essential to effective diplomacy and executive action, the classification and restriction of knowledge are inherently counterproductive and fraught with the risk of corruption.

Ethics and Intelligence

After close to a quarter-century's experience in government, I am convinced that secrets are inherently pathological, undermining reasoned judgment and open discussion. With the exception of relatively limited technical information and some information about plans and intentions, most of what we want to know is readily and cheaply available through the art and science of scholarship and personal interaction.

It is one of the great tragedies of our time that scholarship has lost so much ground, has been forced into mediocrity by the pressures of time, overload, and plain human failure. A lack of ethics and credibility in the academic community leads directly to ethical abuse in the intelligence community, for even when hiding behind secrets, the intelligence community has always been vulnerable to the detection of ridiculous assumptions by articulate and insightful scholars.

A wise man once said, "A nation's best defense is an educated citizenry." One could make the case that knowledge is the foundation for democracy, and that without an "open books" approach to national knowledge, we are destined to become the slaves of the rich, or worse. The purchasing and securing of patents for more fuel-efficient engines, "indestructible" polymeric paints, and other good ideas, solely to protect investments in archaic industrial plants, illustrate the problems that occur when knowledge is treated as property. Individuals end up paying much more for certain products, both because of inefficient production processes and because there is insufficient knowledge of external diseconomies such as pollution and waste.[2]

My proposed paradigm in no way allows for the establishment of a government monopoly on information handling, or government control over the way that we manage data and knowledge. On the contrary, this paradigm forces the issue of "who owns knowledge"? (I maintain it is in the public domain) and severely limits the degree to which any organization, in or out of government, can withhold knowledge from the public.

Ecology and Intelligence

We are our own worst enemy. Although there is a healthy increase in interest by our national leadership in environmental intelligence, it is directed outward. The data obtained by national intelligence about external environmental conditional and practices must be fully integrated with state and local data on environmental conditions and practices. Only in this way can we reasonably assess the "cost" of a specific product in relation to both inefficient production processes that consume raw materials in excess and also produce waste and pollution that "cost" the individual in terms of resources, time, and money required for mechanical disposal, and environmental degradation.

---

[2] For an interesting examination of how an industrial system also undermines the moral foundation of a society—kinship—and thus establishes the foundation for national and industrial decision-making against the best interests of the people *qua* people, see Lionel Tiger, *The Manufacture of Evil: Ethics, Evolution, and the Industrial System* (Harper & Row, 1987).

Taken in combination, what we are doing to the environment through tacit sanction by our *national* energy, trade, defense, housing, and education policies is far worse, every day, than a whole series of Chernobyls.[3]

Evolution and Intelligence

The Cold War cost us both resources and perspective. Because of the Cold War, we paid no attention to "lesser" threats and circumstances which, we are now beginning to recognize, represent a cumulative threat to our survivability and prosperity. There are subtle threats, difficult to observe and understand, and the remedies are also subtle, difficult to articulate and implement. As a result, we are now in the same position as the forest ranger who, for being so intent on avoiding the bear, fails to see the encircling fires. Now both the ranger and the bear are about to be burned alive.

Evolution requires recognition of change, flexibility of posture, and fleetness of adaptation. There are only two ways to "force" evolution: through overwhelming force, a role this nation will never accept (we *could* have turned our forces loose on the Middle East and totally eliminated all weapons in both the Arab coalition and Israel); or through education. This latter approach (the preferred solution for a democracy) requires an educated citizenry. It is now clear to all of us that we are "losing our mind"[4] as a nation. I see national intelligence, and a presidential initiative in conveying to every citizen the nature of the nonmilitary threats to our survival, as the only means of catalyzing our educational system into reform. From education comes evolution—the alternative is deepening depression and chaos, as the nine regions of North America[5] choose to fend for themselves, and ethnic fragmentation takes its toll on the commonweal.

---

[3] Walter Truett Anderson's *To Govern Evolution: Further Adventures of the Political Animal* (Harcourt, 1987), while as yet obscure, is an extraordinary reading.

[4] I take this notion from Chester E. Finn, Jr.'s *We Must Take Charge: Our Schools and Our Future* (Free Press, 1991); two other books of note, both focused on content, character, and culture, are those of Allan Bloom, *The Closing of the American Mind* (Touchstone, 1987) and William J. Bennett, *The Devaluing of America: The Fight for Our Culture and Our Children* (Summit, 1992).

[5] Joel Garreau, in *The Nine Nations of North America* (Houghton Mifflin, 1981), makes a compelling case for the influence of geography on the Western Hemisphere, outlining nine distinct geographical entities with their corresponding ethnic and cultural groupings.

Where Do We Start?

Where do we start? I see intelligence as part of a continuum, or a larger national construct, which must also include our formal educational process, our informal cultural values, our structured information-technology architecture, our informal social and professional networks for information exchange, our political governance system extending not only internationally but down to the state, local, and citizen level; and as traditionally defined, as an integral element of the federal bureaucracy.

Again, with a genuflection toward civil libertarians, I must stress that my "open books" approach to a national knowledge architecture in no way creates a government monopoly or increases government opportunities to impose "necessary illusions;"[6] on the contrary, this approach to knowledge represents a radical departure from the current practice of allowing organizations to conceal and manipulate knowledge against the common interest.

On this basis, one can suggest that Congress and the Executive would be seriously remiss if they were not moving aggressively toward a national open-systems architecture and simple, direct connectivity between public and private educational institutions (e.g. reference librarians and library search systems); corporate marketing and research centers; state and local government information centers; ethnic, religious and other cultural information "gatekeepers;" and, ultimately, any citizen's computer terminal.

This is the long-term objective. A measure of our situation today is the degree to which the intelligence community is integrated with all of the departments of the federal government (Agriculture, Commerce, Education, Energy, Housing and Urban Development, Interior, Justice), not just the traditional national security departments (State, Defense). The answer is not good. In fact, it is very bad, for even the traditional customers must receive their "intelligence" in bulky compendiums of hard-copy, most of it overclassified, too narrowly focused, and untimely enough to be almost useless

---

[6] I take this phrase from Noam Chomsky's *Necessary Illusions: Thought Control in Democratic Societies* (South End, 1989). See also Edward S. Herman and Noam Chomsky, *Manufacturing Consent: The Political Economy of the Mass Media* (Pantheon, 1988).

when contrasted with the flood of "good enough" open-source material (which does not need a mass of security guards to register and control the data). The nontraditional consumers at the federal level receive little or no intelligence support and there is no systematic integration, correlation, or comparison of the open-source information they use with the secret data of the intelligence community.

Priority to People

What steps must we take today to achieve an integrated national intelligence system by the year 2001?

The intelligence community spends too much money on extremely expensive technical collection systems, whose flood of digital information cannot be processed by existing or planned methods and personnel. Less than 10 percent of what we collect with these systems is processed, calling into question the return on investment. Our analysts are few in number, and generally inexperienced—few analysts responsible for the study of a particular country, for instance, have ever actually lived in that country, learned the language, or gotten to know the social nature and cultural character of the people about whom they are supposed to be "expert."

Our analysts are also cloistered away from their customers, the policy-makers and the action officers, and have little significant interaction with their academic, industrial, and foreign counterparts—in part because of security restrictions and in part because intelligence management refuses to the give them the time to travel, train, and reflect. Analysts are instead chained to their desks, force-fed a dry diet of hard-copy intelligence, deprived of most open-source materials, and expected to "produce" sterile, uncontroversial, "objective" reports.

In my judgment, analysts should spend one-third of their time traveling and training, one-third working directly with consumers (including academic and industrial consumers), and on-third doing *analysis* that may or may not result in a product. We should nurture private-sector analysts as well as government analysts, perhaps by providing joint training programs, joint travel opportunities, and so on.

Priority to Open Sources

I have written in chapter two about our desperate need for a means of managing our unclassified and open source capabilities that is untainted and unbiased by direct association with the traditional intelligence community. Elements of the government now dealing with open sources should be consolidated under such a program and granted an independent charter to enable them to support not only the intelligence community, and the remainder of the Federal government that has been starved for information, but also the private sector and even foreign organizations as appropriate.

Such a program would not be successful without a direct Congressional charter and separate program, and I therefore recommend that Congress follow the precedent it created with Special Operations/Low Intensity Conflict, and create a Consolidated Open Source Program. A significant portion of the funds in this program should be used to build upon the funds appropriated for the National Security Education Act of 1991, and used to dramatically upgrade educational programs (beginning in elementary school) and industrial information resources devoted to our knowledge of the physical, political, economic, and cultural environment.

Priority to Open Systems

The issues of privacy and computer security aside, there is much to be said for accelerating the electronic connectivity of the Nation; as quickly as possible every government action officer should be accessible through Internet-like channels, and every university professor, high school geography or history teacher, business executive, and student should be part of a national network of readily identifiable individuals with common interests.

The National Research and Education Network initiative is a good one, but as I and others have written, if we do not provide for the rural roads and comfort stations needed by *individuals*—including the millions that do not yet own or know how to use a computer—this initiative will be of little value to the broad population of literate persons requiring rapid access to multi-media knowledge. I would move the government, including the national security structure, to an unclassified open systems baseline, and sharply reduce the production and dissemination of classified information while increasing the availability of government-collected and government-generated information to the public through electronic channels.

Consumers of intelligence—including the highest policy-making officials whom the multi-billion dollar community considers its most important customers—have often stated, they would rather have an unclassified surrogate that is "good enough" to work with, than a highly classified and extremely accurate photograph or report which they cannot use with their counterparts. Analysts should be able to use classified information to inform themselves and validate their views, but they should focus production efforts on the unclassified side, providing information which can not only go to individual government consumers, but which can also go into the public domain through the open architecture.

Redefine National Security

A Presidential Blue Ribbon Commission, including representatives of various industries, academic sectors, and major Departments of government, should be brought together to redefine national security and our strategic objectives as a Nation. The Rudman Commission has been plagued with internal problems and will not produce the visionary findings that are needed. Some progress was made in this direction by National Security Review 29. The results, which include significantly increased emphasis on the environment as a "target" for collection and analysis, are never-the-less inadequate in that we have not truly come to grips with what our changed national strategy should be, nor what changes should take place in relations between our government and the private sector, between our Nation and other nations, and between U.S. non-governmental organizations and foreign or international non-governmental organizations.[7]

---

[7] I hold the view that government cannot abdicate its role in nurturing our culture and its educational foundation—that statecraft is indeed soulcraft—and that government expenditures are less important with respect to what they actually purchase in services and more important in terms of their influence on the private sector. Government expenditures should establish a foundation that encourages private sector outlays in positive ethical and environmental directions. Among the books that have influenced me are George Will, *Statecraft as Soulcraft: What Government Does* (Simon & Shuster, 1983); William Lind, *Cultural Conservatism: Toward a New National Agenda* (Institute for Cultural Conservatism, 1987); Herbert Stein, *Governing the $5 Trillion Economy* (Oxford, 1989); Albert L. Malabre, Jr., *Within Our Means: The Struggle for*

In brief, as nuclear and conventional forces cease being the arbiters of power, as many (but not all) nation-states regress to pre-sovereign conditions; and as other forces, (economics, environmental changes, and ideo-cultural movements) come to the fore as key areas of competition and challenge, we need to redefine who our national intelligence consumers are. In economic warfare, our private sector (industry, academia, and citizenry) provide the "troops" and thus requires the kind of intelligence support that national intelligence has previously provided to the tactical commander. Simultaneously, in ideo-cultural competition, it is primarily private sector organizations that require an improved understanding of their "competition" and of the demographic playing field upon which they are competing. We no longer need multi-billion dollar investments in systems designed to cover strategic nuclear missiles; instead, we need a multi-billion dollar investment in national knowledge architectures and global collection, analysis, and dissemination sources and methods which are *open, free,* and *unclassified.*

These thoughts are consistent with those of Mitch Kapor and his concept of a National Public Network.[8] My point is a simple one: national power ultimately stems from the people, even if that power might be abdicated by the people or stolen by the rich and political. Knowledge is power, and one could say that the people require and will obtain knowledge in one of two ways: by participating in a cooperative venture in which the government facilitates and nurtures information exchange, in much the same way that it facilitated inter-state commerce; or through revolution, in which the people, aided by hackers, "break open" the vaults of knowledge and refuse the government and private sector organizations their current privilege of concealing or keeping from the marketplace knowledge which merits dissemination and exploitation.

Economic Recovery After a Reckless Decade (Random House, 1991); and David M. Abshire, *Preventing World War III: A Realistic Grand Strategy* (Harper & Row, 1988). The latter book, despite its title, is a superb description of how the president should and could take charge of long-term policy planning across all dimensions of our domestic and foreign environment.
[8] As found in the *Whole Earth Review*, Issue #74, page 72.

Protection of Privacy

For those concerned about the protection of privacy, with civil libertarian issues, I would again stress that my concept of national intelligence is focused on collecting predominantly open information about conditions and entities beyond our borders, for the purpose of informing our public and private persons; my concept does not call for the collection of information about people within our borders—in fact, were knowledge about our people necessary (e.g. for demographic studies, census reviews, etcetera) I would be the first to call for "electronic aliases" in which it would be illegal to associate a true name with any compiled information about more than one person. By stressing the predominance of *unclassified* information, we essentially provide our public with an "open books" approach to knowledge and government management, while significantly increasing the synergy between private sector data and public sector data.

The Real Revolution

As civilization has evolved, and the sources of power have changed over time, from tribal mass to political force to financial leverage, each era has faced the challenge of adapting to change. We have reached a turning point, one where the ultimate source of power is finally recognized—knowledge. I conclude with an observation from Will and Ariel Durant, who in their lifetime of studying civilizations, east and west, north and south, came to the following realization:

> *"The only real revolution is in the enlightenment of the mind and the improvement of character, the only real emancipation is individual, and the only real revolutionists are philosophers and saints."*[9]

We are a smart people, but a dumb Nation, and this is something we must change if we are prosper and be secure in the 21st Century.

---

[9] Will and Ariel Durant, *The Lessons of History* (Simon & Schuster, 1968), page 72.

Part II:
From War to Peace

There is, of course, a global system. But it is not what most people imagine it to be. Efforts to prevent, limit, end, or settle wars, whether by armies or peace activists or anyone else, require some understanding of the system within which the war is taking place. If our map of the system is obsolete, picturing it as it was yesterday, rather than as it is fast becoming, even the best strategies for peace can trigger the opposite. Twenty-first century strategic thinking, therefore, must start with a map of the global system of tomorrow.

Alvin & Heidi Toffler[1]

Part II contains five chapters and covers the period 1995-1999 during which the intelligence community successfully avoided implementing any of the major recommendations from the National Performance Review sponsored by President Clinton and Vice President Gore, or from either of two bi-partisan, Congressionally-mandated commissions, the Commission on the Roles and Capabilities of the United States Intelligence Community, and the Commission on Protecting and Reducing Government Secrecy.

Interestingly, during this same period there was an internal revolution within the military, where the terms "asymmetric warfare" and "information operations" came into vogue. The emerging military concept of "information superiority", despite being largely lip service to the concept of getting the right information to the right person at the right time, helped legitimize more radical perspectives on intelligence. The open source intelligence points of contact within the theater commands are going to be the catalyst for broader reform.

---

[1] Alvin and Heidi Toffler, *War and Anti-War: Survival at the Dawn of the 21st Century* (Little Brown, 1993), page 241.

Chapter 6, "TAKEDOWN: The Asymmetric Threat to the Nation", summarizes the findings of the 1998 Army Strategy Conference, and concludes that we face four distinct threats or challenges to our national security in the 21st Century, and therefore require four distinct "forces" *only one of which is a traditional military force.* This chapter also touches on the intelligence implications as well as the need for new divisions of labor between the active duty and reserve forces, and between the government and the private sector.

Chapter 7, "Open Source Intelligence: The Private Sector & National Security" provides an executive overview of why both government and business executives need to demand improved open source intelligence support and outlines private sector capabilities to provide very substantial global coverage and near-real-time intelligence.

Chapter 8, "Relevant Information: The Emerging Revolution" is a strategic examination of what is wrong with today's government doctrine for keeping policymakers, acquisition managers, and commanders informed. It identifies three major deficiencies: the lack of collection management staffs, the lack of access to open sources of intelligence, and the lack of a genuine all-source analysis and fusion capability at the departmental and command levels.

Chapter 9, "Virtual Intelligence for the Diplomat and the War-Fighter" is an in-depth look at the concept of "virtual intelligence", a concept that fully integrates the private sector into national intelligence support to decision-making. In three parts, this chapter examines what we need to know and why; the perils and promise of information technology; and the opportunities to create—through a national information strategy—a rewarding content-based partnership between government and the private sector.

Chapter 10, "Information Peacekeeping: The Purest Form of War" outlines an operational approach to the use of intelligence as a substitute for munitions. The elements of information peacekeeping are open source intelligence, information technology, and electronic security. Information peacekeeping is the operational counterpart to the virtual intelligence community—together they comprise the two critical elements of a national information strategy with global reach.

TAKEDOWN:
The Asymmetric Threat
to the Nation

You may not be interested in war, but war is interested in you.

Trotsky

Can America be defeated through asymmetric means that strike at the known Achilles' heels of the military, as well as key nodes in the largely unprotected civil infrastructure?

A recent Army conference provides a strong answer: YES. This leads me to propose not one, but *four* distinct "forces after next", each with a distinctive mix of reserve and civil counterpart elements.

I also take the opportunity to present ideas for new distributions of responsibility between the government and the private sector, and between the active and the reserve components of our armed forces.

"Challenging the United States Symmetrically and Asymmetrically: Can America be Defeated", was the focus of the Ninth Annual Strategy Conference hosted by the U.S. Army War College in 1998, and the findings were clear: "No, we cannot be defeated" by symmetric attack and "Yes, we can be defeated" by asymmetric attack. [1]

---

[1] Hosted by MajGen Robert H. Scales, Jr., Commandant, and opened by LtGen Paul K. Van Riper, USMC (Ret.), the conference brought together what may be the single largest collection of iconoclasts and "out of the box" thinkers who are both available to the Department of Defense, and allowed to speak publicly on this important question. Dr. Earl H. Tilford, Jr., Director of the Strategic Studies Institute, led the team that conceptualized and organized this superb event.

The Threat: Four Warrior Classes, Not One

World War II spawned what President Eisenhower called the U.S. "military-industrial" complex, and America's way of war for the 20th Century was confirmed. Despite lessons from Viet-Nam and pressures from Congress that ultimately resulted in the creation of Program 11, Special Operations and Low Intensity Conflict capabilities, the U.S. military machine today remains just that—a machine that stresses the procurement of fewer and fewer astonishingly expensive weapons systems and mobility platforms, each less and less useful across the spectrum of violent peace and hidden war that confronts us now and into the 21st Century.

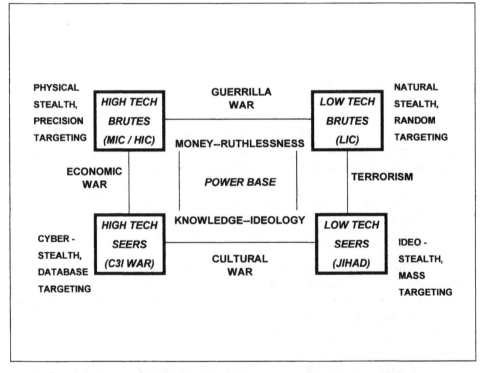

Figure 18: Four Warrior Classes Confronting America

The figure above provides an illustrated short-hand description of the four warrior classes we must confront in the 21st Century.

Without going into great detail here,[2] suffice to say that we are only moderately prepared, both in our war-fighting capabilities and our intelligence capabilities, to deal with the first of these four warrior classes, the "high-tech brute". Each of the other three warrior classes represents a different kind of intelligence challenge, a different kind of deterrence challenge, a different kind of victory challenge. The "way of war" of these three warrior classes, the kinds of war they choose to fight and at which they excell, represent what we call the "asymmetric" challenge to America in the 21st Century.

The Bottom Line

In the largest sense, the conference called into question Joint Vision 2010, and documented the need for abandoning the force structure—but not the budget—required to fulfill—simultaneously—two Major Regional Conflicts (MRC) and a minor contingency (the "2+" approach). Although not endorsed by all present, the strategic vision offered as a substitute might be the "1 + iii" approach—one MRC, one low intensity conflict or law enforcement support scenario, one major humanitarian relief operation, and one major electronic campaign—either in the offense or the defense—"1 + iii", simultaneously.

The most difficult issue confronting most of the participants was not that of threat identification, nor even that of response development, but rather the more ambiguous political issue of "whose job is it?" According to many present, the U.S. military must not allow itself to be distracted from its primary responsibility to prepare for, deter, and win conventional wars. However, all present appeared to recognize that the U.S. government is not trained, equipped, and organized to deal with three of the four threat classes, and therefore the larger challenge may be internal to the U.S. government as a whole—developing concepts, doctrine, and organizational means of working across legal, cultural, and budgetary boundaries.[3]

---

[2] This typology was first articulated in detail in the author's "The Transformation of War and the Future of the Corps", in *INTELLIGENCE: Selected Readings—Book One* (Marine Corps University, AY 1992-1993).

[3] This conclusion bears a striking similarity to the conclusion of the Navy's Technology Initiatives Game 1991, after which Vice Admiral Reynolds reported to the Chief of Naval Operations that technology was not the challenge. Instead, the organizational difficulty in developing new concepts and doctrine represented the greatest challenge to adaptation, as discussed in the author's earlier "C4I: The New Linchpin" (*Proceedings*, July 1992).

A Naval Officer Opens

LtGen Paul K. Van Riper, USMC (Ret.) set the stage for the conference with hard-hitting remarks about how the past fifty years have left us with a defense decision-making system that has forgotten how to plan, cannot adapt to change, and is incapable of stimulating a serious dialogue. From Joint Vision 2010 to "dominant battlefield awareness", we are burdened with the proverbial naked emperor.

With specific reference to information operations and asymmetric warfare, LtGen Van Riper stated in no uncertain terms that we have no one who can really define what information superiority means or how we achieve it—we have substituted pablum publications for strategic thinking; and wishful thinking about how we want to wage war, in lieu of realistic planning.[4]

Desert Storm (the Gulf War), seen by many to be the catalyst, the vindication, or the culminating point for the so-called Military Technical Revolution, must be considered with great caution. The enemy may have suffered a tactical defeat, but at the strategic level not only retained power, but grew in influence in both the Arab and Islamic worlds. In particular, the failed promises of aviation have not been scrutinized, and too many senior decision-makers continue to believe that strategic and tactical aviation can preclude the need for placing infantry at risk.

---

[4] Our acquisition of systems continues to be characterized by a complete avoidance of the tough issues of intelligence and logistics supportability. Major programs, such as the Army's multi-billion dollar communications program, continue to "assume" that all needed data will be provided in digital form by the U.S. Intelligence Community or "other" sources, and continue to avoid planning for either the hard task of discovering and digitizing critical external information (including maps and other foreign area information), and also the hard task of communicating with coalition partners who do not have space-age computers and the kind of bandwidth that the U.S. considers commonplace.

The Historical Perspective

Several distinguished historians[5] examined lessons from the past, but were perhaps most helpful in provoking thoughts for the future:

- Mobility is more important than mass.

- Technology is worth little in the absence of timely and insightful intelligence, and geospatial data at a useful level of resolution.

- Tools must fit the target—we cannot afford to take out hundreds of small targets with extremely expensive high precision munitions.[6]

- Time and space are much more available to our enemies than to ourselves—and can be traded for bodies and bullets.

- The enemy's objective is to get us to spread ourselves too thin—yet we persist in starting every confrontation that way: spread too thin.

---

[5] Dr. John F. Guilmartin, Jr. of Ohio State University; Colonel Robert Dougherty of the U.S. Military Academy; and Dr. Donald J. Mrozek of Kansas State University.

[6] According to unclassified internal reports in the aftermath of the Gulf War, the U.S. Navy exhausted its supplies of precision munitions within the first eight days of firing. At the time there was also discussion of the cost difference between an 8" round from a battleship ($800) and a Harpoon missile ($80,000), and also of the disconcerting evidence then appearing that many of our "precision" munitions actually missed the target—either because of internal design flaws, or the absence of adequate targeting data from the U.S. Intelligence Community. Subsequently, in an attack on a Saudi Arabian terrorist based in Afghanistan, the U.S. expended $79 million dollars worth of precision munitions to kill 26 people and wound 40 while failing to kill the terrorist. This sum is very close to the annual operating cost, including salaries for the crew, of a battleship carrying the much cheaper (and actually much more reliable) 8" rounds.

The Threat Today—Non-State and State

Seven speakers provided a comprehensive review of the non-state threat today. Their most telling observations are summarized below:

- We are our own worst enemy—continuing to procure computers which are wide open to errors & omissions, inadvertent destruction of data, insider abuse, and outside attack (the least of our problems).[7]

- U.S. vulnerabilities to asymmetric attack are largely in the civil sector, and include bridges, levees, dams; power and telephone switches; and downlinks for the U.S. Intelligence Community and operational commands. Most vulnerable of all are the data managed by banks and major logistics elements including fuel suppliers.[8]

- Our enemies will succeed by waging war between the seams in our legal system, not our operational capabilities.[9]

- Time favors the enemy using any kind of information virus.[10]

- Our future enemies will not be stupid—they will choose carefully between stand-off, indirect (anonymous) and hands-on attacks.[11]

---

[7] The author, in "TAKEDOWN: Tools, Targets, & Technocracy". The paper is available at http://www.oss.net/TAKEDOWN.

[8] *Ibid.* Admiral Arthur K. Cebrowski, then J-6 of the Joint Chiefs of Staff, first articulated the military's vulnerability through the private sector with his staff and public briefings on "sanctuary lost". Winn Schwartau, author of *INFORMATION WARFARE: Chaos on the Electronic Superhighway* (Thunder Mouth Press, 1994), is his civilian precursor.

[9] Mr. Edmund M. Glabus, Aegis Research Corporation, "Blindsided by Viruses: Unconventional Weapons of Mass Destruction"

[10] *Ibid.*

[11] Dr. Steven Metz, Strategic Studies Institute, "Trans-National Threats"

- The political, economic, and technological climate favors an increase in terrorism and asymmetric attack. This will lead to the privatization of security, the militarization of the police, and the gendarmnification of the military.[12]

- Our existing criteria for victory are impossible to achieve (decisive victory, limited casualties).[13]

- Our existing force structure is vulnerable to superior asymmetric maneuvering in time, space, and materials (e.g. infrasonic waves easily penetrating armor to harm personnel).[14]

- We continue to be vulnerable to well-informed campaigns to manipulate the international media and our home public's perceptions, especially with regard to atrocities and casualties.[15]

- Our Achilles heel in future overseas deployments will be our dependence on volunteer civilian contractors essential to the maintenance of complex technologies beyond the abilities of our uniformed personnel—as soon as they are terrorized, we lose our cohesion.[16]

- When all is said and done, most men, and especially men from non-Western cultures and less-developed areas, are capable of taking great pleasure in great evil—the human

---

[12] Dr. Stephen Sloan, University of Oklahoma, "Terrorism and Asymmetry"

[13] Dr. Robert J. Bunker, California State University, "Five-Dimensional (Cyber) Warfighting: Can the Army After Next be Defeated Through Complex Concepts and Technologies" (Strategic Studies Institute, 10 March 1998). Although very difficult to read, this paper briefs better than it reads, and was—in the author of this article's mind--the most exciting paper presented in the entire conference.

[14] *Ibid.*

[15] Col Charles Dunlap, U.S. Strategic Command, "Asymmetrical Warfare and the Western Mindset"; this officer is also the author of the very influential article, "How We Lost the High Tech War of 2007", *The Weekly Standard* (29 January 1996).

[16] *Ibid.*, in luncheon remarks.

factor cannot be ignored and cannot be underestimated as a cause and a sustaining element in conflict.[17]

The three speakers addressing state-on-state conflict offered several useful insights:

- One man's limited war is another man's total war—U.S. perceptions of "information operations" as a form of warning or limited attack are completely at variance with Russian perceptions of C4I attacks as "core" attacks against the very survival of the state.[18]

- It is not enough to win in the field—you must also win strategically.[19]

- Lessons to be drawn from the Gulf War include the essential nature of coalitions; the critical value of public support that can only be achieved if policies and objectives are explained and make sense; and the importance of timing in identifying and responding to challenges.[20]

- Related to states, but going beyond states, one speaker identified the following six functional areas of concern:[21]

---

[17] Mr. Ralph Peters, distinguished author and retired LtCol, USA, in "Our New Old Enemies". His earlier article, "The New Warrior Class", in *Parameters* (Summer 1994), ranks with Col Dunlap's (*supra* note 15) as one of the seminal works in considering the nature of modern war.

[18] Dr. Stephen J. Blank, Strategic Studies Institute, "Major State Strategies: Russia". Dr. Blank also noted that today's information warriors appear to overlook the "dead hand threat" of pre-programmed launch in the event C4I links are cut. Dr. Blank also commented that under such circumstances, the imminent potential of a U.S. information warfare attack could provide an incentive for a nuclear first strike.

[19] *Ibid.* Implicit throughout the conference, in the remarks of many speakers, was the sense that the Department of Defense in particular, and the U.S. government in general, have completely lost all understanding of how to think strategically.

[20] Dr. Stephen C. Pelletiere, Strategic Studies Institute, "Regional State Competitors: Middle Eastern Candidates".

[21] Dr. Kori N. Schake, "Other Possible State Competitors: Have You Thought About ____?"

- Anti-U.S. coalitions such as Iran-Iraq; or an Asian economic block;

- New borders and contested new states such as a Kurdish Republic challenging Turkey, Iraq, and Saudi Arabia—or Kosovo (90% Albanian, within Serbia);

- Regime changes such as may emerge within North Korea, Egypt, and Saudi Arabia;

- Conditions inhibiting the use of U.S. forces;

- Critical dependence on allies; and

- Criminalization of governments such as has occurred in Colombia and Mexico.

Summary Conclusions

The concluding panel began with a summary of the event by Dr. John Allen Williams of Loyola University in Chicago, and the following is noteworthy:

> *Getting into their heads is more important*
> *than getting into their bytes.*

This observation by Dr. Williams is based on the numerous references throughout the conference to the fact that an *understanding* of potential enemies, their circumstances, and especially their cultural context, is perhaps more vital than any technological advantage. Indeed, the whole point of the conference seemed to be that our technology is *not* an advantage in asymmetric warfare, but rather a vulnerability, and that the only recourse we have to defend ourselves under these circumstances is a greater *understanding* of the threats, and hence an ability to address their root causes intelligently, in time to avoid conflict.

Dr. Williams provided a very succinct summary of the conference, and additional observations. His summary:

- We must respect the utility of history.

- U.S. will continue to have great difficulty in dealing with complexity and non-linear conditions, especially since our expensive systems are driving us in one direction and reality is often found in the other direction.

- Reserve sources have important roles to play—but we have not really defined what they can do in pursuing asymmetric strategies.

- There is some question about the ability of the U.S. to combat certain challenges, including domestic terrorism and ambiguous threats.

Expanding upon his summary observations, Dr. Williams brought forward four additional areas requiring further consideration:

- Fallacy of misplaced concreteness—we are too quick to accept our programmed systems and our approved force structure as a given of value.

- Offensive asymmetry—we have not explored the areas where we have an advantage.

- Nature of the planning process—does not deal with unanticipated radical shifts.

- Civil-military relations—need to examine the role of the military officer in educating the civil sector and advocating specific strategies for dealing with threats to the Nation.

MajGen Timothy Kinnan, Commandant, Air War College, was trenchant and to the point: we cannot afford the existing force structure, but the services are like rats in a box, eating each other over the allocation process. We need to move away from 2+. He went on to say:

> *Technology will not replace boots on the ground....its greatest contribution may be to let us all work together in real time and finally begin the process of integrating all of our components in a sensible fashion.*

MajGen Scales, host of the conference, closed with several points that should guide our future deliberations:

- States are unlikely to risk outraging the U.S.—"that's not the deal." They know where to draw the line between pushing for maximum gain and goading the elephant into extreme anger.

- Today's military appears to be splitting between Navy-Air Force reliance on air power, and Marine Corps-Army reliance on ground power as the fulcrum for victory.

- We clearly need to rethink and create a new military— must look beyond 2010. Ten years is the blink of an eye— we can take it slow on technological reforms and investments for a decade, see what time brings.

- The issue is one of balance—of how to achieve interdependence rather than interoperability. Need to start with a vision, not rush, think it through.

- Soldiers cannot be policemen—calls for totally different mind-sets, cultures, and reactions under fire; there are good reasons why soldiers are precluded from domestic employment.

> *People have a longer lead time than machines.*

If we focus on people, our priorities for the next decade or two should be:

- Leader development
- Training & education
- Doctrine
- Experimentation

The Way Ahead

Nothing in this chapter should suggest that anyone at the conference endorsed the following proposal for the future of the Department of the Defense and other elements of our national security structure. Their insights, however, would appear to clearly support the need for a more *balanced* national security force structure. The figure below shows the strategic and operational context for thinking about our future force structure.

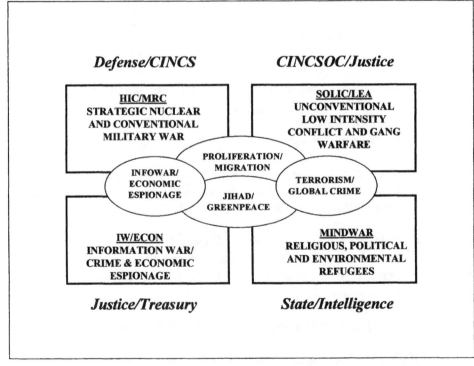

Figure 19: Realignment of Operational Defense Responsibilities

We must, in brief, create four "forces after next", each trained, equipped, and organized for dealing effectively with one of the four warrior classes facing us in the 21ˢᵗ Century. It will be difficult for us, because three of the four "forces" will not be military at all, but rather skilled at transnational law enforcement, feeding people, and the minutia of electronic crime and economic espionage. To accept this, and to lead this charge from in front, is the challenge facing the Secretary of Defense and his most senior military officers now serving.

Allocating the Existing Budget

I propose that the existing Department of Defense budget, with some increase, be gradually—over the next six years—realigned and allocated as follows:

- 60% (roughly $153.6 billion a year) to existing strategic nuclear and conventional forces, excluding special operations and low intensity conflict.[22]

- 20% (roughly $51.2 billion a year) to CINCSOC, with the caveat that no less than 5% (25% of the allocated amount or roughly $12.8 billion a year) be earmarked for direct support, including full-time civilian manpower, to transnational law enforcement. [This 5% for law enforcement agencies is left with CINCSOC rather than lumped with the final 10% for electronic security because the intent is to have a military-based bridge spanning the gray areas between para-military and coalition operations, and direct support to law enforcement.]

- 10% (roughly $25.6 billion a year) to the Secretary of State, and specifically to a revitalization of the U.S.

---

[22] Among other things, this cut should require a dramatic—indeed a draconian—reduction in U.S. subsidization of arms sales abroad, and a termination of virtually all U.S. foreign military aid. The level of U.S. aid to specific countries need not be reduced, but it should be converted into peacekeeping dollars under the oversight of the Secretary of State.

Information Agency, the Peace Corps, and selected sustainable development initiatives intended to deter and preclude conflict, including civil war, stemming from shortages of water, food, and other resources including civil order.[23]

- 10% (roughly $25.6 billion a year) to the Attorney General, who will serve as Executive Agent for a number of government departments responsible for various aspects of electronic security and counterintelligence within the U.S. and around the globe.

Active-Reserve Force Mix

The role of the Reserve—both the Ready Reserve and the National Guard—is very important. One can even suggest, given the following proposed alignments, that the role of the Reserve in the 21st Century is two to three times more important than it has been in the past.

- In conventional units, the active force must restore its ability to fulfill intelligence, military police, combat support, and combat service support functions, with no less than 75% of all required capabilities in the active force, and 25% in the Reserve.

- In low-intensity conflict and missions in support of transnational crime-fighting, the split should be closer to 50-50, with the Reserve providing the bulk of the foreign

---

[23] Our leadership and its intelligence community continue to down-play the environmental imperatives even though in isolated instances (e.g. Secretary of State Christopher (a Democrat), and before him Secretary of State Baker (a Republican)) we declare that the environment is a national security priority. Rwanda-Burundi were not about a "clash of civilizations"—they were about a shortage of water and food, combined with a break-down of the state, which caused the tribes to fall back into traditional forms of organization and traditional forms of violence, in seeking to secure adequate resources—never mind that this required the mass murder of "lesser" beings. The best "intelligence report" in this area remains the annually-produced *State of the World* from the Worldwatch Institute, under the leadership of Mr. Lester R. Brown (W.W. Norton, 1997).

area officers, linguists, and 90-180 day multi-lingual personnel with unique skill mixes needed for SOLIC and transnational criminal interdiction missions. A Law Enforcement Reserve within the National Guard (with special training and certification) is specifically envisioned.

- For missions in support of the Department of State and international missions of mercy, dealing with religious, political, and environmental refugees, the Reserve becomes vastly more important than the active force, and a 25-75 mix is appropriate. Major new Reserve units with regional, linguistic and civil affairs skills should be formed and ready for short and mid-term deployment in support of non-combat humanitarian assistance and sustainable development missions.

- Finally, to deal with the rapidly growing challenge of providing for electronic security and counterintelligence— for the protection of U.S. intellectual property upon which our national security and national competitiveness are founded, it is appropriate to return to a 50-50 mix, with uniformed and civilian active duty experts providing for a disciplined and knowledgeable "continuity of operations"—and the Reserve can be placed throughout the communications and computing industry, serving as a "network in place" of citizen-soldiers who understand the threat and can move easily between military and civilian occupations.[24]

The above discussion of the active-reserve mix should inspire a broad dialogue about completely redefining the nature of the Reserve. Only a small portion of the reserve force must be trained, equipped, and organized to conduct traditional conventional military operations—indeed, it may be that the largest portion of the reserve force need not be in uniform, and perhaps need not be pre-selected and pre-trained. Instead, we may find—and this is especially true of requirements for foreign area specialists and other experts—that we need a

---

[24] This is the Swiss model, in which all civilian communications nodes have trained military reservists in key positions.

vastly expanded concept of the reserve force which allows for the short-term contract hiring of any expert, anywhere in the world, without clearances and without the "recruit" needing a shave and a haircut or even basic military training!

Government-Private Sector Mix

After putting its own house in order, the greatest difficulty facing the military, and the U.S. government, is the determination of how best to divide responsibilities for dealing with serious threats, between the government and the private sector. Here the following are suggested as rough rules of thumb that might inspire specific legislative and financial incentive programs.

- Conventional military operations, 75% government, 25% private sector sustainment.

- Low intensity conflict/transnational crime, 50% government, 50% private sector (with special emphasis on private sector reporting responsibilities and auditing of records and containers in support of law enforcement and compliance).

- Refugee and cultural operations, 50% government and 50% private sector (with special emphasis on nurturing overt action and information peacekeeping operations by private sector non-profit groups).

- Information operations and defending against economic espionage, 25% government and 75% private sector (the government can set the standards and provide oversight for testing and certification laboratories, but the private sector must be made to realize that it bears the ultimate responsibility for protecting its own intellectual property).

In considering the role of the private sector in contributing to national security and the defense of the Nation across a spectrum of complex and often ambiguous threats, it merits emphasis that a classified threat is not an actionable threat to the private sector. As Senator Daniel Patrick Moynihan and

100

others have noted, there are significant policy and economic costs to secrecy, and among them, is our inability to communicate to our most important allies— our own private sector—the nature of the threat and the role they must play in defending America against such threats.[25]

Thinking Inside the Box

The resulting division of dollars and responsibilities might look something like this:

HIC/MRC
60% Existing DoD Budget
75% Active/25% Reserve
75% USG/25% Private Sector

SOLIC/LEA
20% Existing DoD Budget
50% Active/50% Reserve
75% USG/25% Private Sector

IW/ECON CI
10% Existing DoD Budget
50% Active/50% Reserve
25% USG/75% Private Sector

MINDWAR
10% Existing DoD Budget
25% Active/75% Reserve
50% USG/50% Private Sector

Abbreviations:

HIC	High-Intensity Conflict
MRC	Major Regional Conflict
SOLIC	Special Operations/Low Intensity Conflict
LEA	Law Enforcement Agencies
IW	Information Warfare
ECON CI	Economic Counterintelligence

Figure 20: Creating a Truly National Defense Community

---

[25] *Cf. SECRECY: Report of the Commission on Protecting and Reducing Government Secrecy* (Washington, D.C. 3 March 1997).

About Intelligence

Intelligence has traditionally been ' an after-thought within the Department of Defense, and we continue to build extraordinarily expensive weapons and mobility systems without regard to either strategic intelligence generalizations (acquiring systems limited to a few countries, or without regard to mobility constraints characteristic of most areas of operation), and without regard to whether or not we have the sensor-to-shooter architecture, and the equally vital global geospatial data (which we lack at the appropriate level of resolution for fully 90% of the world).[26]

> *Getting into their heads is more important*
> *than getting into their bytes.*

An important part of avoiding and resolving all conflicts which threaten the national security and national competitiveness of the United States of America, in the 21st Century, will revolve around giving the Director of Central Intelligence (DCI) the urgently needed authority to rationalize our national intelligence roles and missions and related capabilities. This community includes three important but mis-guided agencies (the National Security Agency, the National Reconnaissance Office, and the National Imagery and Mapping Agency), all using the bureaucratic stone walls within the Pentagon to avoid meaningful oversight. We process less than 6% of the signals we collect, and less than 10% of the classified imagery we collect. We spend $12.6 billion dollars a year on collecting classified imagery, and only $10 million a year on buying commercial imagery urgently needed by our peace-keepers and war-fighters. We continue to accept the complete absence of maps for most of the world at the 1:50,000 level where fires are coordinated and lives are saved.

---

[26] The official unclassified briefing by the National Mapping and Imagery Agency acknowledges that 90% of the world is not available at the 1:50,000 level (10 meter resolution) at which most military operations are coordinated. At this time the best maps available for the Third World, where most contingency operations are executed, are from the former Soviet Union, which has 1:100,000 coverage of most of the Third World, with contour lines, at roughly $300 a map sheet. Commercial image maps, with contour lines, can be obtained for roughly $6-10 per square kilometer, at the 1:50,000 level. Despite defining a requirement for $250-500M a year, NIMA only receives $10M a year for commercial sourcing.

A Balanced National Defense

The National Security Council (NSC) may or may not be the place from which to provide for day-to-day oversight of a balanced national defense. If the President were to re-define and enhance the duties of the Deputies Committee, and give both the Attorney General and the Secretary of State the broader charter they require, this might be a good solution. CINCSOC and the Assistant Secretary of Defense for Special Operations and Low Intensity Conflict also require special handling, possibly by integrating SOLIC and International Security Affairs under a new Under Secretary of Defense for Peacekeeping, who would then serve as a second DoD member of the Deputies Committee.

Whatever management forum is chosen, with the advice and consent of the Congress of the United States, we urgently need to set this plan in motion. The time has come to increase dramatically the operational reach and spending authority of both the Attorney General and the Secretary of State, while also down-sizing our conventional force structure and simultaneously doubling our SOLIC capabilities.

Until the Secretary of Defense acknowledges the vital role of the DCI, and fences the intelligence budget under the pre-eminent authority of the DCI, we cannot strike the proper balance between collection and processing, between secrecy and intelligence, and between an obsessive focus on traditional conventional enemies, and a more informed focus on the vastly more subtle— and vastly more difficult—threats and opportunities which face us in three of the four warrior classes.

Only DoD has the talent, the discipline, and the resources to fund this revitalization, but DoD must accept—and demand—the engagement of the Attorney General and Secretary of State, and of the DCI, in bringing about a renaissance in American national security. DoD cannot be forced into this— but if DoD will take the lead here, it will do far more to assure our national security in the 21st Century than it is now doing.

Open Source Intelligence: The Private Sector & National Security

...the concept of UN intelligence promises to turn traditional principles on their heads. Intelligence will have to be based in information that is collected primarily by overt means, that is by methods that do not threaten the target state or group and do not compromise the integrity or impartiality of the UN.[1]

If it is 85% accurate, on time, and I can share it, this is a lot more useful to me than a compendium of Top Secret Codeword materials that are too much, too late, and requires a safe and three security officers to move around the battlefield.[2]

Overview

National Security policy, acquisitions, and operations can be greatly enhanced and advanced through the use of Open Source Intelligence (OSINT) available from the private sector. Several aspects of post-Cold War politico-military issues lend themselves to an increased use of OSINT to assist policy-makers, acquisition program managers, and operational commanders:

---

[1] Hugh Smith, "Intelligence and UN Peacekeeping" in Survival (36/3, Autumn 1994), page 39, as cited by Sir David Ramsbotham, "Analysis and Assessment for Peacekeeping Operations" in Intelligence Analysis and Assessment (Frank Cass, 1996).

[2] Paraphrase of comment by Navy Wing Commander who led the lead flight over Baghdad, made at Technology Initiatives Game 1991, where author served as chairman of the National Intelligence Cell.

1) Contingencies tend to arise in lower Tier nations (per PDD-35) where U.S. classified capabilities are least applicable or largely unavailable.

2) Warning of these crises has not required classified collection.

3) These issues have required increased reliance on international organizations and non-traditional allies with whom information must be shared, which is difficult if not impossible with classified sources.

4) The "information explosion" has increased the amount of available information, while also creating a new "intelligence gap" between what needs to be known, and what can be processed and exploited.

OSINT, like all other intelligence sources, is more than information. It represents a careful sifting, selecting, analyzing and presenting of open source material on a timely basis. OSINT should be a valuable contributor to "all source" intelligence, although it continually gets short-shrift throughout the intelligence and policy communities.

Properly developed and implemented, the OSINT support process for national security decision-making should include SI/TK buffers and full security assurances, proper attention to copyright compliance, access to all foreign language sources as well as automated translation technologies, very strong emphasis on source validation, and full access to supporting materials by NS analysts and action officers.

OSINT can help national security decision-makers in two ways: (1) crisis support; and (2) support to on-going operations, bringing to bear in both cases the best and most relevant open sources to respond to established national security decision-support needs with OSINT rather than just information. OSINT includes global geospatial data and global logistics information.

Bureaucratic misperceptions notwithstanding, OSINT is not free to current users and is not being supplied by the Intelligence Community to the national security community in any significant way. However, a modest investment by national security elements themselves in OSINT can significantly multiply the effectiveness of current classified intelligence capabilities while simultaneously improving general intelligence support to policy makers, acquisition managers, and warfighters.

National Security and Open Source Intelligence

Faced with ever-increasing requirements for intelligence support—particularly in lower priority countries where classified capabilities have not been focused and operational funds have not been pre-programmed—the U.S. military has discovered the unique value of commercial imagery and developed EAGLE VISION and JOINT VISION. Commercial imagery is but one small portion of the remarkable range of open sources that can support national security policy-makers, acquisition program managers, and operational commanders. This chapter proposes that our national security community develop a concept of operations for providing open source intelligence (OSINT) to all elements of the national community, both here in the United States and overseas.

OSINT is uniquely suited for support to national security operations because OSINT relies exclusively on information and expertise obtained through legal and ethical means. This gives OSINT greater utility and flexibility in working with Congress, with foreign coalition partners, and with civilian agencies not routinely cleared for classified information. There are four primary reasons for this:

First, contingencies have tended to arise in lower Tier countries (as defined by PDD-35)—such as Haiti or Somalia—where the United States is paying much less attention overall and where national collection resources are least likely to provide much useful information, especially at the outset of a crisis. These are also areas where analytical expertise has been cut back into order to meet demands within the top Tiers and the Hard Targets. As the current DCI himself has observed, the Intelligence Community cannot now cover the hard targets and also provide global coverage.

Second, the lead-ups to these issues have not relied on highly classified intelligence as was often the case during the Cold War. Many of these situations—physical conditions in Somalia, the existence of a junta in Haiti, Milosevic's early statements of his intentions re Bosnia, refugee flows into Goma, Zaire—have been evident from unclassified sources.

Third, these issues have emphasized recourse to international organizations and broad diplomatic and military coalitions beyond the bounds of the United States' traditional allies and intelligence partners. These are not instances in which much classified intelligence can be easily used, given the increasing need to share information across a broad spectrum of partners.

Fourth, the "information explosion" has increased the amount of available information, while also creating a new "intelligence gap" between what needs to be known, and what can be processed and exploited. Both producers and consumers of intelligence are being flooded with information of mixed value, and both lack the expertise and tools to filter, distill, summarize, visualize, and digest the "nuggets".

OSINT has the advantages of providing a great deal of the intelligence that national security (NS) community would find useful as soon as the crisis breaks; of being available to the decision-makers independently and without waiting for the DCI and CIA to sort out their own priorities and needs; and of being more easily used within day-to-day operations in terms of sharing it with politico-military partners or coalition forces not cleared for classified.

OSINT Characteristics—Intelligence, Not Information

OSINT, also known as unclassified intelligence or, in the business community, as "decision support" or "business intelligence", must be carefully distinguished from open source information (OSIF), which is acquired in support of both the OSINT process carried out by the private sector, and the all-source process carried out by the U.S. Intelligence Community. OSIF consists of volumes of multi-media and multi-lingual information gathered for further processing and consideration. OSINT, in sharp contrast, integrates world-class human expertise with an integrated human-technical process to produce only "just enough, just in time" intelligence—information tailored to support a specific decision. The OSINT process includes four key elements:

1) ***Discovery.*** "Knowing who knows" and "knowing where to look" are the heart of a global OSINT process, which leverages distributed centers of expertise and archival knowledge. 80% of the information needed to create OSINT useful to NS is not online, not in English, and not available within the US.

2) ***Discrimination.*** Careful discrimination between good and bad sources, current and outdated sources, relevant and irrelevant sources, and finally, between cost-effective and cost-prohibitive sources, is part of the unique value of the OSINT process.

3) ***Distillation.*** The most important value added by the OSINT process is that of distillation, so that the final OSINT report can be as short as a paragraph or a page, and can communicate to the decision maker the essence of the collective wisdom pertinent to the decision under consideration. The OSINT process permits the out-sourcing of first echelon analysis, and allows world-class expertise to placed in the service of the in-house analysts and their NS customers.

4) ***Delivery.*** The best intelligence is the world is useless if it cannot be delivered to the customer in a timely fashion, in a media compatible with the in-house system, with adequate provision for security, and in a format that can be easily understood.

In other words, OSINT, if done correctly and systematically by knowledgeable professionals, is as rigorous, timely and focused as any other intelligence source available to decision-makers.

OSINT is not a substitute for classified "all-source" analysis. However, if the term "all source" is to have any true value then it must include OSINT where necessary and applicable. OSINT is often the only intelligence available during routine times and as the necessary first body of knowledge when the national intelligence community and policy makers are shifting toward the increased coverage required by crises. OSINT is widely acknowledged as an essential element for:

1) *Tip-off.* The most experienced intelligence analysts acknowledge the vital role played by open sources in tip-off regarding intentions, new weapons systems, and emerging crises.

2) *Context.* The expertise and historical knowledge to assess a situation rapidly, especially in a lower tier country or in an arcane issue area of limited historical interest to the U.S. government, is available from private sector experts whose decades of knowledge have been funded by others and can be tapped on a "just enough, just in time" basis.

3) *Collection Management.* A solid OSINT foundation is essential to those responsible for classified collection management, both within the consumer agencies and within the producer elements, because it permits the focus of classified capabilities on "the hard stuff".

4) *Cover.* Even when classified intelligence is available, OSINT can be used to protect sources and methods while still communicating essential insights and key findings to coalition partners, the press, and the public.

The Substance of OSINT

The greatest obstacle to improved use of open sources is not that of access, which is freely or inexpensively available to all, but rather that of acknowledgment. The two most erroneous perceptions among experienced national security professionals who should know better are that open sources are "merely a collection of newspaper clippings" (in the words of a senior Intelligence Community official) or "the Internet" (in the words of a general officer).

On the one hand, neither the national security community nor the U.S. Intelligence Community have properly inventoried the full range of private sector offerings, and neither has a credible foundation for identifying, evaluating, and exploiting a complex mix of "just right" open sources, softwares, and services. At the same time, both within the intelligence producer and the intelligence consumer communities, there is a reluctance to accept the fact that the U.S. Intelligence Community is no longer the sole source of critical information, nor the best source for open source information.

Sources. Representative sources include those associated with Current Awareness (e.g. Individual Inc.); Current Contents (e.g. ISI CC Online); Directories of Experts (e.g. Gale Research, TELTECH); Conference Proceedings (e.g. British Library, CISTI); Commercial Online Intermediaries (e.g. DIALOG, STN); Risk Assessment Reports (e.g. Forecast International, Political Risk); Maps & Charts (e.g. Russian military maps at the 1:100,000 level with contour lines, from East View Publications); and Commercial Imagery (e.g. SPOT Image, Radarsat, Autometric).

Software. Representative software which is commercially available and which an OSINT provider can integrate off-site, not requiring the client to buy new technology, include Internet Tools (e.g.Copernic.com or Net Reality); Data Entry Tools (e.g. Vista, BBN); Data Retrieval Tools (e.g. RetrievalWare, Calspan); Automated Abstracting (e.g. DR-LINK); Automated Translation (e.g. SYSTRAN); Data Mining & Visualization (e.g i2, PATHFINDER); Desktop Publishing & Communications Tools (many options); and Electronic Security Tools (e.g. SSI, IBM Cryptolopes, many emerging offerings).

Services. Representative services from the private sector include Online Search & Retrieval (e.g. NERAC, subject-matter and foreign language experts

111

listed in Burwell Worldwide Directory of Information Brokers); Media Monitoring (e.g. BBC, FBIS via NTIS); Document Retrievel (e.g. ISI Genuine Document); Human Abstracting (e.g. NFAIS members); Telephone Surveys (e.g. Risa Sacks Associates); Private Investigations (e.g. IGI, Kroll, Parvus, Pinkerton, INTELYNX); Market Research (e.g. SIS, Fuld, Kirk Tyson); and Strategic Forecasting (e.g. Oxford Analytica).

This token listing barely scratches the surface, and illustrates the importance to decision-makers of ensuring that its OSINT providers are able to document their investment in following the rapidly expanding, often changing, and frequently unstable nature of the open source world.

Beyond this depiction of the variety of open sources, software, and services that can be applied to the answering of requirements from consumers and producers of intelligence, is the distinction between those unclassified data resources which are readily available within the U.S. Intelligence Community; within the rest of the government; within the nation (i.e., in the private sector with its universities, information brokers, businesses, media, and other information activities); and within the larger global information community. It is absolutely essential that each intelligence producer and consumer have a "map" of this larger knowledge terrain, and a strategy for assuring their ability to discover, discriminate, distill, and digest critical open-source information and intelligence.

The Mechanics of OSINT

The OSINT provider must bring to bear the optimal combination of government-friendly security and understanding, with private sector savvy of open source copyright, foreign language capability, and source validation issues.

Security. The OSINT provider's key personnel must hold Top Secret SI/TK clearances, and be eligible for any compartmented clearances as required. Individual sources can hold SI/TK, Top Secret, and SECRET clearances—or no clearance at all—and this qualification can be treated similarly to language and subject matter qualifications. The OSINT provider should serve many clients and provide NS client with the same kind of obscurity and discretion that a bank provides its most valued private accounts. The OSINT provider should have a Sensitive Compartmented Information

Facility (SCIF) in its building and have Intel-Link and STU-III connectivity as desired. By using fully cleared personnel for the requirements process, and then balancing between in-house and sub-contract personnel who are not privy to the identity of the client and are also operating under non-disclosure contracts, the OSINT provider can fully protect the client's equities. When finding an expert (or several experts) to respond to a particular requirement, the OSINT provider should not reveal the requirement to the expert or contract with the expert until the client has reviewed a resume of the expert's qualifications and approved employment of the expert for the specific requirement.

Copyright. The OSINT provider should handle copyright through a combination of full compliance, in which the OSINT provider, without revealing the identity or interest of the client, acts as its agent to pay the copyright clearinghouse or obtain a copy through legal and ethical means; and the more common second means of avoiding copyright violation, by abstracting key ideas and data points with full citation. The OSINT provider should avoid the need to classify documents or otherwise restrict their handling to avoid honoring copyright—the client should receive products that are legally and ethically of the highest standard, and also receive indemnification from the OSINT provider with respect to copyright.

Foreign Language. Apart from languages spoken by the core management team, the OSINT provider's approach to foreign language qualifications should be identical to its approach to substantive qualifications. It was as the suggestion of OSS Inc. that *the Burwell Worldwide Directory of Information Brokers* added to its publication an index of foreign language and foreign database capabilities. Many other capabilities, such as the Monterey Institute of International Studies, use graduate students with native fluency in Arabic, Russian, Vietnamese, Korean, and many other languages. A few select technology companies offer advanced foreign language browsing and data extraction technologies with applications already developed for Russian, Chinese, Japanese, Arabic, French, German, Thai, and Spanish. Others can be readily developed.

Source Validation. The normal concern of military professionals with source validation, report integrity, and the reliability of the process upon which the open source intelligence reporting is based merits special attention.

1) The OSINT provider should employ the traditional rigor of the intelligence community analysis process, in that every source should be clearly and explicitly evaluated in terms of its authority, currency, and confidence level. In particular, the OSINT provider should be conscious of personal, political, cultural, and other biases associated with Internet, commercial online, offline, and individually-produced source material.

2) The true OSINT provider is in the business of discovering, distilling, discriminating, and delivering open source intelligence. This is a completely different process with significantly more value than the process of open source information discovery and delivery. *Open source information steals your time, open source intelligence buys you time!* The greatest value that the true OSINT provider can offer is that of first echelon technical processing (de-duplication, weighting, clustering, and summarization) and first echelon human analysis by experts who can be relied upon to evaluate and discriminate and also to distill intelligently. *In practical terms, this means that the over-burdened all-source analyst or decision-maker can avoid being overwhelmed by open sources because the true OSINT provider offers a complex filtering mechanism that relies primarily on subject-matter experts, and incidentally on technology.*

3) At the same time, the OSINT provider should offer a deliverable that permits the all-source analyst or policymaker to "drill down" to original source documents if they wish. For instance, if a question is asked and the OSINT provider supplies a one paragraph answer,

beneath that one paragraph answer, in HTML format or in hard-copy, as desired, should be the expert report, the commercial online documents, the Internet search results, and the memorandum of conversation for a verbal inquiry, if that is what the analyst or policymaker desires to have delivered.

4) The true OSINT provider should strive to serve as the "trusted agent" for the client, and specialize in "knowing who knows", "knowing where to look", and also in the value-added evaluation of sources and first echelon analysis which pre-processes open source for the all-source analyst. Every source used should be identified and available for scrutiny.

All-Source Access. The OSINT provider is a support activity. While it is capable of serving as the open source intelligence stovepipe, at no time should the OSINT provider assume the role of the in-house librarian, all-source analyst, or staff action officer. Initially, as a new client and their personnel become familiar with the quality and range of the OSINT provider's capabilities, there will be a tendency to "drill down" into the underlying sources. Eventually, as the value and the reliability of the process are proven, the supported analysts and policymakers will place greater and greater reliance, and value, on the fact that *the OSINT provider will deliver the briefest possible answer, in the shortest possible time, at the lowest possible cost—and will focus on answering the question of the moment rather than on inundating the analyst with unfiltered source material.*

Specific OSINT Support to National Security

There are two tracks for OSINT support to national security operations:

Crisis Support. In crisis support, a surge effort can tap a wide variety of private sector sources and services, and provide the policy-makers and commanders with quick but relatively comprehensive intelligence on the situation, to include personality studies, estimates of intentions, and rapid response air head and other logistics assessments.

On-Going Operations. On a routine basis, the policy-makers, acquisition managers, and commanders can receive periodic awareness reports, on-call QuickSearch services, access to experts on demand, and strategic forecasting support. Such support can be tailored to cover specific issue areas, specific named areas of interest, and specific technologies, system counter-measures, or vendors.

Crisis Support is illustrated below with a listing of the responses actually developed by OSS Inc. during "the Burundi exercise" requested by the Aspin/Brown Commission on Intelligence. The requirements were posed at 1700 on Thursday, 3 August 1995; private sector capabilities were tasked by 1500 on Friday, 4 August 1995; all requested materials were delivered to the Commission offices by 1000 on Monday, 7 August 1997.[3]

1) ***Strategic Orientation.*** Oxford Analytica provided a series of two-page assessments created over a two-year period for the World Bank and Prime Ministers around the world.

2) ***Academic Experts.*** The Institute of Scientific Information and citation analysis were used to identify the top experts available for immediate debriefing. Such individuals have a global network of life-

---

[3] The exercise is described in vague terms on page 88 of Preparing for the 21st Century: An Appraisal of U.S. Intelligence (report of the Commission on the Roles and Capabilities of the United States Intelligence Community, also known as the Aspin/Brown Commission). The two critical findings of the Commission on Intelligence with respect to open sources were that the U.S. Intelligence Community itself is "severely deficient" in lacking access to open sources and that this should be a "top priority for funding"; and—most pertinent to military operations—that intelligence consumers should not refer to the U.S. Intelligence Community any questions which can be answered "predominantly" by open sources. In the future, each intelligence consumer will be expected to develop their own open source intelligence capabilities, and to refer for classified collection only those questions that cannot be answered by the private sector.

long contacts, including top government and business officials in-country.

3) ***Journalists on the Ground.*** LEXIS-NEXIS was used to identify journalists of varying nationality who had been on the ground recently and were intimately familiar with personalities and the situation. Such individuals publish less than 10% of what they know, and have current appreciations for personalities, logistics, corruption, and other key factors of high interest to the Country Team.

4) ***Conflict Orientation.*** Jane's Information Group, of the United Kingdom, provided a very authoritative and easy to use map of tribal areas of influence, one page orders of battle for each tribe, and one paragraph summaries of all articles about the Burundi situation published by Jane's in the preceding two years.

5) ***Military Maps.*** East View Publications provided a listing of all immediately available military maps created by the former Soviet Union, at the 1:100,000 level and with contour lines. This is especially important because 90% of the lower tier countries have not been mapped by the United States below the 1:250,000 level.

6) ***Commercial Imagery.*** Belatedly but no less importantly, SPOT Image Corporation confirmed that it had available in its archives 100% of Burundi, cloud-free, and immediately available for the creation of military maps, precision munitions

117

targeting packages, and aviation mission rehearsal systems.

On-Going Support can accommodate a variety of recurring needs from policy-makers, acquisition managers, and commanders. Although each requirement will vary in its depth, priority, and mix of needs, the following four kinds of generic open source intelligence services have been established:[4]

Current Awareness. There are several private sector options for obtaining daily one page listings of key news stories matching specific profiles. These can be combined with Internet monitoring services (e.g., watching the discussion groups on Angola and Zaire) as well as the monitoring of academic and industry journals for "current contents." The consumer can then select full-text access or file full-text elements for later access—and this is all delivered in HTML format with technology embedded (de-duplication, clustering, weighting) and subordinate to a subject-matter expert's summary analysis and selective judgment. Foreign language and off-line sources of particularly high value can also be programmed for coverage.

QuickSearch Help Desk. With this service, the consumer has the option of calling, faxing, or sending electronic mail to obtain additional information, while also specifying a not-to-exceed price within an existing basic ordering agreement. This, like all aspects of good OSINT support, can be tasked and delivered via existing SI/TK channels which do not require any further investment in alternative unclassified architectures, or costly A-B multi-level switch augmentation. The Help Desk is able to access the full range of commercial online services (adding the value of both knowing which international services to use, and also the skilled searching knowledge which

---

[4] Mr. Jan Herring, Executive Vice President (Designate) of the OSS Business operating group, developed this practical and integrated concept for applying proven intelligence processes to unclassified information. Mr. Herring served a distinguished career in the U.S. Intelligence Community, retiring in 1988 after final service as the National Intelligence Officer for Science & Technology. He went on to be the founder of the U.S. business intelligence community, and was responsible for establishing the business intelligence units—all relying only on legally and ethically available information but applying the intelligence collection management and analysis processes to the unclassified information—for Motorola, Ford, Phillips Petroleum, NutraSweet, General Dynamics, Southwestern Bell, and Monsanto.

reduces costs from unproductive search strategies), and is also able to access the full range of international gray literature sources. It is important to emphasize that this concept does not rely on a single information broker or document acquisition source, but is optimized instead to identify and utilize those intermediaries who specialize in particular geographic or functional areas of inquiry and thus have decades of knowledge about both sources and search strategies, which cannot be replicated inside the U.S. government.

Experts on Demand. The full-service OSINT provider must offer a highly efficient process for identifying and utilizing world-class experts in any area of interest. This process should combine the use of selected intermediaries such as Oxford Analytica (strongest in the political-economic arena) with independent citation analysis and exploitation of its own (or a superior provider's) international network of open source intelligence experts. The bottom line: within a day or two a top expert can be identified who can be relied upon to produce an extremely informed analysis, benefiting from direct access to in-country indigenous sources as well as unpublished materials, which answers the question.

Strategic Forecasting. The proper approach to strategic forecasting combines automated citation analysis, automated content analysis, and selective exploitation of expert judgments. This combination allows very high-value products to be delivered for a tenth of the cost of the standard "beltway bandit" approach, and within a week to ten days instead of months or a full year.

Why Pay for Open Source Intelligence?

The nature of OSINT leads many to question why they should have to pay for it. After all, aren't these sources that are publicly available? There are several substantial reasons that justify a relatively modest expenditure for OSINT:

1) ***"Open Source" Does Not Mean "Free."*** No matter who undertakes to collect, sift and assess open source information in order to create OSINT—an outsider or an in-house analyst, there are inevitable costs associated with it in terms of time, access to on-line databases, etc.. Selected sources may indeed be

119

"free", and also full of bias, inaccurate, untimely, or focused away from the policymakers specific needs. The process of sifting, selecting, analyzing, and presenting open source intelligence is what adds great value, and the very best sources will not be free.

2) ***OSINT Is an Intelligence Community Stepchild.*** Under current practice, analysts are largely expected to undertake OSINT on their own, as time allows: reading newspapers and magazines; checking FBIS; perhaps attending the occasional conference. But none of this is supposed to detract from keeping on top of all classified sources and producing necessary analysis. The ultimate result is that necessary OSINT is given short shrift if not ignored completely. If "all source" is to have any value, then it must include OSINT. But if OSINT is going to make the contribution that it could, then it must be treated as seriously as other collection disciplines (imagery, signals, etc.), with its own dedicated resources. The key difference between OSINT and the other disciplines is that most if not all of these resources are most effective if left within the private sector. In fact, OSINT is not about the "privatization of intelligence", but rather about nurturing an emerging private sector capability to provide OSINT support to each of the classified disciplines (overt HUMINT, commercial imagery, overt broadcast and print monitoring) while also providing first-echelon historical and contextual analysis to the all-source analyst and action officer.

3) ***The IC Is Not Providing OSINT.*** The problems noted above are not unique to the

national security consumers for intelligence. They are endemic to the Intelligence Community. Our national security decision makers suffer, in effect, from a twofold loss: the short shrift given to OSINT overall, and the prior claim that CIA and the White House alone put on most intelligence resources. Private sector OSINT offerings can help the IC optimize its classified collection and production, but the IC should not be expected to be the bill-payer for OSINT needed by intelligence consumers. The Commission on Intelligence was quite clear on this point: intelligence requirements that can be met "predominantly" through open sources are the responsibility of the consumer, not of the Intelligence Community.

4) ***OSINT Is an Intelligence Multiplier and Cost Saver.*** If OSINT is undertaken systematically and with proper management and focus, it can be responsive to a very large number of the tasks and questions that national security decision-makers might pose. This frees up much more expensive classified intelligence resources for those issues for which they are uniquely suitable and ultimately saves costs as these classified means are not tasked to address queries that can be answered more efficiently and more quickly by OSINT. Further, the greater ability to use OSINT more freely saves both time and costs, while significantly expanding national security policy options, acquisition efficiencies, and operational effectiveness.

5) ***OSINT Is A Resource Multiplier and Public Value.*** The range of multi-lingual and multi-media open sources and services is so varied in

terms of coverage, reliability, and relatively low cost, that a truly professional OSINT endeavor can save our national security community at least as much as it costs in preventing the waste of internal man-hours and funds against less than excellent sources, while also increasing the quality of the information available to policy-makers, acquisition managers, and commanders.

Recommendations

I recommend that we establish a policy, acquisitions, and operations focal point for addressing national security needs for OSINT as a community, including oversight and programming authority for both the Services and the theater commands. This focal point can examine national security intelligence requirements, including those from major commands supported by Joint Intelligence Centers; quickly identify those which can be met through OSINT rather than more expensive and harder to task classified systems; and begin the process of earmarking one half of one percent of the Department of Defense's total budget for OSINT.

We should develop a complete concept of operations for OSINT support to national security operations as quickly as possible and possibly in time to impact on the current legislative cycle for authorizing and appropriating funds for national security operations.

We should systematically identify critical intelligence requirements, including the elements of scope, timeliness, and reliability of sources, for each of the major national security consumer communities—policy-makers, acquisition managers, and operational commanders; and then translate these requirements into a carefully constructed and justified concept of operations and proposed program for meeting national security needs for OSINT—this is especially obvious and fruitful in relation to existing commercial imagery capabilities to satisfy military needs for wide area surveillance, 1:50,000 combat charts, precision munitions guidance, and aviation mission rehearsal imagery.

Open source intelligence support works best when two conditions are provided for:

Analyst and Action Officer Training on Open Source Options. As the Commission on Intelligence noted in its report, the ability of all-source analysts to access open sources is "severely deficient". Analysts know so little about what is available from open sources, that the support process is significantly enhanced if analysts receive training about their open source options prior to being asked to participate in all-source decisions that draw on open sources. This makes the all-source analyst much more effective at specifying their needs and understanding the deliverables. The same holds true for action officers who are either dealing directly with private sector OSINT providers, or developing their all-source requirements for submission via the chain of command.

Maximum Flexibility. Analyst and action officer needs are virtually unpredictable, and it is not helpful to force upon anyone a generic package of services or even a Chinese menu of one profile, ten search units, or whatever. Each analyst and action officer should be able to specify their needs and receive tailored open source intelligence support (under cost guidelines and with management approvals, which ensure that the subject-matter and financial guidelines of the program are satisfied).

Therefore, the national security concept of operations should provide for the integration of OSINT training into all standard civilian and military training and education programs, and especially the training of acquisition program managers, commanders, and their respective staffs. A mix of electronically accessible self-paced study, easy to use handbooks, online directories of sources and services, and mobile training teams could be defined to provide surge and on-going training at the entry, middle, and senior levels.

Funding Profile

For less than one percent of the Department of Defense budget (roughly $2.7 billion a year), national security needs for *both* open source intelligence and electronic security enabling interaction with private sector communications and computer service providers, can be fully satisfied. This chapter focuses on the open source intelligence support issue, and proposes a budget of $1.5 billion a year (leaving $1.2 billion a year for much-needed enhancements to the electronic security and counterintelligence program) to meet our documented but as yet unfunded needs for maps, foreign area studies, critical technology futures, and other related essential elements of information amenable to resolution within the private sector.

Since the Secretary of Defense controls roughly 85% of the total national foreign intelligence program (86% according to the Commission on Intelligence, "over" 80% according to the HPSCI *IC21* Report), the Secretary of Defense has the option of boldly accelerating this entire program by realigning $1.5 billion a year, ramping up from an initial realignment of $250 million in 2001.

At full operational capability, a $1.5 billion national Open Source Intelligence Program (OSIP) could fully satisfy NS needs for tactical maps, provide a global architecture for OSINT support to coalition and contingency operations, augment NS overt collection capabilities in most Embassies and especially in lower tier countries, and provide for a robust program of direct OSINT support to key policy-makers, acquisition managers, and commanders.

It merits emphasis that this new capability will not duplicate nor compete with nor relieve DIA of its existing all-source responsibilities. In fact, this program, offers great relief directly to the all military consumers of intelligence, while allowing DIA to optimize its scarce resources against "the hard stuff".

2001	2002	2003	2004	2005	2006
$250M	$500M	$750M	$1B	$1.25B	$1.5B

Figure 21: Proposed Funding Profile for Open Source Intelligence

The Community Open Source Program is on record as stating that the National Foreign Intelligence Program (NFIP) spends 1% of its budget on open sources, and that this returns 40% of the all-source product.

A national security initiative to increase the investment in open sources from 1% to 6% (of the NFIP) will have a significant positive impact on defense intelligence production as well as defense policy, acquisition, and warfighting.

At a more detailed level of examination, below is a short list of representative OSINT opportunities with rough cost levels per year at final full funding level:

Description of Open Source Intelligence Capability	Cost/Year
Commercial Imagery for Mapping, Targeting, and Mission Rehearsal	$250M
JOINT VISION ground-stations for each CINC and Service Center & follow-on all-source procurement (10 @ $5M each)	$50M
NATO/PfP, UN, and Ad Hoc Coalition OSINT Support	$100M
Creation of NS OSINT Cells (JCS, CINCs, Services, 15 @ $10M each)	$150M
Creation of NS-wide OSINT Training Program	$25M
Creation of Internet Seeding/Sponsorship Program	$25M
OSINT Analysts at Embassies with Funds to Buy Local Knowledge Legally and Ethically (100 @ $500,000 each)	$50M
Strategic Forecasting OSINT Support (10,000 @ $25,000 each)	$250M
Experts on Demand (One Day at a Time/25,000 @ $6,000)	$150M
QuickSearch Investigations (300,000 queries @ $1000 each)	$300M
Integrated Current Awareness Profiles (50,000 @ $2,500 each)	$125M
Contingency/Crisis Surge Support (10 @ $2.5M each)	$25M
TOTAL	**$1.5B**

Figure 22: Detailed Spending Plan for $1.5B/Year OSINT Budget

These numbers are merely illustrative. There are roughly 100,000 SI/TK workstations around the world, and at least that many analysts and action officers who require "just enough, just in time" OSINT support. It bears emphasis, repeatedly, that these modest funds will result in dramatic improvements in general intelligence support to NS policy-makers, acquisition managers, and commanders, and that this support and the additional funding are required above and beyond the existing budget of the Defense Intelligence Agency and the Defense Technical Information Center.

A Final Note

What is important to recognize about the OSINT process is that it significantly reduces most of the overhead costs and the atrophy of capabilities associated with "standing armies" of intelligence collectors and producers (including those maintained by second-tier private sector bureaucracies). It does this by relying on finding the very best experts (with particular citizenship and clearance or foreign language qualification as required), and tapping into their knowledge and sources—knowledge and sources funded over decades by others and thus available to the client for the marginal cost of short-term exploitation. With this OSINT foundation, the very capable, very expensive, and often difficult to exploit classified capabilities can be freed up to attack the most difficult intelligence challenges, and can be exploited in the context of the fuller understanding of the target derived from OSINT.

Relevant Information:
The Emerging Revolution

The next information revolution is well under way. But it is not happening where information scientists, information executives, and the information industry in general are looking for it. It is not a revolution in technology, machinery, techniques, software, or speed. It is a revolution in CONCEPTS. So far, for 50 years, the information revolution has centered on ... the "T" in IT. The next information revolution asks, What is the MEANING of information, and what is its PURPOSE? And this is leading rapidly to redefining the tasks to be done with the help of information, and with it, to redefining the institutions that do these tasks. ... We can already discern and define the next... task in developing an effective information system for top management: the collection and organization of OUTSIDE-focused information.

Peter Drucker[1]

Existing doctrine identifies Information Superiority as a key element of success. Information Superiority is comprised of Information Operations (active measures to affect adversary information while protecting one's own), Relevant Information, and Information Systems. The doctrinal definition of *information fusion* acknowledges that no one capability exists to meet the commander's needs for fusion, while the doctrinal definitions of *information gathering* and *information requirements* acknowledge the value of information acquired from international and non-governmental organizations while not addressing the existence of commercial fee-for-service sources. Intelligence doctrine includes *open source intelligence* as one of seven types of

---

[1] "The Next Information Revolution", *Forbes ASAP* (24 August 1998), page 46.

127

intelligence,[2] but does not acknowledge the nature and value of fee-for-service commercial open sources. This chapter proposes enhancements to existing doctrine in order to provide for information collection, sharing and analysis capabilities that are needed but do not exist.

Today's decision-maker, from the President and the Secretary of Defense down to the most junior commander, lacks both a focused collection capability for obtaining all Relevant Information, and a reliable "all-source" analysis system able to fuse secret and non-secret sources into distilled, reliable and timely "intelligence."[3] The current staff process for any decision-maker relies almost completely on a stream of "free" inputs received from counter-part bureaucracies, international organizations, and private sector parties pursuing their own agendas. At the same time, the narrowly focused secret or restricted steam of information is often afforded direct access to the decision-maker without being subject to in-depth staff scrutiny and proper integration with unclassified official and external information. Functionally today's staff process lacks the organization, knowledge and funding necessary to methodically obtain information from specific international and other non-governmental organizations or to manage the collection of original information from external sources. Over-arching both these limitations, there is no top-level Relevant Information analysis staff organization that is able to provide the decision-maker with filtered, fused and analyzed "all-source" decision-support.

The emerging revolution is changing the nature of the relationships between private sector providers of fee-for-service information and both the intelligence community and the operational community, at the same time that it is mandating a resumption within the operational community of its inherent

---

[2] "There are **seven primary intelligence source types**: imagery intelligence, human intelligence, signals intelligence, measurements and signatures intelligence, open source intelligence, technical intelligence, and counterintelligence." *Joint Publication 2-0*, page 24.

[3] The conventional understanding of "intelligence" as information that is inherently classified is incorrect. Data is the raw print, signal or image. Information is data that has been collated into a generically useful product that is generally broadcast. Both the *New York Times* and most of what is now called "intelligence" are actually unclassified or classified *information*. **Intelligence** is information that has been deliberately discovered, discriminated, distilled, and delivered to a decision-maker in order to answer a specific question. Most intelligence is *not* classified.

responsibility for directly managing both all-source collection and all-source production.

General Problem Description

The problem begins with our current concepts and doctrine for achieving Information Superiority. Below is the current 21st Century approach as adopted by Joint Vision 2010. While this is a Department of Defense perspective, it is representative of the general philosophy for information acquisition of the U.S. Government as a whole.

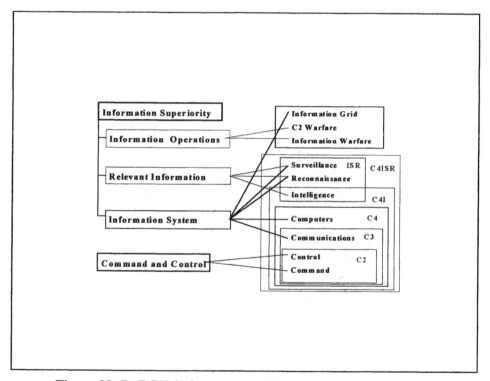

Figure 23: DoD/USG Concepts and Doctrine for Information

Missing from this depiction is the necessary high-level emphasis on standards for external information-sharing, on sources of information external to the U.S.-built architecture, and on needed functionalities for deriving *meaning* from the information. Of particular concern is the doctrinal assumption that all Relevant Information will come from government-owned surveillance, reconnaissance, or intelligence assets.

There are essentially four major "gaps" on the substantive (content) side of Information Superiority, known doctrinally as Relevant Information. These gaps involve the collection, sharing and analysis of information from all sources. Information comes not only from traditional classified intelligence sources, but also from open sources of information (e.g., from the private sector) and from restricted sources of information (e.g., from international organizations and counterpart organizations).

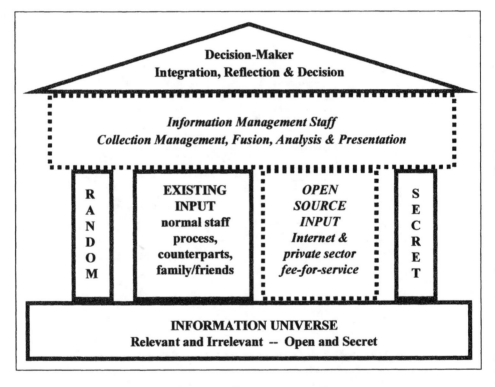

Figure 24: Relevant Information Elements

Addressing these gaps and re-asserting operational control over information collection, sharing, and analysis, would significantly improve our posture with respect to strategy and threat reduction, net assessments, force structure, and operational readiness.[4]

Figure 24 depicts the current situation.[5] Random information includes whatever reaches the decision-maker directly, without staff filtering and outside the decision-maker's established circles. Existing input represents the current "standard" information feed of "free" sources. The secret channel represents either secrets or "internal restricted" information.

Today's normal input streams are missing:

1) methodical, reliable and transparent (overt and beyond reproach) information-sharing with a wide variety of international and non-governmental agencies as well as both home and host government agencies engaged in operations overseas;

---

[4] One could go so far as to suggest that an Undersecretary for Information is required, responsible for policy and acquisition oversight of Information Operations, Relevant Information (both secret and non-secret), and Information Systems. This is not an original thought—the last time this was seriously considered was during the tenure of The Honorable Dwayne Andrews as Assistant Secretary for Command, Control, Communications and Intelligence (C3I). What *is* original this time and implicit throughout the paper, is the urgent need to get away from a C3I system that emphasizes Departmental information technology as the driving force and intelligence as the sole source of external information. Instead we need an Undersecretary of Information whose primary focus is the Relevant Information needs of the decision-maker (from platoon commander up to the President) and whose primary solutions are oriented toward the acquisition and exploitation of external sources of information with minimalist investments in internal technical architectures.

[5] Figure is based on an original drawing by Col Earl Madison III (now serving on the Joint Chiefs of Staff [J-8]), with the missing functional elements conceptualized by the author and by LtCol Ian Wing (Chief of Defence Force Fellow, Australia). In the "information age" the continued absence of doctrine and related organizational and financial resources for acquiring Relevant Information from external organizations including commercial fee-for-service providers and quasi-hostile international organizations is the single most dangerous deficiency in all of joint doctrine.

2) fee-for-service open sources such as commercial imagery and related processing and analysis services from the private sector.

At the same time, the existing staff process is missing the ability to manage information collection so that the information responds fully to all mission areas:

3) the ability to triage requirements to allocate demands across information openly-collected by other organizations, outsourcing to private-sector open-source research providers, and assignment to covert, classified information-gathering services;

4) top-level Relevant Information analysis staff able to integrate *all* source streams, including the classified, into distilled and coherent briefs for the decision-makers.

These four deficiencies suggest that Information Superiority, if it is to be achieved, requires doctrinal changes in how we provide for the collection, sharing, and analysis of Relevant Information. *Providing these capabilities is an inherent responsibility of command that cannot be delegated to the U.S. Intelligence Community or to the functional staffs.*

This chapter focuses on Relevant Information, not on Information Systems or Information Operations. It merits comment that Relevant Information requires a Global Information Management approach that puts the end-user first while also focusing on what raw information sources are available externally as well as internally.[6]

---

[6] Paul Strassmann, former Director of Defense Information, has provided a very useful doctrinal, financial, and political guide to proper Information Systems development and maintenance in his book, *The Politics of Information Management: Policy Guidelines* (Information Economics Press, 1995). See especially page 401 on the role of C4I, page 429 on the "smoking gun" precepts that place technology acquisition subordinate to policy needs, and page 447 on the command and control requirements or the future developed by General Colin Powell in response to a request from then Assistant Secretary of Defense Dwayne Andrews. The recommendations focus exclusively on management and technology policy and *assume* that the data is a "given". Although there are passing references in the original document to internal and external fusion

The following quotation from the Aspin/Brown Commission on Intelligence report, *Preparing for the 21st Century: An Appraisal of U.S. Intelligence*[7] is especially trenchant:

> *The Commission believes that intelligence agencies should not satisfy requests for analysis when such analysis could be readily accomplished using publicly available sources....*

The message is clear: policy-makers, commander and acquisition managers are on their own when it comes to collecting, processing and analyzing open source information. Users of intelligence must decide for themselves how good they want their non-secret information sources to be and how good they want their process to be for collecting, sharing and analyzing Relevant Information. Today's doctrine, policy and financial resource allotments do not provide for the acquisition of overt external information.

Emerging Solutions

Our model for enhancing doctrine for collecting, sharing and analyzing Relevant Information is one that can—without the clandestine and covert aspects of secret intelligence collection—also be adopted by international organizations, non-governmental organizations, non-profit organizations and

---

(Action 40), commercial communications (Action 76), external interoperability (Action 78), resolving the ambiguity of intelligence fusion at various levels (Action 106) and redesign to substitute locally-generated information for ported information (Action 111), there are no references to actually linking the end-user's question ("what's on the other side of the hill?") with real-world sources such as commercial imagery. Corporate Information Management, championed most ably by Mr. Strassmann, refers to information entered by an element of the organization. In early 1992, after reading much of Mr. Strassmann's published work, the author developed the concept of Global Information Management, with the specific intent of moving toward a global C4I2 (information and intelligence) architecture that provided for one-time data entry by any individual or organization while making possible global access. The delivery aspect is consistent with Mr. Strassmann's concepts for a "survivable browser" at the small unit level. What no one has been willing to take on, either within the U.S. Intelligence Community or within the joint operational forces, is the issue of "who, what, why, when, where, and how" we actually *acquire* Relevant Information.

[7] (1 March 1996), page 17.

the business community at large. In brief, we are about to enter the third wave of decision-support analysis.

The first wave, emergent during World War II, was known as Operations Research (OR). This was the agricultural and skilled foraging or "data mining/sharpshooter" stage of analysis. The second wave, emergent following World War II, has been known as "all-source" analysis and been relegated to the intelligence community. This was the industrial or "factory" model of analysis.

The third wave is just now emerging in the Global Disaster Information Network (GDIN) supported by the Vice President of the United States and accepted by the United Nations as a complement to the UN's own ReliefWeb; the U.S. Pacific Command (USPACOM) Virtual Information Center (VIC); the U.S. Atlantic Command (USACOM) Future Collaborative Information Environment (FCIE); the U.S. Special Operations Command (USSOCOM) concept of operations for a "white knights" cadre (as opposed to the existing "black knights"); and in the Australian initiative to create a national open source intelligence network that links the military, law enforcement, business and trade collection and analysis capabilities.

All of these new initiatives suggest that we might soon see a Relevant Information approach that takes the best of the two earlier approaches and elevates true all-source analysis to the Battle Staff/Chief of Staff level of operations. This senior expert staff analysis capability will not replace existing all-source intelligence analysts nor existing mission area specialists. It should not require additional structure, but it might benefit from a new military occupational specialty series equally divided between all-source collection management, civil-military information-sharing, and all-source fusion. It could benefit from an interim consolidation of selected intelligence, gaming, and operations analysts.

In the course of nurturing this emergent third wave of Relevant Information analysis, policy, command and acquisition leaders need to consider the establishment of four substantive enhancements to their existing Information Superiority practices:

FIRST, they need to develop within their staffs the necessary knowledge of what is available from the private sector on a fee-for-service basis, together with the necessary financial resources, security protocols and contract management skills needed to take full advantage of open sources and services. Since most government organizations are accustomed to information as well as intelligence being a "free" good, this will require significant changes in how resources are earmarked for Relevant Information.

SECOND, since direct open-source procurement through individual staffs will not be cost-effective, they need to develop an *integrated information collection management* capability that is fully responsive to all staffs and especially to those staffs that are accustomed to being ignored by the intelligence community (e.g. logistics). This information collection management process must assign information collection requirements to internal staff elements (e.g. a special cell for Internet exploitation, or the Command library augmented by a commercial online searcher), to external capabilities in the private sector (e.g. to commission a ground reconnaissance, an overhead image, or a foreign broadcast transcript and translation), or to the intelligence community for classified collection.

THIRD, they need to learn from the International Committee of the Red Cross (ICRC) and other international organizations how to institutionalize methods for both collecting open information "on the ground" and for sharing such information in ways that do not endanger the participants or in any way impugn the integrity of the information-sharing process.

> *"...the concept of UN intelligence promises to turn traditional principles on their heads. Intelligence will have to be based in information that is collected primarily by overt means, that is by methods that do not threaten the target state or group and do not compromise the integrity or impartiality of the UN."* [8]

Since most government organizations do not have trained liaison elements and do not have ready access to an external Web-based network for information-sharing with international organizations, a shift to open source intelligence will require both funding realignments and the development of new protocols. The Civil Affairs specialists in the U.S. military pride themselves on avoiding the taint that accompanies traditional intelligence collectors (even

---

[8] Hugh Smith, "Intelligence and UN Peacekeeping", *Survival* (36/3, Autumn 1994), page 39.

routine military patrols) and have developed their own culture for overt information collection and information-sharing. More needs to be done to merge their concepts and doctrine with those of the international organizations represented within GDIN, in order to develop a new operationally-oriented concept, doctrine and table of organization and equipment for fully exploiting external sources of information in complex peacekeeping and disaster relief environments. These changes should not require new structure but would definitely require new attitudes within every command.[9]

FOURTH, (and this may be the most difficult), decision-makers need to come to grips with the urgent need to establish an integrated Relevant Information management capability that is not buried within any single staff function (such as intelligence). The kind of skilled analysis typical of some all-source intelligence analysts and of some operations research analysts, needs to be brought together in a staff element that reports directly to the Chief of Staff or the Deputy Commander/Deputy Director. Such a staff must be able to integrate three major information streams fully: the classified or internal restricted stream; the open source or commercial stream; and the existing staff stream that passes along and filters information provided at no cost from counterpart and varied external organizations. This shift to a Relevant Information management process will require changes in command and staff doctrine as well as corresponding changes in tables of organization and related training programs. Such a process must also subordinate Information Systems to its needs rather than continue today's practice of assuming that the data will be available and that "inter-operability" is the primary challenge.

Recently there have emerged several useful constructs for the substantive side of Relevant Information collection, sharing and analysis. From these constructs, one might establish a new generic approach to all-source information collection, sharing and analysis that provides:

1) The ability to share information with a complex range of international and non-governmental organizations, using a

---

[9] The state of the art in pro-active Information Operations, as practiced in Bosnia by the Commanding General of the 1st Infantry Division, is outlined in Garry J. Beavers and Stephen W. Shanahan, "Operationalizing IO in Bosnia-Herzegovina" in Alan D. Campen and Douglas H. Dearth, contributing editors, *CYBERWAR 2.0: Myths, Mysteries and Realities* (AFCEA Press, 1998), pages 267-275.

network and protocols that provide assurance to all parties that the information being shared will be handled with due care and will *not* be mis-used for intelligence or covert action purposes. *This must always be a two-way channel.*

2) The ability to leverage the considerable access and expertise and technology available to the private sector, without having to invest in commensurate personnel, training and in-house technology installations.

3) The ability to obtain *distilled* information and applied *analysis* at the top of the decision pyramid rather than having to rely on scattered analysis within varied functional or source pipelines or, alternatively, permit narrowly-focused classified analysis to "end run" the more fragmented mission-area staff analyses.

Implementation Issues

There are a number of practical implementation issues that merit discussion.

FIRST, as the Aspin/Brown Commission on Intelligence determined, the U.S. Intelligence Community is *not* the place where open source collection, sharing and analysis should be conducted on behalf on the departments and agencies of government.[10]   The properly restrictive nature of classified collection, sharing and analysis precludes any possibility of the U.S. Intelligence Community—even if it wanted to—becoming the focal point for open source exploitation and international information sharing. Doctrine must be updated to reflect the findings of the Aspin/Brown Commission on Intelligence and to provide commanders and their staffs with an information management capability for collecting, sharing, and analyzing Relevant Information.

SECOND, the task of open-source collection, sharing and analysis is more complex than any existing operational organization is capable of executing effectively even if financial resources were immediately available.

---

[10] *Supra* note 7.

This is not a function that can be delegated to librarians and then forgotten. Librarians are part of the solution, but only a small part. Internal effectiveness in open source collection, sharing and analysis requires, at a minimum, dedicated personnel for requirements analysis, collection management, Internet collection, commercial online collection, primary research coordination, external services contracting and in-house quality control and presentation management (from an all-source operational perspective).[11]

THIRD, and this is a particular strength of the commercial open source sector, it is essential that both operational and intelligence analyses avoid the traditional tendency to focus only on orders or battle or the specifics of unstable situations. A broad-based Relevant Information management approach must ensure that information is collected, shared and analyzed in the political-legal, socio-economic, ideo-cultural, techno-demographic and natural-geographic domains. Only in this manner can historical and contextual "grist" be fully exploited.

FOURTH, the government must stop trying to re-invent the wheel and focus on commercial-off-the-shelf offerings. Two of the most important categories of tools to emerge in recent years are those dealing with collaborative work and those dealing with geospatial information. Both are pertinent to the Relevant Information arena. It is important that government not confine itself to adoption of "knowledge management"[12] solutions, as these are limited to technical approaches to internal data and do not address the critical issues associated with external information and human communications.

FIFTH, it is necessary to budget money to support the fee-for-service element of a coherent and effective Relevant Information capability. In

---

[11] A detailed discussion is provided in "Concept for Creating a 'Bare Bones' Capability for Open Source Support to Defense Intelligence Analysts," at http://www.oss.net/DIAReport.

[12] "Knowledge Management" is a term of art now used instead of "data mining" or "data warehousing". Examination of the literature about "knowledge management" establishes its focus on internal information rather than external information or integrated external and internal information. This term also fails to capture the human and informal communications aspect of the larger network requirement.

general, such a budget must be divided equally between procuring internal capabilities and out-sourcing.[13]

SIXTH, open-source intelligence gathering must not be allowed to damage U.S. national interests by allowing inference about the subject areas of interest—operational security must be an integral aspect of every collection, sharing and analysis action. On the technical side, anonymous Internet search access, firewall protection and very strong constantly updated anti-virus measures will be essential to any command interacting with the external information environment. At the same time that the command protects itself, however, it must also respect the intellectual property rights of the private sector. Means will have to be found for compliance with copyright, especially when open source materials are to be integrated into unclassified intelligence products for dissemination to coalition and civil partners.

Conclusions

Summing it all up then, we can end with the following key points:

1) Relevant Information has four content-related elements that are not yet represented in existing concepts, doctrine, tables of organization, or financial resource management:

    a) Management of tasking to all sources of Relevant Information
    b) Network for leveraging information collected overtly by international and other external organizations
    c) Doctrine and funds for leveraging commercial fee-for-service open sources and services vital to mission support

---

[13] The DoD-level budget is provided at the conclusion of chapter 7; the CINC-level budget of $1.5M/Year was recommended to the U.S. Special Operations Command on 25 February 1999 as they began reflection on what budget to earmark for their newly-formed Open Source Intelligence Cell, and has subsequently been provided to the CINC OSINT Working Group that has been formed to address operationally-oriented issues that the Washington-area intelligence bureaucracies have refused to take on since 1992.

    d) Command-level information fusion and analysis capability

2) The U.S. Intelligence Community is not in the business of resolving any of these four deficiencies—they are the responsibility of the commander or agency head.

3) There are a number of real and emerging constructs that can, if melded together in a sensible manner, contribute to the creation of a generic global information and knowledge operations network.

4) The private sector has much to offer government, not only in the form of collaborative tools and commercial imagery and geospatial data collection and processing, but also in the way of advanced concepts and tools for collecting and processing open source intelligence and for creating organizational intelligence.

5) This Relevant Information capability cannot exist in isolation from real-world sources and services that are only available from the private sector.

6) This Relevant Information capability cannot exist in isolation from the real-world sources and insights available to the IO/NGO, business, media and academic communities—the architecture must be *global* and *open*.

7) This Relevant Information capability will take money, but no more than 1% of any organization's total budget.

8) A generic solution is available now, is inexpensive, and will pay great dividends in terms of strategic effectiveness, threat reduction, net assessments, force structure and operational readiness.

Virtual Intelligence
for the Diplomat and
the Warfighter

(W)hen it comes to the direction of human affairs, all these universities, all these nice refined people in their lovely gowns, all this visible body of human knowledge and wisdom, has far less influence upon the conduct of human affairs than, let us say, an intractable newspaper proprietor, an unscrupulous group of financiers or the leader of a recalcitrant minority

Both the assembling and the distribution of knowledge in the world at present are extremely ineffective, and thinkers of the forward-looking type whose ideas we are now considering, are beginning to realize that the most hopeful line for the development of our ... intelligence lies rather in the direction of creating a new world organ for the collection, indexing, summarizing, and release of knowledge....[1]

Introduction

In an age characterized by distributed information, where the majority of the expertise is in the private sector, the concept of "central intelligence" is an oxymoron and its attendant concentration on secrets is an obstacle to both national defense and global peace. The underlying threat to peace and prosperity — the cause of causes — is the ever-widening chasm between policymakers with power and private sector experts and participants with knowledge. Neither classified information nor information technology alone can bridge this gap — but both can make a positive contribution if they are managed within a larger information strategy that focuses on content as well as connectivity and enables policymakers to draw upon the expertise available in

---

[1] H. G. Wells, *World Brain* (Adamantine, 1994), page 109, 120.

141

the private sector. We thus require a strategy to create a "virtual intelligence community" able to both inform governance and also carry out a new kind of virtual diplomacy, "information peacekeeping". Information peacekeeping can help avoid and resolve conflict and represents the conceptual, technical and practical foundation for successful virtual diplomacy — virtual intelligence "is" virtual diplomacy and also virtual warfighting.

This chapter presents the concepts of "virtual intelligence" and of "information peacekeeping". Part I discusses the nature of conflict as an analysis problem — what do we need to know and how. Part II examines the perils as well as the promise of information technology as now developed and applied by governments and corporations — why we are substituting technology for thinking but also, how can technology help us think and also gain access to external expertise. Finally, Part III discusses the "information archipelago" comprised largely of private sector communities of expertise; defines a theory of "information peacekeeping"; and outlines a specific strategy for creating a "virtual intelligence community" which can both inform governance and conduct "information peacekeeping" operations — how we harness distributed expertise from the private sector and use information technology tools. The chapter concludes that the "core competency" for both diplomats and warfighters must be the management of information *qua* content — its discovery, discrimination, distillation and dissemination as intelligence. It follows from this that diplomats and warfighters must take the lead in developing a national information strategy as an element of national power and also master the art of "information peacekeeping". For both commanders and intelligence professionals the implications are more ominous: learn new tricks or face the prospect of losing budget share commensurate with one's limitations.

Part I:
What Do We Need To Know And How?

The policymaker needs an intelligence-support system that is directly related to their daily schedule; that provides just enough intelligence just in time, at the lowest possible level of classification; and that enables direct access to private sector experts whenever needed. This system must be firmly grounded on a foundation of complete global geo-spatial data at the 1:50,000 level and must provide the policymaker with both strategic generalizations and a full range of multi-dimensional assessments including a full understanding of the cultural, technological and geographic aspects of a potential or on-going conflict. Organizationally, this system must fully integrate the information available to civilian, military and law enforcement authorities as well as business leaders; and it must offer a seamless architecture which transitions easily from domestic to international locations under conditions of both peace and war. Above all, it must allow the policymaker to deal with emerging threats on a "come as you are" basis and to harness private sector expertise in real-time.

Unclassified Intelligence. Intelligence is information that has been discovered, discriminated, distilled and disseminated in a form tailored to the needs of a specific policymaker at a specific time and place. Intelligence is most often *not* classified and its utility tends to decrease dramatically with every increase in its level of classification.[2] In today's global environment, intelligence that can be shared and that does not compromise the political standing of the sponsors of the intelligence by relying on covert means is vital.[3]

---

[2] This is a generalization. As one reviewer of an earlier version of this chapter has noted, the record of ULTRA during World War II clearly shows the value of certain kinds of restricted intelligence. In the author's experience across all disciplines, there are indeed a few (a *very* few) signals and human intelligence operations whose extraordinary value is directly translatable into action through communication to a very small number of decision-makers, but as a whole, "intelligence" *qua* tailored answers to important questions (or early warning of unanticipated plans and intentions of import) is vastly more valuable when its security classification is not permitted to interfere with the natural need of the inherent content—the message—to be shared and disseminated with those who have a need to know but have not been inducted into the secret society.

[3] "If it is 85% accurate, on time, and I can share it, this is a lot more useful to me than a compendium of Top Secret Codeword materials that are too much, too late, and require a safe and three security officers to move around the battlefield." Paraphrase of comment by Navy Wing Commander who led the lead flight over Baghdad, made at Technology Initiatives Game 1991, where the author served as chairman of the National Intelligence Cell. See also Sir David Ramsbotham, "Analysis and Assessment for Peacekeeping Operations" in *Intelligence Analysis and Assessment* (Frank Cass, 1996), and especially his citation of Hugh Smith, "Intelligence and UN Peacekeeping" in *Survival* (36/3, Autumn 1994), page 39, to wit: "...the concept of UN intelligence promises to turn traditional principles on their heads. Intelligence will have to be based in information that is collected primarily by overt means, that is by methods that do not threaten the target state or group and do not compromise the integrity or impartiality of the UN."

IDEA: Require every "intelligence" report to offer varying degrees of classification beginning with unclassified, to clearly mark all paragraphs with their inherent level of classification, to footnote primary and secondary customers and their telephone numbers and to specify in detail the open sources and experts as well as the classified sources which were drawn upon to create the report. Provide consumers with an electronic means of documenting whether they actually read the report and an electronic means of grading the report (at its various levels of classification) in real time.

Just Enough. The policymaker does not have the time or the inclination to digest vast quantities of information, however much they may feel that only their intellect could possibly comprehend all the nuances. The successful analyst supporting the policymaker will have gained their trust and understanding and will provide "just enough" intelligence to permit the policymaker to grasp the essence of the value-added information (i.e. insights the policymaker did not already have) and to provide the analyst with guidance if additional detail or other related analytical paths are to be pursued.

IDEA: Require that intelligence be delivered via Web-like applications that begin with a paragraph and allow the policymaker to drill down to a page or a longer document, or to navigate into original sources if desired. This is completely distinct from the "Intel-Link" concept, which does nothing more than convert the intelligence production fire-hose into electronic form. This idea also requires aggressive commitment to the digitization of supporting documentation and hence facilitates inter-agency access to basic multi-media and multi-lingual raw information sources. This idea can be applied on behalf of the large number of policymakers who require hard-copy products, by automating the production process so that four levels of details are provided.

Just in Time. Twelve month research plans and eighteen month editing cycles have made most "intelligence" (actually no more than classified information) irrelevant to the day-to-day needs of the policymaker. The policymaker needs intelligence that is pertinent to the decisions they are

144

making that very day (including decisions that set in motion longer term endeavors by others).[4]

> IDEA: To the extent that the policymaker is willing (some operators are worse than spies in their obsession with secrecy), ensure that the daily agenda of the policymaker is electronically available to all analysts supporting them, kept up to date and used as the electronic "hot link" foundation for providing intelligence support. As the policymaker looks at their daily agenda on their screen, they should see a little "icon" that says, in essence "Intelligence Available" and from that be able to go directly to a paragraph, then to a page and then to supporting documentation or a short video.

Direct Access. In the 21st century, the "acme of skill" for the master analyst will be the ability to put a policymaker with a hot question in direct touch with a world-class expert (generally in the private sector) who can create new knowledge on the spot and in a few minutes "cut to the chase" and provide the policymaker with an informed judgment in real time that is tailored to the precise nuances of concern to the policymaker.[5]

---

[4] Mr. Paul Evan Peters, Executive Director of the Coalition for Networked Information, has articulately related this fashionable phrase, perhaps first associated with logistics, to global networks for networking information. Speaking to the International Document Acquisition conference in 1994, he noted that it makes no sense to archive vast volumes of material centrally if one can reach out and get exactly what is needed on a "just in time" basis. To this the author would add two observations: first, that only 10% of what one needs is generally online, although online means can be used to reach experts who have access to the other 90%; and second, that the most exciting aspect of distributed information is that *someone else* bears the cost of creating and updating such information as *is* available online, and for maintaining the expertise which can generate "just in time" products at a fraction of the cost that would be required if one were to maintain a centralized think tank intended to cover all topics all the time. Such distributed expertise also tends to be vastly more current, deeper, more insightful, and indeed cheaper than "central intelligence" funded by the taxpayer.

[5] The most common objection to this idea, generally from intelligence analysts rather than the policymakers themselves, has been founded on an extreme reluctance to reveal their organizational interest or the nature of their question. The reality is that most issues that are "hot" are hot for everyone—CNN and the Maryknoll nuns are all asking about the same issue. The author has generally found that policymakers "just want the damn question answered" and are not really concerned about what others might

IDEA: Using existing Web technology, including security technology, establish a "virtual intelligence community" directory and forum that is constantly updated by the Institute of Scientific Information and OSS so as to permit any analyst or indeed any policymaker to quickly identify and exploit world-class experts in any topical area.[6]

Earth Map. The policymaker, their counterparts and staffs all require an accurate map of those portions of the earth under consideration at any given time. This is not only essential as the foundation for decision-making, it is vital as the foundation for fusing information from various collection disciplines (imagery, signals, human) and for automating the visualization of information in the aggregate. Hard as this is for most Commanders-in-Chief and their staffs to understand, none of us have the world mapped accurately or comprehensively. The United States has less than 10% of the world mapped at the 1:50,000 level (10 meter resolution with contour lines) and most of that is severely out of date.[7] In both Somalia and Burundi, the next best alternatives to

---

speculate about their interest. Finally, it has been the author's experience that private sector experts are by definition discreet, for they understand the value of discretion as it pertains to future business.

[6] While there are various ways of establishing who the world-class experts are in any given discipline, by far the most reliable is that provided by the Institute of Scientific Information (ISI) and its exclusive international, multi-lingual database of those who have not only published in peer-reviewed journals, but also been cited by their peers in a manner which easily establishes their general influence and credibility. These experts in turn generally know their peers in government and non-government institutes and organizations that are world-class authorities but cannot publish.

[7] The EARTHMAP Report, signed out in October 1995 by Undersecretary of State Tim Wirth and other principals, represented an eighty-person multi-agency finding that specified the critical nature of comprehensive global mapping in support of economic and environmental initiatives. Unfortunately, despite the fact that the President of the United States considered economic initiatives important enough to create a National Economic Council, and his Secretary of State (then Warren Christopher) publicly elevated the environment to the high table of national security, the U.S. Intelligence Community and the Department of Defense (first the Defense Mapping Agency and then the National Imagery and Mapping Agency) have both chosen to ignore the EARTHMAP Report and declined to respond to the urgent civilian agency needs for maps in support of peacemaking and diplomacy. They are also ignoring increasingly insistent demands from the U.S. theater Commanders-in-Chief for wide-area surveillance such as can only be obtained from commercial imagery sources. In

tourist maps are previously classified Soviet military topographic maps at the 1:100,000 level, only recently made available through a U.S. company, East View Publications.

> IDEA: Earmark $250 million dollars a year to the Department of State with which to procure commercial imagery sources and related processing services in support of both peacekeeping initiatives and EARTHMAP Report requirements of other civilian agencies. These commercial imagery sources will still require orientation (ortho-rectification) using either precision imagery from the National Reconnaissance Office or positioning of key features using hand-held Global Positioning System (GPS) receivers, but such a fund would be responsive to civilian and peacekeeping requirements without being subject to realignment by unappreciative intelligence and defense bureaucrats and would help resolve decades of active neglect in this area.

Strategic Generalizations. The policymaker requires strategic generalizations with which to plan and direct operations. Analysts and their managers too frequently inundate the policymaker with thousands of "current intelligence" updates and also exaggerate the threat, for lack of a model of analysis which requires them to address the peacekeeping environment in a comprehensive manner which readily brings out useful generalizations.

- In 1989, after the Marine Corps Intelligence Center (now Activity, MCIA) was established, a review of available Central Intelligence Agency (CIA) and Defense

---

November 1999 the National Imagery and Mapping Agency declared in a press release that it was earmarking $100 million over five years for the procurement of commercial imagery. This is nothing more than a continuance of the *status quo* and a callous disregard for increasingly troublesome shortfalls. The established requirement for commercial imagery was articulated in 1996 as $250 million per year at the 10 meter level of resolution, and in 1997 as $500 million per year at the one meter level of resolution — hence the current NIMA program addresses less than 10% of the requirement, a failing grade by anyone's standard. The source of the publicly discussed estimates was a Deputy Director of this same organization — one can only conclude that their senior management is in disarray and/or being prevented from accomplishing its mission by staff politics within the Office of the Secretary of Defense.

Intelligence Agency (DIA) production was found[8] to contain no intelligence of general value to the Marine Corps. Everything was a "snapshot" (generally dated) of a specific weapons system, personality, organization, event, or location.

- A more useful model for integrated analysis was developed and tested, with the finding that *the threat changes depending on the level of analysis and also upon the relationship between the military capability being considered and the pertaining civil and geographic factors in the area of operations.*

- Below is a high-level view of the model:[9]

	Military	Civil	Geographic
Strategic	Sustainability	Allies	Location
Operational	Availability	Instability	Resources
Tactical	Reliability	Psychology	Terrain
Technical	Lethality	Infrastructure	Atmosphere

Figure 25: Concept for Integrated Intelligence Analysis

---

[8] By the author, then the founding Special Assistant and Deputy Director of the Center, the newest national intelligence production facility in the United States.

[9] A complete copy of the model, including war-fighter definitions of high, medium, and low degrees of difficulty for each of 107 factors (43 military, 35 civil, and 29 geographic) is now available to U.S. government personnel as Appendix F-1 in *Open Source Intelligence: Professional Handbook 1.1* (Joint Military Intelligence Training Center, October 1996). The author's contribution to the model (developed by a team) was significantly influenced by Edward N. Luttwak and his book *STRATEGY: The Logic of War and Peace* (Harvard, 1987), where he demonstrated the inter-relationship between weapons systems at different levels of war, each perhaps irrational in isolation, but most sensible when considered as part of the whole.

Two examples of this model's utility are offered because its implications are so important to policymakers dealing with complex conflict situations.

- **Middle Eastern Tank Threat.** In a test case discussed with the appropriate analysts from all of the major intelligence agencies in the U.S. government, MCIA discovered that the tank threat in a particular Middle Eastern country, historically classified as *high* because it was comprised of Soviet T-72 tanks, at the time the most powerful main battle tanks other than US tanks, changed dramatically depending on the level of analysis — **it was only *high* at the technical level (lethality).**

  - **At the tactical level (reliability),** because of very poor troop training, the long-term storage of most tanks in the open and the cannibalization of tanks at random for parts, the threat fell to *low*;

  - **At the operational level (availability),** because of the quantity of tanks scattered around the country, the threat rose to *medium*; and

  - **At the strategic level (sustainability),** where various constraints would not permit this country to sustain tank operations for more than two weeks, the threat again fell to *low*.

MCIA considered this very significant to the perspective of the policymaker or commander making decisions about the over-all structure of the force to be deployed to this region, even in the absence of related information about civil and geographic factors.

- **Integrated Analysis.** In a second example, which illustrates the importance of civil and geographic factors to the over-all analysis of any peacekeeping situation or related acquisition and employment decisions, the

149

Commandant of the Marine Corps asked MCIA to evaluate the Marine Corps requirement for a follow-on procurement of the M1A1 tank. MCIA examined civil and geographic factors for the sixty-nine countries (now eighty) that comprised the expeditionary environment and discovered these "strategic generalizations":[10]

- **Intervisibility (Line of Sight Ranges).** 91% of the countries in the Marine Corps environment offered line of sight distances of 1,000 meters or less, making the M1A1 irrelevant to operations in those countries;

- **Cross-country mobility.** 79% of the countries offered *zero* cross-country mobility; the terrain would require all mobility platforms to use normal roads (most of which have bridge loading limitations of 30 tons or so, making the M1A1's 70-ton weight a distinct liability);

- **Ports.** 50% — fully half — of the countries did not have a port usable by a U.S. Navy or Maritime Pre-Positioned Force (MPF) ship — they lacked an adequate depth, turning radius and/or piers and cranes. This means that the 70-ton M1A1 would have to be off-loaded in mid-stream using scarce and often-inadequate landing craft.

---

[10] *Overview of Planning and Programming Factors for Expeditionary Operations in the Third World* (Marine Corps Combat Development Command, March 1990) was a unique first effort for the U.S. Intelligence Community as a whole in that it developed strategic generalizations founded on a close working relationship with the warfighter customers who specified the sixty-nine countries to be considered; defined the military, civil, and geographic factors of greatest interest to them as well as their perception of what constituted high, medium, and low degrees of difficulty; and also relied exclusively on open sources of information while publishing the results in unclassified form. It is available today as a recurring global coverage study, *Expeditionary Factors* (FOUO/RESTRICTED).

A similarly strategic observation was subsequently made with respect to aircraft, which are designed by the U.S. Navy for the U.S. Marine Corps based on a standard aviation day that is warm (around 65°F) and with average humidity.

- The Marine Corps aviation day is in fact *hot* (routinely over 80°F) with very high humidity. Translation: Marine Corps aviation can carry half as much half as far than the book says it can — both range and lift are dramatically reduced under these conditions...yet policy makers and the military commanders that advise them consistently fail to plan for this reality. This is of special concern with respect to Non-Combatant Evacuation Operations (NEO).

- MCIA also discovered that :

  - most U.S. Embassies were well beyond the round-trip range of the CH-46 from a naval platform at the five fathom line even at optimal performance;

  - most countries in the Third World can out-gun the standard U.S. Navy five-inch gun with their existing shore batteries; and

  - the allies are completely lacking in digital imagery and 1:50,000 combat charts for operations in 90% of the world[11], as well as

---

[11] The 90% figure has not changed in the seven years since the study was done. In September 1996 official unclassified briefings from the Defense Mapping Agency (now the National Imagery and Mapping Agency) documented the fact that while most of the world is charted at the 1:1,000,000,000 level and much of it at the 1:250,000 level, down at the 1:50,000 level (10 meter resolution) where the hard work of coalition and fire support coordination takes place, only 10% of the world is available, and this is generally old data. For the specific Marine Corps study, we found that of our 69 countries of high interest, most in the Third World, we had no 1:50,000 maps at all for 22 countries; old 1:50,000 maps for the ports and capital cities only for another 37 countries, and very old 1:50,000 coverage for ten countries.

200 ship-years behind in shallow-water (100
fathom and less) hydrography.

Why is this so important? The sad fact is that policymakers are often
ignorant of the realities of the military, civil and geographic elements in
relation to one another and the levels of analysis and this ignorance leads to
woefully inadequate estimates of what it will take to achieve stated objectives.
At the same time, the military and their policy masters are largely uninformed
as to the "intangible" aspects of the situation and the military itself is generally
is not trained, equipped and organized for operations which require that they
deal with people rather than kill them.[12]

IDEA: Post the Marine Corps study for easy access by both
policymakers and the public.

Multi-Dimensional. The policymaker is poorly served when analysts
focus only on the political-legal situation, or the military situation, or even —
to the extent they can gain access to the necessary open sources — on the
economic situation. Every emerging and on-going conflict has a multi-
dimensional nature and must be understood across a spectrum that includes
sociological, economic, ideological, cultural, technological, demographic,
natural and geographic conditions. At the same time, culturally astute experts
must study the aspects of human development and the local psychology and
these informed judgments must be factored into the decision-making process.

The average analyst[13], pre-occupied with cutting and pasting
miscellaneous "current facts" and lacking access to sources of cultural and

---

[12] We still do not have a proper Table of Organization and Equipment for a unit to
handle refugees and prisoners of war — in the Gulf War, this became an undesirable
duty for the nearest infantry battalions. In particular, such tables as exist for reserve
units do not provide for the communications and computing equipment, nor the special
personnel, needed to rapidly debrief individuals and enter the findings into the larger
information architecture.

[13] The "average analyst" in this article is generally the government analyst, trapped in a
bureaucratic system which demands and rewards a form of work where it is presumed
that the classified and other government-provided sources represent all information that
is pertinent, and production is recognized in relation to a master plan addressing generic
requirements rather than specific day to day needs of the ostensible customers for the
analysis.

other forms of "intangible" intelligence as well as access to tools for visualizing complex integrated problem sets, is rarely if ever going to provide the policymaker with insights into the multi-dimensional nature of the conflict and the consequently unanticipated consequences of revolutionary change in the non-traditional dimensions such as the ideo-cultural or techno-demographic.

For this reason, it is essential that we have two required analysis models — the first focusing on the levels of analysis and the inter-relationship between military, civil, and geographic sources of national power; the second focusing on the dimensions of national power:

- Political-Legal
- Socio-Economic
- Ideo-Cultural
- Techno-Demographic
- Natural-Geographic

Consider Figure 26 as a matrix of the kinds "indications & warnings" country study and related policies should take into account.[14]

IDEA: First, do a case study of a single country and completely re-define the idea of a "Country Study" so as to move far beyond the cursory coverage of the CIA *World Fact Book* or the useful but largely "tangible" and also highly fragmented Army *Country Studies*. Then develop a Web-based network of sites and publications organized by country and within country so as to allow any policymaker to quickly access multi-lingual and multi-cultural perspectives in each of these matrix areas, using only open sources of information which can be easily shared with coalition and non-governmental partners. Use automated gisting and clustering technology to quickly visualize the aggregate data while comparing "points of view" from different sites and organizations.

---

[14] The figure is revised and improved from an original developed by the author in his first graduate thesis, *Internal War: A Framework for the Prediction of Revolutionary Potential* (Lehigh University, May 1976).

	Political-Legal	Socio-Economic	Ideo-Cultural	Techno-Demographic	Natural-Geographic
Perception	Isolation of elites; inadequate intelligence	Concentration of wealth; lack of public disclosure	Conflicting myths; inadequate socialization	Acceptance of media distortions; inadequate education	Reliance on single sector or product; concentrated land holdings
Identity	Lack of elite consensus; failure to define priorities	Loss of economic initiative; failure to do balanced growth	Loss of authority; failure to provide and honor national myth system	Failure to accept and exploit new technologies and new groups	Failure to integrate out-lying territories into national system
Competence	Weak or inefficient government; too much or too little bureaucracy	Break-down of fiscal, monetary, development, or welfare policies	Humiliation of leaders; loss of confidence by population	Failure to enforce priorities, with resulting loss of momentum	Failure to prepare for or cope with major natural disasters
Investment	Ego-centric or parochial government	Excessive or insufficient mobility; lack of public sector	Cynicism; opportunism; corruption	Failure to nurture entrepreneurship or franchise all groups	Failure to preserve or properly exploit natural resources
Risk	Elite intransigence; repression; failure to adapt	Failure to deal with crime, especially white collar crime	Failure to deal with prejudice; desertion of intellectuals	Failure to develop national R&D program	Failure to honor human rights; failure to protect animal species
Extroversion	Ineffective tension management; failure examine false premises	Structural differentiation; lack of national transportation	Elite adoption of foreign mores; failure to deal with alienation	Failure to develop comms infrastructure, shared images	Failure to explore advantages of regional integration
Transcendence	Foreign control of government; arbitrary/excessive Government	Loss of key sectors to foreign providers; loss of quality control	Media censorship; suppression of intellectual discourse	Failure to control police, army, or terrorists; failure to employ *alphas*	Failure to respect natural constraints or support organic growth
Synergy	Failure to assimilate all individuals or respond to groups	Status discrepancies; lack of economic motivators	Absence of sublimating myths; failure of religion	Failure to provide program and technology assessment	Failure to distribute benefits between urban and rural
Complexity	Garrison, industrial, or welfare states	Unstable growth; excessive DoD $$	Cultural pre-disposition toward violence	Excessive urbanization, pollution, development	Lack of land for expansion, inefficient land use

Figure 26: Framework for the Prediction of Revolution

Come As You Are. Finally we must come to grips with the fact that "the water's edge" is as dangerous to our security as the "iron curtain" once was, in that it is imposing — on our governmental policy organizations and on our national and law enforcement intelligence communities — a dangerous and probably catastrophic barrier to the development of seamless lines of communication and shared knowledge about transnational criminal gangs and terrorist organizations moving freely between overseas and domestic locations; major religious as well as cult organizations and alien-smuggling operations; and individuals participating in economic espionage, information terrorism and information vandalism, in association with international partners, be they governments, corporations, gangs, or other individuals. Consider the following illustration:[15]

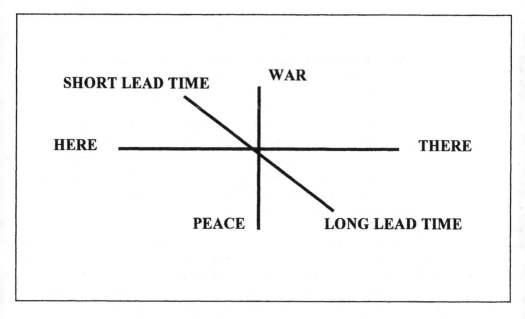

Figure 27: "Come As You Are" Environment for War and Peace

---

[15] Mr. John Peterson, President of the Arlington Institute, developed the original two-dimensional matrix to show how we are too focused on "war, over there" while failing to develop our capabilities for defending ourselves here at home, within a "violent" peace. The author has added the third dimension of time.

What does this figure imply for how we devise policy and execute operations? It has two meanings:

- First, it demonstrates the urgency of creating a seamless architecture for linking policymakers, financial authorities, law enforcement, the military and all others including non-governmental organizations, into a global information network where shared knowledge is the foundation for preventing conflict and damage to mutual interests including financial stability. Conflict is no longer simply unilateral, military, or "over there".

- Second, it emphasizes that conflict avoidance and resolution against the emerging threats represent "come as you are" situations and that we do not have the luxury of time to gradually recognize threats, devise means of monitoring them and finally come to consensus on means of dealing with them, after which the means can be gradually constituted. An underlying implication of this lack of time is that we must find a means of harnessing all available citizens as voluntary sensors in a global "warning system" and that we must engage all available expertise from the private sector so as to be able to respond rapidly to threats beyond the *ken* of the conventional government policymaker, bureaucrat, or analyst.

What does this mean in terms of what we need to know and how? It means that we now have to cover a much vaster range of "threats" (and also opportunities), each much more subtle, more diffuse, more obtuse, than the traditional conventional threat we have grown to rely on for our feeling of security (that we understand our world). As we discussed in Chapter 3, the U.S. Intelligence Community is neither prepared, nor inclined to become prepared, for this more complex world. At the same time, the private sector now offers a "virtually" unlimited range of open sources, systems and services, which are directly applicable to meeting the needs of international policymakers and that have the added advantage of avoiding the constraints associated with classified information.

Part II:
Perils & Promise Of Information Technology

Information technology up to this point has been a resource drain and ultimately reduced the ability of government to hire and retain world-class experts. Information technology has imposed on the policymaker financial, productivity, secrecy and opportunity costs. The "iron curtains" between classified information technology systems, policymaker information technology systems and private sector information technology systems have created a wasteful and counter-productive archipelago of information, which the policymaker needs but cannot access electronically. Billions of dollars are being wasted through a lack of coordination and standardization and a lack of focus on requirements analysis, human productivity and the need for easy access to multiple remote multi-lingual and multi-media databases. Information technology continues to offer extraordinary promise, but only if the policymaker begins to *manage* the technology rather than abdicate technology procurement decisions to technologists far removed from the core competencies of the policy environment.

Information technology, in relation to "content", appears to have swamped the end-user with three waves, each of which has left the end-user less productive and less informed than they were before having information technology imposed on them.

- The "first wave", when electronic publishing and electronic storage of data first became possible, brought with it two major negatives:

  - Because computer memory was so limited, the end-user was turned into a "virtual slave" to the computer and obliged to master all manner of arcane commands with which to feed the "c prompt"; and

  - Because librarians were focused on hard copy and technologists were focused on processing generic bytes, the computer industry developed

157

without any strategy for data classification and data archiving.

- The "second wave", when increasingly sophisticated word processing and database management programs became available, also brought with it two major negatives:

  - Because the programs were so sophisticated, end-users were required to either spend a significant amount of time in training, or to forego most of the features offered by the programs; and

  - Because the programs kept changing and managers kept allowing the technologists to specify ever-more sophisticated programs for use, the end-user ended up losing access to much of their legacy data and spending a great deal of time re-entering data to satisfy the changing formats and features of the new programs.

- Now comes the "third wave", in which the Internet is touted by the most optimistic as well as the least principled (two different classes of advocate) as the be-all and end-all for meeting the information needs of the policymaker, with, again, two major negatives:

  - Because the Internet is such an interesting environment and new programs do indeed have a lot of power, analysts are disappearing into the void, either hopelessly lost or hopelessly addicted to wandering in cyberspace; and

  - Because the Internet does offer a superficial amount of information on virtually any topic, albeit with no real source authentication or validation, it has become the "classic comics"

158

of knowledge and too many otherwise thoughtful professionals are accepting the Internet as the first *and* last stop in their quest for information.

In summary, today information technology is part of the problem, not part of the solution. However, the fault does not lie with the technologists, but rather with the managers who have abdicated their responsibility for the direction of technology and its proper applications in support of core competencies.[16]

- **At the strategic level,** we must manage information as the core value — what Paul Strassmann calls "knowledge capital™" and use information technology to reach across national, organizational and disciplinary boundaries.

- **At the operational level,** we must radically alter how we manage both security and procurement, as both are now hobbling information technology by placing barriers in the way of connectivity and state of the art capabilities, while we simultaneously avoid investing in advanced electronic security oversight of *insider* activity.

---

[16] In 1991 Admiral Jerry Tuttle, USN, the "Rickover" of the information age, sponsored Technology Initiatives Game 1991 at the Naval War College. A number of flag officers and senior field grade officers participated. The two most dramatic conclusions reported to the Chief of Naval Operations:

- Technology is not the showstopper — <u>management</u> is where we must change the way we do business.

- Architecturally we must define a completely new paradigm of what information we need, how we handle it, and how it is delivered to the user; this new paradigm must include an information architecture (vice a system/command architecture) approach, must extend to include commercial and coalition capabilities, and must integrate Geographic Position System (GPS) data.

- **At the tactical level,** we must dramatically realign dollars from the collection of classified information, to the discovery, discrimination, distillation and dissemination of unclassified information.

- **At the technical level,** we must accept that our classified base of analyst workstations is a given and stop trying to create a duplicate architecture of unclassified machines which the analysts and policymakers will never use — instead we must rely on private sector Sensitive Compartmented Information Facilities (SCIF) to serve as the "air gaps" for introducing unclassified information into the classified system. At the same time, we must invest in our global Embassies (of all nations) and their related corporate offices and establish a Global Information Management (GIM) concept of operations.[17]

Returning to the field of imagery and global geospatial data to illustrate the perils of badly managed information technology, one can observe:

- Billions have been spent to collect repetitive snap-shots of (then) Soviet missile silo doors, at the same time that the mapping satellite constellation was canceled and the Defense Mapping Agency was forced to create an enormously cumbersome processing system to digest synoptic and relatively microscopic classified images. The system is as a result poorly suited to integrating commercial imagery sources that have now far outpaced

---

[17]The practical and intellectual contributions of Paul Strassmann, and his prolific documentation of the critical role of information technology in the context of management ("information technology makes bad management *worse*"), make him the *virtual* Chief Information Officer of the United States. His insights into information pay-off, the business value of computers, the politics of information management, and the economics of information are essential to devising and implementing any national-level improvements. The author has extended Mr. Strassmann's original concept, Corporate Information Management (CIM), to the global context—one time data entry, global access.

national assets in terms of diversity of utility and breadth of availability.

- SPOT Image Corporation has most of the earth already in its archives, generally 100% cloud-free and less than three years old....yet the U.S. Intelligence Community refuses to realign funds to meet the stated need[18] of the National Imagery and Mapping Agency (NIMA) for $250 million dollars a year to buy commercial imagery; the Office of the Assistant Secretary of Defense has refused an even more modest request from NIMA for $25 million a year; the appropriate authorities continue to refuse to create a separate funding line for the procurement of commercial imagery; and NIMA compounds this problem by refusing to acknowledge the EARTHMAP Report and the geospatial needs of the Departments of State, Commerce, Treasury and other key elements of the government concerned with peace and prosperity.

- In the absence of a means for integrating *existing* commercial global geospatial data into a global multi-media database, automated data fusion between distinct sources and disciplines remains an impossibility. *Global geospatial data at the 1:50,000 resolution level is literally the foundation for information sharing and integration and automated value-added processing and — ergo — the foundation for virtual intelligence, virtual diplomacy and information peacekeeping.*

Now what of the promise of information technology? One can focus on three areas: generic functional requirements for individual workstations; generic organizational methods for routine, reliable and responsive access to

---

[18] NIMA today is allocated around $30 million a year on the procurement of SPOT (10 meter) and other (Russian 2 meter, Indian 5 meter, Canadian radar 25 meter) image data. Despite a clear awareness within NIMA of the urgent need to spend heavily for wide-area surveillance coverage from commercial imagery, severe bureaucratic obstacles continue to exist in this area.

global data and expertise (including data definition standards); and collaborative information-sharing across boundaries.

Generic Functional Requirements

Data entry	Data routing and records management
• Selective text and image extraction • Hard copy scanning including color • Audio transcription/translation	• Automated clustering Automated gisting • Automated weighting • Automated routing, filing and purging
Data retrieval	**Database construction and management**

• Very large unstructured multi-media database search
• Automated access to and querying of distributed databases
• Menu-driven multiple database/multi-level security access programs
• Natural language query conversion to all legacy search systems
• Automated flagging of data changes
• Retrieval of like images despite angle of look and shades of gray differences
• Understanding of numeric variations and equivalents
	• Free form database construction
	• Automated database maintenance
	   Automated verification and cleansing
	• Automated text extraction
	• Automated tagging of data elements with level of classification and source
	• Fully integrated text and images
	• Automated and ad hoc hot links
	   Automated records management
	• Individual entry protocols for voice and video

Data collection and exploitation	**Knowledge base construction and management**
• Desktop publishing • Graphics and briefing aids • Global electronic mail • Graphical visualization • Integrated modeling & simulation • Automated statistical analysis • Expert pre-screening of indicators Automated flagging of "hot" words and changes in content over time • Digital map overlays • Automated overlay maintenance	• Menu driven access to previous queries • Automated repeat queries • Menu driven flagging of key words, profile extensions • Gradual automated and user-assisted development of key links and concepts
"Intelligence" collection management	**Administrative and security management**
• Automated collection asset inventory and status • Automated matching of assets and requirements • Automated "tasker" • Automated tracking of satisfaction/tickler • "Alternative collection strategies" generation • Raw/finished collection evaluation toolkit	• Documents control/bar coding • Electronic "marking" of classification • Automated sanitization to any level • Automated comparison of reports • Automation of all forms and reports • Automated name traces • Automated access/query audit trail • Automated virus eradication • Smart in-boxes • Instant retrieval of contingency plans and archived inter-agency info.

Figure 28: Generic "All-Source Fusion" Workstation

The single most helpful contribution to the productivity of all those supporting policymakers across national and organizational boundaries would be the stabilization of their individual workstations and their means of accessing multi-lingual and multi-media data. At a minimum, organizations must put a stop to the practice of duplicative and counter-productive investments in varying kinds of "all source fusion workstations" which ultimately divide rather than unite data and people.[19]

Figure 28 lists illustrative examples of generic requirements, which should be part of joint government-corporate efforts to establish an international information technology standard that contributes to individual productivity:[20] The technologists will be quick to say "we can do that", but there are two realities that continue to escape them:

- Human productivity and human nature cannot afford to learn a different application for each function and task. These are basic functions and tasks, which must be integrated and intuitive.

---

[19] While serving as a founding member of the Advanced Information Processing and Analysis Steering Group of the Intelligence Research and Development Council (U.S.), the author observed that virtually every "black" compartmented program appeared to be allocating around $10 million a year to building its own "all source fusion workstation". Since the data domains were compartmented, the procurement system was essentially funding between 10 to 20 different programs, at a cost of $100-200 million a year, intended to build 10-20 different versions of the same generic workstation. During this period the author also completed a second graduate thesis, *Strategic and Tactical Information Management for National Security* (University of Oklahoma, May 1987) and much of that work has influenced the author's perceptions on the vertical and horizontal disconnects that permeate the entire U.S. government information kaleidoscope.

[20] The requirements were developed by the author in 1986 while serving as Project Manager for "Project GEORGE (Smiley)" on the Artificial Intelligence Staff, Office of Information Technology, Central Intelligence Agency. A similar requirements document, "Computer Aided Tools for the Analysis of Science & Technology (CATALYST) was developed by the Office of Scientific and Weapons Research (OSWR) under the leadership of Dr. Gordon Oehler — they were promptly informed by the Office of Information Resources that their requirements, which required Sun and other UNIX workstations, could not be accommodated because "CIA" had decided to go with IBM and the PC 2 architecture. They are only now, 20 years later, catching up.

- Crazy things happen when multi-media and multi-lingual data is needed that can only be obtained from multiple remote sources. No technology should be considered acceptable until it has been fully tested against real-world data sources and real-world data processing needs of the end-user.

It is essential that *policymakers* present a united front, across all boundaries, with respect to generic functional requirements for the most important tool in the arsenal of the diplomat, commander, and policy-maker: the electronic information machine.

Doctrine for External Access

Writing in *Forbes ASAP* in August 1998, Peter Drucker, the dean of business process gurus, took the time to focus on something that intelligence professionals have understood for centuries: the heart of the matter is *not* what you already know, or "internal" information, but rather what you *don't know"*, or "external" information. Drucker's article,[21] does a very fine job of pointing out the fundamental mis-steps American management has taken in the past few decades, first with its over-emphasis on information technology, and then with its more recent emphasis on "business process reengineering" and "knowledge management"—the latter two nothing more than alternative expressions for "stirring the internal pot". Drucker writes:

We can already discern and define the next...task in development an effective information system for top management: the collection and organization of OUTSIDE-focused information. All the data we have so far, including those provided by the new tools, focus inward. But inside an enterprise—indeed, even inside the entire economic chain—there are only costs. Results are only on the outside. The only profit center is the customer whose check hasn't bounced. But as regards the outside (customers, and, equally important, noncustomers; competitors and, equally important, noncompetitors; markets; technologies other than those already in place in one's own industry; currencies; economies; and so on) we have virtually no

---

[21] Peter Drucker, "The Next Information Revolution", *Forbes ASAP*, 24 August 1998, page 24.

data. Few businesses use even the little information that is available or pay enough attention to demographics. And even fewer realize that the most important datum for planning and strategy is reliable information on whether the share of income that customers spend on their industry's products or services is increasing or declining.

Everything Drucker says about business is true ten times over for government.

The private sector offers the policymaker an extraordinary range of world-class expertise at very low cost and with the ability to create new knowledge on demand. In most cases having to do with Third World conflicts, traditionally very low priorities for classified intelligence capabilities, the private sector is the essential source for expertise needed by the policymaker. At the same time, the policymaker can acquire a new appreciation for information as a "munition" or a means by which to alter the balance of power in a conflict through an alteration of the balance of information.

The following illustrates the "information archipelago"— essentially distributed private sector expertise and knowledge—that exists today, the vast majority of it in the private sector:

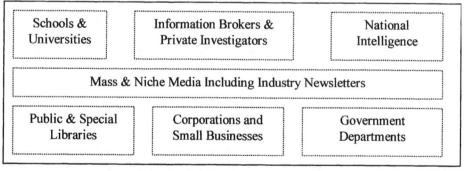

Figure 29: The Information Archipelago

In contemplating this Archipelago, the policymaker should consider the following key findings:

- *The expertise contained within each of the sectors is created and maintained at someone else's expense.*

- The expertise that is maintained in these other sectors is constantly subject to the test of market forces and tends to be more current with respect to both sources and methods than the government's archives and analysts.

- The cost of this expertise, when the policymaker is able to surmount security and procurement obstacles, is on the order of $10,000 for a world-class report which is concise and actionable and delivered overnight, inclusive of the cost of identifying and validating the best choice of expert.

- Such published information as is available to the policymaker through either online retrieval or hardcopy document retrieval represents less than 20% and more often less than 10% of what is actually known by the individual experts.

- The most significant deficiency in national intelligence today as it pertains to providing the policymaker with just enough, just in time "intelligence", is the lack of direct access to the human expertise available in the private sector.

There are many examples of worthy private sector sources and capabilities that can be harnessed to meet the needs of the policy maker, but for the sake of this chapter a practical case study pertinent to foreign affairs and national defense will be described.

On the afternoon of 3 August 1995, a Thursday, the author was testifying to the Commission on Intelligence regarding the importance of dramatically improving government access to open sources. At the end of the day, at 1700, the author was invited to execute a benchmark exercise in which the U.S. Intelligence Community and the author would simultaneously seek to provide the Commission with information about the chosen target, Burundi.[22]

---

[22] The exercise is described in vague terms on page 88 of *Preparing for the 21st Century: An Appraisal of U.S. Intelligence* (report of the Commission on the Roles and Capabilities of the United States Intelligence Community). What the report does not

By 1000 the morning of 7 August 1995, a Monday, the following was delivered to the Commission offices via overnight mail:

- **From Oxford Analytica,** a series of two-page executive reports drafted for their global clients at the Chief Executive Officer level, outlining the political and economic ramifications of the Burundi situation;

- **From Jane's Information Group,** a map of Burundi showing the tribal areas of influence; a one-page order of battle for each tribe; and a volume of one-paragraph summaries with citations for all articles about Burundi published in the past couple of years in *Jane's Intelligence Review, International Defense Review* and *Jane's Defense Weekly.*

- **From LEXIS-NEXIS,** a listing of the top journalists in the world whose by-line reporting on Burundi suggested their intimate familiarity with the situation;

- **From the Institute of Scientific Information (ISI)** in Philadelphia, a listing of the top academics in the world

---

mention is that the comparison was so shockingly graphic that the staff initially decided to avoid the issue of open sources entirely, calling the exercise "unstructured and invalid". This "denial" was common knowledge within 48 hours and subsequent correspondence with the Chairman was evidently successful, as a three person sub-panel of Members was created, and the report ultimately contained a number of very significant comments on the critical importance of improving access to open sources of information. Perhaps even more significant than its findings on the critical nature of open sources for the U.S. Intelligence Community, was the Commission's conclusion that intelligence questions that could be answered predominantly by open sources, should be answered by the consumers themselves — by the home organizations of the policymakers needing the intelligence. This is an important recommendation that validates much of this chapter's thrust, because the reality is that most policymakers do not have, today, a staff or a fund with which to define their requirement, manage the collection, and then apply the value-added techniques of intelligence analysis necessary to convert open source information into open source intelligence. Policymakers can no longer excuse their ignorance by claiming reliance on secrets that do not materialize — they *must* take responsibility for collecting and producing open source information.

publishing on the Burundi situation, together with contact information;

- **From East View Publications in Minneapolis,** a listing of all immediately available "Soviet" military topographic maps for Burundi, at the 1:100,000 level.

- **From SPOT Image Corporation,** it was determined that SPOT could provide digital imagery for 100% of Burundi, cloud-free and less than three years old, at a ten meter resolution adequate for creating military maps with contour lines at the 1:50,000 level as well as precision-munitions guidance packages and nape of the earth interactive aviation and ground mission rehearsal simulation packages.[23]

The above effort was described by one very senior Hill staff manager as "John Henry against the steel hammer—only John Henry won." The "steel hammer", the U.S. Intelligence Community, had nothing of substance because Burundi was at the very bottom of its priority list and its capabilities were not suited for surge coverage of this obscure and remote area that had here-to-fore been irrelevant to U.S. interests. It is, however, very important to stress again and again that open sources are *not* a substitute for spies and satellites, but rather that both common sense and fiscal realities suggest that it is imperative that the policymaker be able to exploit open sources to the fullest in their public diplomacy, military acquisition and economic competitiveness roles, while relying on classified intelligence — classified intelligence presented in the *context* of open sources — for those unique insights and details that cannot be obtained through other means and which in fact are demonstrably so precious as to warrant the risk and cost of espionage.

---

[23] SPOT Image Corporation was not part of the author's consortium of open source providers during the week of its competition but was belatedly identified and its offerings with respect to Burundi reported. It merits comment that for all the talk about U.S. one meter imagery becoming available in the near future, it will take the U.S. commercial imagery providers at least a decade to replicate the industrial strength system that SPOT has in place today, including multiple satellites with two-day revisitation capabilities, seventeen ground stations, and virtually the entire world already available in the archives for immediate exploitation.

So, with respect to external access and the creation of an architecture through which policymakers can obtain open source intelligence from the private sector, the next two figures outline the core ideas for the *information merchant bank* ®.

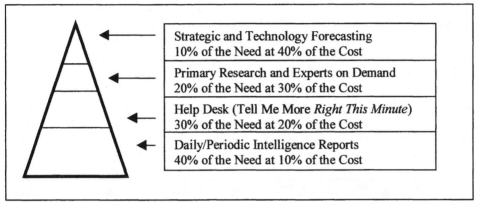

Strategic and Technology Forecasting
10% of the Need at 40% of the Cost

Primary Research and Experts on Demand
20% of the Need at 30% of the Cost

Help Desk (Tell Me More *Right This Minute*)
30% of the Need at 20% of the Cost

Daily/Periodic Intelligence Reports
40% of the Need at 10% of the Cost

Figure 30: Four Levels of Open Source Intelligence Service[24]

Daily Intelligence Briefs. The lowest level of service is the *Daily Intelligence Brief* that builds on a quality process that integrates multi-lingual access to Internet, commercial media and trade and industry journals as well as conference reports, dissertations, and new books in order to provide to each individual policymaker (or supporting staff employee) a concise digest of highly focused current news pertinent to their explicit *individual* responsibilities — each entry comes with a route to obtaining the full text document.

Help Desk (Online Search & Retrieval). The next level of service, the Help Desk, provides rapid response search and retrieval services that can access the Internet, all major commercial online services (including international and foreign language online services as well as international electronic databases that are not necessarily "online" but can be exploited

---

[24] As conceptualized by OSS EVP (D) Mr. Jan Herring, charter member of the Society of Competitive Intelligence Professionals and widely-regarded as the "father" of business intelligence in the United States, and as implemented at www.oss.net.

remotely) and hard-copy references including general literature such as is available in a major library.[25]

Primary Research (Experts on Demand). At the third level, even more expertise can be applied to a policymaker's problem by systematically identifying and then contracting with individual experts who can bring to bear decades of experience and immediate access to all manner of electronic and hard copy sources (as well as their own network of experts and assistants). The economic benefits of out-sourcing decision support to such experts cannot be understated — this essentially allows the policymaker to harness expertise that has been maintained at someone else's expense and that has proven itself in the marketplace through peer citation and public success. Oxford Analytica, which uses the Dons of Oxford University as a *de facto* "Intelligence Council", is the only organization of its kind and an integral part of any comprehensive effort to take advantage of the knowledge available in the private sector.

Strategic Forecasting (Including Technology Forecasting). Finally, at the fourth level, strategic studies and forecasts, including forecasts of scientific and technical trends and opportunities, can be obtained by using the capabilities of the Institute of Scientific Information (ISI) to quickly identify and select from world-class experts on any topic. This unique organization is the sole source in the world of both citation analysis data, which covers all significant peer-reviewed journals in the world (i.e. it is international and multi-

---

[25] In the early 1990's the Central Intelligence Agency created a list of all public journals to which its analysts had access through their library or through subscription, and then established the accessibility of these journals via electronic means. They found that roughly one-fifth were available through LEXIS-NEXIS, one-fifth through DIALOG, one-fifth through other online services or other electronic databases, and two-fifths were not online. Most customers for information services do not realize that most information brokers rely largely on either LEXIS-NEXIS or DIALOG, not both in tandem, and have limited access to the larger range of international online sources, while having almost no access at all to a complete collection of hard-copy references. At the same time, very few customers for information services understand that the best value in searching comes from employing a searcher who has *both* access to a full range of international sources, *and* subject-matter expertise—otherwise, the customer pays for the searcher's learning curve and false trails. The *Burwell World Directory of Information Brokers* is an essential reference for those doing their own "general contracting", as it provides both a subject-matter index to information brokers, and an index to brokers speaking a foreign language and familiar with specific foreign databases.

lingual) as well as essential technology for mapping specific disciplines and identifying key individuals and centers of expertise. In combination with a wide range of other open sources, systems and services, relatively low-cost strategic forecasts can be developed.[26]

Below is an illustration of a basic internal clearinghouse, followed by a brief description of its core functions.

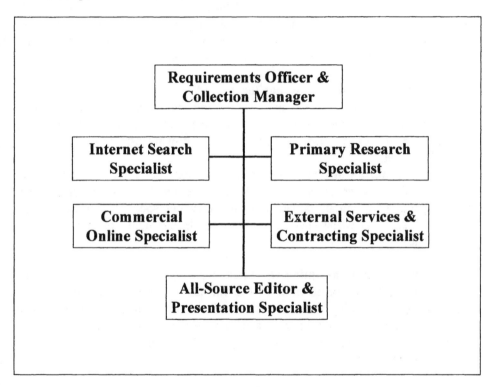

Figure 31: Open Source Intelligence Support Cell

---

[26] It is unfortunate that most organizations turn to very large accounting, legal, or market research organizations, to spend hundreds of thousands of dollars for huge compendiums of *information*, when they would be much better served by using a clearinghouse — the information merchant bank® model — to focus very carefully on their most important questions, and then obtain "just enough just in time" *intelligence*, generally for a fraction of what they would pay for the more comprehensive but less useful compilations of assorted facts and figures.

Any organization can establish its own clearinghouse for gaining access to external expertise and knowledge. It may not be as effective as using a "virtual" intelligence center provided by a global leader in open source exploitation, but it will assuredly improve — significantly improve — day to day decision support and hence contribute to the effectiveness of the organization.

The key is to recognize that the primary focus for such a cell is *solely and exclusively* that of service as a clearinghouse—getting the internal requirement for information properly defined, *knowing who knows* outside, and bringing the two together through a deliberate process.

The "cell" is scaleable, but the key idea is to avoid at all costs the creation of a centralized unit with increasing numbers of employees that attempt to actually do the research and develop the intelligence itself. Instead, the focus for *each* of the specialists must be on "knowing who knows"[27]

The Internet specialist keeps track of external Internet experts who are also subject-matter experts, for instance in regional, scientific, or military domains, and who can be called upon to carry out specific searches of the Internet. This specialist also monitors the development of new Internet technologies.

The commercial online specialist must understand in strategic terms the relative utility and price value of the various commercial online offerings and focuses on retaining the appropriate information broker or brokers, each with the necessary expertise at particular online services, as well as a complementary knowledge of the language and /or foreign databases as well as the subject matter area.

The primary research specialist is expert at using a combination of citation analysis, association and other directories and direct calling to rapidly

---

[27] This excellent phrase is one that the author credits to Dr. Stevan Dedijer. Dr. Dedijer, a member of the original Office of Strategic Services, is considered by many in Europe and elsewhere to be the intellectual father of the concept of business intelligence. He spent many years in Sweden as a professor at the University of Lund, and is now in retirement in Croatia (his birthplace) where he is writing his memoirs and occasionally lecturing on intelligence matters to the Croatian military and police.

get answers to questions that cannot be addressed through accessing published information, but rather require either access to "gray literature" that is legally available but only if you know where to go for it, or to a human expert who can construct the answer in real time by drawing on their historical knowledge and access to various unpublished sources, including human sources.

The external services specialist is a master of the marketplace and follows all of the niche providers who offer narrowly focused sources, software or services; this person can also serve as the contracting expert for the cell.

Below are some of the standard niche services that are common to the private sector:

Some Types of Open Source	Some Types of Open Software	Some Types of Open Service
Current Awareness	Internet Search Tools	Commercial Online Search & Retrieval
Current Contents	Data Entry Tools	Foreign Language Media Monitoring
Subject-Matter Clearinghouses (Univers.)	Database Construction and Management Tools	Human Document Abstracting and Indexing
Conference Proceedings and Papers	Data Retrieval, Routing and Records Management	Document Translation
Direct Access to Commercial Online	Automated Document Abstracting and Indexing	Gray Literature Discovery and Retrieval
Contextual Awareness/ Cultural Orientation	Automated Document Translation	Experts on Demand
Document Acquisition	Knowledge-Base Construction & Mgmt.	Primary Research (Telephone Surveys)
Subject-Matter Commercial Databases	Data Mining and Visualization Tools	Private Investigation and Direct Debriefings
Risk Assessment Reports	Desktop Publishing Tools	Market Research
Expert and Association Directories	Multi-Media Communications Tools	Strategic Literature and Technology Forecasting
Photographic Archives	Digital Imagery Processing	Hard-Copy Global Map and Chart Procurement
Digital Data Archives	Electronic Security and Administration Tools	Commercial Imagery and Map Production

Figure 32: Niche Capabilities Offered Within the Private Sector

"Market research" and "studies & analysis" are generic categories where in many cases the customer cannot rely on the provider. In general, providers of such services who have major investments in permanent personnel will *not* take the trouble to systematically identify world-class experts or fully survey external online and hard copy sources. It is an unfortunate reality that such organizations are constantly seeking to assign existing employees, whether or not they are fully qualified to address the specific inquiry, and to avoid paying for direct support from niche providers such as those who specialize in specific languages, citation analysis, patent records search, etcetera.

Information technology continues to offer the policymaker significant opportunities for acquiring and managing knowledge with which to avoid conflicts and resolve conflicts, as well as to identify and exploit opportunities for mutual peaceful advantage, but it will not be part of the solution until the policymaker recognizes that in the age of information, the management of information technology is an inherent function of command and not something that can be delegated to technologists.

It is also critical that the policymaker focus on content and access to external expertise and multi-lingual data as well as value-added services rather than on internal information handling systems that tend to require more effort to "feed" than they return in value-added.

In the age of information, the cost of communications and computers (hardware and software) has already declined dramatically. Now the cost of content is leveling off and is about to begin declining. The major added value in the next two decades — and information technology has an important but not an exclusive role to play in delivering this added value — will come from:

- **Discovery.** Policymakers have power and they should spend their time reflecting and deciding when they are not in negotiation and in face to face communication with their counterparts. It is for the "virtual intelligence community" to meet the policymakers needs for discovering as much of the raw information as is necessary to meet the policymakers needs for "just enough just in time" intelligence.

174

- **Discrimination.** A major value-added function is that of discriminating between valid and invalid information, through a constant process of source validation, generally a labor-intensive process requiring genuine human expertise as well as new developments in automated understanding. A cost element can also be provided here, by giving the customer the benefits of superior knowledge in selecting sources of equal content but lower prices.[28]

- **Distillation.** This is the essence of "intelligence" in that it combines research judgments that first discover and discriminate and then it adds expert subject matter knowledge to distill the broader effort into "just enough" intelligence — intelligence being information which is tailored to the needs of the policymaker and tightly focused on helping the policymaker with a specific decision at a specific time and place.

- **Dissemination.** Often the timing, length and even the format of the delivered product can be decisive in determining whether the intelligence contained in the document (or oral presentation, or video, or electronic mail, or whatever) is received by the intended policymaker, and compelling enough to support action. There is far more to dissemination than simple delivery.[29]

The above is not intended to make a case for the use of open sources from the private sector to the exclusion of either unclassified information or classified information from government sources. Indeed, the ideal situation emerges when both the policymaker and the intelligence community use open

---

[28] There are a number of major media providers that can be accessed through the Internet for free, or through commercial online services for a fee. This is but one example.

[29] In a most engaging way, (then) National Security Advisor Frank Carlucci told a group of mid-level CIA analysts in the 1980's that the ideal intelligence briefing for President Ronald Reagan would be "a five minute video, five minutes before his meeting". This remains a superb statement of the requirement, and one that the intelligence community has yet to acknowledge or address.

sources to the fullest extent possible, but with intelligence methods applied to produce open source intelligence, *then* task the classified systems for such information as is truly critical; and finally utilize open sources to protect classified findings but inform those who require information support but to whom classified information cannot be disclosed.

Conclusion

The day of the decision-maker oblivious to intelligence is over. Decision-cycles are compressing in time and extending in scope. All intelligence systems must be geared to cold-starts, surges, and answering specific questions from specific decision-makers. In the face of ambiguous unconventional threats, if we do not reform our community, major intelligence failures are waiting to happen.

Intelligence technology must not be left to technologists. Open sources are overtaking classified sources in a complementary manner. A significant amount of government intelligence collection and analysis can now be out-sourced to the private sector. Virtual intelligence communities are now a reality made possible by information technology and especially the Internet. The key is to mobilize all knowledge sectors (experts and knowledge created and maintained *at someone else's expense*).

Information *qua* intelligence is now a major "weapons system" in the arsenal of the sovereign state. "Knowledge about knowledge" is the core competency of the 21st Century intelligence professional.

Information Peackeeping:
The Purest Form of War

Information is a substitute for violence.

Alvin Toffler

Information Peacekeeping is the neglected aspect of Information Operations, a new concept that up to this point has focused exclusively on Information Warfare, and avoided dealing with the substance of All-Source Intelligence, or the proactive possibilities of Information Peacekeeping. Information Peacekeeping is the active exploitation of information and information technology so as to achieve national policy objectives without violence. The three elements of Information Peacekeeping are, in order of priority, open source intelligence; information technology; and electronic security & counterintelligence. Information Peacekeeping is the strategic deterrent as well as the tactical force of first resort for the 21st Century. Virtual Intelligence, a supporting concept, is the foundation for informed policy-making, judicious acquisition management, effective contingency planning and execution, and timely public consensus-building. By its nature, Information Peacekeeping must rely almost exclusively on open sources and services available from the private sector; this requires the crafting of a new doctrine of national intelligence that places the critical classified contributions of the traditional national intelligence communities within the context of a larger global information community. Information Peacekeeping is the purest form of war, but most traditional warriors will be reluctant to accept its most fundamental premise: that intelligence is indeed a virtual substitute for violence, for capital, for labor, for time, and for space. Information Peacekeeping is in effect both a strategy for government operations and a national security strategy with global reach; consequently it has profound implications for how we train, equip, and organize our government and our military.

Introduction: Intelligence As Munition

Time and time again, the U.S. defense and intelligence communities rush to spend billions on technology, while routinely ignoring the challenges and the opportunities inherent in human collection, open-source collection, foreign area expertise and human all-source analysis. We do it in mobility systems, in weapons systems, in command-and-control systems and in intelligence systems. Sadly, leaders in all corners of the Department of Defense (DoD), at all levels, continue to abdicate their responsibility for *thinking* at the strategic, operational, tactical and technical levels, and have surrendered their forces to the mindless flow of self-generated bits and bytes.

This is not the place to repeat original thinking from earlier writings, but it *is* the place to emphasize the fact that a majority of the U.S. military leadership still does not "get it". The Revolution in Military Affairs is a joke. It is nothing more than lip service, substituting astronomically expensive systems with no sensor-to-shooter guidance nor any relevance to three of the four warrior classes, for outrageously expensive systems with no sensor-to-shooter guidance and dated relevance to one of the four warrior classes. The three warrior classes we must confront in this new era are: the low-tech brutes (transnational criminals, narco-traffickers, terrorists); the low-tech seers (ideological, religious, and ethnic groups unable to accept conventional relations among nations); and high-tech seers (a combination of information terrorists or vandals, and practitioners of economic espionage). Most of our training, equipment, and operational doctrine are completely unsuited to meeting the threat from these three warrior classes. Perhaps even more disturbing is the fact that our national "order of battle" must now fully integrate our government civilian agencies and our private sector information reserves, but we have no one in a leadership position who is willing or able to deal with this harsh and urgent reality.

The real revolution is being led by a few original thinkers who have yet to be heard on Capitol Hill and whose thoughts are a decade from influencing fruitful changes in how we train, equip, and organize our Nation for war. Alvin and Heidi Toffler were among the first to articulate the fact that information is a substitute for wealth and violence, for capital, labor, time, and space.[1]   Pilots and ship drivers may never forgive Martin Libicki for reframing their platforms as delivery vehicles for intelligence-driven operations.[2]   Winn Schwartau overcame his Hollywood and rock-and-roll past ultimately to inspire a Presidential Commission on Critical Infrastructure Protection.[3] Colonel James Clark blew past the nay-sayers, with support from a very wise Vice Chief of Staff of the Air Force, to bring EAGLE VISION in as an operationally effective means of putting real-time commercial imagery into tactical service— something the National Reconnaissance Office (NRO) and the National Imagery and Mapping Agency (NIMA) refused to contemplate and still resist at every level.[4]

Information Peacekeeping, the subject of this chapter, is the purest form of war. It shapes the battlefield, it shapes the belligerents, and it shapes the bystanders in such a way as to defeat the enemy without battle—in such a way as to achieve U.S. policy objectives without confrontation and without bloodshed. Sun Tzu would approve.[5]

---

[1]   See specifically Alvin Toffler, *PowerShift: Knowledge, Wealth, and Violence at the Edge of the 21st Century* (Bantam, 1990), and Alvin and Heidi Toffler, *War and Anti-War: Survival at the Dawn of the 21st Century* (Little Brown, 1993).

[2]   One of the most intelligent and revolutionary writings pertinent to military doctrine is Martin J. Libicki, *The Mesh and the Net: Speculations on Armed Conflict in a time of free silicon* (National Defense University, 1994).

[3]   Schwartau's first book, *Terminal Compromise*, was considered by his lawyers to be so controversial that he was required to publish it as a novel.   His follow-on, *INFORMATION WARFARE: Chaos on the Electronic Superhighway* (Thunders Mouth Press, 1994), set the stage for global discussion and is widely credited with awakening both the international press and the international military to this critical issue area.

[4]   EAGLE VISION/JOINT VISION is a ground station transportable in a single C-130 that is capable of taking real-time feeds from both SPOT IMAGE (10 meter) satellites and national satellites.   Today it can feed directly into aviation mission rehearsal systems and allow interactive three-dimensional fly-through practice. If the Army will pay attention and hook up its 18-wheeler topographic vans to one of these ground stations, they may find that they can produce 1:50,000 combat charts with contour lines on a "just enough, just in time" basis.   As tactical capabilities to exploit commercial imagery expand, it will be increasingly difficult for NIMA and the NRO to justify their existing budgets and production costs.

[5]   "The acme of skill is to defeat the enemy without fighting."   This widely-accepted mantra has not yet influenced how we structure our military force packages.

DEFINITION: A Strategic View of Information Operations

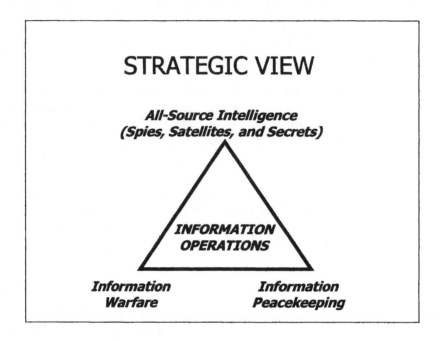

Figure 33: Strategic View of Information Operations

At the strategic level Information Operations must be seen as a triangle in which all-source intelligence, information warfare, and information peacekeeping are seamlessly integrated and inherent in all aspects of military and civilian operations.

Perhaps the most important aspect of information operations in the 21ˢᵗ Century is that it is not inherently military; instead, civilian practitioners must acquire a military understanding and military discipline in the practice of information operations, if they are to be effective.

Information Operations tends to be viewed as a strategic form of Information Warfare, and this is a much-too-narrow view which deprives the policy-maker, acquisition manager, and commander of two-thirds of the "firepower" represented by a more accurate and well-rounded understanding of Information Operations.

All-Source Intelligence is the critical classified element of Information Operations that assures all parties being supported that they are receiving essential indications and warning intelligence, current intelligence, and estimative intelligence, to name just a few kinds of all-source intelligence.

Information Peacekeeping is the active exploitation of information and information technology so as to achieve national policy objectives. The three elements of Information Peacekeeping, in order of priority, are: open source intelligence; information technology; and electronic security and counterintelligence.

Information Peacekeeping is a *strategic deterrent* that significantly increases the ability of the practicing nation to avoid and resolve conflict in relation to all four warrior classes and across the complete spectrum of government operations—not only military but diplomatic, commercial, agricultural, etc.

All three aspects of Information Operations—the obvious one of Information Warfare and the two less obvious aspects of All-Source Intelligence and Information Peacekeeping—share one critical component: open-source intelligence.

No aspect of Information Operations can be conducted effectively without full access to a cooperative private sector that controls the vast majority of national knowledge resources—the "information commons."[6]

Once thought of in this light, it becomes evident that the center-of-gravity for Information Operations is in the civil sector—in the private sector.

---

[11] Lee Felsenstein of the Interval Research Corporation is the originator of the term "information commons."

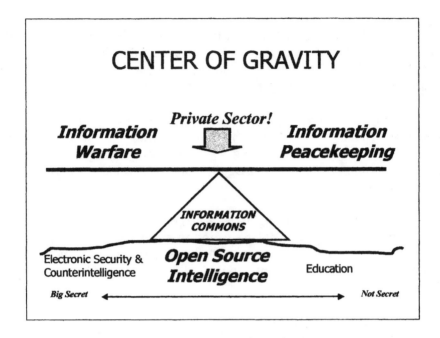

Figure 34: Center of Gravity for Information Operations

Interestingly, this perspective also makes it clear that the importance as well as the presence of secrecy declines dramatically as one moves from the left "warfare" side of the equation, to the right "peacekeeping" side of the equation. In fact, as is now generally recognized, fully eighty percent of the intelligence "solution" comes from open rather than classified sources, and it is incumbent on the consumers of intelligence—not the producers—to harness these *open* sources.[7]

---

[7] Over the years authoritative speakers including Mr. Ward Elcock, Director of the Canadian Security and Intelligence Service; Dr. Gordon Oehler, (then) Director of the highly-regarded DCI's Non-Proliferation Center, and many others, have generally agreed that even for topics as seemingly difficult as terrorism and proliferation, open sources of information comprise roughly 80% of all-source solution. In fact open sources can contribute as little as 10-20% (mostly targeting assistance for denied area coverage by classified sources), and as much as 95-99% (strategic economic intelligence). The official National Foreign Intelligence Board finding, based on input from the Community Open Source Program Office (COSPO), is that the U.S.

Information Peacekeeping:
The Heart Of Information Operations

Information Peacekeeping is the active exploitation of information and information technology—in order to modify peacefully the balance of power between specific individual and groups—so as to achieve national policy objectives. The three elements of Information Peacekeeping, in order of priority, are: open-source intelligence (providing useful actionable unclassified information); information technology (providing "tools for truth" that afford the recipient access to international information and the ability to communicate with others); and electronic security and counter-intelligence (a strictly defensive aspect of Information Operations).

To understand what this means, it is useful to specify what Information Peacekeeping is *not*. Information Peacekeeping is not:

- the application of information or information technology in support of conventional military peacekeeping operations, or in support of United Nations, coalition, or diplomatic operations.

- the development and execution of traditional psychological operations or deception operations that strive to manipulate perceptions in order to achieve surprise, or to cause actions to be taken that would not have been taken if the true circumstances were known.

- covert action media placement operations, covert action agent of influence operations, or covert action paramilitary operations

- clandestine human intelligence operations or overt research operations.

Intelligence Community, and most specifically the Central Intelligence Agency, spends 1% of its total budget on open sources, and for this amount of money receives 40% of its input to the all-source process. Imagine what they could do if they spent 5%!

183

Although Information Peacekeeping is not to be confused with clandestine or covert methods, there are gray areas. Information Peacekeeping may require the clandestine delivery of classified or open source intelligence, or the covert delivery of "tools for truth" such as the traditional radio broadcast equipment, or the more recently popular cellular telephones and facsimile machines. Information Peacekeeping may also require covert assistance in establishing and practicing electronic security and counterintelligence in the face of host country censorship or interference.

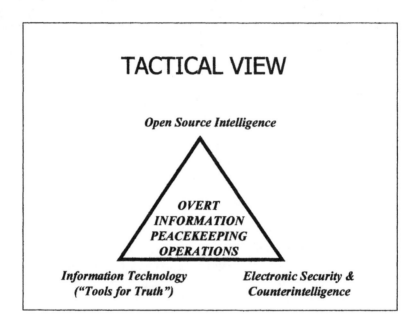

Figure 35: Elements of Overt Information Peacekeeping Operations

On balance, then, Information Peacekeeping is by its nature most powerful and effective when it relies exclusively on open sources of information, the delivery of open-source intelligence, and on overt action. Under these conditions, it is incontestably legal and ethical under all applicable rules of law, including host country and non-Western cultural and religious rules of law and custom.

Information Peacekeeping is the tactical "force of first resort" for 21ˢᵗ Century operations, and every theater and every major command, must have an order-of-battle able to conduct overt Information Peacekeeping Operations in all three of its major aspects.

Existing staff functions are not adequate to this challenge at this time. Taking each of the major staff elements for a theater command in turn:

-- J-1 (Administrative). Generally includes handling of refugees and prisoners of war. No concepts, doctrine, or "order-of-battle" for treating information as either a munition or a critical logistics elements. Of most immediate concern: no J-1 (or G-1 or S-1) appears to have at hand an approved Table of Organization and/or Table of Equipment for handling humans who are placed under military care in a tactical environment.

-- J-2 (Intelligence). Generally reactive and apathetic—takes whatever it can get from classified national intelligence systems. Does not have the concepts, doctrine, funding, security permissions, or "order-of-battle" for going out and *getting* open-source intelligence with which to provide direct support to theater operations.

-- J-3 (Operations). Focuses strictly on placing munitions on target, positioning troops, and planning movements. Does not have concepts, doctrine, or an "order-of-battle" with which to use information as a substitute for munitions or men. Note that the execution of Information Warfare attacks, or the conduct of Psychological Operations, do not count and do not have the same effect as Information Peacekeeping Operations.

-- J-4 (Logistics). Focuses on beans, bullets and band-aids. Not responsible for evaluating or considering how full or empty the various constituencies are with respect to information essential to their mission. Imagine how effective a command might be if its information requirements—and those of its coalition partners and civilian agency counterparts—were treated with the same seriousness as fuel stocks or critical spare parts for fighter aircraft.

-- J-5 (Plans/Other). Focuses on plans in isolation. Is not held accountable for declaring specific plans to be unsupportable due to a lack of intelligence or maps. The fact is that most theater contingency plans have made no provision for acquiring the necessary open-source intelligence—including commercial imagery—because everyone is assuming that national capabilities will suffice and will be made available. This is fiction.[8]

    -- J-6 (Communications). Focuses on administration of limited bandwidth and assignment of limited communications and computing resources, as well as subsequent oversight of the entire architecture. Is not held accountable for considering how the theater will communicate with coalition and civilian partners who are not equipped to U.S. standards, and is at the same time burdened by a vast and very expensive C4I architecture designed by the military services, all of whom assumed that the U.S. would always be fighting a unilateral military action in which all parties have the necessary clearances to be part of the largely classified theater command- and-control system. In particular, the J-6 is not held accountable for ensuring that externally acquired data, including maps and other hard-copy multi-lingual data, and external information nodes, including non-governmental groups, can be fully integrated into the larger Information Operations environment within which the CINC must operate.

    Others can focus on the information technology and electronic security aspects of Information Peacekeeping—this chapter will conclude with an examination of the most important aspect of Information Peacekeeping: the use of open source intelligence to understand, shape, and dominate the knowledge terrain in the "battle area".

GEOSPATIAL GAPS:
The Achilles' Heel of Information Operations

    In the over-all scheme of information operations, there is no greater debility than the almost total lack of global geospatial data at the 1:50,000 level.

---

[8] One of the best actions General Phil Nuber, (then) Director of the Defense Mapping Agency, ever took was to attempt—without lasting success—to get the theater commanders to evaluate their contingency plans using the established C-1 to C-4 status reporting system. Most theaters would get a failing grade on most plans because they are not being held accountable for planning the future supply of information and maps in the same way that they must plan for men, materiel, and munitions.

- This is the level necessary for tactical movement of troops under fire, for the coordination of combined-arms support, for the targeting of precision munitions, and for the simulation of three-dimensional nape-of-the-earth approaches for sensitive aviation missions.

- It is also the level at which automated all-source data fusion (the Holy Grail for all intelligence technocrats) and automated multi-source data visualization become "real".

The National Imagery and Mapping Agency (NIMA) acknowledges that it has less than 10% of the world at this level, and has no plans for acquiring commercial imagery in order to create a global geospatial database at this level.[9] As the Defense Mapping Agency (DMA) discovered during the Gulf War, NIMA is also incapable of creating 1:50,000 maps—even with full support from commercial imagery sources—in less than 60-90 days.[10]

The broad nature of the deficiency can be defined as follows:

- For Africa, where many of our unexpected contingencies occur, we do not have acceptable mapping data for thirteen countries including Ethiopia, South Africa, and Uganda.

- For Asia and the Pacific, an area many consider central to our economic future and also highly subject to regional disturbances, we do not have acceptable mapping data for twelve countries, including China, Indonesia, and Papua New Guinea, nor for the four major island groups including the contested Spratly Islands.

---

[9] Based on official NIMA briefings at the unclassified level.

[10] As was widely discussed in official circles at the time, General Nuber had to make a personal appeal to General Schwarzkopf for realignment of national imagery assets to collect precision points with which to make maps. At the same time, the U.S. Air Force gave up on national imagery as its main source of wide-area surveillance and targeting imagery, and began buying vast quantities of commercial imagery directly—without DMA assistance or coordination.

- For Europe and the Mediterranean, Greece and Turkey remain completely uncovered, despite their importance to NATO, their traditional rivalry, and the role of Turkey in relation to the former Soviet Republics, Iraq, and Iran.

- For the Western Hemisphere, our own "back yard", we lack acceptable mapping data for thirteen countries, including Argentina, Colombia, Mexico, and Paraguay.

This deficiency will continue to exist for the next decade or two—and beyond—unless there is a deliberate decision made at the Presidential level, with full support from the Joint Chiefs of Staff, to resolve this deficiency immediately. The cost for resolving it has been estimated by knowledgeable senior leaders of NIMA at between $250 million and $500 million a year in commercial imagery procurement for the next five to six years.[11] This cost would cover, among many other important priorities, complete 1:50,000 coverage of China, the Amazon, and Africa. In combination with the planned shuttle mission in 2002 to collect precision points (Digital Terrain Elevation Data) for the entire Earth, this will allow the United States to have a phenomenal intelligence and Information Operations advantage, as the only

---

[11] Mr. Doug Smith, Deputy Director of NIMA, stated in 1996, at the fifth international symposium on "Global Security & Global Competitiveness: Open Source Solutions", that an estimate of $250 million a year was on the mark. In 1997 he revised this estimate upward toward $500 million a year (the increase reflects the greater cost of now available 1-meter commercial imagery). Despite his best efforts, however, neither DoD leadership nor the Executive Office of the President are willing to address this critical deficiency—and NIMA as a body has gone so far as to stonewall the *EARTHMAP Report* of October 1995 in which Undersecretary of State Wirth, among other leaders of the civilian elements of government, called for rapidly acquiring global geospatial data at this level of accuracy and detail. The obstacles appear to be two-fold: a real ignorance at the theater level about the utility of existing SPOT IMAGE capabilities, and a real reluctance at the Office of the Secretary of Defense level to buy commercial imagery from a French source—preferring instead to wait for the constantly post-poned offering of U.S. commercial imagery at the one meter level of resolution (the author believes this will not be available to the degree SPOT IMAGE data is, until about 2010). At the same time, everyone except EAGLE VISION aficionados continues to ignore the fact that one meter imagery comes with enormous—enormous—bandwidth, storage, time of transmission, and cost burdens which we cannot afford in the foreseeable future. One meter is a "designer" image option, not an industrial image option.

country in the world with a complete accurate map of every significant portion of the Earth at the 1:50,000 level.

It merits constant reiteration that, in the absence of geospatial data at the 1:50,000 level, policy options are severely constrained. Precision munitions cannot be used until the imagery and mapping data is collected and processed; Special Operations units and drug interdiction teams are at a major disadvantage; conventional military and law enforcement operations cannot be properly planned and executed; humanitarian assistance and other coalition operations are handicapped—the list goes on and on.

There is no one today, at any level of the military and certainly not within the White House or any other Cabinet department, who is willing and able to make this case before the Secretary of Defense and the President of the United States—hence we continue to plan for the future with our "eyes wide shut".[12]

CONCLUSION: *New Doctrine for a New Era*

Information Peacekeeping is in effect both a strategy for government operations and a national security strategy with global reach; consequently it has profound implications for how we train, equip, and organize our government and our military.

In the final analysis, we must come to grips with the fact that our government today is an Industrial-Era government, woefully inadequate in all respects as to the management of internal information and the acquisition and exploitation of external information. This in turn renders us wastefully ineffective in the planning and execution of global influence operations, both those that use information and those that use violence or other means.

---

[12] "Eyes Wide Shut" was the editorially assigned title for an article about this matter in *WIRED Magazine* (August 1997). The author's complete views on this grave deficiency were articulated in an invited presentation to the Third Congress of the North American Remote Sensing Industries Association "Exploring the Four Pillars: Government, Community, Market, and the World", Washington, D.C., 22 May 1997. See www.oss.net/Papers/speeches/NARSIA22.html for an outline of the speech.

If we continue to muddle through, then low-tech brutes will continue to slip through our crude defenses, low-tech seers will continue to be invisible to our warning networks, and high-tech seers will spend the next twenty years freely practicing information terrorism and vandalism, or plundering our electronic intellectual property and digital storehouses of wealth.

This is what government information-driven operations might look like if we were to conceptualize a "Third Wave" government focused on leveraging information to protect national security and enhance national competitiveness:

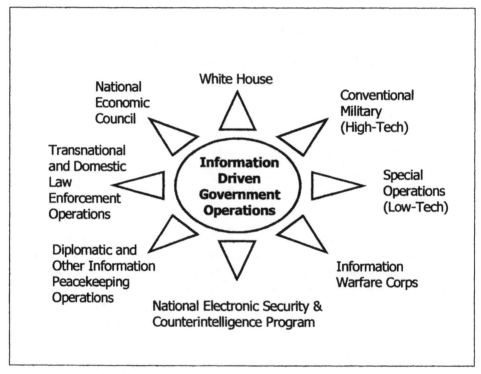

Figure 36: New Government Information Operations Concept

Part III:
Creating a Smart Nation

These people, these politicians, these statesmen, these directive people who are in authority over us, know scarcely anything about the business they have in hand. Nobody knows very much, but the important thing to realize is that they do not even know what is to be known. ... They are so unaccustomed to competent thought, so ignorant that there is knowledge and what knowledge there is, that they do not understand that it matters.

Maynard Keynes[1]

Part III contains five chapters and covers the near-term future, defined for this book as the period 2000-2010. The political science literature is quite clear on the fact that it takes a minimum of six years for an organization to complete substantive change, assuming that the organization at all levels desires to undergo such change. It has been my experience, and it is now my conclusion, that when one is dealing with both a bureaucracy and secrecy, each aspect adds an additional six years for a total of eighteen years. This being the U.S., where we have a plentitude of money, love all things technical, and like to do things the hard way, I would add an additional six years for a total of twenty-four. Rather nicely, this tallies perfectly with Senator Daniel Patrick Moynihan's observation in his recent book, *Miles to Go*, that it took him a quarter century to implement substantive changes in U.S. social policy.[2] As the open source revolution began in 1992, one cannot expect deep change in U.S. intelligence to take effect until roughly 2010-2016.

---

[1] Maynard Keynes, as cited by H. G. Wells, *World Brain* (Adamantine UK, 1994), page 81.
[2] Daniel Patrick Moynihan, *Miles to Go: A Personal History of Social Policy* (Harvard, 1996).

Chapter 11, "Strategy, Policy, Intelligence & Information" lays out the larger context within which we might create a "Smart Nation". Some new thoughts, on the changing nature of command and control and the changing relationship between politicians and the people (or business leaders and their clients) are presented. It is a summary or "capstone" chapter between the first two parts and the concluding third part of the book.

Chapter 12, "National Intelligence: Dollars and Sense" begins with a historical overview of intelligence reform endeavors, and a side-by-side comparison of the most recent reform efforts, and then goes on to provide the only publicly-available explicit recommendations for *reducing* the U.S Intelligence Community budget by $11.6 billion a year, while earmarking $1.6 billion a year for restoration against new priorities. *I believe that ultimately the U.S. Intelligence Community budget should be preserved at its current level of funding, gradually restored, but only after draconian changes in how we do business—changes that will only come about if we demonstrate "tough love" over a sustained period, beginning now and lasting at least a decade.*

Chapter 13, "Presidential Intelligence" is the centerpiece of the book in that it sets forth, in an executive format suitable for a President or CEO, fourteen specific changes that must occur in America if we are to become a "Smart Nation". Our future intellectual competence requires that we create a truly *national* intelligence community, one running from "school house to White House". The President of the United States is the *only* person with the programmatic and political authority sufficient to lead this reform endeavor.

Chapter 14, "The National Security Act of 2001" begins with a review of the Senate and House versions of the National Security Act of 1992 that was not brought forward for a vote, and then presents, in language suitable for easy adoption and rapid submission to Congress, a proposed bill for the implementation of the broad national intelligence reforms recommended by the author.

Chapter 15, "Reinventing National Intelligence: The Vision & The Strategy", provides a concluding overview of the "big ideas" that have been brought forth in the book, and relates these to the needs of the business community, academia, the media, and the most important element of all, the "intelligence minuteman": each citizen.

192

Strategy, Policy, Intelligence & Information

Introduction

This chapter outlines both the requirement for, and a recommended approach to, the creation of a National Information Strategy. Despite the fact that we have leaders in both the Administration and the Legislature who understand the critical importance of information as the foundation for both national security and national competitiveness at the dawn of the 21st Century, our leadership has failed to articulate a strategy and a policy that integrates national intelligence (spies, satellites), government information, and private sector information objectives and resources.

In the Age of Information, the absence of a National Information Strategy is tantamount to abdication and surrender--the equivalent of having failed to field an Army in World War II, or having failed to establish a nuclear deterrent in the Cold War.

This chapter is both an orientation for citizens and bureaucrats, and a call to arms for policy makers and legislators. It is a fundamental premise of this book that in the Age of Information, the most important role of government—at the Federal, State, or Local level—will be the nurturing of the "information commons"

National security will be largely a question of protecting information infrastructure, intellectual property, and the integrity of data; national competitiveness will be completely redefined—corporations and individuals are competitive in a global economy—it is the role of nations to be "attractive" to investors. How nation's manage their information commons will be a critical factor in determining "national attractiveness" for investment in the 21st Century.

This chapter addresses and defines in a summary fashion the challenge of change; the information commons and information continuum; the theory and practice of intelligence in the age of information; the ethical, ecological, and evolutionary implications of this approach; the need to reinvent and integrate national intelligence (spies and satellites) into a larger network of distributed intelligence largely accessible to citizens; and finally, the concrete elements that must comprise the National Information Strategy.

The Challenge of Change

As we enter the 21st Century, we are faced with several order of magnitude changes that defy resolution under our existing paradigms and organizational or policy structures.

The most obvious challenge to government as a whole is the changing nature of the threat. Since the rise of the nation-state (with citizenship, taxation, and standing armies); the most fundamental national security issue for governments has been the sanctity of borders and the safety of citizens and property abroad. Physical security maintained by threat of force was easy to understand and easy to implement. Today, we face a world in which transnational criminal gangs have more money, better computers, better information, and vastly more motivation to act and to act ruthlessly, than most states. Perhaps even more frightening, we face a world in which we are allowing technology and limited policy understanding to create very significant masses of dispossessed and alienated populations—including sizeable elements within our own borders; and at the same time we are ignoring our government's obligations to provide for home defense, for electronic civil defense, in the private sector.

There is another important change requiring government diligence, and that is the change in the role of information as the "blood" of every enterprise, every endeavor. Three aspects of this change merit enumeration: first, each citizen, whether they are conscious of this fact or not, is increasingly dependent on accurate and timely information in order to be fully functional; second, the "information explosion", like a major climatic change, is making it difficult for citizens accustomed to slower times and simpler tools to adjust to the requirements of life in the fast lane of the information superhighway; and finally, most citizens, stockholders, and business managers do not realize that we have national telecommunications, power, and financial networks that have

194

been designed without regard to security or survivability. It is not safe, today, to work and play in cyber-space, and we do not even have a body of law that requires communications and computing providers to assure their customers that their services and products are safe and reliable!

In brief, we now have an information environment in which every citizen needs to be a collector, producer, and consumer of "intelligence", or decision-support; and at the same time we have an extraordinarily complex and fragile information infrastructure which can be destroyed, disrupted, and corrupted by single individuals or small groups now capable of attacking our information infrastructure nodes through electronic means or simple physical destruction--and able to do so anonymously.

Defining The "Information Commons"

The "information commons"can be viewed—as the public commons for grazing sheep was once viewed in old England—as a shared environment where information is available for public exploitation and the common good. There are three major information "industries" that must contribute their fair share to the commons if the commons is to be robust and useful.

The first, relatively unknown to most citizens, is the U.S. intelligence community, traditionally associated with spies and satellites. In fact, between 40% and 80% of the raw data going into the final products of the intelligence community comes from "open sources", from public information legally available. Unfortunately, this $30 billion dollar a year community buries its open source acquisitions in the "cement overcoat" of classification, with the result that most of the useful public information about foreign affairs and commerce that is acquired by the intelligence community at taxpayer expense is not in fact made available to the citizen-taxpayer.

The second, well-known to most citizens as a massive bureaucracy that generates regulations and imposes taxation, is the government. The government is *not*, however, known for making information available to the public, and this is an extraordinary failure, for it turns out that the government is not only acquiring enormous stores of information at taxpayer expense, on every imaginable topic, but the government also serves as a magnet for vast quantities of information that it receives "free" from other governments, from think tanks, lobbyists, universities, and every other purveyor of a viewpoint desiring to influence the bureaucrats that comprise the government. In the age of information, governments must transition from the industrial model (vast bureaucracies attempting to deliver goods and services using a hierarchical structure to control resources) to the "Third Wave" model (small expert nodes nurturing distributed centers of information excellence). There are some significant capabilities within government intended to address this issue, including the National Technical Information Service (NTIS) in the Department of Commerce and the Defense Technical Information Center (DTIC) in the Department of Defense, but by and large government information is *out of control*. If the intelligence community is a $30 billion a year information industry, then the U.S. government can safely be assumed to be at least a $300 billion a year information industry.

The third "industry" capable of contributing to the information commons is the most important, the most diverse, and the most dynamic—it is the private sector. This has extraordinary implications for both governance and enterprise in the 21st Century, because of four characteristics of "knowledge battle" in the 21st Century that governments must recognize if they are to do their part: first, 90-95% of knowledge is open, not secret—governments that continue to believe in secrecy as the paramount element of executive action will fail; second, the center of gravity for national security and natoinal competitiveness is in the civil sector—governments that continue to rely on their military and their police and exclude from consideration the role of private sector capabilities, will fail; third, information today is *distributed*—governments that persist in relying upon "central intelligence" structures will fail; and finally, information is multi-lingual—governments that do not invest in analysts and observers able to move easily in multi-lingual environments will fail. If the intelligence community is a $30 billion a year industry, and the U.S. government is a $300 billion a year industry, the private sector can safely be assumed to be a $3 trillion a year industry—do we see a pattern here? The national information community, in short, is comprised of three concentric circles of investment that are not, at this time, contributing a single datum to the "information commons".

The Information Continuum

The "information continuum" for any nation is comprised of the nine major information consuming and information producing sectors of society:

schools, universities, libraries, businesses, private investigators and information brokers, media, government, defense, and intelligence.

It is very important to understand three basic aspects of the information continuum:

First, each organization within each sector pays for and controls both experts and data that could contribute to the information commons. Perhaps most importantly from the taxpayer and government point of view, these distributed centers of excellence are maintained at no cost to the government.

Second, it is important to understand that what any one organization publishes for sale or for free, whether in hard-copy or electronically, represents less than 20%—often less than 10%—of what they are actually holding in their databases or is known to their employees.

Third, and here we begin to set the stage for why a National Information Strategy is essential, it is vital that both citizens and bureaucrats realize that across this information continuum there are "iron curtains" between the sectors, "bamboo curtains" between organizations in each sector, and "plastic curtains" between individuals within organizations.

The role of government in the 21st Century is to provide incentives and to facilitate the sharing and exchange of information between the sectors, the organizations, and the individuals that comprise the national information continuum—and to work with other governments to create an international and transnational information commons.

Schools and universities have both expert faculty and willing student labor as well as significant electronic storage facilities. They also tend to have a multi-lingual population that can do very fine data filtering and data entry work. Two examples: the Monterey Institute of International Studies (MIIS), which uses graduate students fluent in Russian, Korean, Vietnamese, and Arabic to maintain the world's best database on the proliferation of nuclear, chemical, and biological weapons; and Mercyhurst College, which uses undergraduate students to produce newsletters on narcotics trafficking and other trends on interest to law enforcement agencies. Universities can also provide technical assistance and project assistance—one very fine example of this capability, which provides direct support to local government agencies as well

197

as small and medium-sized businesses, in the InfoMall developed by Syracuse University.

Libraries represent "distributed knowledge" in the best possible way, and not only provide direct access for citizens, but also skilled librarians who can serve as intermediaries in global discovery and discrimination. Examples of unique contributions in the library arena are represented by the University of Colorado, which created Uncover Reveal to distribute electronically the tables of contents of all journals it processes; the Special Libraries Association that brings together corporate and association librarians; and the Library-Oriented List Service developed by Mr. Charles Bailey, Jr.

Businesses not only hold significant amounts of data that they generate themselves, including customer preference data that could contribute to aggregate industry studies; but they also pay for great quantities of data, such as market surveys, which could after a short passage of time be eligible for sharing with smaller businesses and universities. One of the challenges facing nations that desire to be attractive to international investors is that of creating "information-rich" environments within which corporations can be globally competitive. One way of doing this is by developing information consortia and protocols for releasing into the information commons such data as might have already been exploited by the company that collected it or paid for it, but which could now have a residual value for the larger community.

Private investigators and information brokers are addressed separately because they play a unique role in a global economy driven by information, in which information is—as Alvin and Heidi Toffler have noted—a substitute for wealth, violence, labor, and capital. The capabilities of these *focused* information firms is extraordinary, and provide a high return on investment.

It is important to note that one of the most significant changes to occur in relation to government information in the past two decades is that the "information explosion" and the free market economy have led to the establishment of private sector capabilities which are superior to traditional government collection and processing mechanisms. Examples of "best in class" private sector "intelligence" capabilities include Oxford Analytica, with its global network of human experts monitoring political and economic events world-wide; FIND/SVP, able to acquire any document anywhere; Investigative Group International, one of the world's best corporate investigative firms;

Burwell Enterprises, publisher of the *Burwell Directory of Information Brokers*; Dow Jones Interactive, the premier "first stop" in commercial online searching; and the Institute of Scientific Information, publisher of the *Science Citation Index* and the *Social Science Citation Index*, both extraordinary means of identifying current and emerging knowledge and the experts behind the knowledge.

The utility of media information for policy, economic planning, military contingency planning, and law enforcement is almost always severely under-estimated. In fact, journalists, and especially investigative journalists, are extraordinarily talented, energetic, and well-connected individuals who produce very significant and accurate reports which can be integrated into finished reports on virtually any topic. It also merits comment that most journalists only publish roughly ten percent of what they know. James Baker, former Secretary of State among other important positions, notes in his memoirs that "In terms of fine-turning our own work, staying abreast of the press commentary was particularly important." Colin Powell, in his own book, notes that when he was Military Assistant to then Secretary of Defense Casper Weinberger, he "preferred the *Early Bird* with its compendium of newspaper stories", to the "cream of overnight intelligence" that was delivered to the Secretary by a Central Intelligence Agency (CIA) courier each morning.

In a direct and practical example, the U.S. Southern Command, working with the Los Alamos National Laboratory, was able—at very low cost—to exploit Latin American investigative reporting such that tactical interdiction missions could be planned and executed based primarily on media reporting. This is not to say that media sources are superior to classified intelligence, only that they cannot be discounted and are especially useful to those in the private sector and in much of government who are not authorized access to classified information.

Finally we have the government, including state and local governments and their information holdings, the Department of Defense, and the intelligence community. These will not be examined in detail. However, it bears mention that in the absence of a policy supportive of information archiving and public dissemination—and the means for implementing that policy—vast stores of information reaching the U.S. government, including information collected and processed by contractors to the U.S. government, are being "buried" each day, needlessly depriving the public of significant information resources. For those in government who are overwhelmed by their own internal "information explosion", and at a loss for how to handle their archiving, Freedom of Information Act (FOIA) requests, and the complex issues of copyright, there *is* a solution: NTIS.

Intelligence in the Age of Information

Now, having explored in general terms the elements of the information commons and the information continuum, we must focus on the specifics of intelligence in the age of information. Among the core concepts that government and private sector information managers must adopt and promulgate:

- Espionage, whether by governments or corporations, is less cost-effective that intelligent exploitation of open sources. Unfortunately, most intelligence communities are trained, equipped, and organized to do secrets, and they are not well-positioned to collect and integrate open sources—-public information—-into their analysis and production processes. This needs to be changed and is addressed at the conclusion of this chapter.

- The best target for the application of intelligence methods (requirements analysis, collection management, analytical fusion, forecasting, visualization of information) is *not* a competitor organization or country, but rather the customer or people and the larger environment (political, cultural, etcetera).

- Decision-support (intelligence) is the ultimate objective of all information processes. One must carefully distinguish between *data*, which is the raw text, signal, or image; *information*, which is collated data of generic interest; and *intelligence*, which is information that has been tailored to support a specific decision by a specific person about a specific question at a specific time and place. Most government information and so-called intelligence products are so generic as to be relatively useless in directing action. Only when information serves as the foundation for intelligence, can its cost be justified.

200

- Distributed information is more valuable and yet less expensive than centralized information. The art of information governance is the 21st Century will focus on harnessing distributed centers of excellence rather than on creating centralized repositories of information.

- "Just in time" information collection and intelligence production is far less expensive and far more useful to the consumer of intelligence than "just in case" collection and archiving.

- The value of information is a combination of its content, the context within which it is being used, and the timeliness with which it is obtained and exploited. This means that information that has been used by an organization declines in value when taken out of context and after time has passed. This in turn means that there is every reason for an organization to barter, share, or sell information (e.g. market research) once it's "prime" value point has passed....this is especially important to an organization as a means of increasing its acquisition of new information which—in its own context and time—has greater value than when it was lying fallow in the information commons.

- The new paradigm for information acquisition is the "diamond paradigm", in which the consumer, analyst, collector, and source are all able to communicate directly with one another. The old paradigm, the "linear paradigm" in which the consumer went to the analyst who went to the collector who went to the source, and back up the chain it went, is not only too slow, but it is not workable when you have a fast-moving topic with many nuances that are difficult to communicate. Today and in the future, the information manager's greatest moment is going to be when a consumer can be put in direct touch with exactly the right source who can answer the question directly, at low cost, by creating new knowledge tailored to the needs of the consumer, at that exact moment.

201

- The most important information resource is the employee. Every employee must be a collector, producer, *and consumer* of information and intelligence. This is called the "corporate hive" model, and is the foundation for a creating "smart nation". If every personnel description does not list as task number one: "collect and report information useful to the organization", and if organizations do not provide a vehicle (e.g. Lotus Notes or OracleX) and a protocol for sharing information among employees, then by definition the organization is "dumb".

- Published knowledge is old knowledge. The art of intelligence in the 21st Century will be less concerned with integrating old knowledge, and more concerned with using published knowledge as a path to exactly the right source or sources who can create new knowledge tailored to a new situation, in real-time.

- The threat (or the answer) changes depending on the level of analysis. The most fundamental flaw in both intelligence and information today is the failure to establish, for each question, the desired level of analysis. There are four levels of analysis: strategic, operational, tactical, and technical. These are in turn influenced by the three major contexts of inquiry: civil, military, and geographic.

Ethics, Ecology, & Evolution

Our "industrial age" concept of intelligence and information has relied heavily on a centralized, top-down "command and control" model in which the question virtually determined the answer, and the compartmentation of knowledge—its restriction to an elite few—has been a dominant feature of information operations. The true value of "intelligence" lies in its informative value, a value that increases with dissemination. The emphasis within our government, therefore, should be on optimizing our exploitation of open sources, increasing the exchange of information between the intelligence community, the rest of government, and the private sector; and the production of unclassified intelligence. This could be called the "open books" approach to national intelligence.

As we move forward in time within the 21st Century, we must ask ourselves some fundamental questions. How do we define national security? Who is the customer for national intelligence? What is our objective? There appears to be every reason to discard old concepts of national security and national intelligence, and to focus on developing integrated nation-wide information and intelligence networks which recognize that national security depends on a solid economy and a stable environment; that the center of gravity for progress in the future is the citizen, not the bureaucrat; and that our objective must be to enable informed governance and informed citizenship, not simply to monitor conventional and nuclear threats.

I am convinced that the "ethics" of national intelligence requires a dramatic reduction in government secrecy as well as corporate secrecy. After twenty years as an intelligence professional, I am certain that secrets are inherently pathological, undermining reasoned judgement and open discussion. Secrets are also abused, used to protect bureaucratic interests rather than genuine equities. Consider the following statement by Mr. Rodney B. McDaniel, then Executive Secretary of the National Security Council:

Everybody who's a real practitioner, and I'm sure you're not all naive in this regard, realizes that there are two uses to which security classification is put: the legitimate desire to protect secrets, and protection of bureaucratic turf. As a practitioner of the real world, it's about 90 bureaucratic turf; 10 legitimate protection of secrets as far as I'm concerned.

A wise man once said "A nation's best defense is an educated citizenry." I firmly believe that in the age of information, national intelligence—unclassified national intelligence—must be embedded in every decision, every process, every organization. The "ethics" of openness need to apply to the private sector as well as to the government. Universities should *not* be allowed to hold copyrights or patents if they are not able or willing to disseminate knowledge or commercialize technology. Corporations should *not* be allowed to monopolize patents solely to protect archaic production processes.

The environment in which we live, in which we hope to prosper and secure the common defense, is our most important intelligence target, and our most neglected intelligence target. Our traditional intelligence community, and our more conventional government information community, both appear reluctant to take on the hard issues of honestly evaluating the larger context within which we export munitions, keep the price of gasoline under two dollars a gallon, permit unfettered gang warfare and exploitation within our immigrant communities, and so on. At what point are we going to establish an architecture for integrating federal, state, and local data about the natural environment, and for producing useful strategic analyses about specific political, economic, and cultural issues? The following paraphrased observation by Ms. Ellen Seidman, Special Assistant to the President on the National Economic Council, is instructive:

> *CIA reports only focus on foreign economic conditions. They don't do domestic economic conditions and so I cannot get a strategic analysis that compares and contrasts strengths and weaknesses of the industries I am responsible for. On the other hand, Treasury, Commerce, and the Fed are terrible at the business of intelligence--they don't know how to produce intelligence.*

Taken in combination, what we do out of ignorance to our environment each day through our existing energy, trade, defense, housing, transportation, and education policies is far worse than a whole series of Chernobyls.

Finally, if the Nation is to evolve, if it is to "harness the distributed intelligence of the Nation", as Vice President Al Gore has taken to saying in his many speeches on the National Information Infrastructure, then we must come to grips with the fact that we are "losing our mind" as a Nation, and that education is the "boot camp" for national intelligence. We must catalyze our educational system, including corporate training and continuing education programs, and realize that openness is a powerful catalyst for bringing to bear the combined intelligence of every citizen and resident—instead of "National Intelligence" (spies and satellites) bearing the burden for informing policy, we should rely upon "national intelligence" (smart people), and use our distributed network of educated scholars, workers, information brokers, journalists, civil servants, and soldiers as the *foundation* for smart policy. Upon such a foundation, spies and satellites can add a decisive value—without such a foundation, spies and satellites are irrelevant.

Power to the People

There is one final observation to make, illustrated in Figure 37: the "power" of intelligence no longer stems from spies and secrecy, but rather from open access and open knowledge.

Whereas during the Cold War our leaders made the decisions based on secrets and a largely unilateral decision-making process, with little regard for other nations or non-state actors, today decision-making is from the people, a "bottom-up" process that is decidely multi-cultural, transnational, and based on open sources of information and intelligence.

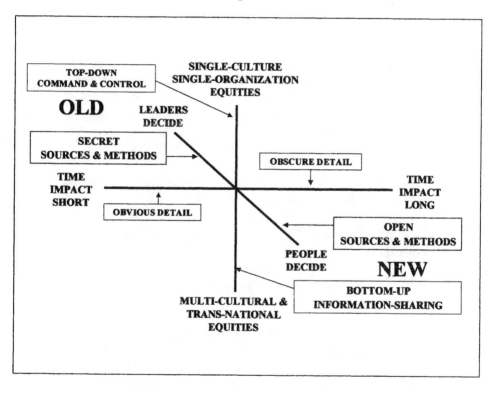

Figure 37: Intelligence Power from the People, to the People

Significantly, this new foundation for national and global intelligence power also takes a much longer-term view of its interests.

The Elements of a National Information Strategy

There are four elements that must be integrated into a National Information Strategy:

- **Connectivity.** The National Information Infrastructure is a good start. We need a Digital Marshal Plan for the rest of world, not only to nurture prosperity and reduce the chances of conflict, but also to facilitate our capture of greater amounts of multi-lingual, multi-cultural information.

- **Content.** This is where we are weakest, and it is this aspect of the strategy that is most important to creating a "Smart Nation." We must have a deliberate program to nurture centers of excellence, both within the United States and overseas, that serve as portals for both data acquisition (digitization) as well as information development and intelligence production.

- **Coordination.** We need to establish standards for generic workstation functionalities as well as their related Application Product Interfaces (API) that are completely open by legislative fiat, as well as standards for data definition and data integration. We also need to coordinate our investments in information technology research & development across industries, states, and federal agency boundaries.

- **C4I Security.** We have gotten a good start on protecting the Critical Infrastructure of the Nation, but since the private sector is the center of gravity for national security and national competitiveness in the age of information, it is essential that Congress legislate new standards of private sector "due diligence", and make this as enforceable aspect of corporate fiduciary responsibility.

Reinventing National Intelligence

Now we can finally turn to the reinvention of the national intelligence community as traditionally defined, for in reinventing this community, we can inspire the reinvention of government information and the establishment of a national information commons.

By and large, the elements of the national intelligence community--the Central Intelligence Agency (CIA), the National Security Agency (NSA), the National Reconnaissance Office (NRO), the Defense Intelligence Agency (DIA), the Federal Bureau of Investigation (FBI)—have all performed to expectations. Where we have gone awry was with our expectations. We focused this community on Soviet secrets, and we funded this community to collect and process Soviet secrets. Everything else was secondary, and by and large, everything else received—no surprise—virtually no attention.

Unfortunately, the national intelligence community, in developing approaches to "denied area" collection requirements, became obsessed with technology, and ultimately ended up substituting technology for thinking. At the low end, an exclusive reliance on the polygraph machine destroyed the art and craft of counter-intelligence. At the high end, the billions of dollars spent on satellites capable of collecting images and signals led to cost-cutting in other critical areas, with the most unfortunate loser being analysis. The community failed to invest in processing technologies, such that less than ten percent of the images and signals collected by this technology are actually processed, and the community went short on analytical expertise, hiring young people just out of college because they were cheap, rather than investing modestly (say, one percent of what is being spent yearly on satellites) in order to hire true experts who have proven themselves in the private sector over time.

What is to be done?

To this we now turn our attention in detail.

National Intelligence: Dollars & Sense

"The restructuring and reconceptualization of intelligence—and military intelligence as part of it—is a step toward the formulation of knowledge strategies needed either to fight or forestall the wars of tomorrow."

Alvin and Heidi Toffler[1]

For a decade now, the United States of America has undergone a series of reviews of its national and defense intelligence programs. Sadly, in the words of one very qualified commentator, what we have learned in this decade of review is that U.S. intelligence may be "too broke to be fixed". Whether or not one agrees, it is clear strong measures are needed if U.S. Intelligence is to rise to the challenges and opportunities of the future.

This chapter provides a proposed program for the 21st Century, a program that is unique—and more promising than previously proposed attempts to fix the community on the margins—because it encompasses the full range of capabilities and insights extant in the "virtual intelligence community" of the 21st Century—a community that fully integrates classified national intelligence, unclassified government information and research, and private sector open sources and services.

The U.S. Intelligence Community is an essential element of national power, but only if it is firmly grounded in the context of a larger *national* intelligence.

---

[1] Alvin and Heidi Toffler, *WAR AND ANTI-WAR: Survival at the Dawn of the 21st Century* (Little Brown, 1993), page 164.

Presentation of the Program

I present the program by first summarizing important past and current reviews of the U.S. Intelligence Community; then by discussing how $11.6 billion a year in savings can be achieved as a means of funding $1.6 billion in necessary offsetting increases while also reducing the deficit by $10 billion a year; and finally by discussing, in moderate detail, several strategic changes in organization and focus.

Historical reviews, spanning the period from 1949 to 1992, have generally addressed the poor relationships between the U.S. Intelligence Community and the Departments of State and Defense; the over-all lack of adequate management authority and capability within the U.S. Intelligence Community; and general short-falls in counterintelligence, overt collection, linguistic training, and various other functional areas.

The current reviews of significance include the National Performance Review (NPR), whose recommendations have still not been implemented by the U.S. Intelligence Community; the two most focused and comprehensive reviews—the Commission on Intelligence and the IC21 Study from the House Permanent Select Committee on Intelligence—and two complementary reviews: the 20th Century Fund Task Force and the Commission on Secrecy.

In general terms, the first three reviews agree that there is an urgent need to enhance U.S. Intelligence Community functional integration and program coherence; to reassess and improve responsiveness to a wider variety of customers for intelligence; to modernize and integrate information handling across all agencies and disciplines; and to significantly modify and improve personnel, security, training, and the exploitation of open sources and/or outsourcing alternatives offered by the private sector.

The 20th Century Fund Task Force review is noteworthy for its blunt assessment that the U.S. Intelligence Community is of declining usefulness to policymakers, and suffers from an imbalance between military and civilian efforts. The findings of the Commission on Secrecy are vital to any future program because they addresses the Achilles' heel of national intelligence, a culture of secrecy run amok, and costing at least $6 billion a year.

In the middle part of the presentation, bridging the gap between critical reviews and practical change, we offer an explicit list of savings goals intended to reduce the annual U.S. Intelligence Community budget from $30 billion a year to $20 billion a year, while also providing for $1.6 billion a year in offsetting increases for eight urgently needed new initiatives—three within and five outside the intelligence program.

A fundamental premise reflected in this proposed program is that significant change will not come about within the U.S. Intelligence Community in the absence of a radical reduction of its funding such that "business as usual" becomes impossible to sustain.

In combination—a radical reduction of funding for traditional systems that will *increase* their productivity by finally forcing new and better practices upon the entrenched bureaucracies—and a relatively modest but still substantial infusion of funds for non-official cover clandestine operations, electronic counterintelligence, open source exploitation, and a modest University of the Republic—I believe that a complete "make-over" is yet possible, and that the U.S. Intelligence Community *can* be constructively guided in achieving the new efficiencies and establishing the new capabilities necessary to meet the challenges and opportunities of the 21st Century.

The fact that this program can simultaneously contribute $10 billion a year to the reduction of the national deficit is both politically powerful as an incentive, and fiscally exciting as a means of enhancing the strategic power of the country as a whole. It should also serve as a wake-up call for the many professional bureaucrats pretending to be intelligence officers but continuing to ignore both public and Congressional expectations for substantive reform.

My proposed program for intelligence and counterintelligence in the 21st Century focuses on three major areas where reform can provide the Nation with a strategic intelligence advantage.

First, it is essential that the U.S. Intelligence Community restore its ability to access open sources and harness the "virtual intelligence community"—probably a $1 trillion a year endeavor—so that its secrets can be in proper context, and we can focus our spies and satellites on "the hard stuff". It is a fundamental precept of intelligence reform as we have defined it, that we

211

cannot revitalize our classified capabilities without first establishing our links and our role *in relation to* the larger world of unclassified government information and private sector knowledge. At the same time, it is critical that the U.S. Intelligence Community be redefined and extended so that it can provide appropriate intelligence and counterintelligence support to the Legislative Branch as well as the Executive Branch; to the Departments of government concerned with national competitiveness as well as national security; and to those elements in the private sector that comprise the foundation of our national power through private enterprise and the creation of intellectual property.

The extended concept of national intelligence in the 21st Century must fully integrate the data, information, knowledge, and wisdom available to the worlds of statecraft, scholarship, business, society in general, and the traditional but insular world of spies and satellites. For this reason, a national knowledge strategy, and a University of the Republic that brings together leaders of all our national knowledge communities, comprise the essential foundation for national security and national competitiveness in the 21st Century.

Mindful of the above, it is important to stress that the individual departments of government must be guided in establishing fully competent internal open source intelligence collection and processing capabilities suited to their needs. At the same time, it is imperative that the special capabilities represented by the Library of Congress, the Congressional Research Service (CRS), the National Technical Information Service (NTIS), and the Defense Technical Information Center (DTIC), as well as other centers of expertise in government, be firmly and quickly guided into a more productive network or consortium arrangement that allows both the government and the public to do effective data mining from the vast taxpayer-funded information stores which are generally not readily accessible today, even by our own government archivists.

Second, it is imperative that both the Director-General of National Intelligence (DGNI) and Director of *Classified* Intelligence (DCI)—one an old position with a dramatically expanded new role, the other an old position with a new title and more narrowly focused role—be given the program authority they require to be effective. Although the concept of a Director of National

Intelligence (DNI) has been surfaced in the past, it has always been brought forth in a debilitating context, one limited to *indirect* authority over inherently classified capabilities. This chapter presents a coherent approach to empowering the existing DCI through a combination of both *explicit* program authority and a more narrow focus, while creating a DGNI who is empowered through a combination of clearly defined programmatic authority over the DCI; a much-expanded National Intelligence Council (NIC) that is above and outside the U.S. Intelligence Community bureaucracy; and a Global Knowledge Foundation (GKF) that uses a $1 billion a year capitalization fund to leverage—in a non-intrusive and non-regulatory way—the $1 trillion a year "virtual intelligence community".

Four equal offsetting increases totaling just over $1 billion a year are proposed in relation to the GKF:

- to provide improved access to open sources for the U.S. Intelligence Community;

- to nurture and enhance distributed centers of excellence in the "virtual intelligence community";

- to fund the procurement of commercial imagery to meet the needs of both the military and civilian elements of the U.S. government; and

- to create a prototypical open source intelligence architecture for coalition operations centered around the Partners for Peace and the North Atlantic Treaty Organization (NATO). As a whole, the GKF gives the DGNI a catalyst for assuring adequate intelligence support to four major communities: public diplomacy and governance; global military and coalition peacekeepers; transnational law enforcement; and competitive enterprises of any nationality that pay U.S. taxes and employ U.S. citizens.

Third, and finally, we come to the U.S. Intelligence Community itself, a community of good people trapped in a bad system—a bad system which

213

represents a half-century of political, security, procurement, and disciplinary ("stovepipe") compromises that leave us with an unmanageable mess—or as James Schlesinger put it in 1971, just over a quarter-century ago, a conglomeration of "unproductively duplicative" collection systems and a general failure in forward planning to coordinate the allocation of resources. Little has changed, at root, since 1971.

Our proposed program, therefore, focuses on careful rationalization of the management of the community, adopting and extending the Congressional proposals for two Deputy Directors of Classified Intelligence (DDCI) and three Assistant Directors of Classified Intelligence (ADCI), to arrive at a single DCI, a single DDCI, and five ADCI—each of the latter responsible for integrating the critical functions of collection, production, infrastructure, research & development, and counterintelligence. The fragmentation of community management is addressed by consolidating authority and resources in three offices—the Office of Intelligence Management, Personnel, and Budget (OIMPB) and the Office of Intelligence Communications and Computing (OIC2), both under the ADCI for Infrastructure; and the Office of Intelligence Research & Development (OIR&D), under the ADCI for Research & Development.

The changes in community management, in turn, permit a streamlining of the Central Intelligence Agency (CIA) so that it may focus on its original core mission—strategic all-source analysis with a unique preeminence achieved through direct access to classified collection capabilities—the CIA is redirected toward focusing exclusively on all-source, and the core Directorate of Intelligence, augmented by the Community Open Source Program Office (COSPO), and half the National Collection Division (NCD) are reconstituted as the National Intelligence Agency (NIA), with additional augmentation in the form of a restored Office of Imagery Analysis and realigned Offices of Signals and Measurements & Signatures Analysis. A new Clandestine Service Agency (CSA), and a consolidated Technical Collection Agency (TCA), in combination with the National Imagery and Mapping Agency (NIMA) and (independently) the Federal Bureau of Investigation (FBI) constitute the four pillars of the revitalized and powerful *classified* intelligence and counterintelligence community of the 21st Century. The Foreign Broadcast Information Service (FBIS) is transferred in its entirety to the U.S. Information Agency (USIA), the latter reconstituted as an overt media-focused collection and dissemination organization.

Three offsetting increases are proposed within the U.S. Intelligence Community—$250 million a year for new costs associated with creating the CSA under complete non-official cover conditions; $150 million a year for the FBI to properly execute the responsibilities of its new Electronic Security and Counterintelligence Program; and $150 million a year for the FBI to take the lead in transferring intelligence technologies and methods, as well as modest funding for direct access to open sources, to the state and local law enforcement and economic authorities.

It merits emphasis that the FBI, with some assistance from the NIC (now outside the classified community) will be the most important element of the U.S. Intelligence Community in the 21ˢᵗ Century, because it will be responsible for the survivability of our national communications and computing architecture, the protection of our intellectual property, and the creation of a state and local intelligence community focused on economic development and law enforcement. It will also be the critical element of a global transnational law enforcement network which serves as the intelligence underpinning to the major war in the 21ˢᵗ Century, that between governments, and gangs.

We conclude this chapter by briefly discussing geoeconomic intelligence, military and international peacekeeping intelligence, law enforcement intelligence, and national counterintelligence as the core elements of national competitiveness. Taken together, these four aspects of national intelligence and counterintelligence comprise the recommended new directions for the U.S. Intelligence Community, and constitute a 180° alteration of course—away from the past, and toward the future—a future in which the "virtual intelligence community" integrates the knowledge of statecraft, scholarship, business, and society in general.

Historical Intelligence Reviews

The table that follows is based on a historical review by the Congressional Research Service, setting the stage without further comment.

YEAR	REVIEW
1949	**First Hoover Commission** • Adversarial relationships between CIA, State, and the military
1955	**Second Hoover Commission** • Counterintelligence & linguistic training deficiencies • CIA to replace State in procurement of foreign publications
1961	**Taylor Commission** • Failure in communication, coordination and overall planning • No single authority short of the President capable of coordinating the actions of CIA, State, Defense, and USIA
1971	**Schlesinger Report** • "rise in…size and cost [with the] apparent inability to achieve a commensurate improvement in the scope and overall quality…" • "unproductively duplicative" collection systems and a failure in forward planning to coordinate the allocation of resources
1976	**Church Committee** • DCI should have program authority and monies for national intelligence should be appropriated to the DCI rather than agencies • Recommended second DDCI for Community Management • State must improve overt collection of economic and political data • Raised issue of separating clandestine/covert ops from analysis
1992	**Boren-McCurdy** • National Security Act of 1992 (not adopted, Defense opposed) • DNI, two DDNIs, consolidate DIA and INR analysts with CIA

Figure 38: Historical Intelligence Reform Reviews[2]

The next major review of the U.S. Intelligence Community is noteworthy for two reasons: it was an integrated element of the National

---

[2] Prepared by Richard A. Best, Jr. and Herbert Andrew Boerstling of the Congressional Research Service, dated 28 February 1996, and included as the final appendix to the *IC21: Intelligence Community in the 21st Century* report of the House Permanent Select Committee on Intelligence, 4 March 1996. Amy B. Zegart's recent book, *Flawed By Design: The Evolution of the CIA, JCS, and NSC* (Stanford, 1999), is a very worthy look at how the military opposed the creation of the CIA and therefore orchestrated a genesis that left the Agency handicapped from the very beginning—flawed by design.

Performance Review (NPR)[3], an endeavor with the full weight of the President and the Vice President; and it has been successfully ignored without penalty by the entire U.S. Intelligence Community:

01	**Enhance Intelligence Community Integration** • The end of the Cold War and the constrained fiscal environment in the U.S. create an imperative for the 13 components of the Intelligence Community to act more effectively and more efficiently as a team.
02	**Enhance Community Responsiveness to Customers** • A 40-year emphasis on the Soviet Union allowed the Intelligence Community to develop a repertoire, which was not dependent on a close relationship with its customers. That is no longer the case today, and NPR makes recommendations for improvements in this area.
03	**Reassess Information Collection to Meet New Challenges** • The analytical issues the Intelligence Community faces are far more diverse and complex today, requiring new focus and new techniques to meet the intelligence needs of the policymakers.
04	**Integrate IC Information Management Systems** • The Intelligence Community lacks the connectivity and interoperability in its information systems to do its job efficiently and effectively.
05	**Develop Integrated Personnel and Training Systems** • This recommendation focuses on organization development and training issues within the Intelligence Community
06	**Merge the President's Intelligence Oversight Board with the President's Foreign Intelligence Advisory Board** • The roles of these two oversight bodies are sufficiently similar that small savings and some efficiencies can be achieved by combining them.
07	**Improve Support to Ground Troops During Combat Operations** • Numerous studies of intelligence support during the Gulf War focused on agency or service-specific support issues. This issue outlines a reinvention lab effort which proposes an integrated approach to studying support to ground forces during combat operations.

Figure 39: NPR Recommendations on Intelligence

---

[3] Al Gore, *Creating a Government that Works Better and Costs Less: The Report of the National Performance Review* (Plume, 1993), pages 249-251.

In dramatic contrast to the encompassing and strategically important ideas reflected in the NPR, below is the current "reinvention" program for the U.S. Intelligence Community, almost all of which are "intentions" pertaining to "housekeeping" rather than "accomplishments" pertaining to "core missions". We assign space in this chapter to list these, not because of their merit, but because they comprise, in any commander's mind, proof positive of the deliberate subversion of presidential intent by the U.S. Intelligence Community.

01	Consolidating Imagery Intelligence
02	Integrating Military and Intelligence Satellite Acquisition
03	Reforming Intelligence Community Human Resource Management
04	Consolidating Intelligence Collection Activities
05	Consolidating Office Space
06	Consolidating Warehousing
07	Privatizing Supply and Equipment Acquisition
08	Franchising Microelectronics Production
09	Reinventing Travel
10	Reinventing Community Courier Service
11	Reinventing Training and Education
12	Reinventing Excess Equipment Reutilization
13	Reinventing Security
14	Reinventing Foreign Language Activities

Figure 40: Going Through the Motions on Reinventing Intelligence

Warehousing? Supply? Travel? No real professional can help but be appalled by this list, or by the specious verbosity which accompanies each of these in the glossy publication which purports to document the "progress" of the community in Phase II of the NPR—words like "work with", "assess", "identify", and "encourage". There is no vision, no commitment, and no accountability in this endeavor, and in most military commands, such results would be grounds for the immediate relief of those responsible.[4]

---

[4] These observations are based on examination of *National Performance Review, Phase II Initiatives: An Intelligence Community Report* (September 1995). The U.S. Intelligence Community approach to NPR appears to reflect a deliberate assumption by senior Department of Defense bureaucrats (NRO, NSA, NIMA) that they will continue to own national intelligence, at its present level of funding, and need not be concerned

It is a sad fact that the Director of Central Intelligence (DCI), even one with the President's personal support and some staying power, simply does not have the authority over senior management appointments, program funds, and day-to-day relations with the men and women of the U.S. Intelligence Community, to effectively implement a coherent program for change. Even a DCI with vision and grit is helpless with the present situation because it is a "given" within the U.S. Intelligence Community that neither Congress nor the President can appear to be "soft" on intelligence or defense, and therefore the present level of funding will continue. Unfortunately, the present level of funding is part of the problem—it is an obstacle to change. It is imperative, as Congress considers the results of the three most recent and professional reviews, summarized below, that it come to grips with the *reality* of national intelligence management.

The U.S. Intelligence Community is not going to change unless two things happen:

- its budget is incontrovertibly cut by one third; and

- a single individual has incontestable authority over the remaining monies across all member agencies.

Figure 41: The *Reality* of National Intelligence Management

Current Intelligence Reviews

We have been fortunate in having three excellent public reviews and one really good private review commissioned and completed in the past four years, and each has made substantive recommendations, all of which are thoughtful, and most of which merit immediate implementation. However, if Congress is not mindful of the *reality* above, there will be no change, and the

---

by any intelligence reform proposals. There is a disturbing lack of urgency or crisp thinking at the highest levels, and a real blindness to the depth of change outside the cement bunker.

U.S. Intelligence Community will continue to muddle through, wasting $30 billion a year of the taxpayers funds, while simultaneously fostering the very dangerous illusion that we have a national intelligence capability suited to the challenges and opportunities of the 21st Century.

Topical Area	Commis. on Intelligence	IC21 Study (HPSCI)
Role of Intelligence	Support diplomacy, military operations, defense planning.	Too *ad hoc* today, lacks coherenc can be self-serving.
Policy Guidance/ Requirements Process	State and Defense dominate guidance, consumers group needed	Declining intelligence base and lo focus on future; system-driven
Response to Global Crime, Support to Law Enforcement	Need more coordination of operations overseas, more sharing of information	Need more information sharing a training, global operation coordination.
Organizational Arrangements/ Communications	DDCI/CIA and DDCI/CM, increases DCI authority	Authorized three ADCIs for maj functions of collection, productio infrastructure.
Central Intelligence Agency	Needs better management at all levels	Must move Centers to DCI leve improve quality of personnel
Budget Structure and Process	Substantial realignment needed to aggregate functions, DCI does not have staff, tools, or procedures for performing budget management	Stove-pipes dominate resource rather than analysts or end-use CMS should have withholdi authority and evaluation ability
Intelligence Analysis	Must improve focus on consumers, and on open sources	CIA's core function; assum departmental capabilities okay
"Right-Size" and Rebuild	Consolidate senior executive service, liberal force reduction	Rationalize NFIP, JMIP, a TIARA, guide by function
Military Intelligence and Support to DoD	DoD needs a single *staff* focal point for managing intel support	D/DIA to be Director Milita Intelligence
Technical Collection	Endorses NIMA, need more coordination of intel and DoD	Technical Collection Agency a Technical Development Office
Clandestine Service	Merge DoD HUMINT into CIA HUMINT	Separate entity reporting directly DCI, CIA feeds it
International Cooperation	Burden sharing in space operations	Not addressed, but notes need to b more open source imagery
Cost of Intelligence	Cost reductions are possible but need better process to find; states that 96% of USIP is in DoD	States that DoD controls 86% of t resources; DCI lacks authority
Accountability and Oversight	Extend tenure of members of the oversight committees.	Ease or eliminate tenure limits.

Figure 42: Summary of Findings of Two Key Reviews

The above table provides comparative extracts in the major areas covered by both the bi-partisan Commission on Intelligence and the IC21 Study conducted by the House Permanent Select Committee on Intelligence. In general terms, these two key reviews found that the role of the U.S. Intelligence Community is in question; that the requirements process is in disarray; that collection and production management require significant improvement; that clandestine operations need a new structure; and that the single greatest obstacle to coherent management is the fact that between 86% and 96% of the U.S. Intelligence Program (USIP) is under the direct control of the Secretary of Defense and unresponsive to leadership from the DCI.

PROBLEMS

- **Declining Usefulness to Policymakers**
  - Atrophying Analytic Capabilities
  - Inadequate Foreign Policy Interaction
  - Costly Clandestine Service
  - Mediocre Economic Intelligence
- **Imbalance Between Military and Civilian Efforts**

RECOMMENDATIONS

- **Better Staffed Open Diplomatic Presence**
- **Enhanced Policy & Analytic Capabilities**
  - Double size of analysis population
  - Move NIC closer to policy
  - FFRDC for academics & private sector analysts
  - Rotate personnel
  - Narrow clandestine focus
  - Priority for economic intelligence
- **Greater Intelligence Sharing & Cooperation**

Figure 43: Summary of 20ᵗʰ Century Fund Findings[5]

---

[5] While the author has read the 20ᵗʰ Century report with appreciation, this figure is adapted from the summary of the report included in the OSS '96 presentation by Mr. Arnold E. Donahue, on "Evolving Trends in U.S. Intelligence".

Of the various private sector endeavors, one stands out and is summarized in Figure 43, that of the 20th Century Fund Task Force. Although the report suffers from the typical public perception that the clandestine service is expensive (it actually costs a fraction of the technical collection capabilities), their observations are among the best coming from the private sector. *The 20th Century Fund has hit on the most important threat to the U.S. Intelligence Community—not that of a budget cut, but rather—that of becoming obsolete and irrelevant in the face of "good enough" alternatives from the world of open sources.* [6]

Finally, we come to the findings of the Commission on Secrecy, which are included here because they are fundamental to the reinvention and reconstitution of the U.S. Intelligence Community.

---

1. Greater openness increases public understanding
2. Secrecy is a form of regulation—must define limits
3. Excessive secrecy degrades policy by encouraging leaks
4. Need single executive office to coordinate policy
5. Need much greater awareness of electronic threats
6. Secrecy founded on concern about ethnic ties[7]
7. Roughly $6 billion a year is spent on protecting secrets

Figure 44: Observations from the Commission on Secrecy

The Commission on Secrecy drives home the fact that a great deal of the existing secrecy—and its attendant costs—are both unnecessary, and harmful to the national interest.

True secrets—and the risky or expensive means to collect them—could be reduced with a positive net contribution to the political, the military, and the economic health of the Nation.

---

[6] (20th Century Fund Press, 1996), with background papers by Allan E. Goodman, Gregory F. Treverton, and Philip Zelikow.

[7] This one is in the historical appendix of the report rather than the full report.

There are three aspects of the Commission on Intelligence and the IC21 reviews which merit emphasis, especially in relation to the findings of the Commission on Secrecy:

- Neither review examined the fundamental disconnect between classified information, government information that is unclassified, and private sector information, other than to say, in both cases, that we should import more unclassified information ("open sources") into the classified system.

  - *On the one hand, we practice such excessive secrecy as to actually handicap our policymakers and acquisition managers.*

  - *On the other hand, we have no architecture for connecting the classified intelligence analysts to the wealth of open sources— including commercial imagery—available from the private sector, nor even, for that matter, to the vast quantities of unclassified information available to the rest of the government.*

  - *In other words, we still have not come to grips with the totality of our intelligence management challenge and hence are not ready to function effectively—as a government—in the information age.*

- Neither review addressed counterintelligence as a major problem area.

- Neither review addressed electronic vulnerabilities or the need for a major investment in electronic security and counterintelligence, both within the government as whole (e.g. Treasury, Federal Reserve Board), and within the private sector nodes that are critical to national security and national competitiveness: financial, power, communications, and transportation.

The report of the Commission on Secrecy is especially noteworthy for two reasons:

- It suggests that the U.S. Intelligence Community—as well as its operational counterparts who thrive on using secrecy to avoid public scrutiny—will never be able to fully integrate themselves into the larger world of unclassified government

223

information and private sector open source information until there is a dramatic reduction in secrecy.

- It explicitly notes that secrecy is costing the tax-payer at least $6 billion a year in fiscal costs, with an incalculable additional multi-billion dollar a year amount associated with the opportunity costs of keeping critical information from those who do have a need to know.

A complete reading of all five reports[8] is recommended for all who care deeply about the future of the U.S. Intelligence Community, but in the absence of a major debate that engages the public, it is virtually certain that the early years of the 21st Century will see a continuation of occasional clandestine scandals, technical launch failures as well as continued complaints from commanders unable to get wide area surveillance, and mediocre analysis that fails to warn, illuminate, or empower the policymaker.[9]

Reducing and Realigning the Budget

In 1993 (then) DCI James Woolsey told Dr. Loch Johnson that the U.S. Intelligence Community budget could safely be reduced to $20 billion a year over time.[10] It is time that both Congress and the Administration get down to

---

[8] In addition to the NPR and 20th Century Fund reports cited earlier, the three reports are *Preparing for the 21st Century: An Appraisal of U.S. Intelligence* (Report of the Commission on the Roles and Capabilities of the United States Intelligence Community), 1 March 1996; *IC21: Intelligence Community in the 21st Century* (Staff Study, Permanent Select Committee on Intelligence, House of Representatives), 4 March 1996; and *SECRECY* (Report of the Commission on Protecting and Reducing Government Secrecy), 3 March 1997.

[9] There are many excellent books and papers not cited in this chapter, but relevant to the discussion of the future of the U.S. Intelligence Community. Most of them are listed in Mark M. Lowenthal, *The U.S. Intelligence Community: An Annotated Bibliography* (Garland, 1994). Two recent books not listed, which bear on reform of the clandestine service, are Evan Thomas, *The Very Best Men* (Simon & Schuster, 1995), and David Corn, *BLOND GHOST: Ted Shackley and the CIA's Crusades* (Simon & Schuster, 1994). See also my annotated bibliography in this book.

[10] This was announced publicly by Dr. Loch Johnson during his keynote speech to OSS '94, and is based on his interview with DCI Woolsey of 29 September 1993. Dr.

the business of giving this country an intelligence community that can be counted on for the future. It is a *blessing* that we can and must save $10 billion a year in the process![11]

"We will never get the funds for procuring commercial source imagery, nor will we be able to alter the information processing or dissemination architecture, for so long as the national imagery collectors and the map producers' believe that the technical collection budget will remain essentially stable—at its current level of funding."[12]

Figure 45: Impact of Excessive Funding on Mindset Inertia

It is important to emphasize—again and again—that serious change will not take place within the U.S. Intelligence Community if the present funding level is maintained. It is clear from extensive discussions at all levels and across all agencies that there is such a pervasive culture of both secrecy and "we know best", that only a major shock wave will succeed in freeing the U.S. Intelligence Community as a corporate body from its present state of mindset inertia.

First, though, let us be clear about what budgets we are talking about. In this chapter the term U.S. Intelligence Program (USIP) is used to refer to the totality of the U.S. Intelligence Community budget, to include the National Foreign Intelligence Program (NFIP), the Joint Military Intelligence Program

---

Johnson, unique for having served on the professional staffs of both the Church Committee and the Commission on Intelligence, is the dean of intelligence reform professionals. The Woolsey interview was prior to the Commission on Intelligence.

[11] The Quadrennial Review that DoD underwent in the 1990's could not have been undertaken in the absence of a certain decline in the defense budget. National bureaucracies do *not* improve with time, size, or dollars—they improve when dramatic change is required of them by external forces that they cannot ignore.

[12] Personal conversation with a very senior professional with current access to both of these communities, and a sound understanding of their culture and their budget.

(JMIP), and the Tactical Intelligence and Related Activities (TIARA) Program.[13]

INTELLIGENCE PROGRAM	Dollars
U.S. Intelligence Program (Bare Bones)	**29.3B**
National Foreign Intelligence Program	**16.4B**
National Reconnaissance Program	6.4B
Community Cryptologic Program	3.4B
Central Intelligence Agency	3.2B
General Defense Intelligence Program	2.0B
Other Departmental Activities	1.4B
Joint Military Intelligence Program	**3.6B**
Defense Advanced Reconnaissance	1.7B
Defense Mapping Agency	.8B
Other DoD	.6B
Tactical Intelligence and Related Activities	**9.3B**
Air Force Tactical Intelligence	4.0B
Army Tactical Intelligence	2.8B
Navy Tactical Intelligence	1.8B
Other DoD Tactical Intelligence	0.7B

Figure 46: General Summary of U.S. Intelligence Program

The information above does not include the full cost of the Federal Bureau of Investigation (FBI), the Department of State with its Bureau of Intelligence and Research (INR) and its many overt collectors world-wide, the U.S. Information Agency (USIA)[14], the Drug Enforcement Administration (DEA), the intelligence elements of the Departments of Treasury or Transportation, or the national laboratories of the Department of Energy. It also does not include the cost of at least 50,000 military personnel fulfilling intelligence functions, many of them in signals intelligence. Overall, then, the above figure does not reflect roughly (very roughly) $5 billion a year in

---

[13] This listing is based on information published by the Commission on Intelligence and subsequently annotated by the Federation of American Scientists.

[14] USIA is now completely integrated into the Department of State. I believe this was a grave error because the unique cultural and personal characteristics required for the more informal media and "man on the street" mission will not survive the formalistic protocol-oriented mentality within the Department of State.

additional military intelligence personnel costs, and another $15 billion or more in civilian counterintelligence, overt non-intelligence collection, and energy intelligence costs. Hence, we can state with assurance that the "real" U.S. intelligence budget, not counting overt information collection and processing, is probably closer to $50 billion a year than $30 billion a year, but for the purposes of this chapter, set the figure at $30 billion a year.

Here are the circumstances that not only demand change, but also make change possible:[15]

- Absence of a dominant foreign adversary
- Emergence of many small, diverse, and less predictable threats
- Increasing reliance on coalition peacekeeping and joint warfare
- Greater availability, accessibility, and reliability of open sources of information including commercial imagery
- Exploding commercial communications and a rapidly maturing Internet
- Increasing government reliance on commercial off-the-shelf technologies
- Increasing technological capabilities of rapid reaction small satellites
- Fiscal and political pressures to downsize and streamline government
- Emphasis on more responsive and performance-oriented government

---

Figure 47: External Changes Impacting on Internal Changes

The nature of the defense and the intelligence communities today, created over the half century since the end of World War II and focused almost exclusively on the former Soviet Union and its strategic nuclear and conventional force, merits emphasis. Neither defense nor intelligence are trained, equipped, and organized to confront—nor inclined to change quickly in order to confront three new classes of threat we face today:

1) **Transnational criminal organizations** far more ruthless and pervasive than the Colombian drug dealers—now including the

---
[15] *Supra* note 6.

227

Russian, Chinese, Japanese, Vietnamese, and Mexican warlord criminals, and soon to include Muslim criminal organizations.

2) **Global ethnic and religious groups** with substantial masses of adherents in all walks of life, with legitimate and often extremely complex concerns and requirements.

3) **Economic warriors**, including those engaged in state-sponsored economic espionage, corporate-sponsored industrial espionage, and individual-sponsored information terrorism, information crime, and information vandalism.

In addition to requiring new kinds of capabilities that are effective at collecting and understanding criminal intelligence, cultural intelligence, and economic counterintelligence, we have to come to grips with the fact that these 21st Century threats require a U.S. Intelligence Community that is able to adjust very rapidly to emerging threats and opportunities that cannot be anticipated and for which specific capabilities cannot be designed and implemented in advance of the threat.

What does this really mean? It means that in the 21st Century we need a *dynamic* U.S. Intelligence Community which can quickly down-size or place into dormancy those capabilities that are not needed for extended periods of time, and equally quickly surge its capabilities to meet new requirements on a "come as you are" basis.[16] We can start now. There are, however, two internal obstacles to fundamental intelligence reform: the cultural resistance to change by all those who assume that their present funding levels will continue and they may persist in conducting "business as usual", and the total lack of authority over U.S. Intelligence Program funds by the DCI. There is one other obstacle, perhaps more serious, and that is the mistaken belief within Congress that we

---

[16] Brigadier Richard E. Simkin, *RACE TO THE SWIFT: Thoughts on 21st Century Warfare* (Brassey's, 1985), remains a very worthwhile primer on how we no longer have the luxury of decades in which to study and prepare to counter conventional threats.

cannot afford to reduce the intelligence community budget, nor to increase it—we are locked into a fiscal *status quo* that has the very insidious and very dangerous effort of also locking us into a quagmire of unpreparedness.

Tough Love Budget Cuts

The judgments that follow, about how to achieve $11.6 billion a year in savings, represent very substantive experience at the highest levels by several extremely knowledgeable experts.[17] *Adoption of these numbers by Congress would energize the Intelligence Community, improve national security and national competitiveness, and reduce the deficit by $10 billion a year.*

It serves no purpose to propose a program, which cannot be achieved within existing fiscal boundaries. Here then is an explicit prescription for achieving $10 billion a year in savings, while realigning an additional $1.6 billion per year to address eight critical deficiencies in national and defense intelligence—these are listed first to emphasize that our intent is to *strengthen and extend* the U.S. Intelligence Community.

OFFSETTING INCREASES FOR CRITICAL NEW INTELLIGENCE INITIATIVES	PLUS UP/ PER YEAR
Clandestine Service Agency	+250M
Electronic Security & Counterintelligence Program	+150M
State and Local Intelligence Community Program	+150M
University of the Republic	+50M
Global Knowledge Foundation	+250M
Community Access to Open Sources/Experts	+250M
Commercial Source Imagery Procurement	+250M
NATO Partners for Peace Open Source Architecture	+250M
Total Off-Sets (Increases from within Reduced Budget)	**+1.6B**

Figure 48: Essential Offsetting Increases for National Intelligence

---

[17] As (then) DCI James Woolsey discovered when he attempted to address the issue of whether one meter imagery should be permitted in the private sector, he was at the complete mercy of his staff and the parochial interests represented by the classified imagery pipeline. While there is no "absolute" truth in national intelligence, this chapter is intended to broaden the discussion and force freer thinking outside the box.

It is essential that the congressional appropriations committees, as well as the congressional authorization committees for government affairs and for each department of government ostensibly consuming national intelligence, become involved in scrutinizing this proposed program and challenging the barons of intelligence on both their numbers, and their ultimate value propositions. These proposals *can* be authenticated by Congress, and their adoption *will* force the issue of constructive change.

National and Defense Intelligence Program Element Recommended for Reduction and Realignment	% of USIP	Save/ Year
Human Intelligence	10%	0.75B
• Significantly downsize large and elaborate overseas stations maintained by both CIA and DoD, and establish single integrated country cells, which include NSA, DEA, and FBI.		500M
• Consolidate Service HUMINT activities into a single cadre.		300M
• Privatize FBIS document procurement and translations but retain the FBIS analysis element and its global role in coordinating media monitoring and burden sharing.		200M
• *Offsetting increase for a new Clandestine Service Agency using non-official cover and mid-career hires, with significant increase in law enforcement collection and covert action against rogue nations and transnational terrorist and criminal organizations unresponsive to international law.*		(250M)
Imagery Intelligence	20%	2.50B
• Pause imagery and infrared warning satellite procurement for 3 years to allow drawdown of existing satellite inventories, promotion of increased development and use of non-intelligence capabilities, and re-engineering to smaller and more flexible payloads for some mission needs.		2.00B
• Reduce classified imagery collection by 50% (only 10% of collected imagery is processed today).		500M
• Downsize intelligence image processing and increase reliance on commercial processing and software for data exploitation to better adapt to rapid changes in volume/character of demand.		250M
• *Offsetting increase for the procurement of commercial source imagery to meet CINC needs for military maps, precision guidance, and aviation mission rehearsal; and civilian needs*		(250M)

---

[18] This and the other four offsetting increases which focus on open source exploitation will be managed by the Global Knowledge Foundation.

as outlined in the EARTHMAP Report (October 1995).[18]		
Signals Intelligence	**35%**	**2.75B**
• Downscale on-going NSA conventional SIGINT operations to conform to more diverse decentralized threats		1.00B
• Stretch procurement of replacement satellites in light of inventories and create a centralized ground architecture utilizing evolving sat-to-sat capabilities; posture for quick reaction low-earth-orbit supplements in times of crisis.		1.50B
• Stretch some advanced high volume collection initiatives in favor of small rapid response collection packages.		500M
• *Offsetting increase for the establishment of an open source intelligence architecture serving as the foundation for integrating the NATO Partners for Peace program—includes purchase of commercial imagery.*		(250M)
Production	**10%**	**0.75B**
• Substantially reduce the standing armies of (largely non-expert) production personnel and related resources in favor of increased reliance on commercial open source, first echelon processing, and contract analytical services.		1.00B
• *Offsetting increase for dramatic improvements in access to private sector experts and open sources, to include a new model of analysis, using the "virtual intelligence community".*		(250M)
Infrastructure and Support Services	**25%**	**2.50B**
• Curtail dedicated communications in favor of more robust, technologically innovative, and adaptable international commercial communications and commercial satellites.		500M
• Markedly reduce costly printed product production and distribution in favor of electronic dissemination and storage.		300M
• Commercialize, as far as possible, existing dedicated government-owned launchers and launch facilities.		1.00B
• Make use of COTS software for intelligence applications the norm, and eliminate redundant development of generic applications by multiple compartmented data domains.		500M
• Commercialize many support services such as background investigations, facility security, transportation services, facility and equipment maintenance, supply services, etcetera.		500M
• *Offsetting increase for funding of FBI's Electronic Security and Counterintelligence Program including national testing & certification laboratory and courtesy inspections and vulnerability testing of tax-paying private sector companies.*		(150M)

• *Offsetting increase for transfer of funds, technologies, and methods for intelligence collection and processing to state and local elements, with emphasis on open source exploitation.*		(150M)
International Burden Sharing	**00%**	**0.75B**
• Establish explicit division-of-effort agreements in intelligence with NATO (or portions thereof), Korea, Japan, and Australia/ New Zealand for selected targets of mutual interest.		750M
• Experiment with more limited agreements with Russia and China as well as Latin American, Middle Eastern, and African countries and selected international corporations.		300M
• *Offsetting increase for the establishment of a Global Knowledge Foundation, jointly sponsored by the United Nations and the Summit of Eight, but managed by the USA, to nurture distributed centers of expertise world-wide.*		(250M)
• *Offsetting increase for the establishment of a University of the Republic program, to provide joint knowledge management training to government, industry, and social leaders.*		(50M)

Figure 49: Annual Savings Goals for National Intelligence

All of these proposed savings are informed judgments, but generally notional proposals to move the dialogue forward, and very much in keeping with the personal estimate for former DCI James Woolsey.[19] It adds up—$10 billion a year savings by the year 2004, with a further $1.6 billion realigned internally to fund offsetting increases essential to reconstituting a modern intelligence and counterintelligence community.[20]

---

[19] There are subtleties in the proposed savings program, and what might appear to be obvious errors (e.g. cutting signals intelligence by $3.0 billion when the NSA budget is only $3.4 billion) in fact take into account the various schemes by which DoD conceals the true cost of intelligence, and particularly the enormous redundancies in tactical signals intelligence collection units and equipment, and related manpower and support costs that are not properly represented to Congress.

[20] Naturally such savings must be sought over a period of several years, but they could begin this year—2000—and be fully achieved within four years, by 2004. These savings do not reflect the additional $2-4 billion a year that could be saved by implementing the recommendations of the Commission on Secrecy, nor do they reflect the estimated $3 billion or so per year that could be saved with improvements in information management by consumers of intelligence throughout the U.S. government, and particularly the utilization of commercial-off-the-shelf (COTS) information technologies, and the rapid decommissioning of archaic legacy systems which prevent

Proposed Program for the 21ˢᵗ Century

This proposed program begins with four strategic ideas.

• Open sources are the foundation for national intelligence because they provide context as well as warning or tip-off, and because unclassified intelligence can be used to further international policies and to educate the public. *Do not send a spy where a schoolboy can go.* Open sources invite open cooperation.

• Spies and satellites should focus on "the hard stuff"—however, they cannot be successful without understanding what is already available from open sources, or without using open sources to guide their precision capabilities.

• The *ultimate* purpose of national intelligence is to inform governance rather than to collect secrets—collection within any discipline is a means to an end.

• In the 21ˢᵗ Century the U.S. Intelligence Community must serve the people, their elected legislative representatives, and the entire administrative branch bureaucracy *including the ever-important state and local authorities*—this will require a dramatic redefinition of national intelligence.

Figure 50: Strategic Ideas for 21ˢᵗ Century Intelligence

This vision for intelligence in the 21ˢᵗ Century is has roots in the writings of Pierre Teilhard de Chardin and Quincy Wright: the creation of a

---

even modest exploitation of commercial sources of information, e.g. commercial imagery. It also does not include the much larger savings—perhaps as much as $50 billion a year, that would accrue from savings in major weapons and mobility system procurements that benefited from improved intelligence support, beginning with support for the basic decision as to whether the system was even needed or not.

"Smart Nation" in which each citizen is a consumer of intelligence. *In the age of distributed information, "central intelligence" is an oxymoron.* [21]

It is also important to understand the fact that "intelligence" is not inherently classified or secret—on the contrary, its utility decreases with every increase in compartmentation and restriction.

In an age when information is a substitute for violence, wealth, labor, space, and time, it is simply irresponsible for a Nation to enter the 21st Century without a national information strategy. [22]

How do we implement such a vision? At the higher level of policy, it will require initiatives in three key areas.

---

[21] Pierre Teilhard de Chardin's writing and its relevance to intelligence theory and practice was brought to the author's attention by Dr. Stevan Dedijer, recognized by many as the father of the concept of business intelligence. The article by Quincy Wright, "Project for a world intelligence center", *Journal of Conflict Resolution* (Volume I, Number 1, 1957) was among the readings in the 1986 running of the CIA's " Intelligence Successes and Failures" course as created and taught by Dr. Jack Davis until his retirement.

[22] The following books comprise an executive tutorial on advanced thinking applicable to the reconstitution of national intelligence as an *integrated* element of national knowledge power: Kevin Kelly, *OUT OF CONTROL: The Rise of Neo-Biological Civilization* (Addison-Wesley, 1994); Alvin Toffler, *PowerShift: Knowledge, Wealth, and Violence at the Edge of the 21st Century* (Bantam Books, 1990); Harlan Cleveland, *The Knowledge Executive: Leadership in an Information Society* (E. P. Dutton, 1985); Howard Rheingold, *Tools for Thought: The History and Future of Mind-Expanding Technology* (Simon & Schuster, 1985); Paul Strassmann, *Information PayOff: The Transformation of Work in the Electronic Age* (Free Press, 1985); and Robert Carkhuff, *The Exemplar: The Exemplary Performer in the Age of Productivity* (Human Resource Development Press, 1984). While the authors have gone on to write other exceptional books, these six in combination provide a level of comprehension that cannot be achieved elsewhere.

1. **In collection,** focus classified capabilities very tightly on "the hard stuff" that truly cannot be acquired by any other means *and* is of incontestable importance to national security.

2. **In production,** transfer proven unclassified intelligence methods to the rest of the government (the consumer community and now including the state and local economic and law enforcement authorities) and to the private sector so that they may use these methods to collect open source information (OSIF) and convert it into open source intelligence (OSINT) products of common concern.

3. **In infrastructure,** establish a Global Knowledge Foundation under the oversight of the Vice President (and outside the U.S. Intelligence Community program) to nurture distributed centers of expertise worldwide, and to bring increasing amounts of distributed content online—establish a global knowledge network including a Digital Marshall Plan based on content and human expertise, rather than simple technical connectivity of technical nodes.[23]

Figure 51: Basic Directions for the *National* Intelligence Community

The goal of this coherent policy direction is to assure national security and national competitiveness in the 21st Century through the nurturing of a "virtual intelligence community" that is able to provide to each citizen, to each business person, to each scholar, to each media representative, to each government action officer at every level, a degree of intelligence support unprecedented in the history of the intelligence profession, and unique for being largely unclassified, just enough, and just in time. Such a community can also practice "information peacekeeping".

---

[23] A Digital Marshall Plan for bringing the Internet to the Third World, and accelerating the adoption of digital publishing in all countries, should certainly be one of the Presidential initiatives early on within this funded program. It would also apply to the millions of Americans who do not yet use computers.

Now we turn to specific programmatic initiatives that are recommended for immediate legislative enactment by the Congress, and executive implementation by a non-partisan DGNI and a refocused DCI. We will address a new higher level of national intelligence management in the context of a national information strategy and a harnessing of the virtual intelligence community; the refocusing and strengthening of the management and organization of the classified intelligence community; and the creation of stronger intelligence capabilities, relying heavily on open sources of intelligence, within the rest of the federal government and at the state and local levels of government.

University of the Republic

A means is needed by which to provide for the "higher education" of the leaders of government, industry, and society—including academic and non-profit organization leaders—with respect to knowledge management.[24] A critical vehicle for bringing these leaders together at regular points in their careers, after they have proven themselves through rigorous selection processes and personal commitments in their respective domains, is a University of the Republic.

"If there was ever a moment in history when a comprehensive strategic view was needed, not just by a few leaders in high (which is to say visible) office but by a large number of executives and other generalists in and out of government, this is certainly it. Meeting that need is what should be *higher* about higher education".

Figure 52: Educating Leaders About Knowledge

---

[24] "Higher education" as defined by Harlan Cleveland in *The Knowledge Executive: Leadership in an Information Society* (E. P. Dutton, 1985), especially Chapter 11, "Education for Leadership". The quotation is on page 203. Mr. Cleveland, a Princeton graduate and Rhodes Scholar, has served as an Assistant Secretary of State, U.S. Ambassador to NATO, and President of the University of Hawaii, as well as the Dean of the Hubert H. Humphrey Institute of Public Affairs at the University of Minnesota.

This institution can be a modest coordinating and facilitating organization, numbering no more than 15 positions in terms of permanent staff, but drawing on the permanent personnel of such institutions as the John F. Kennedy School of Government at Harvard University, the National Defense University, the Hubert H. Humphrey Institute of Public Affairs at the University of Minnesota, and at least two major regional educational centers, one in the South and also one on the West Coast.

The Extended National Intelligence Community

The intended result of a national information strategy, aided by a University of the Republic that creates shared cultural, organizational, and management visions among leaders of the various knowledge elements in America, is an extended national intelligence community that encompasses state and local government organizations, business and social (e.g. non-profit, cultural) organizations, federal government collectors of unclassified information and producers of unclassified information and intelligence; and those international governmental and non-governmental organizations— including religious and cultural organizations—that choose to be part of an extended "world brain".

In the age of distributed information, the concept of "central intelligence" is an oxymoron. Information does not automatically lead to knowledge; intelligence does not automatically require secrecy; and computers most certainly do not automatically process information into knowledge or intelligence. We are at a special point in human history, on the verge of understanding relationships between biology, psychology, ecology, and cybernetics. Three ideas and their originators merit special mention as part of the context or "framing" of national intelligence in a new and extended manner:

1. **CoEvolution/Whole Earth (Stewart Brand).** It was Stewart Brand, founder of the *CoEvolution Quarterly* that ultimately evolved into *Whole Earth Review*, who best articulated the idea of coevolution—the symbiotic relationship between elements such that one could not evolve without the other—such that interaction with others accelerated evolution rather than threatened it. Today we must refocus the extended national intelligence community toward identifying and exploiting *opportunities* for accelerated evolution *in relation to external open information nodes*, rather than simply

237

attempting to contain threats to the *status quo ante* through secret sources and methods alone.

2. **Virtual Communities (Howard Rheingold).** Howard, Stewart's natural successor, originally focused on "cool tools" and virtual reality, but soon came to the realization that information technology was perhaps most important for having made possible virtual communities on the electronic frontier.

3. **Corporate Hive (Kevin Kelly).** Kevin Kelly, today editor of *WIRED*, "the" digital generation magazine, authored the seminal work, *OUT OF CONTROL: The Rise of Neo-Biological Civilization.* Abysmally marketed, this brilliant work is one of the hidden nuggets of advanced thinking from the 1990's, and should be read by every information and intelligence professional, and every manager. Kelly is the "Osborne and Gaebler" of cyberspace, and the one person who seems to really understand—and ably explain—how information technology makes a "corporate hive" model of intelligence work, with bottom-up sensing and group intuition as powerful forces which enable "just enough, just in time" intelligence well-suited to the challenges of the 21st Century.[25]

Taken together with the earlier discussion of the three new classes of threat (transnational crime, global ethnic and religious ties, and economic war), these three ideas and their originators shape our understanding of how we must move quickly to create an intelligence and counterintelligence community that is fully extended to all elements of the Nation—both the public and the private sectors—while it is also global in nature, capable of operating in real-time, and empowered by the voluntary harnessing of every citizen-mind, and indeed most world-minds, as part of a living, organic "virtual intelligence community" which is inherently open, legal, ethical, and "conscious".

---

[25] Addison-Wesley, 1994. Cited in note 21 as critical to advanced thinking. It is hard to say enough good things about this book. It is not an easy read—there is some very heavy going—but of all the books the author has read in the past decade, perhaps numbering 500, this is one of a handful that stand out as exceptional.

Federal Knowledge Management

This chapter focuses on restoring the traditional classified intelligence community to its special place within the halls of national power, but mention must be made of the "other" national intelligence community that today is as badly fragmented and poorly managed as is the U.S. Intelligence Community. Completely apart from the repositories of expertise resident in the various departments—and including hundreds of thousands of reports written by contractors as well as access to tens of thousands of private sector experts on direct contract to the U.S. Government—there are several institutions that must at least be mentioned, for they comprise a very valuable portion of the "virtual intelligence community", and the reform of the U.S. Intelligence Community cannot proceed without their full integration into a larger universe of collaborating centers of expertise. These include, without further comment and without this being a comprehensive listing:

- Defense Advanced Research Projects Agency (DARPA)
- Defense Attaché Service (DAS)
- Defense Technical Information Center (DTIC)
- Library of Congress
  - Federal Research Division (FRD)
  - Congressional Research Service (CRS)
- National Aeronautics and Space Administration (NASA)
- National Library of Medicine (NLM)
- National Science Foundation (NSF)
- National Technical Information Service (NTIS)
- U.S. Information Agency (USIA)[26]

National Intelligence Forum for Policy Direction

---

[26] Few seem to know that this organization produces media summaries and analyses that rival if not surpass those done by the Foreign Broadcast Information Service (FBIS) of today's Central Intelligence Agency (CIA). The author has provided invited testimony to the Commission on Public Diplomacy urging that this culturally-astute organization be given a much greater role in overt collection and the analysis of cultural and media issues, presuming we can restore it as an independent agency.

The various recommendations regarding policymaker involvement in guiding national intelligence all recognize that there is a grave deficiency in this area, but tend to return time and again to the National Security Council and to the Defense-State axis as the touchstone for improvements. This is a mistake.

There are three major consumer groups that must be attended to and have in place a senior-level coordination mechanism under this proposed program for national intelligence and counterintelligence in the 21st Century:

1. **National Security—Government Consumers.** This includes the National Security Council in its capacity as the President's coordinator; the Department of State; the Department of Defense; the Department of Justice; and the Department of Treasury. The threats from global crime, and from electronic attacks to our national financial systems, are of sufficient weight to warrant new and equal status for the latter two departments of government. *This also includes each of the counterpart congressional committees.*[27]

2. **National Competitiveness—Government Consumers.** This includes the National Economic Council and the Council of Economic Advisors; the Department of Commerce; the Departments (or Bureaus) of Agriculture, Natural Resources, and Health and Human Services; and those other elements of government such as the Environmental Protection Agency and the Immigration and Naturalization Service that do not receive serious intelligence support today. *As with the first group, this element should also includes each of the counterpart Congressional committees.*

3. **National Security & National Competitiveness—Private Sector.** This includes all infrastructure providers including those based overseas, all corporate entities that pay taxes and employ individuals within the borders of the United States of America[28], and the population at large. The

---

[27] The definitive original and authoritative review of the need to provide improved intelligence support to Congress is found in Britt Snider, *Sharing Secrets with Lawmakers: Congress as a User of Intelligence* (Center for the Study of Intelligence, 1997). This program, by dramatically improving our ability to produce unclassified intelligence, will be most beneficial to the Members of Congress and will have a direct impact on their ability to be more helpful to their business and other constituents.

[28] This is Robert Reich's definition of a "U.S. entity" and it serves very well.

President's Foreign Intelligence Advisory Board (PFIAB) could be reconstituted as the Public Intelligence Advisory Board (PIAB) and serve as the channel for private sector representation at the highest level. For general day-to-day coordination, industry associations and volunteer advisory representatives would be utilized and coordinated by the PIAB. *Here also Congress should be represented, so that the key committees responsible for the various sectors of the U.S. economy are fully engaged.*

The issue of intelligence support to the private sector is one that is contentious but that need not be so if the unnecessary and false premises are stripped away.

- First, it is important to emphasize that the first priority for support to the private sector lies in the arena of counterintelligence, and especially electronic security and counterintelligence that is focused on eliminating economic espionage and the theft of intellectual property; and on the protection of our critical nodes, including enormously fragile financial and other databases, from information vandalism, information terrorism, and information warfare.

- Second, when one understands and adopts the definition of 21st Century intelligence—tailored information created to support a specific decision—most of it not classified at all—it becomes clear that an unclassified intelligence process offers significant dividends to both government consumers who cannot work with classified information, and to the private sector. This is not to say that the U.S. Intelligence Community will provide such intelligence, but rather that it will be a full partner in a larger "virtual intelligence community" which can address the needs of this *much* larger private sector consumer community.

Hence, a properly constituted National Intelligence Forum would have two Senior Inter-Agency Groups (SIG) and one Public Intelligence Advisory Council (PIAC), each representing critical segments of their community at the GS-15/Colonel/Corporate Vice Presidential level.

The management elements of this Forum would consist of the Deputy Secretaries for the government elements, and a reconstructed President's Foreign Intelligence Advisory Board (PFIAB)—renamed the Public Intelligence Advisory Board (PIAB)—focused on properly representing the needs and concerns of the private sector that generates our gross national product and also controls 95% of all of our military communications capabilities. The staff in support of the NIF would be resident with the Director-General of National Intelligence (see below), but the NIF would be a *policy* device with a public element, and serve as the Board of Directors for national intelligence writ large.

National Intelligence Forum		
DepSecs-NS	DepSecs-NC	PIAB
SIG-NS	SIG-NC	PIAC
NS Working Group	NC Working Group	PI Working Group

Figure 53: Organization of the National Intelligence Forum

National Intelligence Management

Congress had the right idea in 1992 when it suggested that the DCI should in fact be the DNI, but at the time Congress was just beginning to understand the open source revolution, and did not go far enough. In the information age, when 90% or more of the critical information is unclassified and at least 75% of it is in the private sector rather than in government hands, a DGNI is required who has global access to *all* information, not only to classified information. Such a person would have policy and budgetary authority over a refocused Director of *Classified* Intelligence (DCI) as well as a new Global Knowledge Foundation (GKF); control over an expanded and elevated National Intelligence Council (NIC); and also *joint oversight but not control* over the substantive aspects of the information collection and processing endeavors of the various departments of government. The DGNI would be the substantive counterpart to the Chief Information Officer (CIO) of the Nation, who would focus on orchestrating information technology (IT) architectures and the general housekeeping aspects related to IT.[29]

---

[29] OMB would have oversight and budgetary authority over all information expenditures by the government. A direct relationship between the DGNI and the Vice

Director-General of National Intelligence				
DGNI Staff	DCI	C/NIC	D/GKF	NIF Staff
U Rep Staff	IC	NIC	GKF	PIAB Staff
OMB	Global ICs	USG	Public/NGOs	Hill

Figure 54: Organization for National Intelligence Management

The DGNI would have Cabinet status in a non-voting capacity, for the purpose of having full access to all policy meetings. Under this concept, the DGNI and the Chair of the National Intelligence Council (NIC) are expected to serve as personal intelligence officers to the leadership of *both* the Legislative and Executives Branches, and to devote a portion of the DGNI's modest staff as well as the full resources of the NIC to ensuring that the President and Vice President as well as the key Committee Chairmen on the Hill are receiving *tailored* intelligence directly related to the issues of the day and provided in "just enough, just in time" fashion"—and much of the intelligence without classification restrictions and hence much more useful for support to political decision-making and public dialogue. The DCI and senior classified intelligence managers will no longer be on public display or serve as the "last word" on intelligence matters, now that a DGNI and C/NIC exist who can place classified intelligence in the context of open source information and *all-source* intelligence.

The Office of the DGNI need not be larger than 200 people in number, roughly divided between five entities: the University of the Republic staff (15); the National Intelligence Forum staff (15); the PIAB staff (10); the National Intelligence Council (60), and the Global Knowledge Foundation (60). The personal management staff of the DGNI (40) would serve as a national intelligence coordination staff in the truest sense of the word, permitting the DGNI to provide direct support to the President and the Cabinet and to the Chairman and Vice Chairman of the committees of Congress, and also oversight and facilitation to the departmental intelligence activities and the

President is recommended, and would infuse the National Information Infrastructure (NII) and the Global Information Infrastructure (GII) with content-oriented support. Ideally, if the President chooses to make the Vice President the Nation's CIO, then the DGNI becomes the most critical supporter, subordinate to the Vice President, of the President's national information strategy and national intelligence infrastructure.

private sector consumers of unclassified intelligence and government counterintelligence support.

Under this concept every government consumer at the federal level would be required to earmark no less than 2% of their total budget to an internal intelligence program—including the cost of acquiring open source information—and to be responsible for meeting those intelligence needs that can be addressed predominantly by open sources.

The DGNI would play a very active role in transferring intelligence methods (e.g. requirements analysis, collection management, source validation, advanced visualization) to the consumer organizations, and also play a very active role in helping them discover, discriminate, distill, and deliver open source information and intelligence internally to their departmental consumers as well as appropriate external consumers such as those responsible for oversight and private sector elements important to national security and national competitiveness.

A very special emphasis would be placed by the DGNI on educating, training, and supporting law enforcement at all levels, and on creating state and local intelligence communities which rely predominantly on open sources of information and intelligence as well as their own collection capabilities including informant networks. The needs of the Chief Executive Officers in the private sector would be addressed by private sector organizations offering business intelligence services, but for policy and counterintelligence coordination, the PIAB would serve as the private sector's focal point at this level.

National Intelligence Council

The National Intelligence Council (NIC) would move *out* of the classified intelligence community and *up* one level to become a broader national intelligence office that has superior access to open sources as well as a much closer relationship with both the consumers and the distributed international centers of excellence in open source information collection and open source intelligence production.

Unlike today's NIC, where the National Intelligence Officers (NIO) are focused on topics rather than consumers, the new NIO would be expanded, and the top-level NIOs would be focused on individual organizational consumers—including state and local consumers and selected critical national economic industry segments, while Assistant NIOs focus on topics.

There would be one other significant change: the National Intelligence Forum (NIF) and the NIC would work closely together to establish both classified and open source collection requirements, and to ensure that classified collection management remains strictly focused on only those critical targets and topics that cannot be addressed by open sources.

Chair, National Intelligence Council				
Vice Chair				
National Intelligence Officers (5 per consumer community)				
Foreign Affairs	Military Defense	Finance & Commerce	Law Enforcement	Environment and Culture
Assistant National Intelligence Officers (2 per topical area)				
WMD	GP Forces	Crime	Terrorism	IW
Political	Economic	Cultural	S&T	Geography

Figure 55: Extending the National Intelligence Council

Either the Chair or the Vice Chair of the NIC should be a four-star flag officer (active or retired). The NIC would play a substantive role in mentoring the departmental intelligence activities, and would be roughly equivalent to the Joint Chiefs of Staff in terms of substantive influence and utility.

Global Knowledge Foundation

The Global Knowledge Foundation (GKF), under the direction of a candidate subject to confirmation, would serve as the administrator of $1.05 billion a year fund for nurturing distributed centers of expertise while also meeting the needs of government consumers for the acquisition and processing of open source information.[30]

---

[30] There is an obvious question which could be asked here, and one which is very welcome as the debate proceeds: "Instead of creating a new Global Knowledge Foundation, would it not be preferable to consolidate the Library of Congress and the

Of the eight offsetting increases proposed within this program, three would be managed within the U.S. Intelligence Community and five (shown below) would be consolidated into a new Global Knowledge Program under the direct oversight of the DGNI.

OFFSETTING INCREASES FOR CRITICAL NEW INTELLIGENCE INITIATIVES	PLUS UP/ PER YEAR
University of the Republic • *Offsetting increase for the establishment of a University of the Republic program, to provide joint knowledge management training to government, industry, and social leaders.*	+50M
Global Knowledge Foundation • *Offsetting increase for the establishment of a Global Knowledge Foundation, jointly sponsored by the United Nations and the Summit of Eight, but managed by the USA, to nurture distributed centers of expertise world-wide.*	+250M
Community Access to Open Sources/Experts • *Offsetting increase for dramatic improvements in access to private sector experts and open sources, to include a new model of analysis using the "virtual intelligence community".*	+250M
Commercial Source Imagery Procurement • *Offsetting increase for the procurement of commercial source imagery to meet CINC needs for military maps, precision guidance, and aviation mission rehearsal; and civilian needs as outlined in the EARTHMAP Report (October 1995).*	+250M
NATO Partners for Peace Open Source Architecture • *Offsetting increase for the establishment of an open source intelligence architecture serving as the foundation for integrating the CIS into NATO under the Partners for Peace program—includes purchase of commercial imagery.*	+250M

Figure 56: The Global Knowledge Foundation

Congressional Research Service under a new Director-General of National Intelligence who manages a separate open source intelligence fund while also overseeing the DCI and the NIC?" It is for the President and Congress to determine how best to proceed—the Global Knowledge Foundation is proposed as a means of clearly articulating its functions apart from the existing capabilities of the Library of Congress and the Congressional Research Service.

The rationale for moving open source intelligence funding out of the U.S. Intelligence Community is similar to the rationale that led to the very successful creation of the Special Operations and Low Intensity Conflict Program (Program 11). However much this program might be supported by Congress and the Administration, the U.S. Intelligence Community bureaucracy and the entrenched practices and cultural biases built up over a half-century will simply not permit the effective administration of these funds within the U.S. Intelligence Program.

The GKF's charter should include language that requires its initiatives to be equally divided in emphasis between support to public diplomacy, national economic competitiveness, defense technology acquisition and warfighting, law enforcement, and national intelligence production.

This would be a non-intrusive, non-regulatory element of government which would use its funds to cover the marginal cost of increasing public access to selected university and other databases that could not afford the increased security and technical load of public access without such assistance; and also to encourage selected private sector open source capabilities through direct procurement of open sources and services on behalf of the U.S. Intelligence Community and government consumers of intelligence. *It would not, however, be a substitute for open source collection and processing by the individual consumers, but rather a strategic and discretionary account under the complete control of the DGNI and responsive primarily to the NIC.*

Location, Location, Location

It is a well-established view in Washington that proximity to the White House and proximity to one's constituents is of the utmost important in determining both influence and long-term success. For this reason, the decisions of former DCI's to give up both the F Street offices of the Intelligence Community Staff and the South-Central campus of three buildings near the Department of State border on being self-destructive. It is bad enough that the CIA campus is across the river and well into Northern Virginia. If Congress supports this program, then it is necessary for Congress to mandate the assignment of at least the South-Central Campus (all three buildings) to the DGNI—one for the DGNI and the NIC, one for the GKF and the University of the Republic, and the third for a multi-purpose secure conference center.

247

Classified Intelligence Community Management

It is misleading to the intelligence consumer, and inconsistent with the realities of the day, to persist in maintaining the position of DCI as it is now defined. Not only does the DCI not have any substantive authority over the elements of the U.S. Intelligence Community, while also lacking access to the vast quantities of open source information that are essential to credibly claim to be producing "all source" intelligence, but the vast majority of intelligence community resources are focused on the collection of classified information rather than the production of all-source intelligence. This position should be renamed to reflect its focus on classified collection, while also receiving the necessary management assistance and program authority it needs in order to be effective.

Director of *Classified* Intelligence				
Deputy Director of *Classified* Intelligence				
ADCI/RD	ADCI/C	ADCI/P	ADCI/I	ADCI/CI
OIRD	TCA	NIA	OIMPB	FBI
	CSA	NIMA	OIC2	

Figure 57: Organization of the Classified Intelligence Community

Following are specific changes that would permit the DCI to be effective as the leader of the *classified element* of the now extended national intelligence community:

1. **DCI and DDCI.** In general, the Director of *Classified* Intelligence (DCI) and the Deputy Director of *Classified* Intelligence (DDCI) should between them, in either order, be a four-star flag officer and a former executive-level civilian with all-source analysis experience. Both should serve terms of at least five years each, with a second term being possible with confirmation by the Senate again being required. We should restore the DDCI to a single position but ask Congress to retain and downgrade the new DDCI for Community Management (DDCI/CM) to an Assistant DCI position responsible for research and development across the entire community (ADCI/RD).

2. **Five ADCI.** We must adopt, with appreciation, the three Assistant Director positions created by Congress (for Collection, Production, and

248

Infrastructure, or ADCI/C, ADCI/P and ADCI/I), integrate the fourth ADCI converted from the second DDCI position, as ADCI/RD; and request a fifth, a new Assistant Deputy Director for Counterintelligence, ADCI/CI. As recommended by the IC21 study, the ADCI/I would assume responsibility for community management functions including budgetary and requirements prioritization responsibilities. Together with an ADCI/RD and the ADCI/CI, this will give the DCI a single principal deputy and five functional deputies. All should be appointed to terms of five years. Their respective mandates are summarized here:

- **ADCI/C.** This single individual would serve as the DCI's principal deputy for collection and would have both collection management and program management oversight responsibilities for the Technical Collection Agency (TCA) and the Clandestine Service Agency (CSA), both described below.

- **ADCI/P.** This single individual would serve as the DCI's principal deputy for production and would have both production management and program management oversight responsibilities for the CIA, now renamed the National Intelligence Agency (NIA) and the National Imagery and Mapping Agency (NIMA). The ADCI/P would also represent the DCI in managing distributed production by the departmental intelligence elements, in establishing international distributed production agreements, and in evaluating all finished intelligence production from all sources including the private sector products prepared for the U.S. government as a whole.[31]

- **ADCI/I.** This individual would serve as the DCI's principal deputy for infrastructure and would have hiring, training, security, and promotion oversight authority for all agencies, as well as direct oversight for the community-wide Office of Intelligence Management, Personnel, and Budget (OIMPB) and Office of Intelligence Communications and

---

[31] In the aftermath of the Gulf War, at least one major review noted that "product" and "system" are now virtually the same. NIMA represents this reality, and could serve as a test-bed for new methods of multi-media electronic publishing, with close coordination between the ADCI/P and ADCI/I as well as all agency heads.

Computing (OIC2). The ADCI/I would be the Chief Information Officer for the classified national intelligence community.

- **ADCI/CI.** This individual would serve as the DCI's principal deputy for counterintelligence, and would have oversight over policies and programs associated with counterintelligence. While the Federal Bureau of Investigation (FBI) would naturally fall within this position's area of interest, it would be from a coordination stand-point, as an executive liaison function, rather than from a management stand-point. This individual, would, however, be responsible for overseeing counterintelligence within the classified intelligence community, throughout the U.S. government, and in the private sector, for the purpose of appraising the DCI of needed improvements and changes in inter-agency and private sector standards and practices. This individual would work closely with the ADDI/I to establish new levels of personnel and electronic security in the U.S. government and in the private sector.

- **ADCI/RD.** This individual would serve as the principal deputy for research & development across all collection, processing, and dissemination systems, with program oversight intended to balance investments between collection and processing, between individual stovepipes, and between internal and external connectivity. This individual would divide their time between direct oversight of the Office of Intelligence Research & Development (OIRD), and representing the DCI to the Defense Advanced Research Projects Agency (DARPA) and other elements of the U.S. government as well as the private sector, with major investments in research & development focused on collection, production, and infrastructure technologies.

3. **Program Authority.** We must reassign to the DCI complete program authority over the budgets for the three combat support agencies which have national-level responsibilities: the National Reconnaissance Office (NRO) and the National Security Agency (NSA)—both combined into the Technical Collection Agency (TCA) recommended by the IC21 Study— and the National Imagery and Mapping Agency (NIMA). The JMIP and

TIARA would remain departmental intelligence programs *after* being subject to the shared reductions outlined in this proposal.

4. **Senior Intelligence Service.** We must adopt Congressional recommendations regarding the establishment of a single consolidated Senior Intelligence Service (SIS) for the national classified community and require that all candidates—including departmental candidates—for promotion to SIS have served at least one tour in another agency and one tour in counterintelligence.

5. **Fenced Program and Savings.** We must fence the USIP, reduced to $20 billion per year by 2001, from further reductions for a period of twenty years from 2001 (i.e. until 2022). We must also egislate an Intelligence Reserve Fund controlled by Congress that permit the restoration of $2 billion per year for each of five years contingent on extraordinary new initiatives being submitted to and found meritorious by Congress.

6. **Bound Responsibility.** We should explicitly relieve the DCI of responsibility for the management of the departmental intelligence programs—these fall under the oversight but not the control of the DGNI—however, the DCI will be accountable, with the DDCI and the various ADCIs, for ensuring interoperability of information media and technologies between the classified and the unclassified worlds, with attendant security.

7. **Office of Intelligence Management, Personnel, and Budget.** We must consolidate management of all personnel, training, and security resources for the community in a single Office of Intelligence Management, Personnel, and Budget (OIMB) under the direction of ADDI(I). This would include pertinent elements of the Directorate of Administration from the Central Intelligence Agency (CIA), as well as general community budgetary and requirements management functionalities.

8. **Office of Intelligence Communications and Computing (OIC2).** We must consolidate management of all resources from U.S. Intelligence Community focused on communications and computing, including the Office of Communications (OC) from CIA/DA, the Office of Information Technology (OIT) from CIA/DS&T, the Office of Information Resources

(OIR) from CIA/DI, and the Information Management Staff (IMS) from CIA/DO.

9. **Office of Intelligence Research & Development.** We should consolidate management of all research & development funds for all compartments in all agencies under the DCI, into a single Office of Intelligence Research & Development (OIRD). This is analogous to the IC21 recommendation of a Technology Development Office, and would include the Directorate of Science & Technology from the CIA, less the Foreign Broadcast and Information Service (FBIS), which would be transferred to the Directorate of Intelligence of the CIA.

National Intelligence Agency

The Nation still requires the capabilities represented by the Central Intelligence Agency (CIA), but its day has come and gone. The U.S. Intelligence Community in general, and the CIA in particular, developed in a hodge-podge fashion over the five decades since its establishment, and the time has come to restore the traditional focus on strategic all-source analysis. To this end, the following specific changes are recommended:

1. **Realign and Elevate Directorate of Administration.** As noted above, spin off the Directorate of Administration (DA) to form the core of the Office of Intelligence Management, Personnel, and Budget (OIMPB) and also the Office of Intelligence Communications and Computing (OIC2) under the oversight of the ADCI/I. All similar functions from other agencies would fall under the oversight of the ADCI/I.

2. **Realign and Elevate Directorate of Science and Technology.** As noted above, spin off the Directorate of Science & Technology (DS&T), less the Foreign Broadcast Information Service (FBIS), to form the core of the Office of Intelligence Research & Development (OIRD) under the oversight of the ADDI/RD. All similar functions from other agencies would be under the oversight of the ADCI/RD.

3. **Dismantle Directorate of Operations.** Begin the process of eliminating the existing Directorate of Operations (DO) by transferring the paramilitary elements to the U.S. Special Operations Command; by amicable severance

of relationships with virtually all existing assets; and by conversion of as many existing clandestine personnel as possible into either overt collectors of open source information, or regional security personnel, with full transfers to other elements of the community or the government.[32] Establish in its place a Clandestine Service Agency (CSA), described in the next section.

4. **Rename the CIA as the NIA.** Rename the CIA as the National Intelligence Agency (NIA), to be comprised of the existing Directorate of Intelligence; the Community Open Source Program Office; and half of the National Collection Division (from the DO). The NIA would also have restored to it the Office of Imagery Analysis and whatever has survived from the National Photographic Interpretation Center,; would have new Offices for Signals Analysis and for Measurements & Signatures Analysis, and would create an Office for Open Sources to work with the GKF in assuring world-class open source support to the all-source collection and production processes.

The Foreign Broadcast Information Service (FBIS), while privatizing its media collection and translation endeavors, would not be reduced in size—instead it would be absorbed by the U.S. Information Agency, expand its international role as a coordinator of joint agreements to monitor both capital city and provincial media, and expand its cadre of multi-lingual analysts who are fully competent at doing content analysis of multi-cultural communications.

Half of the National Collection Division (NCD) would become the operational arm of the DI, and specialize in overt but discreet collection operations which are completely legal, ethical, and necessary and which

---

[32] However much the existing DO managers may wish to deny this, the hard reality is that at least 50% and perhaps as many as 75-90% of their agents and case officers are known to local liaison. It is not possible to run secure operations out of an official U.S. installation with young people who spend money like it is going out of style, do not know the language and culture as well as they should, and clearly operate beyond the bounds of the Department of State and other official cover agencies. The author bases this evaluation on a decade of service as a clandestine case officer, including three overseas tours where the author had a recruiting record five times the regional average, and subsequent overt discussions with the directors or deputy directors of seventeen intelligence organizations world-wide.

require extensive travel, multi-lingual facility, and direct dealings with a wide variety of international personalities in all walks of life. This element could be significantly expanded to provide fruitful employment for the many case officers who are so known to international intelligence agencies that they can no longer serve as clandestine case officers.

The NIA would be Nation's sole strategic intelligence analysis capability, and would limit itself to those questions that cannot be answered by the departmental intelligence organizations (while providing oversight, evaluation, and validation for departmental intelligence findings in lesser areas).

OFFSETTING INCREASES FOR CRITICAL NEW INTELLIGENCE INITIATIVES	PLUS UP/ YEAR
Community Access to Open Sources/Experts • *Offsetting increase for dramatic improvements in access to private sector experts and open sources, to include a new model of analysis using the "virtual intelligence community".*	+250M

Figure 58: Earmarked Funding from the GKF

The NIA would serve as the action arm of the NIC, and be subordinate to the NIC in responding to requirements as well as guidance. The NIC would be the highest analysis body in the Nation, and would deal with 100% of the intelligence requirements of the Nation, at least 75% of which would be fulfilled using private sector analysis or departmental analysis capabilities. The NIA would focus on the 25% of the requirements where the bulk of the raw information must come from classified sources, and a deep interactive relationship with classified collection capabilities is essential to the development of the full analysis.

Clandestine Service Agency

Human nature has not changed, and the Nation will continue to be threatened by rogue nations, transnational criminals, ideological terrorists, and information vandals, all able to wreak havoc on our financial, power, communications, and transportation nodes, as well as all capable of unleashing weapons of mass destruction upon us. We must have a clandestine service, as well as a covert action capability, but it must be both serious in nature (not easily detected by every country in which it operates), and focused on the extremely important secrets which cannot be obtained by technical means or overt means. This new organization, to be designated a combat support organization, should have as its deputy a retired flag officer of three-four star caliber, and as regional deputies retired flag officers of one-three star caliber. All managers of the CSA will remain under cover and will not be exposed to the public.

OFFSETTING INCREASES FOR CRITICAL NEW INTELLIGENCE INITIATIVES	PLUS UP/ YEAR
Clandestine Service Agency	+250M
• *Offsetting increase for a new Clandestine Service Agency using non-official cover and mid-career hires, with significant increase in law enforcement collection and covert action against rogue nations and transnational terrorist and criminal organizations unresponsive to international law.*	

Figure 59: Increase of Funding for Clandestine Service Agency

The CSA would *not* be the focal point for classified intelligence exchanges or classified liaison with the intelligence organizations of other governments—these requirements would be met by a special office within the NIA, perhaps staffed by exceptional former DO officers, by Regional Security Officers (RSO) from the Department of State (perhaps augmented by former DO case officers transferred to the Department of State for this purpose), and at the highest levels with participation from the NIC.

The following specific changes are recommended:

1. **Close the Existing Field Offices.** As quickly as possible, stand down all existing networks of agents, 50% or more of which are known to local liaison, and withdraw all existing case officers from the field.[33]

---

[33] Existing non-official cover (NOC) case officers are presumed to be compromised because of very poor tradecraft by the official cover case officers with whom they have had frequent recurring contacts. Most NOCs can be reassigned to the new CSA and work in other countries, but all will require a transition period and additional training.

2. **Convert Stations to Tactical Analysis and Open Source Collection Sites.** Turn the existing station areas, all certified as Sensitive Compartmented Information Facilities (SCIF) over to the DI, under oversight of the ADDI/I, for conversion into inter-agency forward analysis centers (FAC), with responsibilities for tactical intelligence production in support of the Country Team (this includes economic and demographic or consular intelligence), and tactical collection of open source information. Offer existing DO personnel options for converting to overt status in either an analysis or an overt collection role.

3. **Turn Paramilitary Assets Over to SOCOM.** Turn all paramilitary assets over to the U.S. Special Operations Command, and offer all special operations group personnel a three-year transition period.

4. **Establish Five Non-Official Cover Offices.** As quickly as possible, establish five regional[34] headquarters in five different locations in the United States, to form the compartmented elements of the new Clandestine Service Agency (CSA). Working methodically and with a much-enhanced budget, recruit non-official officers at the mid-career level—people who have established their own cover history and are masters of both the foreign language and the region in which they are to work. Compartment their training with five different training cycles and require full sanitization and student alias identities while in training. Eliminate all ground transportation to and from the training facility, and use military aircraft from randomly selected military airfields to move personnel in and out of the training facility.

5. **Relocate Office of Technical Services.** Retain and enhance the Office of Technical Services but relocate it and establish new methods for providing support to non-official cover personnel.

6. **Relocate Office of Special Operations.** Retain and enhance the Office of Special Operations, but relocate it and provide it with a dedicated cadre of

---

[34] China, Russia, Arabia, Europe, and Emerging Powers. The latter Office would have as its major divisions Pacific Rim, Near East, Latin America, and Africa. Operational personnel would be equally divided among these five offices. The Offices are listed in a deliberate order, which reflects their importance in addressing 21st Century threats.

multi-regional case officers who will never have contact with other official personnel.

7. **Eliminate Office of Medical Services.** Eliminate the Office of Medical Services immediately. Phase down all other elements of the DO, with very selective retention of some personnel to serve as cadre for the CSA's administrative elements.

Technical Collection Agency

As the IC21 Study suggests, we urgently need a single consolidated agency that can integrate all aspects of space-based collection. The challenges extend beyond the existing U.S. Intelligence Community, for there is enormous redundancy and poor planning for integration between classified space assets and those controlled by the National Aeronautics and Space Administration (NASA) and the National Oceanographic and Atmospheric Administration (NOAA), among others—never mind the allies and the opportunities extant in burden sharing between Canadian twenty meter (radar), French five and ten-meter (multispectral and panchromatic) and U.S. one-meter imagery collection. To this end, the following specific changes are recommended:

1. **Integrate NRO and NSA.** Fully integrate the National Reconnaissance Office (NRO) and the National Security Agency, as well as the Measurements and Signatures Intelligence (MASINT) elements. Implement the combined savings goals for signals and imagery outlined in the preceding section.

2. **Three-Tiered Program.** Begin a long-term program, working with the surviving elements of the Defense Advanced Reconnaissance Office (DARO) as well as the Community Open Source Program Office (COSPO), the National Imagery and Mapping Agency (NIMA), and the Global Knowledge Foundation (GKF) to establish a three-tiered program for comprehensive intrusive and non-intrusive aerial surveillance of any target, which fully integrates and can alternate mixes of commercial source imagery, air-breather imagery including drones, and overhead imagery. Focus on integrated signals and imagery operations such that tip-offs and simultaneous coverage of key targets with both means are a matter of routine.

3. **Tactical and Virtual Operations.** Begin a long-term program to address signal interception means that require physical intrusion in a tactical mode; to monitor those aspects of Internet communications that require coverage; and to address the inevitable global availability of unrestricted encryption including modes of encryption that are not obvious such as steganographic processes.[35] Working with the National Imagery and Mapping Agency (NIMA), and all elements of the Department of Defense, establish a global dissemination architecture, which permits remote receipt and production of integrated signals and imagery intelligence products, and places special emphasis on utilizing EAGLE VISION and other capabilities that permit the fullest possible exploitation of commercially sources of imagery and signals.

National Imagery and Mapping Agency

Established by Congress and merging the Defense Mapping Agency (DMA) with various management and processing elements of the imagery community, including the Community Imagery Office (CIO) and the National Photographic Interpretation Center (NPIC), this organization has an extremely important role to play in enabling not only classified intelligence, but all unclassified information, to be accessed and automatically manipulated over time. In brief, the single highest priority for this organization must be the mapping of the earth at the 1:50,000-resolution level, as originally called for in early drafts of the EARTHMAP Report (October 1995). The following specific recommendations are made:

1. **EARTHMAP Report. Adopt the EARTHMAP Report (October 1995)** as an integral guidance document, and refocus NIMA from its limited defense perspective to a truly national perspective.

---

[35] Professor William J. Caelli, FACS, FTICA, MIEEE, Head of the School of Data Communications, Faculty of Information Technology, Queensland University of Technology, Australia, is one of the most thoughtful strategic thinkers in this area. His various papers make it clear that key-escrow schemes and other ill-conceived ideas for giving governments any kind of "control" over encryption are simply the mad delusions of those who have not come to grips with the fact that cyberspace is beyond the control of governments, and that information technology power has devolved to the hands of the individual. Under such circumstances, spies must learn new tricks, and cease their foolish efforts to hold back the tide.

2. **Commercial Source Imagery Procurement.** Utilizing the $250M per year earmarked in this proposed program for intelligence and counterintelligence in the 21st Century, as well as a portion of the $250M earmarked for the NATO Partners for Peace open source intelligence architecture, create a virtual mapping database by the year 2001 that fully integrates the planned NASA shuttle acquisition of Digital Terrain Elevation Data (DTED) with the available commercial source so that 75% of the world is available to all consumers at the 1:50,000 level on demand, and the remainder can be collected and created within 48 hours of demand.

OFFSETTING INCREASES FOR CRITICAL NEW INTELLIGENCE INITIATIVES	PLUS UP/ YEAR
Commercial Source Imagery Procurement • *Offsetting increase for the procurement of commercial source imagery to meet CINC needs for military maps, and civilian needs as outlined in the EARTHMAP Report (October 1995).*	+250M

Figure 60: Funding for Commercial Imagery Procurement

Geoeconomic Intelligence and Counterintelligence

Geoeconomic power is the tangible benefit that emerges from having a "smart nation" that uses a robust national information infrastructure to fully harness distributed centers of expertise. One of the major advantages of this proposed program is that it creates a DGNI with the resources and the orientation necessary to provide both legislative and executive branch leaders as well as private sector leaders with integrated and comparative geoeconomic intelligence. Unclassified intelligence products that legally integrate open source intelligence about U.S. industries in order to provide the essential strategic perspectives—the contrasting of U.S. strengths and weaknesses in comparison with foreign economic strengths and weaknesses, will finally be possible. Three forms of geoeconomic intelligence and counterintelligence will be provided under this new program:

1. **Classified Government Intelligence.** Using unclassified open sources for domestic U.S. sourcing, the DGNI will be able to "illuminate the geoeconomic battlefield" and provide both legislative and executive branch

leaders with the intelligence they need to make good policy and to enforce international sanctions.

2. **Classified Government Counterintelligence.** The single most important element of this program is the Electronic Security and Counterintelligence Program, and the related improvements in the protection of intellectual property that comprise the foundation for U.S. national power in the 21st Century. The electronic sources and methods to be used in protecting the private sector will have to have very good protection and merit classification—the advisories and active measures taken to correct deficiencies in the private sector will require some form of proprietary/for official use only handling, and exemptions from the Freedom of Information Act (FOIA).[36]

3. **Unclassified Information Commons.** The greatest long-term value to the geoeconomic health of the Nation will come from the creation of a robust information commons and the transfer of intelligence technologies and methods to state and local authorities as well as to private sector enterprises that wish to remain competitive by learning how to do requirements analysis, collection management, source validation, and so on, using only open sources, systems, and services.

In general, at least one fifth of the national intelligence capability (both classified and open source) should be devoted to geoeconomic, public diplomacy, and general support objectives for federal policymakers and their corresponding legislators.

---

[36] The FOIA is the single best friend of foreign economic competitors, both state-sponsored and corporate driven, and needs to be completely revised if not eliminated. Only individuals should be permitted to apply under this program, and only for information directly related to their personal privacy.

Military and International Peacekeeping Intelligence

Under this proposed program military intelligence would be consolidated under a Director of Military Intelligence (DMI, also the Director of the Defense Intelligence Agency (DIA)), and the DCI would largely defer to the Secretary of Defense and the DMI for management of the Joint Military Intelligence Program (JMIP) and the Tactical Intelligence and Related Activities (TIARA) program. While a Joint Military Intelligence Command (JMIC) capable of training, equipping, and organizing theater and tactical intelligence units as a cohesive whole is recommended, this suggestion would be subject to the will of the Secretary of Defense.

However, the DCI and the DGNI would advise Congress on an annual basis and at each acquisition milestone for every major weapons, mobility, and command & control system, as to each system's supportability from an intelligence point of view. It would be for the Secretary of Defense and the DMI to devise means to ensure that all systems are supportable with appropriate investments in and planning for real-time sensor-to-shooter interfaces, which is not the case today.

Open source intelligence support to the identification and evaluation of critical commercial technologies would become a major new program managed by DIA on behalf of the acquisition community, as would a major new focus on information peacekeeping—on the use of information as a means of avoiding and resolving conflict.

The DGNI and DCI would also take an interest in the valuable role of the military intelligence cadres as a source for foreign language and foreign area expertise, and would strongly endorse a very significant increase in the numbers of Foreign Area Officers and their continuing employment in assignments related to their area of expertise.

Using the GKF and its control of a separate initiative for the North Atlantic Treaty Organization (NATO) Partners for Peace command and control infrastructure, DIA would develop a global open source intelligence sharing architecture—including full access to commercial imagery and the means for rapidly converting commercial imagery into combat charts, precision-munitions guidance, and nape of the earth aviation mission simulations—that would revolutionize international peacekeeping.

OFFSETTING INCREASES FOR CRITICAL NEW INTELLIGENCE INITIATIVES	PLUS UP/ YEAR
NATO Partners for Peace Open Source Architecture • *Offsetting increase for the establishment of an open source intelligence architecture serving as the foundation for integrating the CIS into NATO under the Partners for Peace program—includes purchase of commercial imagery.*	+250M

Figure 61: Funding for NATO-CIS Open Source Architecture

As part of this and other initiatives under the oversight of the GKF, a major new international burden-sharing consortium for the collection, distributed storage, and processing of multi-media and multi-lingual open source information would be established, with the military as the initial beneficiary, followed by law enforcement and the private sector.

In general, at least one fifth of the national intelligence capability (both classified and open source) should be devoted to unilateral and coalition military and peacekeeping objectives.

Law Enforcement Intelligence

In recent years, it has been fashionable to speak of the need to increase support to military operations (SMO), and this has been a valid response to the grave concerns of commanders who realized in Grenada, in Panama, in the Gulf War, and in many smaller engagements world-wide, that they are trapped between a Department of Defense that does not budget for organic tactical and theater intelligence collection; and a national intelligence community that was not trained, equipped, and organized to support tactical military operations.

Now we find that there is a greater challenge than intelligence support to military operations, and it is the challenge that will dominate and define national intelligence operations in the 21st Century—the challenge of providing intelligence support to law enforcement.

To make possible and accelerate the creation of a seamless architecture which brings together state and local intelligence elements (not just law enforcement, but also economic development and environmental monitoring elements), an offsetting increase is proposed, to be managed by the FBI with oversight from the NIC and assistance from the NIA and the military intelligence community.

OFFSETTING INCREASES FOR CRITICAL NEW INTELLIGENCE INITIATIVES	PLUS UP/ YEAR
State and Local Intelligence Community Program • *Offsetting increase for transfer of funds, technologies, and methods for intelligence collection and processing to state and local elements, with emphasis on open source exploitation.*	+150M

Figure 62: State and Local Intelligence Community Program

It is important to stress that law enforcement must be helped to help itself. At the local, state, national, and transnational levels, we must devote an entire generation to conceptualizing, implementing, and improving law enforcement intelligence collection and analysis capabilities. This must also include international law enforcement intelligence sharing agreements and criminal intelligence collection networks—the FBI should serve as an active catalyst in developing global intelligence exchanges with respect to Chinese, Russian, Vietnamese, Japanese, and Muslim criminal organizations and their intentions.

In general, at least one fifth of the national intelligence capability (both classified and open source) should be devoted to law enforcement intelligence, to include support to state and local authorities.

Counterintelligence

This area has been so neglected that it merits special attention here. While the FBI is the proper focal point for counterintelligence, including counterintelligence investigations of U.S. Intelligence Community employees, the FBI has lacked resources, cooperation from the classified intelligence agencies, and a larger mandate and perspective.

Almost one hundred traitors are listed in *Merchants of Treason: America's Secrets for Sale*[37] for the period 1955-1987. At least another ten to twenty have been identified since then to the public. It is the author's judgment that in combination with the temptations of knowledge gained from running drugs and laundering money during the Viet-Nam era, and a very low quality of life that included over 80 bankruptcies of persons holding Top Secret clearances in just one year in Maryland, that roughly 500 or more individuals now serving or recently retired have provided classified information to unauthorized recipients, generally for money but occasionally for revenge.

Perhaps as many as five hundred internal traitors, including both federal employees and defense contractor employees, remain to be caught.[38]

Figure 63: The Counterintelligence Problem

Counterintelligence must be reinstated as the foundation for national security and national competitiveness. Between the two—intelligence and counterintelligence—the latter is more fundamental because it addresses the protection of the intellectual property as well as state secrets upon with the Nation's strategic standing depend. Open source intelligence, and the combined resources of many great minds in our Nation with no access to "secrets", is an acceptable alternative to classified intelligence *in extremis*—there is, however, no substitute and no salvation when the national counterintelligence effort fails.

This is a strong country, and we have "muddled along", spending close to $30 billion a year on collecting secrets and $6 billion a year on gong through the motions of protecting secrets, but we have not come to grips with the opportunity cost of failed counterintelligence nor have we begun to conceptualize the perils of failed counterintelligence in the information age. As

---

[37] (Dell, 1988).

[38] Since there are many secrets that should not be secret, this number excludes those who leak classified information as part of the "little game" that Washington likes to play. This number also excludes internal spies in the U.S. private sector funded by other countries and other corporations—that number is probably on the order of 2,500 to 5,000.

Alvin Toffler has pointed out in many writings and speeches, when information is stolen, as opposed to a physical artifact, the original copy of the information is still in place—absent effective counterintelligence as well as electronic security, we can waste billions of dollars pursuing technical and other paths that have been compromised.

We need a new theory and practice of counterintelligence that takes into account the vital importance of intellectual property in the private sector; the enormous vulnerability of information now stored in unprotected electronic databases; and the emergence of an unlimited "fifth column" of individuals representing aggressive allies, rogue nations, transnational criminal and religious organizations, and sometimes simply themselves.

Below are a just a few precepts for this renewed focus on counterintelligence.

1. **A larger personnel and information management strategy is required.** We cannot resolve the contradictions of intelligence without an over-arching strategy that includes personnel compensation and quality of life guarantees as well as a comprehensive and sensible approach to the management of a reduced universe of electronic and hard copy "secrets".

2. **Electronic tagging of information is the CI counterpart to mapping the earth.** In the information age, counterintelligence is impossible in the absence of an electronic map of the terrain to be protected, and reliable audit trails and other means of following treason in cyberspace.

3. **Private sector counterintelligence is the foundation for national security and national competitiveness.** The financial, communications, power, and transportation nodes are the "heart" of the nation and require a dramatic improvement in security and counterintelligence. The private sector must bear its own burden, but it should not be expected to do so without legislation defining due diligence, and an active leadership role by the Administration and especially the FBI.

4. **Counterintelligence must be global, inter-agency, and cross-functional.** It cannot be treated as a separate discipline, but rather be as pervasive as "administration" or expense accounting; it must cross seamlessly across

agency and government boundaries (federal, state, and local); and it must move easily across the intelligence disciplines while using all disciplines to support its own collection requirements in a secure fashion.

OFFSETTING INCREASES FOR CRITICAL NEW INTELLIGENCE INITIATIVES	PLUS UP/ YEAR
Electronic Security & Counterintelligence Program • *Offsetting increase for funding of FBI's Electronic Security and Counterintelligence Program including national testing & certification laboratory and courtesy inspections and vulnerability testing of tax-paying private sector companies.*	+150M

Figure 64: Electronic Security & Counterintelligence Program

The FBI has two major front-line elements—one chases criminals and one chases traitors. It needs a third new major front-line element that is devoted to protecting U.S. intellectual property world-wide.

Summary

Here is the "twelve-step" program for the 21st Century.

01	Establish a national information strategy with legislation.
02	Create position and staff for Director-General of National Intelligence.
03	Approve elevation of National Intelligence Council.
04	Create University of the Republic
05	Create Global Knowledge Foundation.
06	Assign South-Central Campus (three buildings) to DGNI.
07	Re-focus and empower Director of *Classified* Intelligence.
08	Approve one DDCI and five ADCIs.
09	Convert CIA into the National Intelligence Agency (NIA).
10	Create Clandestine Service Agency (CSA).
11	Create Technical Collection Agency (TCA).
12	Execute proposed program savings and offsetting increases.

Figure 65: "Twelve Steps" for U.S. National Intelligence

Conclusion

This program is essential to our national security and national competitiveness—only in this way can we create a true extended national intelligence community suited to the 21st Century—one that fully integrates classified intelligence, government information, and private sector knowledge into a "virtual intelligence community" with global reach....and the power to excel at global "information peacekeeping" while providing for assured economic and electronic security at home.

Presidential Intelligence

Dear Mr. President,

Now that you have won election as President of the United States of America, you must come to grips with what may well be the most fundamental topic pertinent to your success as our leader. I refer to the need to make America a "Smart Nation", a Nation that can dominate the intellectual high ground of the information age and in this way both preserve its security and also prosper as a community of individuals, tribes, states and commonwealths.

Being in favor of the Internet or information technology is not only inadequate; it is counterproductive if you do not also have a larger National Information Strategy. As Paul Strassmann, former Director of Defense Information and one of America's most able minds likes to note, "Information technology makes bad management worse". Nor is this about budget priorities, for, as Arnie Donahue, the former Director for C4I in the Office of Management and Budget has noted, "There is plenty of money for ... (national intelligence)." This is about concepts, doctrine, and Presidential leadership.

Executive Summary

Intelligence *qua* warning and understanding will be the crux of tomorrow's world-wide struggle for power. Power is shifting from states to groups, from muscle power to brain power. All aspects of the President's role and relationships are being affected, with bureaucracy being among the first casualties of the Internet. National Security and National Competitiveness each require extraordinary new leaps of both understanding and organization.

The President is handicapped by the existing intelligence bureaucracy, and needs to take a strong leadership role in revitalizing and extending the concept of national intelligence in order to harness the distributed intelligence of the business, academic, media and individual experts in the private sector.

269

There is an enormous gap between the people with power in government, and the people with knowledge in the private sector. There are also major "bed-rock" issues pertaining to the basic and continuing education of the population and the family unit that sustains individuals over the course of their lifetime. Fourteen specific intelligence reforms are described here and recommended for inclusion in a Presidential Directive and related legislation.

No President has ever faced such a complex political, economic, social and technical environment. Building upon a newly empowered and extended national intelligence community, Presidential leadership in establishing a Global Intelligence Council and a Global Intelligence Organization is recommended. In addition, a substantive restructuring of the Presidential staff is recommended to integrate national policy making across security, competitiveness and treasury boundaries, and to provide small staff elements for global strategy, national intelligence, and national research in direct support of the President and the President's immediate subordinates.

Only the President has the programmatic and political authority to serve as the leader of a truly *national* intelligence community, and to correct the severe deficiencies existing today within the government's intelligence bureaucracy. *Intelligence is an inherent responsibility of the Commander-in-Chief, and not something that can be delegated to a political appointee or to the bureaucracy.*

PowerShift

Alvin Toffler introduced the term "PowerShift" in 1990. His book can be considered a primer for those who aspire to govern anything in the 21st Century. Here are just a few of his key concepts applicable to you: [1]

- Knowledge is now the most salient aspect of social control and hence the most important foundation for national power. "Knowledge is the crux of tomorrow's world-wide struggle for power."

---

[1] Alvin Toffler, *PowerShift: Knowledge, Wealth and Violence at the Edge of the 21st Century* (Bantam Books, 1990). These points are drawn from an original seven-page book review by (then) 2ndLt Michael J. Castagna, USMC.

- Power is shifting from states to groups, from muscle power to brain power. "The old Second Wave factories needed essentially interchangeable workers. By contrast, Third Wave operations require diverse and continually changing skills...And this turns the entire problem of unemployment upside down." He goes on to note that any strategy for reducing unemployment (and maintaining America's competitive edge) "must depend less on the allocation of wealth and more on the allocation of knowledge."

- Conflicts of the future will revolve around the quest for knowledge. The skirmishes and battles of the future will be decided by who can collect, analyze, and disseminate intelligence most effectively and efficiently.

- The relationships between politicians and bureaucrats, and between people and politicians, will change dramatically. *Bureaucracies will be among the first casualties within the new information environment.* Governments will become more decentralized and rely to a greater extent on private sector and other non-governmental organizations to fulfill traditional government responsibilities.

- The end of the Cold War does not mean the end of violence. If anything, we should look for the cultural "tribalization" of the world. Irrational hate-mongering ideologies will persevere and require different kinds of political-military responses than we are capable of contriving today.

- In order for nations to maintain their strategic edge, an effective intelligence apparatus will be a necessity. In an environment where both the policymaker and the intelligence collectors are being inundated with information, there is a need to revolutionize intelligence—not only will espionage still be in demand, but economic espionage, and counterintelligence against hostile economic espionage, will be boom businesses.

- The privatization of intelligence capabilities, including overhead imagery and signals collection, open source collection, and also the exploitation of advanced processing and dissemination technologies not now common within governments, will dramatically alter and influence government intelligence capabilities.

Challenge of Change

With Toffler's thoughts as an introduction, let us now review five specific aspects of the changing environment for governance that will challenge any President in the 21st Century—in the new millennium.

1. Threat. There are actually four threat "classes" that the President needs to be concerned about, but the President is inheriting a national security community that is moderately able to handle only one of these threat classes, the one that no longer exists: the high-tech brute nation-state intent on conventional or nuclear confrontation. Neither the Department of Defense, nor the Departments of State and Justice, are suitably trained, equipped, and organized to deal with the other three major threat groups that are "exploding in our face" as we start the new millennium: low-tech brutes including terrorists and transnational criminals; high-tech brains that engage in either economic espionage or information terrorism and crime; and low-tech brains that engage in mass cultural warfare, religious zealotry, and more mundane global trade and environmental skirmishing.

2. Players. As outlined above, and also noted in Jessica Matthews' article for *Foreign Affairs* (January-February 1997), the players that Presidents have to contend with to devise and implement policy have changed dramatically from the days of Franklin Deleanor Roosevelt. Governments can not understand, much less mandate outcomes for, the various issue areas without actively engaging non-governmental organizations. This has two implications for national intelligence: first, that we must "target" these organizations as co-equal to traditional state-based ministries; and second, that we must share intelligence with these organizations in the same way that we have shared intelligence with other governments in order to establish consensual understanding.

3. Money. There will be less and less money for government, especially if government at the Federal level persists in wasting its funds on out-of-date and extremely expensive capabilities spanning the range of traditional

government capabilities from warfare to welfare. In this context, you have to make some dramatic—revolutionary—decisions about the realignment of the funds you do have in hand. Two of your priorities must be the dramatic revitalization of the national intelligence community; and the realignment of a substantial—40%—portion of the Department of Defense budget to fund needed changes in new military capabilities as well as diplomatic and overt action overseas, and also counterintelligence and security law enforcement at home and abroad.

4. Knowledge. After the Gulf War Cable News Network (CNN) magnate Ted Turner is reputed to have told President George Bush he would never be shut out of the skies again. Today commercial imagery and remote sensing capabilities are available for a fraction of the cost of the now badly out-of-date classified imagery architecture, and similar gains have been made across all of the disciplines. In fact, the biggest problem today with respect to national intelligence is that it is, as the Aspin/Brown Commission stated so definitively in 1996, "severely deficient" with respect to its access to open sources of information.[2] "The problem with spies is they only know secrets". *The President and key decision-makers will remain desperately ignorant of history and culture, and desperately lacking in current and estimative intelligence support, if we don't fix the severe imbalances in the intelligence community.*

5. Technology. The information technology underlying government operations was largely procured and expensed (on the hardware side) in the 1970's and 1980's, and we continue to spend 80 cents on the dollar to maintain legacy software systems—billions of lines of code—that have been accumulated and are long overdue for modernization. As Stewart Brand of the Global Business Network has told me, the costs of Y2K compliance are "a mere whiff of the carnage to come." Worse, as the ability of the private sector to provide "extranet" options grows rapidly, we continue to invest in hundreds of government-owned and operated "intranet" solutions, while ignoring the fundamentals of data definition standards. The simple fact about information technology investing today is that it should not be driven by hardware and software decisions but rather

---

[2] Commission on the Roles and Capabilities of the United States Intelligence Community, *Preparing for the 21st Century: An Appraisal of the United States Intelligence Community*, 1 March 1996.

by access and data manipulation decisions across multiple national, cultural, and organizational boundaries. There is another related aspect, that of encryption. As the value of data grows, the value of meta-data will grow exponentially. Meta-data will not emerge, and its value will not be harvested, until the transnational private sector has access to the same level of unencumbered encryption that the National Security Agency now provides for Presidential communications. The center of gravity for both national security and national competitiveness is in the private sector, and for this reason a truly Presidential strategy for meeting the challenges of the 21st century would free encryption; forego further major investments in government-owned hardware and software; and use government spending to inspire order of magnitude greater investments by the private sector in "extranet" solutions that allow you to share data securely with other national governments, state and local governments, and non-governmental entities.

National Security & Competitiveness in the 21st Century

The threat has devolved down to the individual level. National Security must still provide for armed conflict between states as the ultimate arbiter of sovereign prerogatives, but as we found in the 1990's, we must allocate resources to, and be ever vigilant with respect to, armed and ruthless brute terrorists and transnational criminals; ethnic, religious and issue groups with global reach; and electronic espionage, electronic terrorism, and electronic theft.

In Chapter 6 I have summarized both the findings of the 9th Annual Strategy Conference sponsored by the Strategic Studies Institute of the Army War College, and also outlined my proposed budgetary realignments for the Department of Defense. I reiterate only the latter here.

To assure National Security in the 21st Century, we must:

- Reduce to 60% of the present DoD budget those funds earmarked for conventional and strategic nuclear warfare, while dramatically increasing the number of (smaller and simpler) naval, aviation, and ground platforms and also increasing the cumulative precision combat power that can be called upon by any individual combatant.

- Apply 20% of the existing DoD budget to Special Operations and Low Intensity Conflict (SOLIC), with one quarter of that amount (5% of the total existing DoD budget) earmarked for military support to Department of Justice transnational crime and economic espionage operations.

- Apply 10% of the existing DoD budget to Department of State operations including a dramatic revitalization of our Peace Corps and the capabilities represented by the Agency for International Development and the U.S. Information Agency. [3] We must also devise new capabilities for engaging in what I have defined as "information peacekeeping,"[4] while also passing legislation to nurture the growing private sector capability to engage in overt actions promoting democracy and capitalism.

- Apply 10% of the existing DoD budget to Department of Justice operations including the creation of a new Federal Bureau of Investigation division dedicated to the protection of U.S. intellectual property and U.S. business contracts world-wide.

Such a restructuring of our National Security program will have substantial positive implications for the Reserve and National Guard, which will have a greater role than ever before in dealing with the three new classes of threat; and for the relationship between the government and the private sector, as the latter will have to undertake measures in its own defense, while also engaging in new information-sharing and counterintelligence coordination activities.

---

[3] Although the U.S. Information Agency has been integrated into the Department of State, this was a mistake, and this book proposes that USIA be restored as an independent foreign affairs agency, reinforced with the transfer from CIA of the Foreign Broadcast Information Service, and henceforth serve as our primary overt collection and dissemination vehicle for public diplomacy.

[4] As discussed in detail in Chapters 9 and 10.

National Competitiveness in the 21ˢᵗ Century requires the President of the United States of America to depart from conventional wisdom and understand that Nations do not "compete" with one another as much as they must strive to "attract" the best and the brightest individuals from all over the world.

To assure National Competitiveness in the 21ˢᵗ Century, we must:

- Forego any more attempts to restrict, encumber or otherwise handicap encryption in the private sector. Legislation should be passed that makes it a crime for any federal agency, explicitly including the National Security Agency, to seek from any private corporation any form of assistance that in any way reduces the effectiveness of the encryption available in the private sector. This is the only way that America can guarantee to the smart individuals of the world that in America, and through the use of American information technology, the fruits of their intellectual labor will be protected. *This is a reverse "brain drain"* _magnet_ *issue that you cannot overlook.*

- Establish a National Information Strategy that provides tax and financial incentives to all publishers who place all of their content online, while making it more and more attractive for individuals to self-publish but still be part of a global indexing system; accelerates standards for sharable software and data, to include legislation that requires Microsoft and all other software producers to stabilize and make public their Application Program Interfaces (API); and provides a legal framework for nurturing the creation of a national "extranet" in which individuals and organizations can store their data remotely with full privacy assurances, while leveraging meta-data visualization and exploitation technologies that are most beneficial when applied to masses of data from multiple parties.

- Undertake a Digital Marshall Plan to bring the rest of the world, and especially the countries of Africa, Latin America, and the underdeveloped portions of Asia, but also including the American underclass that does not own or use computers, into the 21ˢᵗ Century's information environment. Only in this way can America simultaneously set the stage for its *global* information superiority, while also addressing the emerging schisms between information haves and information have-nots.

• Refocus national, state, and local governance on the education of the individual and the sustenance of the nuclear family with two parents who between them have one full-time job (not two) and can provide their children and community with one full-time care giver and community participant. A wiser man than I once said "An educated citizenry is a nation's best defense. *This is the bed-rock foundation for a Smart Nation.*

National Intelligence Redefined

The U.S. Intelligence Community (IC) emerged from the demands of World War II. The Central Intelligence Agency (CIA) grew from the original Office of Strategic Services (OSS), itself a result of a central coordination group that emerged as a response to Pearl Harbor. Over time, as new opportunities and challenges emerged, we found ourselves with a National Reconnaissance Office (NRO), a National Security Agency (NSA), a National Imagery and Mapping Agency (NIMA), and a variety of standing armies for intelligence collection and production at the tactical and theater levels, in the form of uniformed and civilian forces created by the services, and Joint Intelligence Centers at each of eleven Unified & Specified Commands.

Somewhere in the course of creating this vast $30 billion a year community, "intelligence" became synonymous with "secrets". This is understandable, in part because the Cold War caused the IC to focus on one major threat, the Soviet Union, and the bulk of all information about the Soviet Union was classified because the Soviet Union was a "denied area" and all of our information had to be obtained by clandestine human or covert technical means. It is not, however, advisable for the next President to permit this grave misdirection to be perpetuated.

There are two other very undesirable facts of life associated with the growth of the IC.

First, because of our natural American penchant for technical solutions, when the former Soviet Union blocked our attempts to obtain information through human clandestine means, we resorted to technical means and ultimately allocated over 90% of our intelligence spending to technical collection. In fact, we collect so much that we process less than 10% of what we collect....this is very wasteful.

Second, only the CIA remained a relatively independent agency under the direct control of the Director of Central Intelligence (DCI). Everything else became part of the Department of Defense (DoD), and hence relatively unresponsive to guidance from the DCI. Put another way: the DCI continues to lack the programmatic authority necessary to make trade-offs between collection and production, between technical and human, between secrets and non-secrets.

In short, "national intelligence" today is obsessed with secrets, is predominantly about technical collection, and is not under the direct control of the DCI.

Below I provide two alternative definitions, the first of "intelligence" and the second of "national intelligence". As a twenty-five year veteran of the U.S. defense and intelligence community, I feel quite confident that any President, Cabinet Secretary, or CEO will appreciate the following practical real-world definitions:

- Data: the raw image, signal, or text from a primary event.

- Information: the combination of various forms of data into a generic form that is of interest to more than one person and hence suitable for broadcast.

- Intelligence: information that has been deliberately discovered, discriminated, distilled, and delivered to a single specific decision-maker or decision-making group in order to facilitate a serious decision with political, economic, or social consequences.

The IC does not think or act in these terms. The IC today focuses on distinctions between different kinds of secrets and different kinds of *classified* "intelligence" that are really nothing more than classified *information*.

Now let us consider what is meant by "national intelligence". Today the practical understanding of national intelligence would include only those agencies and service elements that are directly focused on the handling of classified information. This would include the national agencies charged with collecting and exploiting secret images (NRO and NIMA), collecting and exploiting secret signals (NSA), and various organizations focused on all-source analysis, including the CIA, the Defense Intelligence Agency (DIA), the Intelligence and Research Bureau (INR) of the Department of State, the four military service intelligence organizations, and—depending on who is doing the definition—the counterintelligence segment of the Federal Bureau of Investigation (FBI), the secret elements of the various Department of Energy laboratories, and a few bits and pieces that are still not visible to the public.

This definition falls woefully short as we prepare to enter the 21st Century, the century of the "knowledge worker" or "gold collar worker".

Consider the following diagram, first developed by myself while driving back with Alvin Toffler from a very disappointing meeting with the most senior defense intelligence leaders, all of whom wanted to stay in their tiny little "military intelligence" box as they understood it.

Policy Intelligence		
Law Enforcement Intelligence	Coalition Intelligence	Military Intelligence
Business Intelligence/Open Source Intelligence/Academic Intelligence		
Mass & Niche Media Intelligence		
Citizen Intelligence—Intelligence "Minuteman"		
Basic, Advanced, Corporate, & Continuing Education		

Figure 66: Elements of a Truly "National" Intelligence Community

The insight that Alvin and I shared that day was that the nature of bureaucracy—the pigeon-hole nature of bureaucracy—had swamped whatever concept of "national intelligence" might have existed over the history of the IC, and that it was time to begin articulating a new vision of national intelligence, one that fully embraced both the needs and the knowledge of the "distributed intelligence" of the Nation.

In the 1990's, when the Cold War ended and Silicon Valley became more important than Wall Street, we witnessed both the death of bureaucracy as the epitome of government power and policy-making, and the ascendance of the Internet and non-governmental organizations. It is now both possible, and necessary, to integrate all of the elements shown in Figure 66 into a new truly national intelligence community.

What Is To Be Done At Home

I have written throughout this book about the need for intelligence reform and in chapter 12 about the specifics of how much money should be cut from what programs in order to create other new programs. My intent here is to list in outline form fourteen specific Presidential decisions that must be integrated into a single Presidential directive as well as supporting legislation— a new National Security Act of 2001 (the language for which is provided in the next chapter).

1. Authority. Establish the position of Director-General of National Intelligence (DGNI) within the Executive Office of the President. Retain the Director of *Classified* Intelligence (DCI) while also establishing a new Director of Public Information (DPI) to coordinate open sources and methods available within the government and from private sector parties. Transfer programmatic authority for all national-level programs now in the defense budget to the DGNI with the DCI as the day-to-day manager of all classified collection and production activities.

2. Collection. Create the Technical Collection Agency (TCA) recommended by the House Permanent Select Committee on Intelligence (HPSCI), and also a new separate Clandestine Service Agency (CSA) that is based outside of Washington and eschews official cover. Establish two collection management authorities: one under the DGNI to determine what requirements should be assigned to classified collection instead of open source collection; and one under the Assistant Director of Classified Intelligence for Collection (ADCI/C) to determine what classified capabilities should be tasked and with what priorities and at what expense.

Implement the recommendation of the Aspin/Brown Commission that requires government agencies to collect their own open source information.

3. Analysis. The President should mandate two fundamental initiatives:
   a. Elevate the National Intelligence Council (NIC) to the Office of the DGNI and expand it to comprise a total of 60 positions, with five new five-person teams responsible for direct support to foreign affairs, military defense, finance & commerce, law & order, and ecology & culture.
   b. Rename the CIA and revitalize it as the new National Intelligence Agency (NIA), with the following six substantial enhancements to its all-source capabilities:
      (1) Provide funding for the immediate hiring of 200 world-class published experts at the mid-career level.
      (2) Provide funding for the immediate hiring of 1,000 world-class published "external associate analysts" to serve as a combination of open source monitors, surge support all-source analysts, and competitive intelligence (Team B) alter egos.
      (3) Integrate half of the National Collection Division (NCD), the Office of Information Resources (including the library and book acquisition divisions), and an external/foreign liaison section into a new Office for Open Sources (OSS) with a substantial increase in financial and personnel resources as well as a priority claim on direct support from the DPI. Transfer FBIS to USIA.
      (4) Restore the Office of Imagery Analysis (OIA) and the National Photographic Intelligence Center (NPIC) to the NIA from NIMA.
      (5) Realign resources from NSA to create an Office of Signals Analysis.
      (6) Realign resources from appropriate organizations to create an Office of Measurements & Signatures Analysis.

4. Open Sources. Without further ado, honor the recommendation of the Aspin/Brown Commission with respect to open sources by earmarking no less than $1 billion dollars a year to the DGNI for execution by the DPI. These funds, to be taken from within the existing totality of the U.S. intelligence budget, comprise less than one half of one percent of what we spend on national defense each year, and will cover the cost of resolving the existing unfunded deficiencies of the policy, acquisition, operations,

281

and intelligence communities for open source information including commercial imagery and Russian military maps of the Third World.

5. <u>Community</u>. We must have a DGNI that can bring together *all* elements of the truly national intelligence community at the same time that we give the DGNI/DCI team statutory authority over funds, training, security standards, research & development, and all forms of external liaison across all elements of the U.S. Intelligence Community.

6. <u>Embassies</u>. We need to keep the spies out of the Embassies; move inter-agency analysis teams into secure spaces within each Embassy, and earmark at least $50 million a year from within the $1 billion a year OSINT budget for the purchase of local knowledge under legal and ethical terms.

7. <u>Peacekeeping</u>. Both the United Nations and the newly expanded North Atlantic Treaty Organization (NATO) as well as the Partners for Peace confront us with requirements for new forms of intelligence—that is to say, intelligence that is not classified but is to the point—as well as new forms of electronic communications and computation that do not require a trillion-dollar legacy "system of systems" to join. We urgently need to develop a global "extranet" that can accommodate multiple levels of security, an infinite variety of constantly changing information-sharing alliances, and a new level of global intelligence burden-sharing on topics that are incontestably important to all: preventing genocide and mass atrocities, trade in women and children and toxic dumping in Africa, to name just three. In partnership with the United Nations and NATO, with a US-UK axis as the foundation, we should immediately fund and manage a prototype "extranet" for intelligence and information sharing at multiple levels of security and in multiple languages, using only web-based tools.

8. <u>Business</u>. The FBI does not have a division dedicated to the protection of intellectual property and the integrity of U.S. business interests. We need such a division, with three arms: one to focus on global counterintelligence in defense of U.S. business contracts and intellectual property; one to focus on infrastructure protection at large to include the integrity of private sector encryption; and one—based on the existing but modest center—to focus on hot pursuit in cyberspace. I would stress, however, that legislation is required to establish standards of "due diligence" for the business sector, which cannot be protected from its own negligence.

9. State & Local. As the Oklahoma City bombing and the recent scare over terrorists already inside our borders and planning for millennium events demonstrate, we need to fully integrate our state & local authorities within our larger national intelligence community. The *process* of intelligence—requirements management, collection management, source discovery and validation, multi-source fusion, compelling presentation—works, and we must transfer this process and related information technologies down to the state & local levels. We must have a seamless national intelligence architecture that reaches from the streets of New York to the jungles of Indo-China, one that does not allow criminals and terrorists to slip between our legal and database "seams". At the same time, we must do more to educate our citizens, including loyal ethnic and religious groups that have adopted America as their home. Today, for example, there is no "hotline" across the Nation for reporting suspicious activities in relation to millennium terrorism—we need one and it must be multi-lingual and culturally sensitive.

10. Encryption. NSA is still seeking to limit private sector encryption and to negotiate secret back doors with major vendors of computing and communications equipment. This dog will not hunt. In the age of information, the center of gravity for both national security and national competitiveness is in the private sector, and it is the integrity of private sector communications and computing that will decide if our Nation remains the foremost global power in the 21st Century. America must be the one place in the world where smart people can develop smart ideas while being fully confident that the fruits of their labor will be protected in our electronic environment. We must not handicap and seek to penetrate our own business software—to do so is to undermine our own national security and national competitiveness.

11. Covert Action. I have found no better observation to cover this area than that found in *The Blond Ghost* by David Corn. Citing Ted Shakley's deputy in Laos, Bill Blair, he quotes him as saying "We spent a lot of money and got a lot of people killed, and we didn't get much for it." Similar comments, sometimes entire books, call into question most of our violent and largely incidental actions in this arena. There is a place for "one on one" covert action, but I believe that all paramilitary capabilities should be transferred to the U.S. Special Operations Command. At the same time, we should significantly improve our clandestine support to this Command as

well as other theater commands, by establishing operational Stations dedicated to each theater and co-located with the theater Headquarters.

12. <u>Overt Action</u>. David Ignatius, writing in *The Washington Post* in the 1980's, got it right: overt action—the kind of action taken every day by Allen Weinstein's Center for Democracy—is the essence of effectively stimulating lasting improvements in political and economic freedom. We need a combined government-private sector program that dramatically enhances our Peace Corps, expands our Agency for International Development, and restores our U.S. Information Agency—and related initiatives—at the same time that we provide tax and other incentives for private sector overt action. We need to do this for one simple reason: good will at the indigenous local level is *the* major ingredient in protecting both our Embassies and U.S. forces deployed overseas.

13. <u>Mission</u>. The U.S. intelligence community culture and its existing leadership appear committed to the idea that their mission is to collect and produce secrets. I disagree. I believe their mission is to inform policy, acquisitions, and operations leadership, and that they cannot do this effectively if they continue to cut themselves off from the history, context, and current intelligence available from open sources. I am also concerned by the counter-part premise on the part of the consumers of intelligence, who have all abdicated their responsibility for collecting and processing open source intelligence because they think—in grave error—that the U.S. intelligence community is going to deliver whatever they need, on time and in a neat package. At the same time, in an era when power is shifting to non-governmental organizations (NGO) and no government can understand—much less mandate—outcomes, without the active cooperation of the NGOs, we need to accept the fact that our mission now is not just to inform our own government, but also our public, foreign leaders and foreign publics, and key NGO leaders and employees. Intelligence—unclassified intelligence—can and should be the heart of the matter when confronting 21st century challenges to global-national-local security as well as prosperity. Spies and secrets are important elements of what we are about, but they are only a means to the end—the *mission* of the national intelligence community, however defined, is to *inform* policy.

14. <u>Pogo</u>. "We have met the enemy and he is us." Only four Presidents have fully appreciated the value and purpose of national intelligence:

Washington, Eisenhower, Kennedy, and Bush.[5] We are abysmally ignorant as a Nation of what it takes to comprehend the pervasive and complex challenges facing us. We are reluctant to accept the fact that it takes time, money, and talent to understand "externalities"—not just the spread of weapons of mass destruction but the vanishing aquifers here at home and the internationally destructive consequences of unchecked culturally-enervating movies and television.[6] We desperately need a President willing and able to serve as the leader of a truly *national* intelligence community. *Intelligence is an inherent function of command, and cannot be relegated to a subordinate.* The best Presidents have been personally and directly involved in the strategic management of national intelligence.

Global Intelligence Burden-Sharing

As a further aid to Presidential decision-making, I believe the time has come to create a Global Intelligence Council (GIC) and a Global Intelligence Organization (GIO).

The Global Intelligence Council should be an international body responsive to the United Nations but not within its authority or budget, responsible for global intelligence policy and global decisions about burden-sharing with respect to open source collection, selected classified collection missions, and burden-sharing with respect to joint intelligence production activities of mutual interest.

The prevention of genocide and mass atrocities, the reduction of trade in women and children, and the elimination of toxic dumping in Africa are all examples of worthy global intelligence projects.

---

[5] As documented in Professor Christopher Andrew, *EYES ONLY: Secret Intelligence and the American Presidency from Washington to Bush* (HarperCollins, 1995) and his personal presentation to my Global Information Forum conference in 1997.

[6] As one who benefited from living in Singapore during several of my formative years, I have a personal appreciation for the benefits of Lew Kuan Yew's leadership. His views on family and culture, as drawn out by Fareed Zakaria in "Culture is Destiny: A Conversation with Lee Kuan Yew", *Foreign Affairs* (March/April 1994) are very provocative and could inspire a confident and open-minded President to explore ways of inviting this globally-respected leader to help the White House address the complex issues of family, education, community, and cultural cohesion that every President must place at the top of their domestic agenda.

This body should be the focal point for orchestrating a matching $1 billion investment from all other nations into open source intelligence collection and production. The U.S. should commit to making the products from its own investments in open sources available to all those who providing matching funds, however modest, with the same expectation.

Under this approach, and with the active participation of each of the theater commanders-in-chief with regional responsibilities, we would immediately implement "Global Coverage" with daily, weekly, and "as required" reporting spanning the full range of countries and topics represented in the Foreign Intelligence Requirements and Capabilities Plan (FIRCAP). This information, drawing on the considerable capabilities of selected private sector organizations such as Dow Jones Interactive, the *Economist* Intelligence Unit, and others, would be accessible by all participating or authorized individuals through the "extranet" that provides for information-sharing at multiple levels of security with an infinite variety of "by name" working groups.

In addition, at some future date after trust and confidence has been gained in the Global Intelligence Council, there should be a Global Intelligence Organization. This should be an affiliated international body responsive to the GIC but never associated with the United Nations, responsible for overseeing, coordinating, and managing joint clandestine and technical endeavors that integrate—often in isolation from one another—covert capabilities made available by participating nations.

At its best, the GIO will create and manage three international Stations—one in Pretoria focused on Africa, one in Santiago focused on Latin America, and one in Canberra focused on Asia. U.S. satellites, indigenous case officers, and combined US-UK-AUS and indigenous analysis teams will focus on those specific issues that are indisputably of common interest: terrorism, counter-proliferation, crime & narcotics, and trade in women and children, to name just four issues of universal concern.

Intelligence as Education

One of the most gripping insights to hit me while attending the conference on "Intelligence and the End of the Cold War", a conference personally led by President George Bush,[7] pertained to the vital role of intelligence as a form of education for policy-makers. At the same time, I realized that we have failed over the years to create a proper framework for educating our own intelligence professionals as well as our policymakers regarding the role and value of intelligence, and also have failed to educate our public to the levels needed to create a truly knowledgeable and national intelligence community across the boundaries shown in Figure 66.

Four educational initiatives come to mind for any President to consider:

1. University of the Republic. We need a place where the emerging and installed leaders of the academic, business, media, non-profit, and government communities can come together to reflect on strategic issues and form "cohorts" that are then more easily able to communicate across organizational and cultural boundaries.

2. Learning to Learn. We need to deconstruct our entire educational approach and restore both the fundamentals of reading, writing, and arithmetic, and also the on-going capabilities of learning to learn and learning to work with information tools at earlier ages.

3. Continuing Education. In combination with advances in medical technology that will dramatically extended life spans and force retirement ages out into the 70's, 80's and eventually the 90's, it is imperative that we establish new modes of dual-tracked education and employment. The draft must be restored to provide a common foundation of service (not necessarily under arms and with domestic community service as an option) and also stabilize our youth, and we must require that all employers, with incentives from all governments, provide for the continuing education of their employees.

4. Community Education. We have lost the ability to teach one another through community service and volunteer activities. The Boy Scouts of

---

[7] This event was co-sponsored by the Bush School at Texas A&M and the Center for the Study of Intelligence at CIA. It took place in College Station, Texas 18-20 November 1999. The author's summary of the event, and thoughts on its meaning, have been published in "Reflections on Intelligence and the End of the Cold War", COLLOQUY (Security Affairs Support Association, December 1999) and are available at www.oss.net/Papers/white/TexasReflections.doc.

America, to take one example, are dying because two-income families are refusing to make the personal investment of time needed to nurture their own children within the character-building architecture offered by the Scouts. We need to get back to the one-income family and to find new ways of permitting both parents to consider part-time work or alternating sabbaticals that yield parent hours to the community and its children.

Presidential Leadership in the Information Age

No previous President has faced such a complex political, economic, social, and technical environment. Without going into all the details, many of which are covered in my paper on presidential leadership and national security policymaking,[8] it is appropriate here to set forth several recommendations regarding the organization of the National Security Council (NSC) staff. Experienced officers are generally agreed that my earlier views on having a Presidential surrogate to serve as Secretary-General for National Security, with super-Cabinet status and oversight over Defense, Justice, and State, are unlikely to be effective because only the President has the necessary *gravitas* as well as the legitimate political power to render judgment at a cross-departmental level. I will therefore focus here only on the suggested enhancements to the Presidential staff.

At the highest level, I have four recommendations:

- Integrate the National Security Council (NSC) and the National Economic Council (NEC) to create a single combined staff, the National Policy (NP) Staff. More on this in a moment.

- Create a co-equal but very small staff section for Global Strategy (GS), much as suggested by David Abshire in his

---

[8] "Presidential Leadership and National Security Policymaking", funded paper for the 10th Army Strategy Conference, April 1999, published on 17 November 1999 www.defensedaily.com/reports/securpolicy1099.htm and also in Word document format at www.oss.net/Papers/white/S99Paper.doc.

book-length discussion of why such a staff is needed at the Presidential level.[9]

- Create a co-equal but very small staff section for National Intelligence (NI), establishing the DGNI position previously recommended, together with the elevated NIC responding directly to the NP and GS staff with whom it will be co-located.

- Create a co-equal but very small staff section for National Research (NR), establishing the position of Director-General for National Research.[10]

The National Policy element is not central to this discussion except as a top consumer, after the President and the Cabinet, of intelligence services. It merits comment, however, that good intelligence is not helpful in the face of bad policy, and bad policy often flows from the way we are organized.

It is no longer prudent to focus the bulk of the President's core staff on "national security" as defined during the Cold War. Indeed, presidential decisions today require enormous finesse and the balancing of national security, national competitiveness, and national treasury issues, *simultaneously and in consonance with one another*.

Hence, for national intelligence to be most effective, I would like to see the National Policy staff divided into three divisions, each with a Deputy Director General for National Policy, and Associate Deputy Director Generals for each of the named areas of Presidential policy interest.

---

[9] David M. Abshire, *Preventing World War III: A Realistic Grand Strategy* (Harper & Row, 1988).

[10] This is not the place for a discussion of America's desperate plight with respect to original scientific research, nor to discuss the very grave deficiencies in how our government funds research. Suffice to say that this is a strategic issue that merits direct Presidential oversight, and that taken together, National Policy, Global Strategy, National Intelligence, and National Research finally give the President the necessary staff focus for actually guiding America into a secure and prosperous future.

National Security	National Competitiveness	National Treasury
High Intensity Conflict	National Education	Entitlements
Low Intensity Conflict	Sustainable Growth	Global Assistance
Environment	Natural Resources	Internal Revenue
Cyber-War	Infrastructure	Electronic Systems

Figure 67: Proposed Structure for the National Policy Staff

Over-All Illustration of a "Smart" Presidential Staff

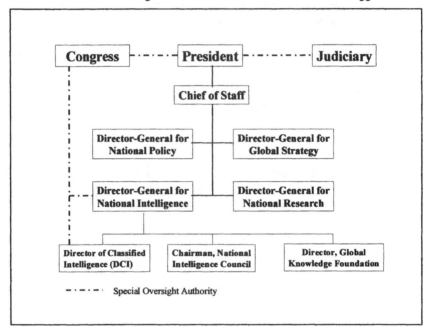

Figure 68: Illustration of Restructured Presidential Staff

"Country desks" and regional responsibilities should remain within the various Departments of government. No single country should merit special handling at the Presidential level.

What I hope will emerge from such a restructuring of the existing staff would be a matrixed policy, planning, and programming process that explicitly coordinates security, competitiveness, and treasury investments in relation to one another, while introducing a structured global strategic thinking capability and substantially improving direct intelligence support to the President.

A situation like Kosovo, for example, would have inspired, several years beforehand, a deliberate calculation of the costs of bombing as well as other *ex post facto* resettlement and rebuilding costs, and would have charted a preventive campaign intended to avoid the genocide and mass atrocities while keeping the cost to the USA modest.

Such a staff approach would place a high value on understanding and utilizing non-military sources of power, while also leveraging the capabilities and contributions of other actors including non-governmental organizations.

The detailed recommendations regarding the Global Strategy and National Research staff elements can be found in the original reference.[11] The details of how a President might improve National Intelligence are all in this book.

There are two other recommendations to make with regard to Presidential leadership in the age of information:

1. Somewhere, perhaps within DoD but even better as an independent element, we must establish an integrated Net Assessments Division and an integrated Operations Division that combine necessary personnel from Defense, Justice, and State so as to effectively oversee both routine programs and crisis response in an integrated manner that is fully responsive to Presidential intent.

2. Somewhere, perhaps within the University of the Republic or the Global Knowledge Foundation, we should place responsibility for nurturing a global as well as a national and state and local program for significantly elevating the quality of academic and corporate and media research and reporting. America has become a "dumb Nation" in many ways, and a revitalized truly *national* intelligence community with a strong educational role and a committed President may well be the fastest way to bootstrap our diverse population into the future.

---

[11] *Supra* note 8.

Summing Up

Intelligence *qua* warning and understanding is the crux of tomorrow's world-wide struggle for power. Power is shifting from states to groups, from muscle power to brain power. The Presidential challenges of the future will all revolve around information. This is changing the relationships between the President and the bureaucracy and between the President and non-governmental organizations. Only four Presidents in our history have understood national intelligence: Washington, Eisenhower, Kennedy, and Bush.

National Intelligence must be redefined away from secrets and toward the more fundamental mission of *informing policy* and most particularly, the President. At the same time, recognizing the growing power of non-governmental organizations, a truly *national* intelligence community must be formed by harnessing the distributed intelligence of the business, academic, media, and individual experts outside of the government.

No President has faced such a complex political, economic, social, and technical environment. Fourteen specific steps related to intelligence and national security are recommended for a new Presidential Directive and enabling legislation needed to revitalize the U.S. national intelligence community. A substantive restructuring of the National Security Council and National Economic Council is recommended, so as to afford the President a National Policy staff that fully integrates national security, national competitiveness, and national treasury calculations; with three additional small staff increments: a Global Strategy staff, a National Intelligence staff, and a National Research staff, all co-located with and in direct support of the National Policy staff and the President. Global leadership initiatives include a Global Intelligence Council, a Global Intelligence Organization, a Global Knowledge Foundation, and a Digital Marshall Plan.

And now we turn to Congress and its authorities in this matter.

National Security Act of 2001

Reform rocks, but only if Congress agrees.

Only the *President* has the programmatic authority to fix the many disconnects and inefficiencies of our existing national intelligence community, and only the President has the political authority to actively solicit from Congress the passage of legislation needed to revitalize the classified national intelligence community while creating the architecture for the "virtual intelligence community" of the future.

Only *Congress* has the power to enact legislation providing statutory authorities and mandates pertinent to intelligence reform and improvements to national security. Congress recognized in the early 1990's that much was amiss and required congressional attention. The National Security Act of 1992 and the Aspin/Brown Commission were two very substantial signs of congressional concern. Both failed to inspire reform.

The National Security Act of 1992, introduced in two variations—one in the Senate as S.2198 by Senator David Boren, Chairman of the Senate Select Committee on Intelligence (SSCI), the other in the House at H.R.4165 by Congressman Dave McCurdy, Chairman of the House Permanent Select Committee on Intelligence (HPSCI), never came to a vote. The Administration—no doubt aided by corporate lobbyists whose companies had much to lose from increased government competence in classified satellite and systems management—provided enough assurances to keep Congress from pressing the point, and then promptly nominated or appointed *five* Directors of Central Intelligence in just over five years.

The Aspin/Brown Commission, one of the compromises made to avoid legislation, served with great honor and intellect for two years, from 1994 to 1996, and reported out a number of very sound recommendations summarized in Chapter 12. None of those recommendations—including the all-important recommendation that the DCI be given the programmatic authority necessary to manage the 85% of the national intelligence community resources now under the Secretary of Defense—have been implemented.

We need a President willing to make national intelligence one of our "top ten" priorities for the 2000-2010 timeframe, and we need a Congress willing and able to devise and enact a National Security Act of 2001.

Since Congress tends to move slowly and draws heavily on its own part records and intentions, this chapter will review both versions of the National Security Act of 1992 as proposed, and then conclude with language for a new National Security Act of 2001 that not only fixes most of the major deficiencies still extant within the U.S. intelligence community, but also creates the architecture for the extended and truly *national* intelligence community.

Director of National Intelligence

In 1992 both intelligence committees agreed that we needed a Director of *National* Intelligence (DNI) with full programmatic authority.

Director of National Intelligence (DNI)
S: Creates separate position from that of Director, Central Intelligence Agency
H: Same

DNI and National Security
S: Makes DNI a non-voting member of the Cabinet
H: Same

DNI and Military Representation
S: Either DNI or Deputy DNI must be active or retired military offices (four stars).
H: DNI may not be an active duty officer

DNI Authority
S: Provides DNI with authority over collection priorities, funds, and personnel throughout the intelligence community.
H: Similar, more pointedly stated.

Figure 69: Congressional Views of DNI in 1992

Although Executive Order 12333 already authorizes the DCI to review and approve National Foreign Intelligence Program (NFIP) reprogramming requests, and to levy tasks and provide guidance, the reality is that only statutory authority over all funds—funds in the base as well as funds in play—can actually empower the DCI or DNI to make *trade-offs* across organizational, disciplinary, and target lines.

There is certainly something to be said to separating the DNI from the position of Director of the Central Intelligence Agency (D/CIA) if—and only if—the DNI actually has the power needed over *all* of the agencies in the intelligence community.

Intelligence Management and Evaluation

Both the Senate and Congress versions of the legislation demonstrated concern over how the community is managed with respect to priorities, requirements, and evaluation.

NFIP Management
S: DNI gets the money rather than the Departments; breaks NFIP out as a separate budget line for authorization and appropriation.
H: Same but requires total budget (not budget detail) to be released as unclassified figure.

Priorities Management & Evaluation Oversight
S: Creates Committee on Foreign Intelligence within National Security Council with NSC principals or deputies as members; responsible for priorities, requirements, and evaluations; includes Commerce.
H: Similar without evaluation function.

Intelligence Evaluation Board
S: Creates independent board under DNI
H: Same

Figure 70: Congressional Views of Community Management in 1992

Congress clearly desires that there be one specific focal point for managing the community. Their proposed solution, however, does not address the fundamental problem with intelligence management today, its concentration on the needs of a quasi-magical "top 100" policymakers. We need a diversified national intelligence capability that is equally nimble and responsive in meeting the needs of the top policymakers; of the thousands of action officer ("desk" officers) who do *not* have codeword clearances and actually do all the work; of the acquisition program managers, both those that decide what to build and those that supervise what is being built; and of operational commanders and their staffs from the national and theater levels, down to the battalions and companies that actually do the fighting and peacekeeping.

The Congressional idea of having customers establish priorities and requirements, and evaluate production, is a good one, but such bodies must have a clear method for ensuring that customers in *every* government agency, at every level of command (strategic, operational, tactical, technical) have a regular as well as an exceptional means for influencing the collection and production of intelligence on their behalf.

The Intelligence Evaluation Board under the DNI is a very good idea and has tremendous potential provided that it is truly independent, understands the theory and practice of program evaluation, and actually carries out its mission across all agencies, disciplines, and target areas. To be credible, the results of the evaluations must be available to all consumer principals— including Department and Service chiefs, theater commanders-in-chief, agency heads, and Ambassadors—as well as Congress, and hence not be classified.

Improving Analysis

Congress was exceptionally thoughtful with respect to the most important weakness of the U.S. Intelligence Community, an area of weakness also stressed by the Aspin/Brown Commission.

The Congressional proposals for analysis in 1992 are all good and need to be reconciled in conference and adopted. They appear on the next page.

Deputy DNI for the Intelligence Community (IC)
S: Creates position, in lieu of existing Director, Intelligence Community Staff
H: Similar, requires Deputy DNI(IC) to be military flag officer

Deputy DNI for Estimates and Analysis (E&A)
S: Creates position to foster inter-agency analysis & estimates capabilities
H: Similar, precludes Deputy DNI(E&A) from being a military officer

National Intelligence Council
S: Provides statutory basis for existence as a collection of senior community advisors
H: Same

Office of Intelligence Analysis
S: Provides for integration of CIA analysts and analysts from other agencies into one office
H: Same

Office of Open Source Information
S: Not addressed
H: Creates a new community-wide office under Deputy DNI(E&A), to procure, coordinate, and disseminate open source intelligence

Office of Warning and Crisis Support
S: Creates new community-wide office under Deputy DNI(IC) to focus on potential threats, identify action options, and provide crisis support to policy-makers
H: Same, without focus on action options

National Intelligence Center "campus"
S: Requires DNI and both Deputy DNIs to sit in same building, to be called the National Intelligence Center
H: Provides for DNI but not Deputies

Figure 71: Congressional Views of Analysis in 1992

There are however two obvious omissions in the legislation that must be mentioned, one dealing with communications and computing, the other with research and development. Both of these areas are in crisis across the government, and especially so within the U.S. intelligence community. Assistant Directors are needed for both arenas, with full control over funds and personnel across agency and service lines.

The system has become the product. This is a simple concept but it is not understood by most intelligence community managers As we move faster and faster toward near-real-time processing of multi-media information, *90% of the information is unclassified and external to the isolated classified systems*, and as our dissemination networks develop parity with the over-capitalized collection networks, two things are going to happen: first, the consumers are going to insist on inter-active access to the databases; and second, the death knell will sound for most hard-copy products. Right now, despite recognized advances in technology, the systems design process and the product planning process are totally divorced; there is no ability to plan multi-media product families; and there is no real integration of system or product planning across agency and disciplinary boundaries.

Each collection discipline today contributes to the fragmentation of the community and continued chaos in its databases for the simple reason that a decade—almost twelve years—after understanding the issue, the community has yet to impose on all collection disciplines the requirement to provide a time and space tag for all raw information *as it is collected*. The Navy does this well with signals intelligence, everyone else is less effective.

At the same time that we provide a geospatial identity for every datum that we collect, there is a second obvious foundation that is needed to permit a true merger of system and product: digital mapping data. A consumer should be able to "fly" or "drive" around the world, zooming in as required. There is no finer intuitive database management structure than that provided by a global map against which all relational databases can be grounded. The EDGE product by Autometric, able to integrate all forms of imagery, photography, and other geospatial data including Russian military maps, is far less valuable to the U.S. government today because both the U.S. Intelligence Community and the U.S. Department of Defense refuse to make the modest investment in procuring the very inexpensive data needed to map the world at the 1:50,000 scale (the tactical scale). As we enter the 21st Century, we still do not have tactical maps or geospatial data for 90% of the world!

Human Intelligence

There are three kinds of human intelligence (HUMINT): clandestine, covert, and overt. The CIA is modestly capable at just one—clandestine HUMINT—and then only when priorities permit the full application of resources, to include sufficient personnel to allow a proper case officer to agent ratio and the full exploitation of tradecraft. There have been significant improvements in the past decade, in both clandestine operations and in covert operations such as were executed in Afghanistan and are now supporting law enforcement in its war on drugs.

There has been a miniscule amount of attention to the need to improve overt capabilities, but the full value of this global resource is generally not appreciated by any community managers, and indeed the resources formerly applied to such extraordinarily valuable projects as the Air Force's collection of overt science & technology literature are being cut down to nothing at the national and service levels.

Congress limited its remedial efforts with respect to HUMINT to the creation of two new executive positions.

Director, Central Intelligence Agency
S: Provides for separate individual in this position while essentially restricting responsibilities to clandestine operations, covert action, and global services of common concern (e.g. secure communications).
H: Same

Assistant Deputy Director of Operations (Military Support)
S: Established new military flag officer position intended to serve as liaison to DoD HUMINT capabilities while extending authority to all HUMINT capabilities in the community.
H: Not addressed.

Figure 72: Congressional Views of Human Intelligence in 1992

Incremental changes in these three vital areas will not be sufficient to prepare us for the challenges of the 21st Century. We must have nothing less than a total "makeover" in each of the three areas.

Direct military augmentation of the CIA's Directorate of Operations, both through long-term assignments of military case officers and also a long-term program to recruit and maintain a cadre of civilian DoD case officers, would be useful.

Since military contingency operations and stay-behind operations do not require the kind of sensitive and on-going tradecraft and reporting requirements that characterize political and economic targeting, there should be much increased utilization of third country "career agents" and ethnic U.S. citizens who might not otherwise be eligible for clandestine assignments.

A much stronger program of mid-career hires and long-term non-official cover "residents" as well as traveling case officers, some with direct action capabilities, must be established. We must do much, much better at maintaining truly clandestine networks that are impervious to curfew restrictions (most Stations stop dead in the water under curfew conditions) and also are responsive to our needs for early warning and pathfinder support to military operations.

Covert HUMINT is a special operations matter most of the time (when paramilitary forces are involved), and requires committed and specially trained military personnel. Given the very genesis of CIA's capability in the original Office of Strategic Services, there is a good case to be made for returning the CIA's paramilitary and psychological warfare capabilities to the U.S. military, and specifically to the Command-in-Chief of the U.S. Special Operations Command (CINCSOC). It would make sense to assign a very senior case officer to serve as his deputy for covert operations, as Chief of Station for a special unit co-located with CINCSOC, and/or as ADDO for Covert Operations, but detailed to CINCSOC.

There are competing views on this matter. One view holds that the real value for the traditional intelligence community is its ability to *take action* and *discreetly* make arrangements for outcomes that are not amenable to public diplomatic overtures. The foundation of discretion is tradecraft, and for this reason it *may* be essential to leave the clandestine and covert services of the CIA under one leader. If so, some sort of Memorandum of Agreement is probably required between CINCSOC and the DCI, one that provides for tradecraft augmentation to special operations forces when required, while keeping the CIA out of the paramilitary business above the squad level.

In any event, we must reinforce the ability of the Department of State to support public diplomacy and overt action by private groups where deemed appropriate. This will be critical to our future success in the "cultural wars" that Bill Lind, among others, has predicted.

300

Overt HUMINT will never be properly handled by people whose culture not only denigrates "unclassified" information, but also devalues and restricts the exploitation and dissemination of what unclassified information they *do* collect by imposing all kinds of handling restrictions associated with *who* collected the overt information rather than *what* the original source was.

The Congressional initiative to integrate management of clandestine HUMINT as well as overt capabilities such as our superb defense attaché system therefore causes concern. Our legitimate overt collectors are starved for resources at the same time that some of them are tempted into indiscretions (*ad hoc* tradecraft) by their frustration with the lack of responsiveness from the CIA to their needs for classified information.

Integrated management of clandestine capabilities, and significant military reinforcement of those capabilities, is called for, but overt capabilities should be under the operational direction of a non-intelligence activity that provides overt collection management and exploitation services across the entire U.S. government.

This is one reason why the House initiative for an Office of Open Source Information is of interest. I would go much further. CIA needs to get its own open source house in order, and should have such an office, but we need something much more comprehensive in nature, such as a Global Knowledge Foundation that is independent of the U.S. intelligence community but able to provide direct open source support to the intelligence community, to the rest of the government, and to the private sector where appropriate in relation to strategic issues of national competitiveness.

Such a capability could be established around the Defense Technical Information Center (DTIC), with DoD as the supporting agent for open source information, and be expanded to include the Foreign Broadcast Service (FBIS) once transferred to the U.S. Information Agency; the National Technical Information Service (NTIS) of the Department of Commerce; the Federal Research Division (FRD) of the Library of Congress, and other selected offices.

This new national consortium, independent of but responsive to the needs of both the intelligence community and the rest of the government, should probably be given its own Program line, just as Congress was moved to create a separate Program for the Special Operations and Low Intensity Conflict arena. Open sources are in precisely the same position as SOLIC once was.

Defense Intelligence

The bills both provide for a separate Assistant Secretary of Defense for Intelligence and finally provide a statutory basis for the military intelligence infrastructure.

Assistant Secretary of Defense for Intelligence
S: Establishes this position to serve as a focal point for accountability; in this way provides for the *de facto* integration of programming and budget oversight functions in relation to national and tactical intelligence activities under the cognizance of the Secretary of Defense.
H: Does not establish position; does require Secretary of Defense to ensure tactical capabilities complement national capabilities, and to establish a Consolidated Defense Intelligence Program (CDIP).

Military Departments
S: Provides statutory basis for intelligence capabilities of the military departments, and distinguishes between the needs of military planners, tactical commanders, acquisition managers, training and doctrine needs, and research & development.
H: Similar

Figure 73: Congressional Views of Defense Intelligence in 1992

Although the Congressional interest in defense intelligence is helpful, there are two related omissions that are of great concern.

First, the bills do not address the urgent need for similar positions of authority over intelligence in the other Departments of government. With the exception of the Departments of State and Energy, the other Departments do not pay due attention to the intelligence function within their own policy and management operations, and this is a serious mistake. In the 21st Century the center of gravity for national security is in the financial and commercial arena—one could add the environmental arena as well—and it is essential that legislation provide a statutory basis for nurturing proper intelligence management authorities across all elements of the U.S. government.

Second, the bills do not address the larger issue of the relationship between overt and internal information and external information and intelligence. Taking the Department of Defense as an example, one can readily see today, as we begin to emphasize "information superiority" as the foundation for victory in future conflicts, that there is a need for an Undersecretary of Information to oversee assistant secretaries for communications and computers, for intelligence, and for information systems as well as internal information management.

This latter oversight is important. The historical differences between the intelligence committees and the armed services or national security committees on the Hill could be strategically diffused if committees responsible for the various departments of government were made full partners in the intelligence restructuring and management process. As we shift from the industrial era to the knowledge era, increased investments in intelligence overall will be necessary and this will only be possible if other Congressional committees are engaged and committed to making their respective spheres of government "smart."

Congress also considered initiatives that would establish a statutory basis for the Defense Intelligence Agency and the National Security Agency, and that would create a new National Imagery Agency—only the latter was actually effected, with the creation of the National Imagery and Mapping Agency, an organization that Congress may dismember at some future date.

Summing up, I would say that Congress has demonstrated its willingness to consider legislation, and that the language that it drafted in 1992 will almost certainly be the starting point for staff drafting the language for a National Security Act of 2001. To this we now turn.

303

107D Congress
1st Session

S. 2001

To amend the National Security Act of 1947 to revitalize and extend the nature of the United States Intelligence Community to provide for improved national security and national competitiveness in the 21st Century.

IN THE SENATE OF THE UNITED STATES

July 4 (legislative day, 1 July), 2001

Mr. Boren introduced the following bill; which was read twice and referred to the Committee on Armed Services, the Committee on Foreign Relations, the Committee on Govenmental Affairs, the Committee on the Judiciary and the Select Committee on Intelligence

---

A BILL

To amend the National Security Act of 1947 to revitalize and extend the

nature of the United States Intelligence Community to provide for

improved national security and national competitiveness in the 21st

Century.

Be it enacted by the Senate and House of Representatives of the

United States of America in Congress assembled,

SECTION 1. SHORT TITLE; TABLE OF CONTENTS.
    (a) SHORT TITLE.—This Act may be cited as the "National Security Act of 2001."
    (b) TABLE OF CONTENTS.—The table of contents for this Act is as follows:

SEC. 2. FINDINGS AND PURPOSES.

(a) FINDINGS.—The Congress makes the following findings:

(1) The principal threat to the United States that prompted the Congress to establish a permanent peacetime intelligence capability at the end of World War II, namely the threat posed to the United States and its allies by the Soviet Union and other Communist States, has now considerably diminished.

(2) At the same time it is clear that the United States is confronted with many diverse and often subtle emerging threats, each requiring new methods and often intense study to understand and deflect.

(3) The existing framework for the conduct of United States intelligence activities, established by the National Security Act of 1947, has evolved largely without changes to the original statutory framework, but rather as a matter of Executive order or directive. In large part this evolution has been prompted by adversity (such as our failure to penetrate the Soviet Union with human sources), advances in technology (offering us the alternative of satellite collection), or incremental "mission creep", rather than reflecting an overall scheme, design, or purpose.

(4) Today, in addition to changing threat circumstances, the United States confronts dramatic changes in the information environment, to wit the "information explosion." Neither the U.S. Intelligence Community as now structured and managed, nor the remainder of the U.S. Government as now structured and managed, is adequate to the task of effectively discovering, discriminating, distilling, and delivering to the appropriate policymakers, acquisition managers, or operational commanders the relevant information necessary for the United States to achieve and maintain information superiority in the 21st Century.

(5) While the Director of Central Intelligence has had an overall coordinating role for United States intelligence activities, under existing law and by Executive Order, in fact, the Director has lacked sufficient authorities to exercise this responsibility effectively, leaving control largely decentralized throughout elements of the intelligence community. Similarly, the Secretary of Defense has historically played a relatively weak role in coordinating intelligence activities within the Department of Defense, while other Departments and Agencies have generally not addressed their intelligence needs from within.

(6) It is apparent that while, on balance, the Intelligence Community has well served United States security interests over the five decades of its existence, it has not, for various reasons including a lack of Presidential interest, performed as well as it might. Civilian and military intelligence are not well integrated; unwarranted duplication remains a problem; severe imbalances exist between investments in technical collection versus technical processing, technical intelligence versus human intelligence, collection versus analysis, and attention to secret sources versus open sources of intelligence.

(b) PURPOSES.—The purposes of this Act are—

(1) to provide a framework for the improved management of United States intelligence activities at all levels and within all intelligence disciplines;

(2) to provide a framework for the improved exploitation of *all* sources of intelligence by establishing the necessary capabilities to fully exploit open sources of intelligence;

(3) to provide an institutional structure that will better ensure that the Intelligence Community serves the needs of the Government as a whole in an effective and timely manner, while also ensuring that individual Government departments and agencies attend to their responsibilities for properly exploiting open sources of intelligence relevant to their mission;

(4) to clarify by law the responsibilities of specific United States Intelligence Community leaders and elements; and

(5) to improve congressional oversight of intelligence activities.

SEC. 3. DEFINITIONS.

The National Security Act of 1947 (50 U.S.C. 401 et seq.) is amended by inserting after section 2 the following new section:

"As used is this Act—

"(1) the term 'commissioned officer of the Armed Forces' does not include a commissioned warrant officer or limited duty officer;

"(2) the term 'Intelligence Community' includes—

"(A) the office of the Director-General of National Intelligence, the office of the Director of Classified Intelligence, the office of the Director of the Global Knowledge Foundation, the office of the Chairman of the National Intelligence Council, the office of the University of the Republic, and the offices of the respective Deputy Directors of Classified Intelligence for Collection Management, Research & Development, and

Counterintelligence (as established under sections 102-105 and sections 201-205 of this Act);

"(B) the National Intelligence Agency (as established by sections 206-214 of this Act);

"(C) the Technical Collection Agency (as established by sections 215-218 of this Act);

"(D) the Clandestine Intelligence Agency (as established by sections 219-221 of this Act);

"(E) the Joint Military Intelligence Program, inclusive of the Defense Intelligence Agency, the Defense Technical Information Center, and all intelligence capabilities within the individual military services and the theater commands (as established or defined by sections 222-228 of this Act);

"(F) the U.S. Information Peacekeeping Fund (as established by sections 306-307 of this Act);

"(G) the intelligence and information collection and processing elements of all other Federal Government departments inclusive especially of all elements assigned overseas and the U.S. Coast Guard;

"(H) on a strictly voluntary basis, all elements of State, Commonwealth, Tribal, Corporate, and Non-Governmental Organizations based in the United States that desire to be in an official information-sharing relationship with the overt liaison elements of the Intelligence Community as defined by this Act.

"(3) the term "intelligence"

"(A) means information deliberately discovered, discriminated, distilled and delivered to a specific policy-maker, acquisition manager, or operational commander, or elements of their supporting staffs, with the specific purpose of supporting a strategic, operational, tactical, or technical decision on behalf of the citizens of the United States of America; and

"(B) is not synonymous with secrets, secrecy, classified information, covert action, espionage, or any other terms traditionally associated with clandestine and covert operations.

Title I—The National Security Council
SUBTITLE A—GENERAL
SEC. 101. ORGANIZATION OF THE NATIONAL SECURITY COUNCIL

Section 101 of the National Security Act of 1947 (50 U.S.C. 402) is amended by adding at the end thereof the following new subsection:

"(h) The National Security Council shall include at all times an Office of the Director-General for National Intelligence, an Office of the Director-General for Global Strategy; and an Office of the Director-General for National Research.

"(i) The Director-Generals of the Offices for National Intelligence, Global Strategy, and National Research (or, in their absence, the Deputy Director-Generals) should, in their roles as principal intelligence, strategy, and research advisors to the President and subject to the direction of the President, participate in meetings of the National Security Council. They shall not be entitled to vote on any policy matter before any Cabinet, Council, or other executive forum."

SEC. 102. ESTABLISHMENT OF A COMMITTEE ON NATIONAL INTELLIGENCE

Section 101 of the National Security Act of 1947 (50 U.S. C. 402) as amended by section 101 of this Act, is further amended by adding at the end thereof the following new subsection:

"(j) (A) There is established within the National Security Council the Committee on National Intelligence (thereafter in this subsection referred to as the 'Committee') that shall be composed of the Directors-General for Intelligence, Global Strategy, and National Research serving in an advisory capacity, the Secretaries of Defense, Justice, State, Treasury, and Commerce, or their respective deputies serving as principals, and such other principal or advisory members as the President may designate.

(B) The President shall designate himself, the Vice President, or any Cabinet principal to serve as the chairman of the Committee, and shall also designate any staff principal within the Executive Office of the President, inclusive of the National Security Council, to serve as Executive Secretary of the Committee.

"(2) The function of the Committee shall be to establish, consistent with the policy and objectives of the President, the overall requirements and priorities for the Intelligence Community within the larger context of the Global Strategy and National Research objectives of the United States and regularly, to assess, on behalf of the President, how effectively the Intelligence Community has performed its responsibilities under this Act."

SUBTITLE B—THE DIRECTOR-GENERAL FOR NATIONAL INTELLIGENCE
SEC. 103. APPOINTMENT OF THE DIRECTOR-GENERAL FOR NATIONAL INTELLIGENCE

There shall be a Director-General for National Intelligence (DGNI) who shall be appointed by the President, by and with the advice and consent of the Senate—

(a)   who shall serve as head of the United States Intelligence Community and shall act as the principal intelligence advisor to the President; and

(b)   who shall exercise direct authority, direction, and control over the following specified agencies (as established by this Act):

> (1)   National Intelligence Agency
> (2)   Technical Collection Agency
> (3)   Clandestine Service Agency
> (4)   National Geospatial Information Agency
> (5)   National Intelligence Council
> (6)   Global Knowledge Foundation
> (7)   University of the Republic

(c) who shall exercise informed influence but not control over the Joint Military Intelligence Program and the general Information Activities of the U.S. Government.

SEC. 104.   RESPONSIBILITIES AND AUTHORITIES OF THE DIRECTOR-GENERAL FOR NATIONAL INTELLIGENCE

At the direction of the President and subject to the requirements established by the Committee on National Intelligence, The Director-General for National Intelligence shall be responsible for providing timely, objective intelligence and counter-intelligence, independent of political considerations or bias and based upon all sources including open sources available to—

(a)   the President

(b)   heads of departments and agencies of the executive branch

(c)   the Chairman of the Joint Chiefs of Staff and senior military commanders

(d)   the Senate and House of Representatives and the appropriate committees thereof

(e)   non-governmental organizations based in the United States or engaged in activities judged essential to the national security of the United States; and

(f)   the people of the United States, so that they may understand the global environment as it affects the security of the United States and requires national policy and strategy decisions intended to assure the security and prosperity of the Nation.

SEC. 105. SUBMISSION OF A SEPARATE BUDGET FOR THE NATIONAL INTELLIGENCE PROGRAM

(a) SUBMISSION OF BUDGET REQUESTS.—Beginning with fiscal year 2002, and for each fiscal year thereafter, the President shall include in any budget request for that fiscal year submitted to the Congress an aggregate amount for the National Foreign Intelligence Program, inclusive of all elements subject to the authority of the Director-General of National Intelligence (as established in section 103 of this Act).

(b) ROLE OF THE DIRECTOR-GENERAL OF NATIONAL INTELLIGENCE.—Any amount authorized to be appropriated, or appropriated, for the National Foreign Intelligence Program shall be considered to be authorized to be appropriated, or appropriated, as the case may be, to the Director-General of National Intelligence, who shall obligate, expend, and allocate such funds within the Intelligence Community in accordance with the appropriate authorization of appropriation Act.

(c) INTERNATIONAL OBLIGATIONS OF THE DIRECTOR-GENERAL OF NATIONAL INTELLIGENCE.—The Director-General of the National Intelligence Program will be the highest appointed official of the United States responsible for intelligence and information matters, and will take precedence over any departmental Chief Information Officers or other knowledge management officers commissioned now or in the future. As such, it will be the responsibility and prerogative of the Director-General of National Intelligence to take such initiatives as may be appropriate, subject to the authority of the President, to establish a Global Intelligence Council or such other international bodies as may be helpful to the furtherance of international information-sharing at the highest strategic levels, or to provide direct support to the United Nations and such other international and regional bodies whose activities are considered to be in the best interests of the United States.

SEC. 106. ELEVATION AND EXPANSION OF THE NATIONAL INTELLIGENCE COUNCIL

(a) The National Intelligence Council shall be elevated to the Office of the President of the United States and shall serve as the senior intelligence body of the government, reporting to and serving at the discretion of the Director-General of National Intelligence.

(b) The National Intelligence Council shall be comprised of no fewer than sixty full-time professionals drawn from any source, and shall be structured to provide the following elements in direct support of the respective government and non-government domains:

(1) Foreign Affairs

    (2) Military Defense

    (3) Transnational Law Enforcement

    (4) Treasury and Commerce

    (5) Culture and Environment

    (c) The National Intelligence Council shall be directed by a Chairman who shall be appointed by the President, by and with the advice and consent of the Senate, seerving concurrently as Deputy Director-General of National Intelligence for Production and who shall have authority, direction, and control, on behalf of the Director-General of National Intelligence, over all production and dissemination matters across all elements of the national intelligence community.

SEC. 107. ESTABLISHMENT OF THE GLOBAL KNOWLEDGE FOUNDATION

    (a) ESTABLISHMENT OF THE GLOBAL KNOWLEDGE FOUNDATION.—A Global Knowledge Foundation is established within the Office of the Director-General of National Intelligence. It shall manage such funds as the Director-General of National Intelligence may allocate, subject to the approval of the President and the consent of Congress, to the procurement and exploitation of open sources of information necessary to fulfill the needs of the National Foreign Intelligence Program.

    (b) ESTABLISHMENT OF DEPUTY DIRECTOR-GENERAL OF NATIONAL INTELLIGENCE FOR GLOBAL KNOWLEDGE.—There shall be within the Office of the Director-General of National Intelligence a Deputy Director-General of National Intelligence for Global Knowledge serving concurrently as the Director for Public Information who shall be appointed by the Director-General of National Intelligence in consultation with the President and Congress.

    (c) RESPONSIBILITIES OF THE DEPUTY DIRECTOR-GENERAL OF NATIONAL INTELLIGENCE FOR GLOBAL KNOWLEDGE. The Deputy Director-General of National Intelligence for Global Knowledge shall serve as the principal liaison of the Director-General for National Intelligence to all overt, legal, and ethical organizations, both in the United States and in other countries, to include both governmental and non-governmental organizations as well as independent individuals, that can offer the United States, under overt, legal, and ethical terms, for free or for fee, useful knowledge.

SEC. 108. ESTABLISHMENT OF THE UNIVERSITY OF THE REPUBLIC

    (a) ESTABLISHMENT OF THE UNIVERSITY OF THE REPUBLIC.—A University of the Republic is established within the Office of the Director-General of National Intelligence. It shall serve as the coordinating body for a distributed program (i.e. without requiring the establishment of a campus or other permanent facilities) whose purpose shall be to bring together selected mid-career and senior managers from across all walks of American life.

(b) PURPOSE OF THE UNIVERSITY OF THE REPUBLIC.—The intent of this program is to create no less than one annual class of graduates, each of whom understands and values the role of intelligence in assuring national security and national competitiveness, and who, by virtue of their participation in this program, henceforth will serve as points of contact for the improved sharing of information across organizational boundaries.

(c) ESTABLISHMENT OF PRESIDENT OF THE UNIVERSITY OF THE REPUBLIC.—There shall be within the Office of the Director-General of National Intelligence a President of the University of the Republic who shall be appointed by the Director-General of National Intelligence in consultation with the President and Congress.

(d) RESPONSIBILITIES OF THE PRESIDENT OF THE UNIVERSITY OF THE REPUBLIC.—The President of the University of the Republic shall serve as the principal liaison of the Director-General for National Intelligence to all overt, legal, and ethical organizations in the United States, and to independent individuals, that are deemed eligible for participation, under overt, legal, and ethical terms, to participate in the program of the University of the Republic.

SUBTITLE C—THE DIRECTOR-GENERAL FOR GLOBAL STRATEGY

SEC. 109. APPOINTMENT OF THE DIRECTOR-GENERAL FOR GLOBAL STRATEGY

There shall be a Director-General for Global Strategy (DGGS) who shall be appointed by the President, by and with the advice and consent of the Senate—

(a) who shall serve as head of the Office of Global Strategy and shall act as the principal advisor on strategy to the President; and

(c) who shall be responsible for coordinating annual strategic reviews of each major department and agency of the U.S. Government such that an integrated unclassified report, *Global Strategy of the United States of America*, will be delivered to Congress no less than 30 working days prior to the State of the Union address to Congress by the President.

SEC. 110. ORGANIZATION OF THE OFFICE FOR GLOBAL STRATEGY

The Office for Global Strategy shall include—

(a) Under the direction of a Deputy Director for Global Strategy, Associate Directors for each of the following:

(1) Strategic Council

315

  (2) Special Projects
  (3) Global Reserve
  (4) Leadership Retreats

`(b) Under the direction of a Deputy Director for Response Management, Associate Directors for each of the following:

  (1) Response Center
  (2) Non-State Actors
  (3) Civilian Reserve
  (4) Public Liaison

Subtitle D—The Director-General for National Research

SEC. 111. APPOINTMENT OF THE DIRECTOR-GENERAL FOR NATIONAL RESEARCH

There shall be a Director-General for National Research (DGNR) who shall be appointed by the President, by and with the advice and consent of the Senate—

(a) who shall serve as head of the Office of National Research within the National Security Council and shall act as the principal advisor on national research to the President; and

(c) who shall be responsible for coordinating annual research program reviews of each major department and agency of the U.S. Government such that an integrated unclassified report, *National Research Program of the United States of America,* will be delivered to Congress no less than 30 working days prior to the State of the Union address to Congress by the President.

SEC. 112. ORGANIZATION OF THE OFFICE FOR NATIONAL RESEARCH

The Office for National Research shall include—

(a) Under the direction of a Deputy Director for Structured Research, Associate Directors for each of the following:

  (1) Classified Research
  (2) Contracted Government Research
  (3) National Laboratories
  (4) Space and Oceanic Research

`(b) Under the direction of a Deputy Director for Distributed Research, Associate Directors for each of the following:

  (1) National Science
  (2) High Performance Computing
  (3) Human Genome and Medical Research
  (4) Research on Educational and Cultural Advancement

TITLE II—INTELLIGENCE ACTIVITIES OF THE U.S. GOVERNMENT

Subtitle A—The Director of Classified Intelligence

SEC. 201. APPOINTMENT OF THE DIRECTOR OF CLASSIFIED INTELLIGENCE

(a) REDESIGNATION OF THE POSITION OF DIRECTOR OF CENTRAL INTELLIGENCE.—The Director of Central Intelligence is hereby redesignated the Director of Classified Intelligence.

(1) Any reference to the Director of Central Intelligence in any Federal law, Executive order, rule, regulation, or delegation of authority, or any document of or pertaining to the Central Intelligence Agency, shall be deemed to refer to the Director of Classified Intelligence unless and except if the Director-General of National Intelligence identifies the law, order, rule, regulation or document as being applicable to that office, in which case it shall be.

(2) There shall be a Director of Classified Intelligence (DCI) who shall be appointed by the President, by and with the advice and consent of the Senate—

(a) who shall serve as head of the United States Classified Intelligence Community, subordinate to the authority of the Director-General of National Intelligence; and

(b) who shall exercise authority, direction, and control, subject to the authority of the Director-General of National Intelligence, over the following specified agencies (as established by this Act):

(1) National Intelligence Agency
(2) Technical Collection Agency
(3) Clandestine Services Agency
(4) National Geospatial Information Agency

(c) who shall, subject the authority of the Director-General for National Intelligence, exercise informed influence but not control over the Joint Military Intelligence Service.

SEC. 202. RESPONSIBILITIES AND AUTHORITIES OF THE DIRECTOR OF CLASSIFIED INTELLIGENCE

(a) At the direction of the President and subject to the requirements established by the Committee on National Intelligence and managed by the Director-General of National Intelligence, the Director of Classified Intelligence shall be responsible for collecting, processing, and disseminating classified information vital to the national security and competitiveness of the United States. In the execution of this office the Director of Classified

Intelligence will be expected to strictly limit the collection of classified information, and classified activities outside the United States, to those that the President and the Committee on National Intelligence have explicitly validated as both unsuited for overt collection, and also vital to the national security and competitiveness of the United States.

(b) The Director of Classified Intelligence, with the advice and consent of the Deputy-Director of National Intelligence and after consultation with the Committee on National Intelligence, the Joint Chiefs of Staff, and the Chairmen and Minority Leaders of appropriate Congressional committees, will appoint the agency heads and deputies of all four elements of the classified intelligence community, and will have veto authority over the appointment of all Senior Executive Service and office director positions within these four agencies.

SEC. 203. APPOINTMENT OF THE ASSISTANT DIRECTOR OF CLASSIFIED INTELLIGENCE FOR ADMINISTRATION

To assist the Director of Classified Intelligence in carrying out his responsibilities under this Act, there shall be appointed by the President, by and with the advice and consent of the Senate, an Assistant Director of Classified Intelligence for Administration who shall have authority, direction, and control over all personnel, security, financial, information technology, and training matters across all elements of the four agencies comprising the classification intelligence community.

SEC. 204. APPOINTMENT OF THE ASSISTANT DIRECTOR OF CLASSIFIED INTELLIGENCE FOR COLLECTION MANAGEMENT

To assist the Director of Classified Intelligence in carrying out his responsibilities under this Act, there shall be appointed by the President, by and with the advice and consent of the Senate, an Assistant Director of Classified Intelligence for Collection Management who shall have authority, direction, and control over collection priorities and resources across all elements of the four agencies comprising the classification intelligence community.

SEC. 205. APPOINTMENT OF THE ASSISTANT DIRECTOR OF CLASSIFIED INTELLIGENCE FOR RESEARCH & DEVELOPMENT

To assist the Director of Classified Intelligence in carrying out his responsibilities under this Act, there shall be appointed by the President, by and with the advice and consent of the Senate, an Assistant Director of Classified Intelligence for Research & Development who shall have authority, direction, and control over research & development programs across all elements of the four agencies comprising the classification intelligence community.

SEC. 206. APPOINTMENT OF THE ASSISTANT DIRECTOR OF CLASSIFIED INTELLIGENCE FOR COUNTERINTELLIGENCE

To assist the Director of Classified Intelligence in carrying out his responsibilities under this Act, there shall be appointed by the President, by and with the advice and consent of the Senate, an Assistant Director of Classified Intelligence for Counterintelligence who shall have authority, direction, and control over all counterintelligence matters across all elements of the four agencies comprising the classification intelligence community.

Subtitle B—The National Intelligence Agency

SEC. 207. APPOINTMENT OF THE DIRECTOR, NATIONAL INTELLIGENCE AGENCY

There shall be a Director of the National Intelligence Agency (NIA), who shall be appointed by the Director of Classified Intelligence with the advice and consent of the Director-General of National Intelligence and after consultation with the Committee on National Intelligence, the Joint Chiefs of Staff, and the Chairmen and Minority Leaders of appropriate Congressional committees. Subject to the authority, direction and control of the Director of Classified Intelligence, with additional oversight and tasking authority from the Deputy Director-General of National Intelligence for Production, the Director of the National Intelligence Agency, serving concurrently as the Assistant Director of Central Intelligence for Production shall be responsible for:

(a) In partnership with the Deputy Director of Classified Intelligence for Collection Management, establishing classified collection requirements responsive to the priorities of the Committee on National Intelligence, the Director-General for National Intelligence, and individual elements of the U.S. government and such private sector activities as warrant classified intelligence and counterintelligence support;

(b) In partnership with the Deputy Director of Classified Intelligence for Collection Management, establishing procedures for guiding and evaluating collection resources created and maintained by the Technical Collection Agency and the Clandestine Services Agency as well as the Global Knowledge Foundation.

(c) In partnership with the Deputy Director of Classified Intelligence for Administration, establishing integrated multi-media and multi-level security information processing capabilities able to both exploit all forms of collected information in unison, to include the on-going definition of and enhancement of a generic all-source workstation toolkit intended to serve as both the government and private sector standard for establishing "information superiority" across all governmental and non-governmental organizations that wish to emulate the standards established by the National Intelligence Agency.

(d) In partnership with the Deputy Director of Classified Intelligence for Research & Development, and in close coordination with the Director-General for National Research, establishing a process for leveraging and influencing private sector research & development activities in the information domains to include cognitive science, cultural and social network theory, and such other humanities, social science, and technical science areas as might contribute to the ability of the United States as a whole to become a "Smart Nation" representative of the highest standards of nation-wide education and continuous learning across all walks of life.

SEC. 208. RENAMING AND REALIGNMENT OF ELEMENTS OF THE CENTRAL INTELLIGENCE AGENCY

(a) The Central Intelligence Agency shall be renamed the National Intelligence Agency, and this organization shall retain control over all personal, equipment, facilities, and other resources now comprising the Central Intelligence Agency, except as noted in section 208(b) and 208(c) below.

(b). Within 90 days of the effective date of this Act as set forth in section 601, the Directorate of Operations is transferred in its entirety to the Clandestine Service Agency as established by section Subtitle D below, except that

(1) the Office of Medical Services is to be completely disbanded within 180 days from the effective date of this Act as set forth in section 601, with the proviso that all of its records are to be examined by the Office of the Inspector General of the National Intelligence Agency, and an unclassified report on any inappropriate practices against U.S. government employees, U.S. citizens, or foreign nationals is to be submitted to Congress within 360 days from the effective date of this Act as set forth in section 601; and

(2) all paramilitary and covert action elements of the Directorate of Operations, both active and reserve, to include all files, are to be transferred to the Commander-in-Chief, U.S. Special Operations Command, within 90 days from the effective date of this Act as set forth in section 601; and

(3) one half of the Division now responsible for national and domestic intelligence liaison shall be retained and integrated into the new Office of Open Source Support as established in section 213.

(c) The Foreign Broadcast Information Service is transferred in its entirety to the U.S. Information Agency as restored by subtitle D.

SEC. 209. REVITALIZATION AND EXPANSION OF THE ANALYSIS CADRE

The Director of the National Intelligence Agency is immediately authorized to hire 200 additional mid-career analysts and 1,000 external adjunct analysts, with funds to be provided by the Director of Classified Intelligence through immediate realignments from whatever elements of the four agencies he might desire to draw upon. In executing this urgent mandate the Director of the National Intelligence Agency is exempted from all existing restrictions on ranks, grades, and salaries, with the proviso that a plan for the revitalization and expansion of the analysis cadre shall be submitted to Congress via the Office of Management and Budget within 90 days from the effective date of this Act as set forth in section 601. The Director of the National Intelligence Agency is required to establish high standards of language and foreign area competency, peer-reviewed publication, and global networking abilities for all new analyst hires, and shall provide to the Director of Classified Intelligence, to the Director-General of National Intelligence, and to the oversight committees of Congress, a monthly report on the composition and competency of the National Intelligence Agency analyst population henceforth and without future relief.

SEC. 210. ESTABLISHMENT OF THE INTERNATIONAL INTELLIGENCE RESERVE

In addition to the 1,000 external adjunct analysts authorized in section 209, the Director of the National Intelligence Agency is directed to establish an international intelligence reserve program in cooperation with the Director of the Global Knowledge Foundation and all governmental and non-governmental organizations desiring to work together toward the establishment of an international intelligence network with established centers of excellence for all topical areas of interest to the National Intelligence Agency.

SEC. 211. RE-ESTABLISHMENT OF THE OFFICE OF IMAGERY ANALYSIS

The Office of Imagery Analysis is re-established, and all elements of the National Imagery and Mapping Agency previously transferred from the Central Intelligence Agency, or subsequently augmented, are to be restored to the National Intelligence Agency within 90 days from the effective data of this Act as set forth in section 601.

SEC. 212. ESTABLISHMENT OF THE OFFICE OF SIGNALS ANALYSIS

The Office of Signals Analysis is established, and the Director of the National Security Agency is directed to transfer within 90 days from the effective date of this Act as set forth in section 601 no fewer than one third of all assigned signals intelligence personnel with all their equipment and facilities, to the operational control of the Director of the National Intelligence Agency, prior to the decommissioning of the National Security Agency and the establishment of the Technical Collection Agency as set forth in Subtitle C.

SEC. 213. ESTABLISHMENT OF THE OFFICE OF MEASUREMENTS AND SIGNATURES ANALYSIS

The Office of Measurements and Signals Analysis is hereby established. All existing offices and capabilities for the management and analysis of measurements and signals intelligence are to be integrated into this new Office within 90 days from the effective date of this Act as set forth in section 601. The remaining capabilities, those associated with direct collection, will be reassigned by the Director of Classified Intelligence to the Technical Collection Agency or the Clandestine Services Agency, at his discretion, within 90 days from the effective date of this Act as set forth in section 601.

SEC. 214. ESTABLISHMENT OF THE OFFICE FOR OPEN SOURCE S

(a) The Office for Open Sources is established from existing resources within the former Central Intelligence Agency. This Office will bring together the following existing elements:

        (1) Central Library and Reference Service

        (2) Map Service

        (3) National Collection Division (one half)

(b) Within the Office for Open Sources a Center for Open Source Support is established. The Director of the National Intelligence Agency will provide 25 positions, all exempt from existing hiring constraints and open to anyone eligible for a clearance, to staff this Center fully within 180 days from the effective date of this Act as set forth in section 601. Individuals assigned to this Center must demonstrate deep competency in discovering, evaluating, and processing external open sources, software, and services, inclusive of commercial imagery and Russian military maps, such as is not now available within the U.S. Intelligence Community. The composition and competency of all personnel assigned to this Center will be included as an attachment to the report on analyst composition and competency as required in section 209, henceforth and without future relief.

Subtitle C—The Technical Collection Agency

SEC. 215. APPOINTMENT OF THE DIRECTOR, TECHNICAL COLLECTION AGENCY

There shall be a Director of the Technical Collection Agency (TCA), who shall be appointed by the Director of Classified Intelligence with the advice and consent of the Director-General of National Intelligence and after consultation with the Committee on National Intelligence, the Joint Chiefs of Staff, and the Chairmen and Minority Leaders of appropriate Congressional committees. Subject to the authority, direction and control of the Director of Classified Intelligence, with additional oversight and tasking authority from the Deputy Director-General of National Intelligence for Production, the Director of the Technical Collection Agency shall be responsible for:

(a)   Under the oversight of the Assistant Director of Classified Intelligence for Collection Management, establishing classified collection capabilities responsive to the priorities of the Committee on National Intelligence, the Director-General for National Intelligence, and individual elements of the U.S. government and such private sector activities as warrant classified intelligence and counterintelligence support, as further defined by the National Intelligence Agency;

(b) Under the oversight of the Assistant Director of Classified Intelligence for Administration, establishing integrated multi-media and multi-level security information processing capabilities able to process all forms of collected information in unison, to include developing new methods for assigning both geospatial and time of information attributes to all information collected by technical information.

(c) Under the oversight of the Assistant Director of Classified Intelligence for Research & Development, and in close coordination with the Director-General for National Research and the Director of the National Intelligence Agency, establish a process for leveraging and influencing private sector research & development activities in the information technology arena, balancing carefully between collection technology and exploitation technology.

SEC. 216. DECOMMISSIONING OF THE NATIONAL RECONNAISSANCE OFFICE

The National Reconnaissance Office is decommissioned and all of its personnel, equipment, facilities, and resources integrated into the Technical Collection Agency, effective from the date of this Act as set forth in section 601.

SEC. 217. DECOMMISSIONING OF THE NATIONAL SECURITY AGENCY

The National Security Agency is decommissioned and all of its personnel, equipment, facilities, and resources integrated into the Technical Collection Agency, effective from the date of this Act as set forth in section 601.

Subtitle D—The Clandestine Service Agency

SEC. 218. APPOINTMENT OF THE DIRECTOR, CLANDESTINE SERVICE AGENCY

There shall be a Director of the Clandestine Service Agency (CSA), who shall be appointed by the Director of Classified Intelligence with the advice and consent of the Director-General of National Intelligence and after consultation with the Committee on National Intelligence, the Joint Chiefs of Staff, and the Chairmen and Minority Leaders of appropriate Congressional committees. Subject to the authority, direction and control of the Director of

Classified Intelligence, with additional oversight and tasking authority from the Deputy Director-General of National Intelligence for Production, the Director of the Clandestine Service Agency shall be responsible for:

(a)   Under the oversight of the Assistant Director of Classified Intelligence for Collection Management, establishing classified collection capabilities responsive to the priorities of the Committee on National Intelligence, the Director-General for National Intelligence, and individual elements of the U.S. government and such private sector activities as warrant classified intelligence and counterintelligence support;

(c)   Under the oversight of the Assistant Director of Classified Intelligence for Administration, establishing integrated multi-media and multi-level security information processing capabilities able to both exploit all forms of collected human information in unison, to include the information available from open sources as provided by Global Knowledge Foundation via the Office for Open Sources.

(d)   Under the oversight of the Assistant Director of Classified Intelligence for Research & Development, and in close coordination with the Director-General for National Research, and the Directors of the National Intelligence Agency and the Technical Collection Agency, establishing a process for leveraging and influencing private sector research & development activities pertinent to clandestine activities and technical collection activities requiring clandestine human intelligence support.

SEC. 219. REASSIGNMENT AND RETIREMENT PROGRAM FOR EXISTING CLANDESTINE PERSONNEL

All existing clandestine personnel including all entry-level personnel now undergoing training, and all existing non-official cover personnel, are presumed to be compromised.   Beginning immediately the Director of the Clandestine Services Agency will establish a three-part program to reassign and retire all existing clandestine personnel including entry-level personnel now undergoing training and all existing non-official cover personnel. The Director of Classified Intelligence will provide all necessary supplemental funding to:

(a) Retire all personnel eligible for retirement within five years from the effective date of this Act as set forth in section 601.   There will be no exceptions.   Retired personnel will be free to apply for any position in government without losing retirement pay if they are selected.

(b) Reassign to the Department of State all liaison officers, reports officers, communications officers, and such other personnel as could reasonably enhance the ability of the Department of State to conduct its mission overseas, to include official liaison with all foreign intelligence services.

Equipment and space in U.S. Embassies overseas will be turned over to the Department of State within 90 days from the effective date of this Act as set forth in section 601. Funds for salaries and related expenses will be reallocated from the Central Intelligence Agency to the Department of State at the same time.

(c) Retrain all remaining personnel for no less than one month and no more than twelve months each, to qualify them to compete for and serve in any appropriate Washington area, U.S. based, or overt foreign position sponsored by the U.S. government, or in position in a non-governmental organizations or in an entrepreneurial position as a founder of a small business. Within two years from the effective date of this Act as set forth in section 601, all remaining personnel will have either been reassigned to a non-clandestine position elsewhere in the U.S. government, with no transfer of funds, or will have resigned voluntarily with whatever financial incentives the Director of Classified Intelligence finds necessary to accomplish this mandated action.

SEC. 220. ESTABLISHMENT OF THE NEW CLANDESTINE PROGRAM

The Director of the Clandestine Intelligence Agency will, within 180 days from the effective date of this Act as set forth in section 601, establish a new non-official cover cadre distributed around the world and having absolutely no contact with any prior clandestine service personnel in the field or in Washington, D.C. Existing training facilities may be used provided that all personnel are flown or driven in and out from varied locations and using appropriate tradecraft. All funds previously allocated to the Directorate of Operations, including half of the Director of Classified Intelligence's Reserve Fund, will comprise the starting budget for the new Clandestine Service Agency.

Subtitle E—National Geospatial Information Agency
SEC. 221. APPOINTMENT OF THE DIRECTOR, NATIONAL GEOSPATIAL INFORMATION AGENCY

There shall be a Director of the National Geospatial Information Agency (NGA), who shall be appointed by the Director of Classified Intelligence with the advice and consent of the Director-General of National Intelligence and after consultation with the Committee on National Intelligence, the Joint Chiefs of Staff, and the Chairmen and Minority Leaders of appropriate Congressional committees. Subject to the authority, direction and control of the Director of Classified Intelligence, with additional oversight and tasking authority from the Deputy Director-General of National Intelligence for Production, the Director of the National Geospatial Agency shall be responsible for:

(a)   Establishing a geospatial database for the entire world at the 1:50,000 tactical level, inclusive of contour lines and all relevant features, within five years from the effective date of this Act as set forth in section 601.

(b)   Establishing a remote printing process capable of producing 250 color-copies suitable for tactical combat use, of any ten standard-sized 1:50,000 map sheets within any single 24 hour period.

(c)   Establishing a web-based process permitting any individual or organization to voluntarily enter the Global Positioning System (GPS) coordinates for their government, corporate, non-governmental, or personal structure into a database available directly to the U.S. and allied governments, and available indirectly to any government or non-governmental organization in segments approved for release by the Director-General of National Intelligence.

(d)   Establishing a process for validating Global Positioning System coordinates submitted into the database.

(e)   Establishing a technology transfer and information-sharing program with qualified U.S. enterprises engaged in all-source geospatial processing activities, such that the bulk of available international geospatial data can be made available to anyone through commercial procurement.

SEC. 222.   INTERNATIONAL OBLIGATIONS OF THE NATIONAL GEOSPATIAL INFORMATION AGENCY

The National Geospatial Agency will be primarily responsible for assuring that all needed foreign geospatial data is available to U.S. defense, law enforcement, diplomatic, and commercial authorities. It will, however, also be responsible for establishing a program that is responsive to the geospatial and mapping needs of all countries of the world and those non-governmental organizations that have multi-national peacekeeping and foreign assistance responsibilities. In acquiring geospatial information from commercial sources, the National Geospatial Agency will ensure that licensing agreements include third parties to whom the National Geospatial Agency might wish to render geospatial and mapping support in accordance with this Act.

SEC. 223.   DECOMMISSIONING OF THE NATIONAL IMAGERY AND MAPPING AGENCY

The National Imagery and Mapping Agency is decommissioned and all of its personnel, equipment, facilities, and resources integrated into the National Geospatial Agency, less that portion transferred to the National Intelligence Agency under section 211 of this Act, effective from the date of this Act as set forth in section 601.

Subtitle F—The Joint Military Intelligence Program

SEC. 224. APPOINTMENT OF THE DIRECTOR FOR JOINT MILITARY
INTELLIGENCE

There shall be a Director for Joint Military Intelligence who shall be appointed by the Secretary of Defense with the advice and consent of the Chairman of the Joint Chiefs of Staff and the Director-General of National Intelligence, and after consultation with the Committee on National Intelligence, the Chiefs of the Services, the theater Commanders in Chief, and the Chairmen and Minority Leaders of appropriate Congressional committees. The position of the Director shall be of sufficient importance and responsibility to warrant the assignment of a full general or admiral from among commissioned officers on the active-duty list or on the retired list with a date of retirement not more than three years prior to their date of appointment. Subject to the influence but not the authority, direction and control of the Director-General of National Intelligence, the Director of the Joint Military Intelligence Service shall be responsible for:

(a) Establishing a program of internal intelligence support for all Department of Defense elements such that the following distinct consumers of intelligence each receive appropriate on-going intelligence:

(1) defense policymakers

(2) theater commanders

(3) tactical military commanders

(4) service chiefs and acquisition managers

(5) coalition and non-governmental partners

(b) Establishing a joint military intelligence service that will integrate all existing personnel, equipment, facilities, and funds now managed by the individual military services and the theater commanders, together with the full integration of all personnel now serving or assigned to the Defense Technical Information Center (DTIC) and the Defense Intelligence Agency (DIA), except that uniformed personnel whose primary military occupational specialty is not intelligence may elect to return to their parent service for reassignment.

(c) Establishing a process for ensuring that all military weapons, mobility, and communications systems are developed and procured with full attention to the diversity of the threat and the geospatial realities of the warfighting and peacekeeping environment, while also being designed, procured and utilized so as to take full advantage of all available information and intelligence during all phases of their operation.

(d) To assist the Director of the Joint Military Intelligence Service in performing his duties and fulfilling his responsibilities, there shall be one

Deputy Director and four Assistant Directors for Joint Military Intelligence each of whom should be at least a Brigadier General or Rear Admiral or civilian equivalent, provided that at least three of the Deputies are uniformed officers from the active duty list or on the retired list with a date of retirement not more than three years prior to their date of appointment.

(1) Deputy Director for Joint Military Intelligence

(2) Assistant Director for Joint Military Intelligence Analysis, double-hatted as the Director, Defense Intelligence Agency;

(3) Assistant Director for Joint Military Intelligence Operations, who shall be double-hatted as the Director of the existing Joint Military Intelligence Program and be responsible for day to day oversight of the Service and Theater intelligence centers;

(4) Assistant Director for Joint Military Intelligence Collection, who shall be responsible for representing the needs of the military to the Director of the Technical Collection Agency, the Director of the Clandestine Service Agency, and the Director of the Global Knowledge Foundation, while also providing day to day oversight of the Defense Attache Program, the Defense Airborne Reconnaissance Program; the Defense Signals Intelligence Program; and such other defense collection activities are managed and staffed predominantly by uniformed military personnel;

(5) Assistant Director for Joint Military Intelligence Administration, who shall be responsible for the administration of the Joint Military Intelligence Service and for all financial, training, facilities, communications, and related administrative matters.

SEC. 226. DECOMMISSIONING OF THE DEFENSE TECHNICAL INFORMATION CENTER

The Defense Technical Information Center shall be fully integrated into the Defense Intelligence Agency within 180 days from the effective date of this Act as set forth in section 601, and shall then be decommissioned.

SEC. 227. INTEGRATION OF THE SERVICE AND THEATER INTELLIGENCE CENTERS

Each of the Service intelligence centers and each of the theater Joint Intelligence Centers shall be fully integrated into the Defense Intelligence Agency within 180 days from the effective date of this Act as set forth in section 601. They shall retain their unique characteristics and shall be under the operational control of their respective Services and theater Commanders-in-Chief, but shall be under the administrative, policy, and financial direction of the Director of the Joint Military Intelligence Service.

SEC. 228.   ESTABLISHMENT OF THE JOINT MILITARY INTELLIGENCE
            SERVICE

There shall be established a Joint Military Intelligence Service to which all existing military intelligence personnel, both uniformed and civilian, shall be transferred within 360 days from the effective date of this Act as set forth in section 601.   In the interim, the Director for Joint Military Intelligence shall have such operational and administrative authority as he may require to immediately begin the process of reassigning personnel to better meet the overall needs of all Department of Defense elements for all-source military intelligence.

TITLE III—INFORMATION ACTIVITIES OF THE U.S. GOVERNMENT

Subtitle A—Role of the Country Team and U.S. Embassy Sites

SEC. 301.   ESTABLISHMENT OF AMBASSADOR AS SENIOR OFFICER FOR
            INFORMATION AND INTELLIGENCE PERTAINING TO HOST
            COUNTRY

The Ambassador of the United States as nominated by the President and confirmed by the Senate is designated the Senior Officer responsible for the direction and quality of all information and intelligence pertaining to the host country to which he or she is accredited.   This responsibility specifically excludes any authority, oversight or contact with technical or clandestine collection elements that might be focused on the respective host country and also excludes any access to raw classified intelligence while specifically requiring that the Ambassador be provided with a copy of all finished all-source intelligence pertaining to his or her host country, in draft and in sufficient time to permit him or her to influence the intelligence report.

SEC. 302.   ESTABLISHMENT OF THE COUNTRY TEAM AS THE TACTICAL
            COLLECTION   MANAGEMENT   AUTHORITY   FOR
            INFORMATION AND INTELLIGENCE PERTAINING TO HOST
            COUNTRY

Each Embassy will establish a Tactical Collection Management Working Group under the oversight of a Department of State Counselor within 90 days of the effective date of this Act as set forth in section 601, and will begin to provide periodic concise guidance directly to the Director-General of National Intelligence, with information copies to all parent agencies of Country Team participants.   It will be the responsibility of the Director-General of National Intelligence, in close coordination with the Country Team and the parent agencies, to assign responsibility for fulfilling the tactical collection management requests through one of four channels:

(1) Tasking and necessary funding authority to the Forward-Deployed Analysis Teams located at the Embassy, as established in Subtitle B;

(2) Tasking to the Global Knowledge Foundation for marketplace procurement;

(3) Assignment of the requirement to the appropriate government department or agency where the requirement is clearly within their predominant area of responsibility and can be met with open sources of information available to them; or

(4) Tasking to the Director of Classified Intelligence in those instances where neither departmental nor open sources are sufficient to satisfy the intelligence requirement *and* the requirement is considered of sufficiently vital importance to national security and national competitiveness so as to warrant clandestine or covert methods.

Subtitle B—Establishment of Forward-Deployed Analysis Teams

SEC. 303. PRECLUSION OF CLANDESTINE STATIONS FROM ALL EMBASSIES.

It is inappropriate and insecure for the United States to rely on official cover and to mount clandestine operations from within its official installations. Within 360 days from the effective date of this Act as set forth in section 601 all clandestine personnel now based within all official installations will be withdrawn from their assignments and retired, reassigned, or entered into a retraining program, and all existing agents will be amicably terminated with the exception of those approved by the Director of Classified Intelligence for placement in a transition program to be handled by a transition cadre of traveling non-official cover officers. The Director of Classified Intelligence, with the explicit approval of the Secretary of State, may leave in place those officers who are declared to liaison *and* whom the Secretary of State or any other parent agency accepts for joining as suitable for assignment to any overt element of the Country Team. All communicators will be transferred to the Department of State.

SEC. 304. REASSIGNMENT OF SENSITIVE COMPARTMENTED INFORMATION FACILITIES

The Assistant Director of Classified Information for Administration will establish a Task Force to inventory and reassign all Sensitive Compartmented Information Facilities back to the Department of State, and will undertake and fund such changes to facilities as may be required to rapidly transfer these spaces to other uses. However, in each Embassy where a Sensitive Compartmented Information Facility exists to house a Station, the Director-General of National Intelligence will have priority in reserving and retaining sufficient Sensitive Compartmented Information Facility space as necessary to meet the needs of the incoming Forward-Deployed Analysis Teams established by section 305 of this Act. In many cases, this may significantly reduce the amount of space to be transferred back to the Department of State.

SEC. 305. ESTABLISHMENT OF FORWARD-DEPLOYED ANALYSIS TEAMS

The Director-General of National Intelligence, in coordination with the principals of the Committee on National Intelligence, will devise a plan and implement a program to place no fewer than five all-source analysts in each major Embassy, three in each intermediate Embassy, and no less than one all-source analyst in all other Embassies. In general, one analyst will be drawn from the ranks of the National Intelligence Agency, one from the Joint Military Intelligence Service, and one from the Treasury or Commerce Departments. Members of the external adjunct analyst cadre are eligible for active duty tours overseas and should be considered. The senior analyst will in each case become the Principal Intelligence Advisor to the Ambassador, and will have a reporting relationship to the Director General of National Intelligence and the Chairman of the National Intelligence Council as well as working relationships with the Director of the Global Knowledge Foundation and the Director of the National Intelligence Agency.

Subtitle C—Establishment of the U.S. Information Peacekeeping Fund

SEC. 306. ESTABLISHMENT OF U.S. INFORMATION PEACEKEEPING FUND

A U.S. Information Peacekeeping Fund is established, to be administered by the Secretary of Defense and implemented by the Commanders-in-Chief of the regional theaters, each acting in cooperation with their respective Country Teams and the U.S. Information Agency as restored in Subtitle D. Within 180 days from the date of this Act as set forth in section 601 the Secretary of State, the Secretary of Defense, and the Director-General of National Intelligence must submit to Congress a plan for realigning—in phases over a ten year period—no less than 75% of all foreign military assistance funds into the U.S. Peacekeeping Fund whose purpose shall be to address emerging and extant causes of conflict between groups.

Subtitle D—Restoration and Enhancement of the

U.S. Information Agency

SEC. 308. RESTORATION OF THE U.S. INFORMATION AGENCY CAPABILITY

The U.S. Information Agency is restored as an independent capability exclusively devoted to overt, legal, ethical information collection and dissemination relevant to public diplomacy and the national security and national competitiveness interests of the United State. The provisions of section XXX of NNNN are rescinded and the original legislation in section XXX of NNNN is restored in force. Within 180 days of the effective date of this Act as set forth in section 601, all necessary actions to effect this restoration should be completed.

SEC. 309. ESTABLISHMENT OF OVERT INFORMATION COLLECTION RESPONSIBILITIES OF U.S. INFORMATION AGENCY

The Foreign Broadcast Information Service is transferred in its entirety to the U.S. Information Agency, together with up to 250 new positions for which former members of the Directorate of Operations are encouraged to apply, especially Reports Officers with high levels of language skill. Effective immediately, the U.S. Information Agency will be the primary vehicle for collecting and reporting overt mass and niche media information inclusive of print, broadcast, and indigenous Internet sites. In cooperation with the British Broadcasting Service, the U.S. Information Agency will submit to Congress a plan for establishing truly global coverage of all overt and multi-lingual publications, broadcasts, and Internet sites pertinent to national security and national competitiveness. The plan should limit government activities to over-all direction and quality control, rely extensively on private sector providers based in the host countries or having representatives in the host countries, ensure a strong program for collecting and translating gray literature, and provide for the dissemination of all resulting reports through established commercial online services as does the BBC.

SEC. 310. ESTABLISHMENT OF OVERT INFORMATION DISSEMINATION RESPONSIBILITIES OF U.S. INFORMATION AGENCY

The U.S. Information Agency will be the primary vehicle for disseminating multi-media and multi-lingual information about all aspects of United States policy, culture, economics, health and any other issues of interest to foreign nationals and non-governmental organizations based outside the United States. The primary purpose of this overt information dissemination program will be to deter and avoid conflict and confrontation between the United States, any group within the United States, and any foreign government or non-governmental group. Special emphasis will be placed on cultural relations and on addressing foreign public perceptions of the United States.

Subtitle E—Expansion of the U.S. Agency for International Development

SEC. 311. ESTABLISHMENT OF OFFICE OF INFORMATION ASSISTANCE

A new Office of Information Assistance is established within the U.S. Agency for International Development. The purpose of this office shall be to nurture foreign entrepreneurs and non-profit organizations including educational institutions by subsidizing their purchase of Internet access, computer equipment, and limited access to English-language content

SEC. 312. ROLE OF THE U.S. AGENCY FOR INTERNATIONAL DEVELOPMENT IN PROVIDING INFORMATION AND INFORMATION TECHNOLOGY ASSISTANCE.

The U.S. Information Agency will realign its resources so as to convert up to half of its existing programs away from agricultural and industrial assistance project and into information and information technology assistance projects within three years from the date of this Act as set forth in section 601.

Subtitle F—Expansion of the U.S. Peace Corps

SEC. 313. EXPANSION OF THE U.S. PEACE CORPS

The U.S. Peace Corps is our Nation's most important and valuable vehicle for demonstrating to indigenous populations around the world our commitment to peace and universal prosperity. The U.S. Peace Corps is a vital contributor to both national security (helping protect our forces overseas by creating good will toward Americans) and national competitiveness (helping increase good will toward U.S. corporations and their products). The President shall include in the next and future budget submissions provision for a doubling of the U.S. Peace Corps end strength by the year 2006.

SEC. 314. ESTABLISHMENT OF OFFICE OF INFORMATION ASSISTANCE

An Office of Information Assistance is established within the U.S. Peace Corps for the purpose of developing projects and related educational materials to be executed by Peace Corps volunteers throughout the world.

SEC. 315. ROLE OF THE U.S. PEACE CORPS IN PROVIDING INFORMATION AND INFORMATION EDUCATION

The U.S. Peace Corps will realign its resources so as to convert up to half of its existing programs away from agricultural and industrial assistance project and into information and information technology assistance projects within three years from the date of this Act as set forth in section 601.

Subtitle G—Establishment of Congressional Centers of Excellence

SEC. 316. ESTABLISHMENT OF CONGRESSIONAL CENTERS OF EXCELLENCE IN EACH STATE AND COMMONWEALTH

A program of Congressional Centers of Excellence is established to be managed by the Librarian of Congress with the assistance of the Director-General for National Intelligence and the Director-General for National Research. Each Senator and Representative, including non-voting Representatives, will nominate one organization in their State or Commonwealth that shall be designated a Congressional Center of Excellence and shall receive funding from the Global Knowledge Foundation sufficient to sponsor one full-time staff member with all necessary information technology needed to participate in the international intelligence reserve program and to serve as a catalyst for their State or District participation in the "virtual intelligence community" created by this Act.

Subtitle H—Establishment of Intelligence Sub-Committees
TITLE IV—CONGRESSIONAL OVERSIGHT

SEC. 401. INCLUSION OF ALL INTELLIGENCE ACTIVITIES WITHIN JURISDICTION OF THE SELECT COMMITTEE ON INTELLIGENCE

Amendment to S. Res. 400 (94th Congress).—Section 14(a) of Senate Resolution 400 (94th Congress) is amended by striking the last sentence in its entirety. All intelligence and information activities addressed by this Act shall be within the jurisdiction of the Senate Select Committee on Intelligence.

SEC. 402. ESTABLISHMENT OF CONGRESSIONAL SUB-COMMITTEES FOR INTELLIGENCE AND INFORMATION

Each Committee in the Senate and each Committee in the House of Representatives will establish a Sub-Committee for Intelligence and Information.

SEC. 403. ESTABLISHMENT OF JOINT NATIONAL INTELLIGENCE AND INFORMATION COMMITTEE

A Joint National Intelligence and Information Committee shall be established consisting of the majority and minority leaders of the Senate Select Committee on Intelligence and the House Permanent Select Committee on Intelligence, and the majority and minority members of the Sub-Committees on Intelligence.

TITLE V—TRANSFER OF FUNCTIONS AND SAVINGS [Deferred]
TITLE VI—EFFECTIVE DATE

SEC. 601. EFFECTIVE DATE.

This Act shall take effect 90 days after its date of enactment.

Reinventing National Intelligence: The Vision And The Strategy

The Vision

In the Age of Information, when individuals have the power to disrupt or destroy national communications and computing systems, and borders are largely irrelevant to global economic competitors, we must dramatically revise our most fundamental concepts of what constitutes war, what constitutes peace, and what constitutes the proper role of the State in the defense of its citizens and its national interests.

We are in an era, as my friends Alvin and Heidi Toffler have documented so well in their most recent books, *PowerShift* and *War and Anti-War*, where information is a substitute for violence and wealth. We are in an era where a small bit of information, obtained at the right time, delivered to the right person, and acted upon in the right way, can neutralize vast arrays of nuclear and conventional capabilities. Indeed, to examine the negative, an information attack is all the more frightening because it can be done *anonymously*.

The age of information has brought us full circle—we now must mobilize entire nations—every citizen of every age and capacity—in order to survive what can only be called "total war". It is not a war of nations—it is a war of organizations and individuals, each using information in an attempt to gain a financial advantage. The nations of the world are either helpless pawns in this new great game, or they are handicapped players, players crippled by out-dated concepts and expensive as well as often useless capabilities.

My vision is the same vision that inspired Pierre Teilhard de Chardin and Quincy Wright and H. G. Wells—a vision of the "Smart Nation" in which every intellect is linked, and the whole is indeed far more potent than the sum of the parts. From "Smart Nation" to "World Brain" to Global Commonwealth.

335

The Challenge of Radical Change

There are five revolutionary changes occurring today. There is the changing threat to national security, in which individual nations are less likely to be the belligerents, and transnational criminal organizations become more powerful, wealthier, and more violent, than many countries. There are the changing demands and expectations of citizens, who now realize that the safety of their children at home is at least as important an element of national security as safety from nuclear missiles. There are the changing fiscal conditions, with fewer people and fewer dollars available for "national defense". Finally, there are two dramatic changes in the private sector: the information explosion, or changing knowledge terrain; and the incredible and constant change characteristic of information technology.

The Battle for Knowledge

War and peace in this era will be decided upon the terrain of information, across the information continuum comprised of schools, universities, libraries, businesses, private investigative and information brokering agencies, print and broadcast media, governments to the state and local level, departments of defense, and last—even least—national intelligence organizations as traditionally defined: spies and satellites.

There are four central characteristics of this new battle for knowledge.

- First, it is an open battle, where 90 to 95% of the information is not secret and cannot be kept secret.

- Second, it is a battle being fought largely in the private sector—the "center of gravity" is in the civil sector, not the government.

- Third, it is a battle where victory will go to those who master the art of harnessing *distributed* intelligence "just in time", rather than those who attempt to centralize and control all knowledge "just in case". The latter is a foolish and impossible task.

336

- Finally, this is a battle where the mastery of different languages, the understanding of different cultures, and the ability to identify, acquire, and exploit hard-copy information, and locate and interview real people in real time, will decide who is rich and poor, who lives and who dies.

The utility of the Internet, and commercial online electronic services, is vastly overrated. 90% of the information necessary for very good decisions has not been digitized and indeed much of it has not been published at all—it is still in the minds of experts waiting to be mobilized, waiting to create new knowledge tailored precisely to the needs of the knowledge warrior.

Spies, Satellites, and Schoolboys

Does this mean that we should stop using spies and satellites? Absolutely not. Human nature has not changed. We will always need methods for discovering the darkest secrets of our enemies. However, to be practical, we should not send spies where schoolboys can go. We must also be conscious of the fact that a major problem with spies is that they only know secrets—they will often overlook the obvious and run grave risks to obtain information—as some American spies recently demonstrated in Paris—which has already been published in the open literature. Commercial imagery satellites will be increasingly important for both military and economic purposes, but most signals and some images will always need special means of collection.

Dr. Joseph Nye, a brilliant man who was served as the Chairman of the U.S. National Intelligence Council and has also been the Assistant Secretary of Defense for International Security, has spoken publicly of the intelligence problem as being like a jig-saw puzzle. The outer pieces of the puzzle are provided by open sources—publicly available information. The inner pieces of the puzzle are provided by clandestine and technical collection. It merits comment that one can neither begin nor complete the puzzle without those open outer pieces. It also merits comment that the information explosion has significantly increased the size and the importance of those outer open sources—most of the traditional intelligence communities of Europe and the rest of the world have not grasped the fundamental and dramatic growth of the importance of open sources to the national defense.

337

Open Sources and Military Warfare

It was my privilege, at the invitation of the Minister of Defense of France, Mr. Francis Leotard, to join Admiral Pierre Lacoste, General Jean Heinrich, and General Jeannou Lacaze in a special conference held in Paris on 23 October 1993 to discuss the need to reinvent intelligence. Subsequently on 18-19 December 1995 I was one of three Americans—the others being Samuel Huntington and Robert Gates—invited to address the French national conference on "War and Peace in the 21st Century." I consider it an honor to be associated with such distinguished officers and authorities, and wish to note for the record that in my judgement, military officers around the world have proven much more open and much more professional about pursuing new methods, than have their civilian counterparts. An American officer, the Navy Wing Commander who led the first flight over Baghdad, has captured the importance of open sources to military operations perfectly: "If it is 85% accurate, on time, and I can SHARE it, that is a lot more useful to me than a compendium of Top Secret Codeword information that is too much, too late, and requires a safe and three security officers to move it around the battlefield." In this era of military operations other than war, open sources are especially useful.

Open Sources and Economic Warfare

One can be amused or shocked by the 1995 cover story in *L'Expansion*, where President William Clinton, (then) Director of Central Intelligence John Deutch, Private Investigator Jules Kroll, and myself were accused of being the central figures in a grand plan to undermine the French economy in particular, and the European economy in general. I can state with certainty that not only are the Americans incapable of organizing themselves that effectively, but the French—and the French defense industry in particular—are much more talented at industrial espionage. Where the French should be worried is in the area of open sources of intelligence, for it is here that the one will gain victory in any battle where victory depends on knowledge. Henri Stiller, Director General of Histen Riller in Paris, has stated that "95% de l'information dont une entreprise a besoin peut s'acquirir par des moyens honorables."[1] He is absolutely correct, and those that persist in paying very high prices for industrial espionage with limited objectives, instead of modest prices for broader open source intelligence coverage, will find themselves bankrupt and defeated. According to Herve

---

[1] 95% of the information an enterprise requires can be obtained by honorable means.

Serieyx, Vice President of the Institut Europeen du Leadership, speaking at the French information industry conference (IDT) in 1993, the French steel industry concentrated its business intelligence endeavors on other steel industries, and completely overlooked the plastics industries of the world as they set about creating plastic substitutes for steel products. Had the French steel industry utilized open sources effectively, they would not have been so terribly routed by their competitors from another industry. It took the Americans eight years to discover the openly-published Chinese manual on how to obtain science & technology information, both classified and open information, and this is simply unacceptably poor performance for any nation.

National Information Strategy

When all is said and done, one finally realizes that there *is* a role to be played by the State—it is to the State that we must look for national leadership, and it is the State that must provide its citizens and its national organizations with a unifying and mobilizing strategy. To be victorious in the total war that characterizes the age of information, each State must have a national information strategy consisting of four pillars: connectivity, content, coordination, and communications & computing security. Like a building, a national information strategy must have all four pillars together, or it will not stand. Individuals and organizations must be electronically connected; they must have access to the maximum possible content—knowledge—using well-coordinated information tools (avoiding waste caused by a lack of interoperability or standards); and they must be able to store and exchange data with confidence in the security, integrity, and survivability of the national communications & computing infrastructure. The latter is a special challenge to the State, for transnational criminals are hiring talented hackers, and hacking tools are now freely available on the Internet to less-talented criminals.

National Intelligence

In the final analysis, every State will need its spies and satellites, but to be truly competitive in the age of information, every State must mobilize all of its citizens and all of its organizations to create a "virtual intelligence community" that is capable of acquiring and exploiting open sources of information faster and cheaper than any other State—upon this foundation, the spies can be decisive. Without this foundation, the spies will be irrelevant.

Salute to the Recipients of the Golden Candle Award

The Golden Candle Award was created in 1992, when the open source intelligence revolution began, as a means of recognizing the pioneers around the world who were contributing to the reinvention of their respective intelligence communities, and the creation of a larger community, the "virtual intelligence community."

OSS '92

Mr. George Marling for his earlier role in developing the HUMINT Committee Open Source Study for the U.S. Intelligence Community.

Ms. Bonnie Carroll, President, Information International Associates, Inc. for pioneering efforts with the National Federation of Abstracting and Indexing Services, and her role as Secretariat to the CENDI (Commerce, Energy, NASA, Defense, Interior) Working Group on Information .

Ms. Diane Webb, Analyst, Office of Scientific & Weapons Research, CIA, for developing the functional requirements for CATALYST (Computer Aided Tools for the Analysis of Science & Technology).

OSS '93

Mr. John Berbrich, Director for Science & Technology, Defense Intelligence Agency, for his attempts to sponsor improved open source exploitation within the defense intelligence community.

MajGen Ken Minihan, Assistant Chief of Staff for Intelligence, U.S. Air Force, for his attempts to sponsor improved open source exploitation with respect to Chinese telecommunications and other matters.

Mr. William Ruh, The MITRE Corporation, for his work on advanced information technology processing initiatives with enormous potential for improving our ability to exploit open sources.

Mr. Alessandro Politi, developer of "Intelligence Minuteman" concept and one of the leading advocates of open source intelligence within the Western European Union.

Mr. Samuel Mercier, advocate for open source intelligence in France and contributor to an understanding of open sources by key French military generals and admirals.

Mr. Rop Gonggrijp, Dutch leader of the Hac-Tic group, founder of <xs4all>, for his role as one of the leaders of the movement to both open and protect international networks.

Mr. Roger Karraker, Author of "Highways of the Mind" in *Whole Earth Review*, the seminal work inspiring the grass roots hijacking of the National Information Infrastructure.

Mr. William McDonald, Hacker-Engineer, for "stuff".

Mr. Paul Hoffman, EarthSeal Entrepreneur, for creating an affordable sticker of the NASA photograph of the Whole Earth that inspired an entire generation of environmentalists and others committed to openness.

OSS '94

Dr. Stevan Dedijer, Office of Strategic Services in Yugoslavia, originator of the field of business intelligence as a discipline, and over-all "wild man" of open source intelligence.

Dr. Douglas Englebart, Inventor, for creating the tools that made possible the Internet and all that followed from electronic mail, graphics, hyper-links, ans mice; and for his current commitment to distributed online collaborative work.

Emmanuel Goldstein, Leader of *2600* hacker community, for his creation of a hacker journal and his sponsorship of the Hackers on Planet Earth conference in New York City that brought over 750 phreakers out in the open.

342

Dr. James Holden-Rhodes, author of *SHARING THE SECRETS: Open Source Intelligence and the War on Drugs.*

Dr. Loch K. Johnson, dean of the intelligence reform movement, for his lifetime of achievement but especially for his seminal article, "The Seven Sins of Strategic Intelligence".

Mr. David R. Young, founder of Oxford Analytica, for creating a viable variation of the *President's Daily Brief* using only open sources of information and addressing the needs of Chief Executive Officers.

Dr. Ross Stapleton-Gray, CIA Internet guru and policy entrepreneur, recognized by the National Science Foundation as one of America's premier cyber-nauts.

U.S. Army 434th Military Intelligence Detachment, for its creation of the first general overview of the utility of open sources to the military.

U.S. Army Project PATHFINDER, under the leadership of Mr. Tim Hendrickson of the National Ground Intelligence Center, for moving forward with the objective of creating a useful analyst's toolkit.

Ministry of the Interior, The Netherlands, for its establishment of an official open source intelligence unit, the first known unit to exist in Europe, and for its development of the centralized discovery, decentralized exploitation model for Internet data mining.

OSS '95

Col Mike Pheneger, USA (Ret.), former J-2 U.S. Special Operations Command, for his paradigm-shattering unclassified exposures of our lack of tactical military maps for 90% of the world, and our enormous over-investment in duplicative and contradictory orders of battle.

Ms. Helen Burwell, Publisher, *Burwell World Directory of Information Brokers*, for her pioneering role in creating the Association of Independent Information Professionals and the international network of professional information brokers.

Mr. Winn Schwartau, Author, *INFORMATION WARFARE: Chaos on the Electronic Superhighway*, for being the first person in America to brief Congress on the possibility of an electronic "Pearl Harbor", and for his sustained efforts to create concepts and doctrine for asymmetric conflict.

Mr. Chris Goggans, Electronic Security Engineer, for "stuff".

National Technical Information Service, for is development of both a web-based electronic access capability and a distributed remote printing agreement with Kinko's.

Jane's Information Group, for its extraordinary overnight support of "The Burundi Exercise" that was instrumental in persuading the Aspin/Brown Commission that open source intelligence is a discipline in its own right.

Eastview Publications, for its extraordinary overnight support of "The Burundi Exercise" that was instrumental in persuading the Aspin/Brown Commission that open source intelligence is a discipline in its own right.

Institute for Scientific Information, for its extraordinary overnight support of "The Burundi Exercise" that was instrumental in persuading the Aspin/Brown Commission that open source intelligence is a discipline in its own right.

LEXIS-NEXIS, for its extraordinary overnight support of "The Burundi Exercise" that was instrumental in persuading the Aspin/Brown Commission that open source intelligence is a discipline in its own right.

SPOT Image Corporation (USA), for its extraordinary overnight support of "The Burundi Exercise" that was instrumental in persuading the Aspin/Brown Commission that open source intelligence is a discipline in its own right.

OSS '96

Colonel (Select) James "Snake Clark, Project Manager for EAGLE VISION, for working around the bureaucracy and delivering a C-130 transportable ground station through which commercial imagery could be immediately exploited by tactical commanders and air crews.

Mr. John W. Fisher III, COTR for Open Source Intelligence Training, Joint Military Intelligence Training College, for his sponsorship of the *OSINT HANDBOOK*.

Mr. Robert Heibel, founding Director, Research and Intelligence Analysis Program, Mercyhurst College, for getting international law enforcement organizations interested in open source intelligence, and for training students in open sources and methods.

Mr. Abram Hoebe, Criminal Intelligence Division, The Netherlands, for innovative exploitation of open sources in countering transnational crime in and around the port of Rotterdam.

Captain Patrick George, Head, Criminal Analysis Bureau, Central Bureau of Investigation, Belgium, for establishing an open source intelligence analysis unit and an open source intelligence network across all of Belgium.

Community Open Source Program Office, Office of the Director of Central Intelligence, for establishing the Open Source Information System.

Director General, Canadian Security and Intelligence Service, for publishing unclassified intelligence and attempting to make optimal use of international open sources of information.

Ministry of Defence, United Kingdom, for the establishment of the Open Source Information Centre in Whitehall.

Swedish Open Source Cooperation Forum, for informally bringing together the civilian, military, business, and academic open source intelligence coordinators, and creating the first national-level coordinating body for the collection of open sources.

Commission on the Roles and Missions of the U.S. Intelligence Community, for its documented findings that U.S. Intelligence Community access to open sources is severely deficient and should be a top priority for funding and a top priority for DCI attention.

OSS '97

Alice Cranor, DIA OSINT program manager and innovator, for her constant advocacy of open source intelligence in support of science and technology collection requirements.

Dr. Vipin Gupta and **Mr. Frank Pabian**, for their extraordinary paper on using commercial imagery to study Indian nuclear testing

Mr. Stephen Aftergood and **Mr. John Pike**, Federation of American Scientists, for the *Secrecy Bulletin* and the *Intelligence Reform* web site.

Mr. Maurice Botbol, founder and managing editor of the *Intelligence Newsletter*, the best open source on global intelligence organizations.

Sgt Elliot Jardines, U.S. Army Reserve, for the publication of *Open Source Quarterly* and his individual attempts to popularize open sources.

Intelligence Community Librarians Committee, for innovation in open source exploitation in the face of institutional resistance.

Monterey Institute of International Studies, for its open source research model using graduate students with native language fluency to screen and extract multi-lingual open source information on proliferation.

Loyola College in Maryland for the Strategic Intelligence web site that serves as a model for a voluntary but substantive web-based resource useful to all students of the intelligence profession.

Maritime Administration, Department of Transportation, for publication of the *Maritime Security Report* series using open sources

Commission on Secrecy for its examination of relative transaction costs between classified and open sources.

EuroIntel '98

Madame Judge Danielle Cailloux, Member of the Comite Permanent de Controle des Services de Renseignements, for her leadership in introducing open source intelligence into Belgian legislation on intelligence reform, and promulgating understanding of open sources of intelligence among senior leaders in the European community.

EUROPOL Drugs Unit, under Mr. Jurgen Storbeck as implemented by Mr. Frans-Jan Mulschlegel, for its establishment of a broad open source intelligence exploitation program.

SPOT IMAGE S.A. (France), for its uniquely robust commercial imagery architecture including two satellites and seventeen ground stations, an offering that was of enormous value during the Gulf War.

Servizio Centrale di Investigazione sulla Criminalità Organizzata (SCICO) della Guardia di Finanza, for its emerging commitment to the use of open sources in the war on organized crime.

Swedish Military Intelligence & Security Directorate, for its establishment of the Long Range Reconnaissance Patrol unit for cyber-space, and its development of innovative methods of discovering and exploiting the 80% of the Internet that is *not* indexed.

The Ministry of the Interior, The Netherlands, for its open source program under the direction of Mr. Frans de Ridder, and particularly its unique status as the only open source unit in the world that is co-equal to clandestine and technical collection units and under the same director of collection.

National Center for Missing & Exploited Children, United States of America, and Mr. Ruben Rodriguez Jr., Director of the Exploited Child Unit, for developing new methods of using the Internet to find and return missing and exploited children to their parents.

Metropolitan Police of London, United Kingdom, and Detective Constable Steve Edwards, for the establishment of the open source intelligence unit within the Intelligence Division, and the extraordinary savings achieved through the

347

use of open sources instead of surveillance team to locate assorted felons and suspects.

i2, Ltd., and in particular to Mr. Mike Hunter, Managing Director, for developing data visualization technology contributing to improved open source exploitation processes.

Captain Patrick Tyrrell, RN OBE MA LLB, Commandant, Defense Intelligence and Security School, for his sponsorship of the open source intelligence movement within the Ministry of Defence, and his authorship of the seminal paper on a NATO/PfP Open Source Intelligence Programme.

OSS '98

Mr. Harry Collier, founding and Managing Director of Infonortics Ltd.; founder of the Association for Global Strategic Information, and a leading practitioner of open source intelligence in support of business and technical objectives.

Dr. Mark Maybury, leader of MITRE's Open Source Processing Research Initiative (OSPRI), for his efforts to develop an integrated web-based system for knowledge development and information-sharing.

Mr. Tom Will, Open Source Program Manager, Defense Intelligence Agency, for spending over $10 million dollars in interesting ways.

The National Intelligence Community of South Africa for its extraordinary renaissance including its successful integration of black revolutionaries into a previously white bastion of secrecy.

Autometric, Inc. for its development of a robust process for integrating all forms of commercial imagery with national imagery to produce digital three-dimensional geospatial information and intelligence.

Colonel Barbara Fast, Commanding Officer, 66th Military Intelligence Brigade, because her senior enlisted personnel insisted we recognize her leadership in exploiting open sources.

PacIntel '99

LCdr Sean Connors, USN, for his role in the development of the Virtual Information Center, U.S. Pacific Command (J-08), a non-intelligence activity sufficiently impressive to have been added to the Battle Staff of the Commander-in-Chief, U.S. Pacific Command.

LtCol Ian Wing, Chief of Defence Force Fellow, Australia, for his leadership and intellectual accomplishments in both authorship on intelligence reform and in the creation and management of Australia's 1998 conference on open source intelligence, an event that brought together over 300 senior participants from across the entire Australian government.

EuroIntel '99

EUROPOL, newly authorized as an independent regional agency, for its definition and advocacy of a regional open source intelligence network in support of European law enforcement.

National Intelligence Service, The Netherlands, for its definition of and advocacy of a European Open Source Intelligence Network.

Office of Strategic Crime Assessments, Australia, for its establishment of an open source intelligence support programme that is a model for others to follow.

OSS '99

None awarded.

OSS 21

Republic of Germany, presented jointly to the BND and the Ministry of Defense for their collaborative effort in creating an inter-agency OSINT architecture.

United Kingdom, presented to the Open Source Information Centre for its role in expanding the original concept beyond the Ministry of Defence to include the Home Office and Law Enforcement Agencies.

Satellite Centre of the Western European Union for its role in demonstrating that regional intelligence has great value, and that commercial imagery and open sources comprise the most essential foundation for such regional intelligence.

Worldwatch Institute, presented to Lester R. Brown for his leadership and the accomplishments of his team of open source intelligence professionals who have demonstrated over a fifteen year period that Global Coverage is not expensive and can be accutely relevant to international policy and behavior.

U.S. Special Operations Command, presented to the Director of Intelligence and Information Operations Center for his leadership and the accomplishments of the Joint Intelligence Center in establishing the first operationally-focused Open Source Cell to provide timely, relevant, and unique support to U.S. Special Operations Forces

U.S. Transportation Command, presented to the Commander, Joint Intelligence Center, for his leadership and the accomplishments of his subordinates in establishing a new model for austerely integrating active duty, reserve, and commercial capabilities to produce open source intelligence in support of a global mission in lower tier countries.

Mr. Philippe Lejeune, graduate of the Master's program in open source intelligence exploitation offered by Mercyhurst College, and now the open source focal point for Interpol, for his persistence in pursuing an unpopular idea. As an individual, he is now the "fourth musketeer" within the European law enforcement open source leadership.

Mr. Dominic Farace, founder and leader of GrayNet, and the foremost champion of Gray Literature acquisition and exploitation.

Nominations of future Golden Candle Award winners should be sent to the author, bear@oss.net..

Bibliographies

A nation's best defense is an educated citizenry.

Introduction

In recent months, as I have reviewed the last three years' worth of articles in the *International Journal of Intelligence and Counterintelligence* and also read several books skirting around the fundamentals of intelligence and in some instances alluding to intelligence reform, I have noticed a very narrow range of sources being cited—this is true of my own works as well. *In essence, we who are writing about intelligence are writing about it in so narrow a context as to be dangerous.* Corporations routinely destroy their productivity by naming technicians as their Chief Information Officers—Nations do something more insidious. Nations put technicians *and* spies in charge of national intelligence, and then wonder why they don't know anything. *The problem with spies is they only know secrets!*

The concept of intelligence *qua* espionage, secrecy, or decision-support cannot be understood or improved upon without reference to a much broader range of sources dealing with the nature of information, the emerging electronic information environment, the challenges facing us in elementary and continuing education, and the over-all global context within which we practice policy and intelligence.

For this reason, I decided to end this book with an annotated bibliography of about half of the non-fiction sources I read in the past decade or so—many deal with intelligence *qua* espionage but most do not. Separately, in the plain bibliography that follows this one, I list all of the speeches and articles from the twenty-two volumes of *Proceedings* that I have edited, for the simple reason that the open source intelligence revolution will inevitably be the catalyst for intelligence reform. Finally, at the very end, I list relevant personal publications and published interviews that led up to this book.

Annotated Bibliography

Information, Crime, Risk, and Hackers
Information, Economy
Information, Environmental
Information, Geospatial and Visualization
Information, Internet and Silicon Valley
Information, Productivity & Politics
Information, Strategic Perspectives
Information, Tactical Methods
Information, Warfare (Cyberwar)

Intelligence
Intelligence, Analysis
Intelligence, Business and Competitive
Intelligence, Coalition and Peacekeeping
Intelligence, Collection
Intelligence, Counter
Intelligence, Covert Action and Paramilitary
Intelligence, Economic Espionage
Intelligence, Foreign Capabilities
Intelligence, Law Enforcement
Intelligence, Military
Intelligence, Policy
Intelligence, Reference
Intelligence, Reform and Future

Management, Acquisition
Management, Future
Management, Leadership
Management, Organizational

Not listed, but relevant to the larger intellectual architecture that needs to be applied to national intelligence, are a broad range of books on 21st Century competitiveness between nations, educational reform, management of the trillion-dollar economy, crime and punishment, and the realities of Presidential and Congressional politics. I hope my comments add value to this limited but interesting collection of books.

Information, Crime, Risk, and Hackers

Hafner, Katie and John Markoff, *CYBERPUNK: Outlaws and Hackers on the Computer Frontier* (Simon & Schuster ,1991).

Three case studies are provided, including one dealing with Robert Morris, son of a distinguished NSA scientist and the person who brought America to a standstill with an epidemic electronic virus. By two distinguished journalists who knew little about hackers but could recognize a great story when they saw one, this is one of the more important early books that erroneously labeled hackers as criminals and electronic criminals as hackers.

Icove, David, Karl Sager, and William VonStorch, *Computer Crime: A Crimefighter's Handbook* (O'Reilly & Associates, 1995).

This is a proper book on preventing, recognizing, and addressing computer crime. It gets high marks from Jim Settle, the top FBI authority on computer crime until his retirement, and now an international consultant in this area.

Levy, Steven, *HACKERS: Heroes of the Computer Revolution* (Dell, 1984).

This is the definitive book on the early hackers, true hackers, and should be required reading for all those people, generally with good intentions, that ignorantly refer to electronic criminals and vandals as "hackers". Steven starts his book with a "who's who" in hacking that includes Lee Felsenstein from Interval, Bill Gates, Steven Jobs, and Woz Woniak, among others, and then goes on in three parts to examine the original night hackers at MIT and other nodes of excellence, then the hardware hackers, and finally the game hackers. *Hackers are a national resource*, and it is only the ignorant who do not understand this.

Neumann, Peter G., *Computer Related Risks* (Addison-Wesley, 1995).

Neumann, founder and moderator of the Internet Risk Forum, is the pope of the legitimate computer risks community. This is the bible.

Slatalla, Michelle and Joshua Quittner, *Masters of Deception: The Gang that Rules Cyberspace* (HarperCollins, 1995).

This is a fun read, but as with the Hafner and Markoff book, reader beware. Erik Bloodaxe, one of the major characters in the book and my friend as well as a trusted security engineer, inscribed this book as follows: "Robert, Hope you enjoy this classic example of 3rd rate speculative fiction. So much for journalistic integrity, eh? /s/. I also know Phiber Optic, and tried to keep him out of jail, even offered to house him and hire him on parole, but to no avail. This is a good story that crosses over frequently into speculative reporting, but it may be better for that, capturing some of the spirit of competition that exists between very talented hackers who by and large do no harm.

Sterling, Bruce, *The Hacker Crackdown: Law and Disorder on the Electronic Frontier* (Bantam, 1992).

This is one of three books I trust on hackers and hacking (Levy and Turkle are the other two trusted authors). Bruce, a very distinguished author in *WIRED* and science fiction circles, went to great lengths to investigate and understand what was happening between hackers exploring corporate systems, corporate security officials that were clueless and seeking scorched earth revenge, and Secret Service investigators that were equally clueless and willing to testify erroneously to judges that the hackers had caused grave damage to national security. Bruce is a true investigative journalist with a deep understanding of both technical and cultural matters, and I consider him superior to anyone in government on the facts of the matter.

Stoll, Clifford, *The Cuckoo's Egg: Tracking a Spy Through the Maze of Computer Espionage* (Doubleday, 1989).

This is an absolutely *riveting* story of how a brilliant physicist, assigned as an initiation rite to track down the reason for a 75 cent error in the computer accounts of the Lawrence Berkeley Laboratory, ultimately identified and nailed an East German electronic espionage specialist. In passing, he outlines with great preciseness the insecurity of the entire U.S. government, military, law enforcement, business, and academic electronic communications and computing network, and reveals the total fragmentation as well as the general ignorance of almost all of the US and international organizations associated with these networks.

Turkle, Sherry, *The Second Self: Computer and the Human Spirit* (Simon & Schuster, 1984).

This is "the" book that described the true origin of "hacking" as in "pushing the edge of the envelope" by writing a complex program in six lines of code instead of ten. This is a really superior piece of work about computer cultures and the people that belong to them. It is a wonderfully readable book with magnificent insights into the psychology of the young people at the bleeding edge of the computer frontier.

Information, Economy

Kelly, Kevin, *New Rules for the New Economy: 10 Radical Strategies for a Connected World* (Viking, 1998).

Building on a series of article for *WIRED* Magazine, Kevin explains ten rules for the new Internet-based economy that make more and more sense as time goes on. From "follow the free" to "feed the web first" and on to "from places to spaces" and "relationship technology", his insights provide an easy to understand map of where the digital economy is going.

Tapscott, Don, *The Digital Economy: Promise and Peril in the Age of Networked Intelligence* (McGraw-Hill, 1996).

After demolishing Business Process Reengineering (BPR) as a necessary element of but insufficient substitute for corporate strategy, organizational learning, or reinvention, the author goes on to address twelve themes central to success in an economic environment characterized by networked intelligence: knowledge, digitization, virtualization, molecularization, integration/internetworking, disintermediation, convergence (a big one), innovation, prosumption, immediacy, globalization, and discordance (another big one). He stressed the need for "busting loose from the technology legacy", the need to dramatically transform both the information management and human resource management concepts and also a turning on its head of how government works—from centralized after the fact "leveling" and gross national security to decentralized, proactive nurturing of individual opportunity before the fact, providing individual security through individual opportunity and prosperity within the network.

Information, Environmental

There is a vast range of literature out there that needs to be brought into the all-source analysis arena. I will list just three representative examples without review. It is clear to me that Lester R. Brown and the Worldwatch Institute should be our *primary* national intelligence node for environmental intelligence, augmented by other nodes around the world, and with very selective classified intelligence support where necessary to detect clandestine and illegal environmental activities that have continental and international repercussions—such as toxic dumping in Africa.

Brown, Lester R., *Tough Choices: Facing the Challenge of Food Scarcity* (W.W. Norton, 1996).

Brown, Lester R., et al., *State of the World: A Worldwatch Institute Report on Progress Toward a Sustainable Society* (W. W. Norton, 1999).

Brown, Lester R., Hal Kane, and Ed Ayres, *VITAL SIGNS 1993: The Trends That Are Shaping Our Future* (W. W. Norton, 1993).

Information, Geospatial and Visualization

These books require no review. They are representative of an entire range of intelligence products that do not exist, and of an entire range of techniques for presenting compelling intelligence that the U.S. Intelligence Community has not yet grasped. These are just the ones I had time to buy and read. There are a number of others now that reflect the enormous progress made in automated geospatial and time data visualization in the late 1990's.

Chaliand, Gerard and Jean-Pierre Rageau, *Strategic Atlas: A Comparative Geopolitics of the World's Powers* (Harper & Row, 1990).

Keegan, John and Andrew Wheatcroft, *Zones of Conflict: An Atlas of Future Wars* (Simon & Schuster, 1986).

Kidron, Michael and Ronald Segal, *The State of the World Atlas* (Simon & Schuster, 1981).

Kidron, Michael and Ronald Segal, *The New State of the World Atlas* (Simon & Schuster, 1991).

Smith, Dan, *The State of War and Peace Atlas* (Penguin, 1997).

Tufte, Edward R., *The Visual Display of Quantitative Information* (Graphics Press, 1983).

Tufte, Edward R., *Envisioning Information* (Graphics Press, 1990).

Tufte, Edward R., *Visual Explanations: Images and Quantities, Evidence and Narrative* (Graphics Press, 1997).

Information, Internet and Silicon Valley

Cringely, Robert X, *Accidental Empires: How the Boys of Silicon Valley Make Their Millions, Battle Foreign Competition, and Still Can't Get a Date* (Addison Wesley, 1992).

A gift from one of the folks he writes about, this is one of the earliest books about Silicon Valley, and is both enjoyable and useful because of its early focus on the mistakes made by IBM, Xerox Park, 3Com, and other "CIA-like" giants, its discussion of the hit and miss and perserverence nature of the early start-ups, and some really big things to avoid like letting venture capitalists or the marketing staff tell you what to offer the public.

Downes, Larry and Chunka Mui, *Unleashing the KILLER APP: Digital Strategies for Market Dominance* (Harvard, 1998).

Twelve principles of killer app design: 1) Outsource to the customer, 2) Cannibalize your markets; 3) Treat each customer as a market segment of one; 4) Create communities of value; 5) Replace rude interfaces with learning interfaces; 6) Ensure continuity for the customer, not yourself; 7) Give away as much information as you can; 8) Structure every transaction as a joint venture; 9) Treat your assets as liabilities; 10) Destroy your value chain; 11) Manage innovation as a portfolio of options; 12) Hire the children.

Evans, Philip and Thomas S. Wurster, *Blown to Bits: How the New Economics of Information Transforms Society* (Harvard, 2000).

Navigation, not content, will rule. Navigators will compete based on reach, affiliation, and richness. Privacy will be a mandated aspect of every offering. Traditional organizations and bureaucracies are unlikely to survive because there is no one there willing and able to "deconstruct" them down to core functionalities and then rebuild them back up with a focus on customer service as the driving force rather than assembly of whatever it was they used to understand as the primary organizing principle.

Gates, Bill, *Business @ The Speed of Thought: Using a Digital Nervous System* (Warner Books, 1999).

No doubt largely written by staff assistants, this book can be considered a watered-down version of Microsoft's game plan for taking over the world, i.e. being the operating system for everything. Each chapter has a useful figure that sums up business lessons and methods for diagnosing one of the aspect's of one's digital nervous system. This is a great airplane book.

Hagel, John III and Arthur G. Armstrong, *net.gain: expanding markets through virtual communities* (Harvard, 1997).

This is a very serious handbook for how to create communities of interest, provide value that keeps the members there, and establish a foundation for growing exponentially from day one.

Lewis, Michael, *The NEW NEW Thing: A Silicon Valley Story* (Norton, 2000).

Great airplane book. The story of Jim Clarke, the only man to have created three billion-dollar ventures—Netscape, Silicon Graphics, and Healtheon. Documents the shifting of power from Wall Street to Silicon Valley, and offers some wonderful insights into the culture. Does not, by virtue of focusing on the one really big success story out of the Valley, begin to address the human waste and carnage from all the failed start-ups.

McKenna, Regis, *REAL TIME: Preparing for the Age of the Never Satisfied Customer* (Harvard, 1997).

This may be one of the top three books I've read in the last couple of years. It is simply packed with insights that are applicable to both the classified intelligence community as well as the larger national information community. The following is a tiny taste from this very deep pool: "Instead of fruitlessly trying to predict the future course of a competitive or market trend, customer behavior or demand, managers should be trying to find and deploy all the tools that will enable them, in some sense, to be ever-present, ever-vigilant, and ever-ready in the brave new marketplace in gestation, where information and knowledge are ceaselessly exchanged."

Rheingold, Howard, *Tools for Thought: The History and Future of Mind-Expanding Technology* (Simon & Schuster, 1985).

Howard, who wears hand-painted cowboy boots and was at the time the long-serving editor of *The Whole Earth Review,* came to my attention through this book, which is an excellent primer for thinking about how technology can impact on thinking.

Rheingold, Howard, *The Virtual Community: Homesteading on the Electronic Frontier* (Addison-Wesley, 1993).

Coming after his book on Virtual Reality, this book solidified in my own mind all of the concepts necessary to implement a "virtual intelligence community."

Rheingold, Howard, *VIRTUAL REALITY* (Summit, 1991).

Howard's second major book is valuable primarily because it begins to explore the issues associated with the integration of humans, machines, and software, and how humans, business, and society in general might be transformed.

358

Stoll, Clifford, *Silicon Snake Oil: Second Thoughts on the Information Highway* (Doubleday, 1995).

"Our networks are awash in data. A little of it's information. A smidgen of this shows up as knowledge....The Internet, that great digital dumpster, confers not power, not prosperity, not perspicacity...Our networks can be frustrating, expensive, unreliable connections that get in the way of useful work. It is an overpromoted hollow world, devoid of warmth and human kindness. The heavily promoted information infrastructure addresses few social needs or business concerns. At the same time, it directly threatens precious parts of our society, including schools, libraries, and social institutions."

Information, Productivity & Politics

Strassmann, Paul, *The Business Value of Computers: An Executive's Guide* (Information Economics Press, 1990).

Way over my head, I would not have appreciated this book if Paul had not first given a brilliant lecture at OSS '96, the keynote presentation, on "Knowledge Capital™" and how to calculate information costs against their actual contributions to corporate profit. In general, one should buy this book to be persuaded of Paul's brilliance, and then hire him to implement the ideas as a strategic consultant. Not for the weak-minded CEO or CIO, as it impales most corporate oxes and concludes that in general, there has been either a negative return on investment, or no discernible contribution to corporate profit, from steadily increasing information technology budgets.

Strassmann, Paul, *Information PayOff: The Transformation of Work in the Electronic Age* (Free Press, 1985).

Paul, former Chief Information Officer for Xerox and later Director of Defense Information, used this book to address the basic issues of employee productivity in relation to information technology. This is one of a very few books, including those by Carkhuff, Cleveland, Kelly, and Toffler, that I regard as fundamental—required reading for anyone with any authority over anything.

Strassmann, Paul, *Information Productivity: Assessing the Information Management Costs of US Industrial Corporations* (Information Economics Press, 1999).

Paul documents the fact that "a very large share of U.S. industrial firms are not productive in terms that apply to the information age." He evaluates and ranks 1,586 firms, and the results are both surprising and valuable.

Strassmann, Paul, *The Politics of Information Management: Policy Guidelines* (Information Economics Press, 1995).

Many of the cartoons published in the *Irreverent Dictionary* came from this book, and I was among those who suggested to Paul that he should publish the cartoons separately. They were, however, essential to this otherwise intimidating book that is nothing less than an operating manual for the Captain of the Virtual Network. The bottom line that I took from this book is that Kevin Kelly is right, our national and international information systems are "out of control" and our policy leaders have abdicated their responsibilities to technicians who do not have the political, economic, or common sense of two ducks and a chicken. As Paul alludes in one of his footnotes, the Network today is somewhat in relationship to the "horseless carriage" stage of the automobile, and we have a very long way to go before policy helps make computers as user-friendly and reliable and interoperable as the telephone and the automobile are today.

Information, Strategic Perspectives

Boisot, Max H., *Information Space: A Framework for Learning in Organizations, Institutions and Culture* (Routledge, 1995).

Together with Edward Wilson's *Consilience* this is the most structured and focused book in this section, and has real applicability as to how one might organize a truly *national* (that is to say, not just spy) intelligence community. Written from a transatlantic perspective, integrating the best of American and European thinking in his references, the author addresses the nature of information, its structuring, the dynamics of sharing information, learning cycles, institutional and cultural contexts, and ends with this thought: that we have spent close to a century "de-skilling" the population to suit assembly line needs and now must spend close to a century "re-skilling" the population to deal with complex information tasks where every action and reaction will be unique.

Branscomb, Anne Wells, *Who Owns Information: From Privacy to Public Access* (Basic Books, 1994).

This is a unique book by a very respected scholar. It methodically goes, chapter by chapter, over who owns your name and address (the U.S. Postal Service does), your telephone number, your medical history, your image, your electronic messages, video entertainment, religious information, computer software, and government information. The answers are not always obvious. A real benchmark.

Carkhuff, Robert, *The Exemplar: The Exemplary Performer in an Age of Productivity* (Human Resource Development Press, 1984).

This book had a profound influence on me, helping me to understand that the functions fulfilled by an employee dealing with "things" are completely distinct from the functions fulfilled by an employee dealing with "ideas", and that completely different educational, training, management, and compensation models are needed for the new "Gold Collar" worker. From this book I realized that virtually everything we are doing in U.S. education and U.S. personnel management and training today is way off the mark and at least a decade if not two or three decades behind where we could be in human productivity management.

Cleveland, Harlan, *The Knowledge Executive: Leadership in an Information Society* (E.P. Dutton, 1985).

This book was a catalyst in changing my own focus from that of reforming the classified intelligence community, to that of creating a "virtual intelligence community" that served as an on-going educational program for government and business leaders. "If there was ever a moment in history when a comprehensive strategic view was needed, not just by a few leaders in high (which is to say visible) office but by a large number of executives and other generalists in and out of government, this is certainly it. Meeting that need is what should be *higher* about higher education."

Collier, Harry, *The Electronic Publishing Maze: Strategies in the Electronic Publishing Industry* (Infonortics, 1998).

Harry is the founder and sponsor of the very interesting Association for Global Strategic Information. His book is as good a review as one could ask for, of "whither electronic publishing." He defines the pieces as consisting of data originators, information providers, online vendors, information integrators, delivery channels, and customers. Overall Harry is quite firm on pointing out that the Internet is not revolutionary and will not transform most medium and small businesses in the near future. He goes over the Internet in relation to established publishers, covers pricing and copyright issues in relation to the Internet, and ends with a discussion of next generation applications and technologies and forecasts.

Foucault, Michel, *POWER/KNOWLEDGE: Selected Interviews & Other Writings, 1972-1977* (Pantheon, 1977).

Some serious food for thought here. Not only is the power to define madness, criminality, and sexuality addressed, but also the active use of criminals, and sex, to suppress and subjugate the populace. Somewhat more difficult to wade through but similar to Norman Cousins, it helped provoke my thinking on how top-down unilateral command based on secrets is inevitably going to give way to bottom-up multicultural decision-making by the people based on open sources evenly shared across networks. This is really very heavy stuff, and it helps call into question the "rationality" of both

361

the Washington-based national security policymaking process, and the "rationality" of spending $30 billion a year on secrets in contrast to what that $30 billion a year might buy in terms of openly-available insights and overt information peacekeeping.

Kelly, Kevin, *Out of Control: The Rise of Biological Civilization* (Addison-Wesley, 1994).

Kevin, a *WIRED* Magazine editor who spoke, with Stewart Brand, at OSS '94, has produced what I regard as one of the top five books of this decade. A very tough read but worth the effort. I had not understood the entire theory of co-evolution developed by Stewart Brand and represented in the *Co-Evolution Quarterly* and *The Whole Earth* until I read this book. Kevin introduces the concept of the "hive mind", addresses how biological systems handle complexity, moves over into industrial ecology and network economics, and concludes with many inspiring reflections on the convergence of biological and technical systems. He was easily a decade if not two ahead of his time.

Kuhn, Thomas S., *The Structure of Scientific Revolutions* (University of Chicago, 1970).

I've had to buy this book three times because I keep misplacing each copy I buy. Every time I wonder how long it is going to take the U.S. Intelligence Community to get it right, I simply have to remind myself that they have not yet had sufficient cumulative pain—pain on the order of a Pearl Harbor or a mass murder of Congress—to force what Kuhn calls the "paradigm shift." Two points are worthy of emphasis: 1) the paradigm shift is always forced and 2) until the paradigm shift occurs, always suddenly, the incumbents can comfortably explain everything with their existing paradigm.

Levitan, Karen B., *Government Infrastructures: A Guide to the Networks of Information Resources and Technologies at Federal, State, and Local Levels* (Greenwood, 1987).

You absolutely do not need to read this book—when I went through it, I worried that I was becoming obsessed with knowledge and going just a bit too far down into the literature. I got two things out of this book: 1) a very nice chart on page xvii that lists the following "rows" in an information infrastructure, from *top* to *bottom*: policy goal, policy resources, policy structures, policy processes, information resources management, information users and producers, information entities, information processes, information technologies; and 2) technology is nowhere near "taking over" anything—the vast majority of the information networking is still personal and informal.

Levy, Pierre, *Collective Intelligence: Mankind's Emerging World in Cyberspace* (Plenum Trade, 1997).

This dude is a heavy hitter, and it says a lot that this one made it over the water from the French original. Clearly a modern day successor to Jacques Ellul (*The Technological Society*) and before him Pierre Teilhard de Chardin. Levy begins with the premise that the prosperity of any nation or other entity depends on their ability to navigate the knowledge space, and the corollary proposition that the knowledge space will displace the spaces of the (natural) earth, (political) territory, or (economic) commodity. He is acutely conscious of the evil of power, and hopes that collective intelligence will negate such power. He ends with a warning regarding our construction of the ultimate labyrinth, cyberspace, where we must refine the architecture in support of freedom, or lose control of cyberspace to power and the evil that power brings with it.

Luttwak, Edward N., *Strategy: The Logic of War and Peace* (Harvard University Press, 1987).

Luttwak's book not only provides articulate explanations of the differences between the strategic, operational, tactical, and technical levels of war, but shows how capabilities combine across mission areas and between levels to create a coherent matrix of mobility, weapons, and communications capabilities. This book inspired my creation of the Marine Corps model for analysis whose subsequent implementation in our first study helped demonstrate that *the threat changes depending on the level of analysis*, and consequently one's plans and capabilities must be firmly oriented not only with respect to the tangible objective, but with respect to the context—the level of action.

Mander, Jerry *In the Absence of the Sacred: The Failure of Technology & the Survival of the Indian Nations* (Sierra Club, 1991).

By the author of *Four Arguments for the Elimination of Television*, this is actually a manifesto for a popular revolution against banks, corporations, and states—a peaceful cultural revolution that has as its objectives the restoration of land ownership to the commonwealth; the acceptance of alternative economic models that optimize group cohesion instead of individual or organizational profit; and the liberation of 3,000 nations of relatively distinct groups from the subjugation imposed by the states that now have sovereign (that is to say, violent coercive) power over the individuals and groups that fall within their imposed territorial claims.

McKibben, Bill, *The Age of Missing Information* (Plume, 1992).

The author taped all the TV shows being broadcast for 24 hours, then watched all of the shows over the necessary time period, and then spend 24 hours alone with nature. There are some well-thought and well-articulated insights in this book. Information is not a substitute for nature. The information explosion is drowning our senses and cutting us off from more fundamental information about our limitations and the limitations of the world around us. Television really did kill history, in that it continually celebrates and rehashes the 40 years of time for which there is television film on background, and overlooks the 4000 years behind that. The worst disasters move slowly, and the TV cameras don't see them.

Neustadt, Richard E. and Ernest R. May, *Thinking in Time: The Uses of History for Decision Makers* (Free Press, 1986).

Together with Luttwak's book, and a few others on cultural frames of reference, this book is an essential point of reference for understanding the analogies and other devices that decision makers use to evaluate information, and hence suggests that there must be certain deliberate actions analysts can take to present compelling intelligence using tailored analogies and terms that strike the correct chord with the individual consumer.

Norman, Donald A., *Things That Make Us Smart: Defending Human Attributes in the Age of the Machine* (Addison-Wesley, 1993).

Technology can make us smart. Or stupid. It can liberate. Or enslave. Norman joins a select group of thinkers advocating a human-centered approach to technology. Inspired (or, more accurately, depressed) by Jerry Mander, he wrote this book to examine the differences between humans and machines, and to establish some ground rules for policy that protected the one and leveraged the other. Norman notes that when technology is not designed from a human-centered point of view, it produces accidents and more often than not the human is blamed. He focuses especially on the distinction between experiential cognition and reflective cognition, and laments that television and entertainment are swamping us with the experiential and not teaching us the reflective. He is concerned that our ever-lengthening chain of technology dependence is forcing us to deal with ever-increasing loads of information at the same time that it weakens our inherent capabilities further. People first, science second, technology as servant.

Rossell, Steven A. et al., *Governing in an Information Society* (Institute for Research on Public Policy, 1992).

There are a whole range of books on "this and that in the age of information." This is one of the most concise, does a nice job of drawing on all the major literature in the 1980's and early 1990's, and explores the issues in relation to governance in a networked environment.

Rothfeder, Jefrey, *Privacy for Sale: How Computerization Has Made Everyone's Private Life An Open Secret* (Simon & Schuster, 1992).

This book is a perfect complement to Anne Branscomb's, and provides a well-told tale, researched in partnership with a private investigator, of just what can be gotten on you through the electronic web within which we all live our lives. This book is the tactical gutter in your face version, Branscomb's book is the academic dissection.

Sale, Kirkpatrick, *Rebels Against the Future: The Luddites and Their War on the Industrial Revolution* (Addison-Wesley, 1995).

Lessons from the Luddites for the Computer Age include: 1) Technologies are never neutral, and some are hurtful; 2) Industrialism is always a cataclysmic process, destroying the past, roiling the present, making the future uncertain; 3) "Only a people serving an apprenticeship to nature can be trusted with machines."; 4) The nation-state, synergistically intertwined with industrialism, will always come to its aid and defense, making revolts futile and reform ineffectual; 5) But resistance to the industrial system, based on some grasp of moral principles and rooted in some sense of moral revulsion, is not only possible but necessary; 6) Politically, resistance to industrialism must force not only "the machine question" but the viability of industrial society into public consciousness and debate; 7) Philosophically, resistance to industrialism must be embedded in an analysis—an ideology, perhaps—that is morally informed, carefully articulated, and widely shared; 8) If the edifice of industrial civilization does not eventually crumble as a result of determined resistance within its very walls, it seems certain to crumble of its own accumulated excesses and instabilities within not more than a few decades, perhaps sooner, after which there may be space for alternative societies to arise.

Shattuck, Roger, *Forbidden Knowledge: From Prometheus to Pornography* (St. Martin's Press, 1996).

Beyond the mundane discussions about secrecy versus openness, or privacy versus transparency, there is a much higher level of discussion, one about the nature, limits, and morality of knowledge. As I read this book, originally obtained to put secrecy into perspective, I suddenly grasped and appreciated two of the author's central thoughts: knowing too much too fast can be dangerous; and yes, there are things we should not know or be exposed to. *Who decides?* Or *How do we the people decide?* are questions that must be factored into any national knowledge policy or any national information strategy. This book left me with a sense of both the sacred and the scary sides of unfettered knowledge. This is less about morality and more about focus, intention, and social outcomes. It is about the convergence of power, knowledge, and love to achieve an enlightened intelligence network of self-governing moral people who are able to defend themselves against evil knowledge and prosper by sharing good knowledge.

Swegen, Hans, *The Global Mind: The Ultimate Information Process* (Minerva UK, 1995).

This is a 211-page essay with no footnotes, bibliography, index, or information about the author. It is a great read, and one can only imagine the author hunched over a pad over the course of a very long Nordic winter with no sun. He starts with "human DNA molecules, which are information carriers, consist of 2300 million nucleotides, which contain the information for nearly one million genes" and goes from there. At the end mind and matter merge, energy, ecology, body and mind come together...and at that point individuals lose some of their individuality, and the global mind turns outward, toward the cosmos.

Teilhard de Chardin, Pierre, *The Phenomenon of Man* (Harper, 1965).

The originator of the term *noosphere* and all this implies.

Toffler, Alvin, *PowerShift: Knowledge, Wealth, and Violence at the Edge of the 21ˢᵗ Century* (Bantam, 1990).

Alvin augments our vocabulary with terms like "info-warrior", "eco-spasm", "super-symbolic economy" and "powershift." He examines the relationship between violence, wealth, and knowledge and concludes that an entirely new system of wealth creation is emerging, as well as entirely new approach to information dissemination that places most of our command and control, communications, computing, and intelligence (C4I) investment in the dump heap with the Edsels of the past. He anticipates both the emergence of information wars at all levels, and the demise of bureaucracy. He cautions us about the emerging power of the "Global Gladiators"—religions, corporations, and terrorists (nice little mix) and concludes that in order for nations to maintain their strategic edge, an effective intelligence apparatus will be a necessity and will "boom" in the 21ˢᵗ Century, with the privatization of intelligence being its most prominent break from the past.

Walshok, Mary Lindenstein, *Knowledge Without Boundaries: What America's Research Universities Can Do for the Economy, the Workplace, and the Community* (Jossey-Bass, 1995).

An industrial sociologist by training, now Associate Vice Chancellor for Extended Studies and Public Service at the University of California, San Diego (UCSD), Walshok begins by challenging universities, exploring the social uses of knowledge, assessing the new knowledge needs of diverse populations, and providing a matrix approach to matching university resources to community knowledge needs. In the second half of the book she focuses on special economic, human, and civic benefits, and ends with her bottom line: neither communities, nor universities, can learn in isolation.

Wells, H. G., *World Brain* (Adamantine, 1994).

First published in 1938, this modern edition is vastly improved by the addition of a critical introduction by Alan Mayne. Very much focused on how a world-brain might alter national policy-making, how Public Opinion or an "Open Conspiracy" might restore common sense and popular control to arenas previously reserved for an elite. The information functionality of the World Brain easily anticipated the world wide web as it might evolve over the next 20-30 years: comprehensive, up to date, distributed, classification scheme, dynamic, indexes, summaries and surveys, freely available and easily accessible. We have a long way to go, but the framework is there. The communication functions of the world brain would include a highly effective information retrieval system, selective dissemination of information, efficient communication facilities, effective presentation, popular education, public and individual awareness for all issues, and facilitate social networking between organizations, groups, and individuals. The world brain *is* the "virtual intelligence community" *qua* noosphere.

Wilson, Edward O., *CONSILIENCE: The Unity of Knowledge* (Alfred A. Knoph, 1998).

Our answer to Levy, but an order of magnitude more practical and steeped in some of the best endnotes I've ever enjoyed. Consilience is the "jumping together" of knowledge across boundaries, and the greatest enterprise of the mind. He begins with an example, showing how biology, ethics, social science, and environmental policy must all come together to properly resolve a global environmental issue, but actually do not—the learned individuals are fragmented into four separate communities, and within those communities further fragmented into nationalities and cliques and jobs, and it is our greater loss for we cannot arrive at the best policy without being able to integrate the knowledge across all these boundaries. He emphasizes that the public must be educated and have access to this unified knowledge, not just the policymakers. He poses, and then answers across the book, this question: "What is the relation between science and the humanities, and how is it important to human welfare?" In my own mind, Edward O. Wilson has defined both national and global intelligence writ large, and done so in way that suggests the "virtual intelligence community" is a very practical and achievable vision.

Wurman, Richard Saul, *Information Anxiety* (Doubleday, 1989).

Ted is the genius behind the TED conferences that cost $3000 to attend, all clear profit because he has created such a convergence of minds across the media, information, technical, and biological sciences that sponsors beg for opportunities to pay for everything. It is a very cluttered book, the kind of thing that happens when an impatient genius wants to fix varying design formats with quasi-logical thinking, but it is definitely worth the effort. The nugget for me was in his observation that while many businesses are devoted to the collection, transmission, or storage of information, there are no businesses he knew of dedicated to enhancing *understanding*. This book is a marvelous problem statement and offers many intriguing thoughts on how to enhance both how you interact with external information sources, and how to add value to the information that passes through you to others.

Information, Tactical Methods

Several books in the "Internet Yellow Pages" and "Do Business on the Internet" genres were originally stacked up for inclusion here but as soon as I realized I could not recommend them for purchase, it became clear they should not be listed. By and large books on the Internet are of very transient value.

Basch, Reva, *Secrets of the Super Searchers* (Eight Bit Books, 1993).

Reva, one of the top five information brokers in the USA, sought out and interviewed 35 professional or gifted amateur *commercial online (fee for service)* searchers and provides in this book a delightful free-flowing conversation with each of them as a "master's class" for intelligence and information professionals.

Basch, Reva, *Secrets of the Super Net Searchers* (Pemberton Press, 1996).

Reva, one of the top five information brokers in the USA, sought out and interviewed 35 professional or gifted amateur *Internet* searchers and provides in this book a delightful free-flowing conversation with each of them as a "master's class" for intelligence and information professionals.

Bates, Mary Ellen, *The Online Deskbook* (Pemberton Press, 1996).

Mary Ellen, or MEB, is the online broker I turn to when I can't solve something in-house. Her book is a working desktop reference, covering the main commercial online services as well as major Internet channels.

Burwell, Helen P., *Online Competitive Intelligence: Increase Your Profits Using Cyber-Intelligence* (Facts on Demand Press, 1999).

This is the most recent guide, by one of the top five information brokers in America. Helen, a past president of the Association of Independent Information Brokers, is also the publisher of the unique *Worldwide Directory to Information Brokers* and perhaps the best connected information broker in the world.

Coleman, Edwin J. and Ronald A. Morse, *DATA: Where It Is and How to Get It* (Coleman/Morse Associates, 1992).

This book, a directory of data sources for business, environment, and energy, is representative of an intermediary product, a hard-copy "portal" to U.S. Government economic experts and the data that taxpayers pay to collect and organize. It provides a valuable service, largely because the U.S. Government stinks at being accessible.

Goldmann, Nahum, *Online Information Hunting* (McGraw Hill, 1992).

If you ever want to scare your children, buy them this book. It covers the minutia of information search strategies for commercial online databases prior to the development of web-based interfaces. A great deal of it is still valuable, and I recommend it mostly because it really captures the complexity of online searching in an era when there is both a flood of information and a dearth of good processing tools.

Martin, Frederick Thomas, *TOP SECRET Intranet: How U.S. Intelligence Built Intelink—The World's Largest, Most Secure Network* (Prentice Hall, 1999).

I was given this book at Hacker's (the MIT/Silicon Valley legal and largely very rich group, of which I am an elected member) by a NASA engineer, went to bed, could not get the book out of mind, got up, and read it through the night. If it were not for the fact that Intelink is largely useless to the rest of the world and soon to be displaced by my own and other "extranets", this book would be triumphal. As it is, I consider it an extremely good baseline for understanding the good and the bad of how the U.S. Intelligence Community addresses the contradictions between needing access to open sources and emerging information technologies while maintaining its ultra-conservative views on maintaining very restricted access controls to everything and everyone within its domain. I have enormous regard for what these folks accomplished, and wish they had been able to do it openly, for a much larger "virtual intelligence community" willing and able to share information. For a spy, information shared is information lost—until they get over this, and learn that information not only increases in value with dissemination but is also a magnet for 100 pieces of information that would never have reached them otherwise, the U.S. Intelligence Community will continue to be starved for both information and connectivity....an SGML leper in an XML world.

Rugge, Sue and Alfred Glossbrenner, *The Information Broker's Handbook* (Windcrest, 1992).

In contrast to Mary Ellen's book, this book is actually for self-starters who are thinking about creating their own small business and covers such excellent basics as the market for information, what an information broker does, the pros and cons of the information business, and then the tools, followed by chapters on marketing, pricing, and project management. Although seven years old now, I still regard this as a good starting point for those who would understand the information brokering business (a small niche within the larger open source intelligence business).

Information, Warfare (Cyberwar)

Baklarz, Ron and Richard Forno, *The Art of Information Warfare* (Professional Press, 1997).

This book, listed with www.amazon.com, is among the ten most popular books on information warfare, and provides a mix of easy to read adaptations of Sun Tzu and other Chinese sayings to issues of computer security, with useful discussions of the importance of all that goes with making information systems safe, secure, and private.

Campen, Alan D. (ed.), *The First Information War* (AFCEA Press, 1992).

As Director C2 Policy in OSD, Alan was intimately familiar with the weapons, tactics and information systems being developed in the Reagan military buildup and foresaw the pivotal role of information in the Gulf War. He may reasonably be considered one of the first offical sponsors of military thinking in this area. This is one of the first serious books to be published in this area, is based largely on the Gulf War experience, and emphasizes command and control, communications, and computer (C4) issues to the detriment of intelligence (I).

Campen, Alan D., Douglas H. Dearth, and R. Thomas Gooden, *Cyberwar: Security, Strategy and Conflict in the Information Age* (AFCEA Press, 1996).

This book is a very fine compilation, spanning a whole range of technical and non-technical aspects of information warfare, and including my own invited chapter on "Creating a Smart Nation: Information Strategy, Virtual Intelligence, and Information Warfare." This is a basic text and those in charge of our information warfare segments today would do well to read it again and again because most of them are focusing on one tiny slice of the IW mission, hot bits.

Campen, Alan D. and Douglas H. Dearth, *Cyberwar 2.0: Myths, Mysteries and Reality* (AFCEA Press, 1998).

This sequel to the first book on cyberwar is even better (and the first one was very good) because it is much more deliberate about addressing strategy and diplomacy (part one); society, law, and commerce (part two); operations and information warfare (part three, where most military professionals get stuck); and intelligence, assessment, and modeling (part four). My chapter on "Information Peacekeeping, the Purest Form of War" appears here, but based on the lack of feedback I suspect all of the contributions in this section are a decade away from being understood with the U.S. Government.

The final part offers four chapters on the future, including an excellent discussion of "Cyberwar: The Role of Allies and Coalition Partners" by Commodore Patrick Tyrrell, then a Royal Navy Captain and now a Commodore responsible for "stuff" in the UK.

De Landa, Manuel, *War in the Age of Intelligent Machines* (Swerve, 1991).

A very early and largely academic-historical-philosophical discussion of the changing nature of the relationships between humans, computers, and war. Written prior to the Silicon Valley explosion, and thus still very concerned about the military dominance of information technology. A good alternative overview.

Thomas, Keith (ed.), *The Revolution in Military Affairs: Warfare in the Information Age* (Australian Defence Studies Centre, 1997).

With an introduction by Andy Marshall, "the man" for net assessments from the old school, this book is a good example of the state of the best thinking currently available within the allied military community. Marshall emphasizes the two twin pillars of future war that are emerging in his world: precision munitions, and information warfare (but meaning information superiority). There are many good observations, for instance on information pathologies within the military, and on the fact that the military is at least a decade (if not two or three) behind the private sector in exploiting state of the shelf information technologies.

Schwartau, Winn, *Information Warfare: Chaos on the Information Highway* (Thunder's Mouth Press, 1994).

This is the original bible, and my former partner (in InfoWarCon) deserves much more credit than he has gotten from Congress or the military or the U.S. business community. He single-handedly foresaw the future (see *Terminal Compromise*) and set about creating the bru-ha-ha that ultimately led to his formal testimony to Congress on the possibilities of an "electronic Pearl Harbor" (his term, not anyone else's) and the subsequent establishment by the White House of a task force for the protection of critical infrastructure. In this book Winn lays out the nature of individual, corporate, and state-sponsored information warfare (including economic espionage and information terrorism or vandalism), and proposes some solutions.

Schwartau, Winn, *Information Warfare: Cyberterrorism: Protecting Your Personal Security in the Electronic Age* (Thunder's Mouth Press, 1996).

This 767-page tome contains a number of new chapters by Winn and over 400 pages from the best of those who spoke at two of our conferences. It includes a directory of "who's who" in cyberspace in relation to information warfare and electronic security, and can be considered the "state of the art" for 1996.

Schwartau, Winn, *Terminal Compromise: A Novel About Computer Terrorism* (Inter-Pact Press, 1991).

There is a level of understanding about the computer "threat" that cannot be achieved by reading learned chapters, and this novel is just plain good. It describes a multi-faceted anonymous information war on the United States launched out of Japan, but get ready for the surprise ending. Still a great book.

Intelligence

Berkowitz, Bruce D. and Allan E. Goodman, *Strategic Intelligence for American National Security* (Princeton, 1989).

This is an even-tempered book, combining a good primer of the nature of the intelligence process with some analytically-oriented thoughts on needed improvements. Their appendix listing things that can go wrong at each step of the intelligence cycle is of lasting value, as is their glossary. Their forthcoming book, *Best Truth: Intelligence in the Information Age* (Yale, April 2000) will assuredly be a major contribution.

Bozeman, Adda B., *Strategic Intelligence & Statecraft: Selected Essays* (Brassey's US, 1992).

While reading this book, every intelligence professional should feel like a bashful second-grader shuffling their feet while being kindly reprimanded by their teacher. This book, a collection of essays from the 1980's, is the only one I have ever found that truly grasps the strategic long-term importance of intelligence in the context of culture and general knowledge. The heart of the book is on page 177: "(There is a need) to recognize that just as the essence of knowledge is not as split up into academic disciplines as it is in our academic universe, so can intelligence not be set apart from statecraft and society, or subdivided into elements...such as analysis and estimates, counterintelligence, clandestine collection, covert action, and so forth. Rather, and as suggested earlier in this essay, intelligence is a scheme of things entire. And since it permeates thought and life throughout society, Western scholars must understand all aspects of a state's culture before they can assess statecraft and intelligence." The 25-page introduction, at least, should be read by every intelligence professional.

Copeland, Miles, *Without Cloak or Dagger: The Truth About the New Espionage* (Simon and Schuster, 1947).

This is one of my two required readings for any aspiring intelligence officer or student of intelligence. An absolute gem across the board, providing insights into both capabilities and culture. The description on pages 41-42 (of the original hard-cover version) of how "Mother" concocted an entire network and got the head of Secret Intelligence to agree its production was worth $100,000 a year (big money in 1946), only to reveal that his source was actually five issues of *The New York Times* "demonstrated not only the naiveté of our nation's only existing group of espionage specialists but the value of ordinary *New York Times* reporting on matters regarded as being of high-priority intelligence interest." Nothing has changed in 50 years.

Dearth, Douglas H. and R. Thomas Goodden (ed.), *Strategic Intelligence: Theory and Application* (U.S. Army War College, 1995).

This is not a well known book, having been published as a limited edition educational work for the defense intelligence school system, but it is well-worth getting—a few hundred copies are still available from Doug at <DHDEARTH@aol.com>. Most of the contributions are exceptional, including John Macartney's "Intelligence: What It Is and How To Use It" and several excellent pieces from Michael Handel, Morton Halperin, and others on warning, surprise, and deception. The last chapters are weak and appear to have been thrown together to justify a "new directions" aspect, but they too are worth reading.

Dulles, Allen, *The Craft of Intelligence* (Signet, 1965).

This is the other required reading. This gem sits on my desk with my dictionary of difficult words and my synonym dictionary. We still do not have an equal to this book. Since Dulles testified to Congress that 80% of the raw material for finished intelligence came from public sources including diplomatic reporting, this book provides an interesting benchmark for understanding the rather pathological impact of technical collection on the larger process of *all*-source collection and analysis.

Herman, Michael, *Intelligence Power in War and Peace* (Cambridge University Press, 1996).

This is the textbook to use if you have really intelligent students. It is not an easy read, between the British language form and the deep thinking, but it is, as Christopher Andrew says, "the best overview" and "surely destined to become a standard work." I liked its attention to components and boundaries, effects, accuracy, and evaluation. More recently Michael has written "British Intelligence In The New Century: Issues And Opportunities." Perhaps most important within his book is the distinction between long-term intelligence endeavors that rely primarily on open sources and serve to improve state understanding and state behavior, and short-term espionage that tends to be intrusive and heighten the target's feelings of vulnerability and hostility.

Johnson, Loch K., *Secret Agencies: U.S. Intelligence in a Hostile World* (Yale, 1996)

Loch is the dean of the scholars competent to address intelligence matters, and his experience as a member of the professional staff of both the Church Committee in the 1970's and the Aspin/Brown Commission in the 1990's uniquely qualify him to discuss and evaluate U.S. intelligence. His chapters on the ethics of covert operations and on intelligence accountability set a standard for this aspect of the discussion. This is the only book I have seen that objectively and methodically discusses intelligence success and failures in relation to the Soviet Union, with a superb three-page listing decade by decade being provided on pages 180-182.

Laquer, Walter, *A World of Secrets: The Uses and Limits of Intelligence* (Basic Books, 1985).

I continue to regard this book as one of the best available textbooks for inspiring informed student and entry-level employee discussion about the intelligence professional and its role in supporting policy-making. The author's conclusion, and the "eleven points" he makes regarding the current status and future of intelligence, continue to be an essential contribution to the great debate.

Lowenthal, Mark, *Intelligence: From Secrecy to Policy* (Congressional Quarterly Press, 1999).

This is an excellent elementary text for the average college student. Over-all it is strong on issues of analysis, policy, and oversight, and weak on collection, covert action, and counterintelligence. The chapter on collection has a useful figure comparing the advantages and disadvantages of the five collection disciplines, and but does not get into the detail that this aspect of the intelligence community—80% of the annual expense—merits.

Lowenthal, Mark, *The U.S. Intelligence Community: An Annotated Bibliography* (Garland, 1994).

Mark is arguably America's foremost intelligence historian, and especially strong on analysis and oversight. The seventy-page bibliography he has put together is useful.

Shulsky, Abram N., *SILENT WARFARE: Understanding the World of Intelligence* (Brassey's, 1991).

I rather like this book, and believe it continues to have value as a primer on intelligence for both students and entry-level employees. Most interesting is the distinction that Shulsky, himself a former defense analyst, professional staffer on the Hill, and sometime Pentagon policy wonk, makes between the "Traditional" view of intelligence as "silent warfare", and the "American" view of intelligence as "strategic analysis."

Intelligence, Analysis

Codevilla, Angelo, *Informing Statecraft: Intelligence for a New Century* (Free Press, 1992)

"It is not too gross an exaggeration that when considering any given threat, DIA will overestimate, CIA will underestimate, and INR will blame the U.S. for it." From his opening chapter and his distinction between static, dynamic, and technical facts, on through a brilliant summary of the post-war spy on page 103 and lengthy sections on how we've gotten it wrong, how we can get it right, and what is needed in the way of reform, I found this book worthy of study. An analyst and political staffer by nature, the strength of this book rests on the premise in the title: that intelligence should be about informing policy, not about collecting secrets for secrets' sake.

Gentry, John A., *LOST PROMISE: How CIA Analysis Misserves the Nation (An Intelligence Assessment)* (Lanham, 1993).

John has written a very personal book, somewhat vitriolic in its attacks on both Bob Gates for politicization and Directorate of Intelligence managers in general for being both ignorant and lacking in courage. It is essential reading for anyone considering improvements in how we do intelligence analysis, and includes an eighteen-point program for reforming both the process of intelligence and the management of intelligence analysis. The figure on page 226 comparing the Traditional, Opportunity-Oriented, and Opportunism-Oriented "Schools" of intelligence analysis is alone worth the price of the book. Includes a number of interesting original internal documents from his fight with DI management.

Intelligence, Business and Competitive

The literature on business intelligence is remarkably under-developed, and just now beginning to emerge. My general assessment of most business intelligence analysts is that they are in the fourth or fifth grade with respect to the process of intelligence. Only 5% of U.S. corporations and 9% of European corporations have a specific business intelligence function established (according to the Planning Forum in the mid-1990's). There are a few centers of excellence—generally specific pharmaceutical or major oil companies—but on balance I believe this arena to be in the "1950's" in contrast to the open source intelligence movement that I regard as ten years ahead of its time.

Ashton, W. Bradford and Richard A. Klavans (ed.), *Keeping Abreast of Science and Technology: Technical Intelligence for Business* (Battelle Press, 1997).

Dick is a genius, and he and Bradford Ashton have pulled together a number of very fine contributions in this book. Still, they sum it up nicely in the concluding chapter: "The formal practice of developing technical intelligence in American business is only in its infancy." They have a nice appendix of sources on scientific and technical intelligence that is missing a few big obvious sources like the Canadian Institute for Scientific and Technical Information (CISTI) and the Defense Technical Information Center (DTIC) as well as the Institute of Scientific Information (ISI) and several smaller sources. On balance, this technical intelligence community is, as Bradford notes, in its infancy. It is U.S. centric, does not yet understand operational security and counterintelligence, is weak of cost intelligence, relies too heavily on *registered* patents, and has too few practical successes stories. Especially troubling is the recent trend within DIA and the Air Force of cutting off all funding for open source exploitation of Chinese and other foreign S&T sources, combined with a dismantling by many corporations of their libraries and most basic market research functions. This book is an *essential* reference and I admire its authors greatly—sadly, they are part of a small minority that has not yet found its full voice.

Bernhardt, Douglas, *Perfectly Legal Competitor Intelligence: How to Get It, Use It and Profit from It* (Pittman UK, 1994).

This is an excellent primer. A subtle underlying theme that is not fully articulated is that of the varying standards across national boundaries of what is and is not legal. In general, and I draw here on work the work of others, the US and UK are most restrictive, with the Germans and Israeli's in the middle (using pretext interviews and other "legal" but deceptive tactics), while the French, Russians, Japanese, Koreans and Chinese are on the lower end of the scale, where anything goes including breaking and entering.

Fuld, Leonard M., *The New Competitor Intelligence: The Complete Resource for Finding, Analyzing, and Using Information About Your Competitors* (John Wiley & Sons, 1994).

This is a serious general text on competitive intelligence, and Leonard is a master. Having said that, I would note that what Leonard does best is work very hard—the practice of business intelligence still lacks a good set of information technology tools for discovering, discriminating, distilling, and delivering packaged business intelligence, and most firms do not have the tools for managing a broadly distributed network of niche experts who are hired on a day to day basis. Fuld & Company Inc., and to a lesser extent the other companies listed in the Open Source Marketplace, are the first wave in what I believe will be a major line of business to business revenue in the 21st Century.

Kahaner, Larry, *Competitive Intelligence: From Black Ops to Boardrooms—How Businesses Gather, Analyze, and Use Information to Succeed in the Global Marketplace* (Simon & Schuster, 1996).

Larry builds his last chapter, "Competitive Intelligence: The Next Generation" around my ideas, so I can hardly complain. This is a good airplane book, a very nicely organized and easy to read overview. In fact, I would say that this book has to be read before reading the books by Leonard Fuld or Brad Ashton and Dick Klavans. One of the things I like most about Larry's book is that it understands and trys to explain that national competitiveness overall—a "Smart Nation"—must be built on a foundation of "Smart Corporations."

McGonagle, John J. Jr. and Carolyn M. Vella, *A New Archetype for Competitive Intelligence* (Quorum Books, 1996).

The authors are serious professionals with several competitive intelligence books behind them, and try in this book to relate the requirements of competitive intelligence to the emerging opportunities of the Internet and information tools—what they characterize and trademark as "cyber-intelligence"™. It's a good book, worth reading.

Meyer, Herbert, *Real-World Intelligence: Organized Information for Executives* (Grove Widenfeld, 1987).

Herb, one of the distinguished speakers at OSS '92, has been Vice Chairman of the National Intelligence Council, and is in my mind one of the top five pioneers of business intelligence in the United States. He started in late 1970's, and his little paperback book is both a gospel and a guide of continuing value. This book was distributed at OSS '92, and continues to be worthy of reading by senior executives who don't do a lot of reading.

Prescott, John E. and Patrick T. Gibbons (ed.), *Global Perspectives on Competitive Intelligence* (Society of Competitive Intelligence Professionals, 1993).

This is the most professional collection of articles on competitive intelligence I know of, with a good mix of both technical intelligence and foreign intelligence information. The Society of Competitive Intelligence Professionals (SCIP), under the day to day leadership of Guy Kolb, has grown from 2,000 members in 1992 to 6,000 in 1999, and it's journal as well as its conferences, set the industry standard. A relatively low standard, but the standard never-the-less.

Sigurdson, Jon, and Yael Tagerud, *The Intelligent Corporation: The Privatization of Intelligence* (Taylor Graham, 1992).

If I recognize anyone as my predecessor in this revolution, it would be Stevan Dedijer from Croatia and Sweden. This book, dedicated to and devised to celebrate Stevan's 80th birthday on 6 July 1991, is a graduate-level yet easy to read collection of articles on the field of private intelligence. Stevan, widely recognized as the father of both business intelligence and social intelligence (I'm surprised he did not focus on cultural and religious intelligence systems as well), has established the standard I have to match. He says: "Nobody has yet built a holistic view of intelligence. There is an increasing need for the integrated study of the human brain, personality, machines, and the social system. There is not yet a method to study how these factors interact with each other." The collection ends with references to the "world brain" that I hope to tap into and empower with OSS.NET. This annotated bibliography is in small part my own tribute to Stevan.

Shaker, Steven M. and Mark P. Gembicki, *The WarRoom Guide to Competitive Intelligence* (McGraw Hill, 1999).

I have mixed feeling about these guys, and their book, but the bottom line is that it makes a contribution and must be read. They address, in a manner understandable by the complete layman, the intersection of competitive intelligence, corporate security, and WarRoom operations. They have a number of very useful and thoughtful figures. The book is unquestionably at the head of the class with respect to WarRoom operations and exploiting information technology and basic planning and execution and visualization concepts. Where I have a real problem with this book is in its advocacy of elicitation and other deceptive techniques, no doubt a hang-over from Steven's days as a CIA case officer. There is absolutely no place in U.S. competitive intelligence for such methods, and any discussion in that direction must be forcefully opposed if we are to succeed in creating a legal, ethical, overt network of intelligence professionals able to reinforce each other in providing open source intelligence to businesses as well as non-governmental organizations.

Stanat, Ruth, *The Intelligent Corporation: Creating a Shared Network for Information and Profit* (American Management Association, 1990).

Well before I got into the open source business Ruth was managing global business intelligence activities, and she wrote the book I would have written if I had had to choose one starting point. This is an essential reference for every manager, both in government and in business as well as in the non-profit arena, and I continue to regard Ruth as the dean of the practical business intelligence educators. Together with Jan Herring, Dick Klavans, Herb Meyer, and Leonard Fuld, she completes the *de facto* U.S. board of directors for real-world business intelligence.

Intelligence, Coalition and Peacekeeping

Pickert, Perry L. and Russell G. Swenson (ed.), *Intelligence for Multilateral Decision and Action* (Joint Military Intelligence College, June 1997).

This book is important as a testament to just how broken the Defense Intelligence Agency is with respect to coalition and peacekeeping intelligence. Fully a year after the Joint Military Intelligence Training Center across the hall published *Open Source Intelligence: Handbook*, these people still had not figured out the fact that open sources of intelligence are the crux of the matter for intelligence support to coalition and peacekeeping operations. I attended the first day of the conference that featured many of the authors as well as a whole flock of Partner for Peace officers flown in for the occasion, and I left greatly saddened by the fact that the whole first day was spent talking about how improvements were needed in sanitizing and disseminating classified intelligence across multi-lateral units. I am told that on the second day of the conference there was no substantive reference to open source intelligence. This book is a good benchmark for evaluating where the DIA bureaucracy is on this important topic: in the basement. (The new CINC OSINT Working Group, by contrast, "gets it.")

Intelligence, Collection

Bamford, James, *The Puzzle Palace: A Report on America's Most Secret Agency* (Houghton Mifflin, 1982).

The book is nothing short of sensational, for two reasons: it is the first and still the only really comprehensive look at global signals intelligence operations as dominated by the National Security Agency; and second, because all of his research was done using only open sources, including unclassified employee newsletters at Alice Springs, and he did a great job of making the most out of legally and ethically available information. James is still around, working on another book about SIGINT, and I believe that only he will be able to top this one.

Burrows, William E., *DEEP BLACK: Space Espionage and National Security* (Random House, 1986).

This is still the only really great book on overhead reconnaissance, and I have been surprised and disappointed to see it overlooked by the mainstream intelligence academics. Contains useful early history on why we got into technical collection (our human spies kept getting killed on arrival as we took the easy route of recruiting from émigré organizations already penetrated by the KGB and GRU). Ends with a passing reference to commercial imagery, a topic that merits its own book.

379

Claridge, Duane R., *A Spy for All Seasons: My Life in the CIA* (Scribner, 1997).

Dewey was a Division Chief when I was a junior case officer, and I continue to admire him. His pocket handkerchiefs were amazing—you could parachute from a plane with one in an emergency. Dewey's bottom line is clear: he concludes that "the Clandestine Services (*sic*) is finished as a really effective intelligence service." He has other worthwhile insights, ranging from the inadequacy of the information reaching CIA analysts from open sources (e.g. Nepal), to the "wog factor" dominating CIA analytical assessments (e.g. Pakistan will never attack India), to the sterile and politically-safe approaches to intelligence by the leadership of NSA and the some of the military intelligence services. My bottom line on Dewey is also clear: he was typical of the case officer talent pool, he tried very hard, and the system still failed. He was a good person in a very bad system.

Sakharov, Vladimir, *High Treason* (Ballentine, 1980).

Not necessarily for students, this paperback from the Ballentine Espionage/Intelligence Library is sensational. I had already been a case officer overseas when I read it, and I read it with real admiration for the Soviet Division and the case officers who had the luxury of doing it "right." From the overseas evaluations to the discreet subway signal of interest in Moscow to the follow-up that resulted in a recruitment in place and an ultimate exfiltration across the desert of Kuwait, this is a magnificent account of "the way it is supposed to be" in the clandestine service. It has a spy's kind of happy ending—really rotten treatment by CIA security blockheads during the resettlement program, a very long drunken period, hit bottom, and finally get clean and work your way free from the system on your own.

Holden-Rhodes, J. F., *Open Source Intelligence & The War on Drugs* (OSS Academy, 1994).

James Holden-Rhodes, an experienced military professional as well as a very respected analyst within two of the Nation's national laboratories focused on the secrets of science, wrote this book to describe his practical experience using open sources of information to create tactical and operational intelligence in support of drug interdiction missions by the U.S. Southern Command and the Drug Enforcement Agency. I printed the book in 1994 for all those attending OSS '94, and it has been subsequently offered to the larger marketplace by the U.S. Naval Institute Press. James is dynamic, thoughtful, and not to be denied. This is the first documented case in which open sources and methods costing roughly $150,000 a year, were proven significantly more timely and capable of producing actionable drug eradication and interdiction intelligence than an equivalent $12 million effort using classified sources and methods.

Thomas, Evan, *The Very Best Men—Four Who Dared: The Early Years of the CIA* (Simon & Schuster, 1995).

I almost broke two fountain pens on this book, and that is close to my highest compliment. Depending on one's mood, it will move any person with a deep knowledge of intelligence to tears or laughter. This is a really superior detailed look at the men that set the tone for clandestine operations in the 20th century: "Patriotic, decent, well-meaning, and brave, they were also uniquely unsuited to the grubby, necessarily devious world of intelligence." From card file mentalities to Chiefs of Station not speaking the language, to off-the-cuff decision making and a refusal to include CIA analysts in strategic deliberations, this is an accurate and important study that has not gotten the attention it merits from the media or the oversight staffs.

West, Nigel, *The SIGINT Secrets: The Signals Intelligence War, 1900 to Today* (William Morrow, 1988).

Nigel has given us a lovely history, and also drawn out a number of themes that have meaning for the future. For instance, the superiority of amateurs from the ham radio ranks over the so-called professional military communications personnel, in the tricky business of breaking patterns and codes; the many "human in the loop" breaks of otherwise unbreakable technical codes, from the Italians with hemorrhoids (not in the code book, spelling it each day broke the code) to the careless Russians. He also touches on security cases in both the U.S. and England. In his conclusion, one sentence jumped out at me: "The old spirit of RSS, with its emphasis on voluntary effort, has been replaced by a bureaucracy of civil servants who preferred to stifle, rather than encourage, initiative." As the current Director of NSA has discovered, NSA today is in mental grid lock, and its culture is oppressive in the extreme.

Intelligence, Counter

Adams, James, *SELL OUT: Aldrich Ames and the Corruption of the CIA* (Viking, 1995).

In this instance I choose to use the following from the book itself: "*Sellout* is the story of America's intelligence community, a community so determined to protect its own, to never admit failure, that it failed to catch Ames, whose spying was done with as much sloppiness as his work for the Agency. The turf wars between the CIA and the FBI and the incompetence of the investigators would mean that the investigation would get nowhere for nearly nine years." During those nine years, Ames rose to become head of the CIA's Soviet Division counterintelligence function, and was able to identify, by name, all of the U.S. penetrations then active within the Soviet Union. All of them are believed to have been executed.

Allen, Thomas B. and Norman Polmar., *Merchants of Treason: American Secrets for Sale* (Dell, 1988).

Roughly 100 American traitors, most of them within the U.S. defense establishment, are itemized in this book, the only such over-all review I have encountered. As I have said on several occasions that I believe we have at least 500-750 additional cases of espionage to discover, at least half of them controlled by our "allies", this book is for me a helpful reminder of the true pervasiveness of betrayal in a Nation where opportunism and financial gain often outweigh loyalty and principle.

Martin, David C., *Wilderness of Mirrors* (Harper & Row, 1980).

This book goes a long way toward explaining CIA's intellectual and operational constipation in the 1950's through the 1970's. It follows James Jesus Angleton, who tied the Agency in knots and went so far as to privately tell the French that the CIA Station Chief in Paris was a Soviet spy, and William King Harvey, who literally carried two six-guns both in the US and overseas "because you never know when you might need them." Included in this book are some serious details about the operations against Cuba, a chapter appropriated titled "Murder Corrupts", and a good account of how Harvey, in perhaps his most important achievement, smelled out the fact that Kim Philby was indeed a Soviet spy. The concluding thought of the book is exceptional: "Immersed in duplicity and insulated by secrecy, they (Angleton and Harvey) developed survival mechanisms and behavior patterns that by any rational standard were bizarre. The forced inbreeding of secrecy spawned mutant deeds and thoughts. Loyalty demanded dishonesty, and duty was a thieves' game. The game attracted strange men and slowly twisted them until something snapped. There were no winners or losers in this game, only victims."

Riebling, Mark, *WEDGE: The Secret War Between the FBI and the CIA* (Alfred A. Knoph, 1994).

I cannot do this book justice, other than to say that I had never understood the depth and stupidity of the bureaucratic hostility between the FBI and the CIA—mostly the fault of the CIA these days but certainly inspired in part by Hoover in the early days—until I read this book; and that it should be required reading for every senior CIA manager. From the FBI's failure to communicate its very early knowledge of Japanese collection requirement on Pearl Harbor via the Germans, to the assassination of President Kennedy, the World Trade Center bombing and the Aldrich Ames case, this book makes me ashamed and angry about how bureaucracy and secrecy subvert loyalty, integrity, and common professional sense on both sides of this "wedgie" contest.

382

Roson, William R., Susan B. Trento, and Joseph J. Trento, *WIDOWS* (Crown, 1989).

"Four American spies, the wives they left behind, and the KGB's crippling of American intelligence." Naturally containing a great deal of bitterness, this is still a worthwhile detailed overview of our national unwillingness to get serious about counterintelligence, and the human cost this failure entails. Especially good on the culture of deception that sets integrity aside in favor of protecting the bureaucracy.

Simpson, Christopher, *BLOWBACK: America's Recruitment of Nazis and Its Effects on the Cold War* (Weidenfeld & Nicholson, 1988).

Very scary stuff. The bottom line is that for the sake of enhancing national security and national competitiveness, the U.S. Government, with approval from the highest levels, funded the wholesale introduction into U.S. citizenship of both Nazi scientists and Nazi participants in genocidal programs who were viewed in many cases as "essential" to our anti-Communist endeavors. The loss of perspective among selected senior intelligence and policy officials, and the long-term influence of this program on our obsession with Communism, give one pause.

Intelligence, Covert Action and Paramilitary

Bittman, Ladislav, *The Deception Game* (Ballentine, 1972).

I have found no better primer on disinformation, propaganda, and influence operations than this paperback.

Corn, David, *BLOND GHOST: Ted Shackley and the CIA's Crusades* (Simon & Schuster, 1994).

Although Ted Shackley was a line case officer, this book is placed within the paramilitary section because his entire career encompassed a series of wars where the CIA played a very tragic and unproductive role. As Shackley's deputy in Laos is quoted on page 163, speaking on Shakley's accomplishments in Laos, "We spent a lot of money and got a lot of people killed," Lair remembered, "and we didn't get much for it." For those seeking to understand the bureaucratization of the Directorate of Operations, both in the field and in Washington, this is essential reading.

Levine, Michael, *DEEP COVER: The Inside Story of How DEA Infighting, Incompetence and Subterfuge Lost Us the Biggest Battle of the Drug War* (Delacorte, 1990).

Above all, this book is a credible indictment of how Washington bureaucracy and political posturing, combined with mediocre intelligence and a determined policy of trying to reduce drug supplies instead of reducing drug consumption, have made a huge mockery of the "war on drugs." There is another underlying theme, that of how the drug war is corrupting our own officers, who either go bad or cast a blind eye as contractors fly drugs into the US enroute to Europe, where they trade them for arms that are then sold to the contras or others at inflated prices CIA is happy to pay.

Stockwell, John, *In Search of Enemies: A CIA Story* (W.W. Norton, 1978).

By the former Chief of the Angola Task Force at CIA, this book is a classic on the Keystone Kops aspects of paramilitary operations as run by the CIA"s Special Operations Group within the Directorate of Intelligence, as well as the lack of contextual judgment that accompanies the CIA's decisions to "get into" local conflicts that are none of our business. Ammunition from the warehouses that doesn't fit the weapons in the field is just the beginning.

Valentine, Douglas, *The PHOENIX Program* (William Morrow, 1990).

This is as good an account I have found of how the CIA got into the business of helping Vietnamese kill each other off one by one. It is a disturbing and valuable book, and I took from it several lessons: 1) CIA puppies with no military background, and military detailees with no law enforcement background, have no business getting into the gutter with foreign thugs; 2) if we support indigenous arrest, torture, and assassination programs they need to have some serious multi-cultural analysis and counterintelligence support lest we simply give one faction the means of killing off the other without regard to our interests; and 3) our general approach to interference in the internal affairs of other nations is corrupt and increases local corruption. We throw money at personalities rather than insight at institutions. We train and equip local units to inflict covert violence, and then wonder why the situation destabilizes further.

Woodward, Bob, *The Secret Wars of the CIA: 1981-1987* (Pocket Books, 1987).

The inadequacy of human sources, the inability of the Directorate of Operations to focus on *internal* threats to the regimes they were helping, the lack of DO knowledge about the international arms market and related financing arrangements, exorbitant payments to agents ($90,000 a year for one senior policeman in El Salvador, this in late 1970 dollars), the bureaucratic infighting (the DO trying to steal a good open source from Adm Inman, then burning the source with the Swedish police when Inman objected)—these are just a few of the gems in this well-documented book. On balance it does not suggest an end to covert action, but rather the need for increased competence.

Intelligence, Economic Espionage

Fialka, John, *War by Other Means: Economic Espionage in America* (W. W. Norton, 1997).

John is a distinguished correspondent for the *Wall Street Journal*, their lead reporter during the Gulf War, and an award-winning investigative journalist in the fields of national security, politics, and financial scandal. The Chinese, Japanese, French and Russians are featured here, together with useful cross-overs into criminal gangs doing espionage on U.S. corporations, as well as overt data mining and other quasi-legal activities that yield far more economic intelligence than most business leaders understand.

Guisnel, Jean, *Cyberwars: Espionage on the Internet* (Plenum Trade, 1997).

Jean, a nationally-respected journalist in France who has covered espionage matters for decades, is the author of one of those rare French books that make it into the U.S. marketplace. Translated into English after great reviews in Europe, it charts the migration of European and Anglo-Saxon intelligence professionals into cyber-space.

Schweizer, Peter, *FRIENDLY SPIES: How America's Allies are Using Economic Espionage to Steal Our Secrets* (Atlantic Monthly, 1993).

One hundred billion dollars annually is one White House estimate of the cost to U.S. businesses imposed by economic espionage carried out predominantly by our allies—France, Israel, Germany, South Korea, and Japan being among the top culprits. Peter Schweizer was the first to really put this issue on the table, and he deserves a lot of credit. Neither Congress nor the Administration are yet prepared to take this issue seriously, and this is a grave mistake, for in the 21st Century information is the seed corn of prosperity, and our allies are eating our seed corn.

Winkler, Ira, *CORPORATE ESPIONAGE: What It Is; Why It's Happening to Your Company; What You Must Do About It* (Prima, 1997)

Ira, a former National Security Agency professional, made a name for himself in his second career as a corporate electronic security specialist by using a combination of common sense and basic work-arounds to penetrate and download millions if not billions of dollars worth of corporate research and development—always at the company's request, and generally with astonishing results. From his antics as a "temp" hire gaining access within two days, to his more systematic attacks using all known vulnerabilities including factory-shipped system administrator passwords that were never changed, he has exposed in a very practical way the "naked emperor" status of corporate America.

Intelligence, Foreign Capabilities

Andrew, Christopher and Oleg Gordievsky, *Instructions from the Centre: Top Secret Files on KGB Foreign Operations, 1975-1985* (Scepter UK, 1991)

Imagine the CIA clandestine mentality and U.S. bureaucracy, as operated by a Soviet-style controlled regime. This is an eye-glazing but very professionally put together testimonial to the fact that much of what the KGB did was pedestrian, pointless, very expensive, and as weak on understanding foreign countries as the US.

Bergin, Anthony and Robert Hall, *Intelligence and Australian National Security* (Australian Defence Studies Centre1994)

We don't see enough books in English on other intelligence communities, in part because they are not often published, in part because we are all very insular. This book groups a number of excellent articles into several major sections dealing with policy, operational intelligence, the wider concept of security, the limits of openness, economic and commercial intelligence, and intelligence requirements for international regimes. The four appendices on intelligence sources are a real disappointment, as they reflect more than anything just how narrowly read most authors on intelligence actually are.

Eftimiades, Nicholas, *Chinese Intelligence Operations* (Naval Institute Press, 1994)

Nick is an experienced sinologist who has worked at the Department of State, CIA, and DIA, and is also a naval reserve officer. His book is well-organized, well-researched, and essential reading for those who would understand how comprehensively the Chinese seek out scientific, technical, and military information in the United States, with a special emphasis on open sources of intelligence.

Hager, Nicky, *Secret Power: New Zealand's Role in the International Spy Network* (Craig Potton NZ, 1996).

This is a wonderful book about New Zealand's signals intelligence service, as good as the *Puzzle Palace* in its own way. Especially charming is the three-dimensional figure of the signals intelligence headquarters showing precisely what functions are on each end of each floor. The two most sensational revelations in this book are that the computers doing the signals targeting are controlled by the Americans and there is no New Zealand oversight or even understanding of what profiles the Americans are installing; and that the signals intelligence service made a deliberate decision not to inform the Prime Minister at the time when they first bought into being an extension of the U.S. signals intelligence empire.

Kalugin, Oleg, *The First Directorate: My 32 Years in Intelligence and Espionage Against the West* (St. Martin's Press, 1994).

Oleg, now a green-card resident of the U.S. is our most personable and enjoyable former opponent on the intelligence speaking circuit, and both Bill Colby and I supported him in his efforts to move permanently to America. His book is a marvelous account on the general details of his formidable career that culminated in his being elected to the Russian Parliament. Page 222, "Kill the dog!", has a special meaning for professionals the world over.

Ostrovsky, Victor with Claire Hoy, *By Way of Deception: The Making and Unmaking of a Mossad Officer* (St. Martin's Press, 1990).

One of my atmospherics books, enjoyable for its description of Mossad training exercises for new Career Trainees, and for its insights into how Israeli fully integrates military assistance carrots and clandestine intelligence follow-ups. Some insights into Mossad's deliberate manipulation of U.S. intelligence and a few allegations regarding U.S. hostage situations where Mossad might have done more but chose not to.

Richelson, Jeffrey T., *Foreign Intelligence Organizations* (Ballinger, 1988).

An essential reference. Focuses on major countries. Needs a companion volume for the smaller powers including Ghana of all places, where a CIA employee was successfully recruited by the "backward" local service.

Sheymov, Victor, *Tower of Secrets: A Real Life Spy Thriller* (Naval Institute Press, 1993).

This book is fun. It provides a look at the career of a KGB officer with a level of detail that makes one thing abundantly clear: the KGB and CIA are more alike than one might think, for the simply reason that they are both bureaucracies. Smoothly presented, enjoyable throughout.

Intelligence, History

Chalou, George C. (ed.), *The Secrets War: The Office of Strategic Services in World War II* (National Archives and Records Administration, 1992).

Twenty four distinguished authors, including Sir Robin Brook from England and William Colby, an original serving member of the OSS and later DCI, provide a really well-developed history of the OSS with special sections on OSS records and OSS research, as well as grouped contributions on OSS operations in various regional areas and reflections on *today's* circumstances. One contributor, Robin Winks, concludes that US intelligence (CIA) is not getting "the right stuff" now for four interlocking reasons: 1) academia by and large no longer cooperates with the intelligence community; 2) academia lost its interest in being helpful when it became apparent that the covert action tail was wagging the intelligence dog; 3) the intelligence community, apprehensive about recruiting from open institutions permitting violent war protests, made the clearance process so convoluted that it began averaging eighteen months; and 4) the agency began to recruit people who badly wanted to join and were willing to put up with a recruitment and clearance process that the best Yale students, the ones who withdrew from consideration, described as "curious, stupid, degrading, and off-putting", with the result that the agency ultimate lost access to "the self-assured, the confident, the questioning, and the adventurous—precisely the qualities that has been so attractive to the OSS—in the process." I myself know from discussions with the head of the office responsible for evaluating incoming Career Trainees, that the standard profile of a desirable candidate has always been "the company man" who goes along, except in two years—1979 and 1982—when they went after "self-starters." Within five years, both those classes lost fifty percent of their numbers to resignation, and I believe that this problem continues to persist. I was in the 1979 class, and hung in there for nine years.

Johnson, Lock K., *A Season of Inquiry: The Senate Intelligence Investigation* (University Press of Kentucky, 1985).

"You see, the way a free government works, there's got to be a housecleaning every now and then." Harry Truman, as cited on the first page of the book. Well, in the U.S. Government, before you get a real housecleaning, it appears you have to build the vacuum cleaner from scratch every few years, and even then you only get the big dirt on the margins. This book is a very important book with all the more value today as we finally get serious about intelligence reform. Loch's professional and extraordinarily detailed account of the entire Church Committee investigation, its findings, White House attempts to avoid reform, and the rather bland outcomes that finally resulted, should be considered the key to understanding where we are today and why we so desperately need legislation to achieve substantive reform. Had Senator Church been chosen by Jimmy Carter as Vice President (Church was favored by the convention, with Mondale and Stevenson tied behind him), who knows what good might have come of his White House service.

Persico, Joseph E., *CASEY—The Lives and Secrets of William J. Casey: From the OSS to the CIA* (Viking, 1990).

Persico has done a wonderful job of capturing Casey's magnificent complexity and intellectual voraciousness. Oddly enough the best quote in there, part of a really excellent over-all description of why the DO does not succeed, comes from Herb Meyer when he was a special assistant to Casey: "These guys have built a system that shuts them off from any intelligence except what you can steal. These people needed to be reconnected to reality."

Westerfield, H. Bradford (ed.), *inside CIA's private world* (Yale, 1995).

Brad, a respected scholar in his own right, was given unique access to all past publications of the CIA's internal journal, *Studies in Intelligence*, and has produced an absolutely lovely collection of the best thoughts inside CIA from 1955-1992, organized into sections for imagery intelligence collection, overt human intelligence collection, clandestine human intelligence collection, human intelligence and its consumers, the analysis function, analysis and its consumers, and counterespionage. I regard this book as an essential supplementary reading for teaching both students and practitioners.

Intelligence, Military

DeForest, Orin, *SLOW BURN: The Rise and Bitter Fall of American Intelligence in Vietnam* (Simon & Schuster, 1990)

This is one of two books I regard as essential to an understanding of our intelligence failures in Viet-Nam. DeForrest was a former military enlisted man who ended up managing a great deal of the prisoner interrogation for a major Agency facility in-country. His story ties together a number of important themes, from the failure of Ivy League types to understand what they were dealing with to the inadequacies (and sometimes the superiority) of vast numbers of "contract" case officers who would normally not have been hired, to the very real value of systematically debriefing all prisoners and entering the results into a database amenable to search and retrieval, something we don't know how to do today. Across every major military operation since Viet-Nam, it has been my experience that we have no table of organization and equipment, completely inadequate numbers of trained interrogators and translators, and no commitment to the tedious but essential work of extracting knowledge from large numbers of hostile prisoners.

Jones, Bruce E., *War Without Windows* (Berkeley, 1987).

Sam Adams may be more famous as the whistle-blower on CIA and U.S. military falsification of the numbers of Viet Cong and regular North Vietnamese army personnel confronting the U.S. in Viet-Nam, but this book is the very best account I have found of the intimate details of how politics, bureaucracy, bad judgment, and some plain downright lying falsified the military intelligence process at all levels of the U.S. military in Viet-Nam.

Katz, Samuel M., *Soldier Spies: Israeli Military Intelligence* (Presidio, 1992).

This is a very fine book about the minutia and the value of a well-rounded military intelligence capability. I was especially impressed by four aspects: the emphasis on prisoner interrogation, the development of easy to install tactical signals collection devices that could be carried in by deep reconnaissance units; the over-all commitment to long-range patrolling; and the commitment to "behind the lines" covert violence using all the tools of intelligence to identify and kill very specific people such as two Egyptian Colonels believed to be guiding Palestinian terrorist actions against Israel. These are all areas where the Americans are very weak, and I consider this book a very helpful "manual" for military commanders who want to take a more active role in guiding defense intelligence into the future.

Mangold, Tom and John Penycate, *The Tunnels of Chu Chi* (Berkeley, 1985). This is required reading for every commander and every staff officer, and for every intelligence professional, both at the entry-level and at mid-career. Two things really hit home from this book: 1) the fact that we were completely clueless about the physical, mental, and cultural toughness and dedication of the Vietnamese who opposed our interference in Viet-Nam; 2) the fact that we are completely unable to detect tunnels under our base camps or in the tactical environment (although new technology is coming along). They dug 200 miles of tunnels by hand, including extensive networks under the major Bien Hoa complex.

Wirtz, James J., *The Tet Offensive: Intelligence Failure in War* (Cornell, 1991).

Jim, a very respected member of the faculty at the Naval Postgraduate School, has provided us with a very well documented study of how the U.S. missed the Tet Offensive in Viet-Name. Among his findings: we knew fully two months in advance at the tactical collection level, with several additional collection successes and some modest analysis successes in the weeks preceding the offensive. We were distracted by Khe Sanh, the commanders did not want to hear it, "intelligence to please" was the standard within the Military Assistance Command Viet-Nam intelligence bureaucracy, and when we finally did grasp, one day before the attack, its true strategic nature, we failed to disseminate the warnings to the tactical commanders with sufficient effectiveness.

Intelligence, Policy

Andrew, Christopher *For the President's Eyes Only: Secret Intelligence and the American Presidency from Washington to Bush* (HarperCollins, 1995).

"Over the past two centuries only four American presidents—Washington, Eisenhower, Kennedy (briefly), and Bush—have shown a real flair for intelligence." This 660-page book documents this assessment, and ends with the conclusion "The presidents in the twenty-first century, like their Cold War predecessors, will continue to find an enormously expensive global intelligence system both fallible and indispensable." His general findings in the conclusion are instructive: presidents have tended to have exaggerated expectations of intelligence, and have frequently overestimated the secret power that covert action might put at their command. For all that failed, both in intelligence not getting it right and presidents not listening when it did, intelligence undeniably helped stabilize the Cold War and avoid many confrontations.

Gates, Robert M., *From the Shadows: The Ultimate Insider's Story of Five Presidents and How They Won the Cold War* (Simon & Schuster, 1996).

I wore out one fountain pen on this book. Bob Gates has served his country, and five presidents, as earnestly and capably as anyone might, and there is much to learn from this book. The level of detail is quite good. He is very critical of the Directorate of Operations for both misbehavior and a lack of management control in relation to Central America, and as one who was there I have to say, he is absolutely right. We disagree on the point of intelligence (he would say, "secrets for the president", I would say "knowledge for the Nation") but I believe we would agree on this: intelligence is important, and intelligence merits deep and sustained interest by the President.

Intelligence, Reform and Future

20ᵗʰ Century Fund, *In From the Cold: The Report of the Twentieth Century Fund Task Force on The Future of U.S. Intelligence* (with papers by Allan E. Goodman, Gregory Treverton, and Philip Zelikow, 1996)

The Director of Central Intelligence now serving refuses to accept the word "reform" and persists in the traditionalist view that only incremental change is needed within the U.S. Intelligence Community. This book, by a very respected team of private sector authorities with experience in the business of intelligence opens by noting that "informed opinion overwhelmingly holds that many of the important questions about the intelligence agencies have yet to be addressed." Their book, and mine, and the books coming out this year by Greg Treverton, the team of Bruce Berkowitz and Allan Goodman, and a group of ten authors including Mel Goodman and Bob White, are part of the responsible effort from the private sector to get the incoming President and the incoming Congress to finally accept their own responsibility for engaging these issues and legislating reform that will never come from within the U.S. Intelligence Community if it is left to its own devices and inclinations.

Adams, James, *The New Spies: Exploring the Frontiers of Espionage* (Hutchinson, 1994).

By the (UK) *Sunday Times* Bureau Chief in Washington, a former defense correspondent, I found this book somewhat disappointing but never-the-less worthy of consideration. Although the author concludes that the end of the Cold War should have produced a massive upheaval and did not, leaving "too many of the old practices intact with little evidence that the intelligence community is ready to face the fast changing, frightening world that lies ahead," my impression was that the author was completely taken in by the party line and overlooked most of the really trenchant intelligence reform literature, including the open source.

Agee, Philip, *Inside the Company: CIA Diary* (Bantam Books, 1975).

I despise what Philip Agee did with this book, endangering the lives of real people and violating his oath as a commissioned officer in the clandestine service. I was also very surprised by the level of detail in the book, and concluded that he intended to betray the CIA well prior to leaving. I've served three overseas tours and three Washington assignments, and from all that time I can barely remember one cryptonym series and not a single true identity. I think Agee took notes and planned ahead to burn the CIA. This is a good diary, and I include it in this bibliography to represent the pedestrian side of the DO—the day to day monotony of going through the motions and doing agent recruitments and agent handling operations in third world countries where the bulk of what one does really does not contribute to U.S. national security or understanding.

Berkowitz, Bruce D. and Allen E. Goodman, *BEST TRUTH: Intelligence in the Information Age* (Yale, 2000).

This book dedicates itself entirely to fixing the underlying process of intelligence. The authors place intelligence in the larger context of information, and draw a plethora of useful comparisons with emerging private sector capabilities and standards. They place strong emphasis on the emerging issues (not necessarily threats) related to ethnic, religious, and geopolitical confrontation, and are acutely sensitive to the new power of non-governmental organizations and non-state actors. The heart of their book is captured in three guidelines for the new process: focus on understanding the consumer's priorities; minimize the investment in fixed hardware and personnel; and create a system that can draw freely on commercial capabilities where applicable (as they often will be). Their chapter on the failure of the bureaucratic model for intelligence, and the need to adopt the virtual model—one that permits analysts to draw at will on diverse open sources—is well presented and compelling. Their concluding three chapters on analysis, covert action, and secrecy are solid professional-level discussions of where we must go in the future.

Eisendrath, Craig (ed.), *National Insecurity: U.S. Intelligence After the Cold War* (Temple University Press, 2000).

A project by the Center for International Policy, founded by Senator Tom Harkin (D-Iowa), this book brings together a series of chapters that are largely anecdotal (but reasoned) pieces from former foreign service officers recalling all the terrible things CIA did or did not do while they were in service. It includes a chapter by Mel Goodman that some thought was to have been a full-blown book. The chapter by Richard A. Stubbing on "Improving the Output of Intelligence: Priorities, Managerial Changes, and Funding" is quite interesting. There is a great deal of truth in all that is presented here—Ambassador Bob White, for example, was in El Salvador when I reported, a graduate thesis on predicting (and preventing) revolution in my past, and I remember vividly our conversation about the need to suppress the extreme right if we were to stabilize the country.

Hulnick, Arthur S., *Fixing the Spy Machine: Preparing American Intelligence for the Twenty-First Century* (Praeger, 1999).

This book has two good features—the author really does understand the personnel issues, and hence one can read between the lines for added value; and the book is as good an "insider" tour of the waterfront as one could ask for. How the book treats the CIA-FBI relationship, for example, is probably representative of how most CIA insiders feel. The book does not reflect a deep understanding of open sources and tends to accept the common wisdom across the intelligence bureaucracy, that all is "generally okay" and just a bit of change on the margin is necessary. In this respect, it is a good benchmark against which the more daring reformist books may be measured.

Johnson, Loch, *Bombs, Bugs, Drugs, and Thugs: Intelligence Challenges in the New Millenium* (New York University Press, 2000)

Above is the working title. Loch, the dean of intelligence reformers and unique for having served on both the Church Committee and the Aspin/Brown Commission professional staffs, addresses in his book the difficulties of conducting intelligence in the post-cold war era and suggests some new ideas for overcoming the current downward trends in both coverage and effectiveness. Although I have not seen this book yet, I am compelled to ensure that it is listed, for Loch is by all measures the longest serving, most committed, and most gracious of the loyal intelligence reformers.

Marchetti, Victor and John D. Marks, *The CIA and the Cult of Intelligence* (Laurel, 1980).

This is one of perhaps ten books from prior to 1985 that I decided to include because of their continuing value. I believe that both history and historians will credit these two individuals with having made a difference by articulating so ably both the clandestine mentality and the problems extant in the lack of oversight regarding proprietary organizations, propaganda and disinformation, and intrusive not-so-clandestine operations.

Moynihan, Daniel Patrick, *Secrecy: The American Experience* (Yale, 1998)

Senator Moynihan applies his intellect and his strong academic and historical bent to examine the U.S. experience with secrecy, beginning with its early distrust of ethnic minorities. He applies his social science frames of reference to discuss secrecy as a form of regulation and secrecy as a form of ritual, both ultimately resulting in a deepening of the inherent tendency of bureaucracy to create and keep secrets—secrecy as the cultural norm. His historical overview, current right up to 1998, is replete with documented examples of how secrecy may have facilitated selected national security decisions in the short-run, but in the long run these decisions were not only found to have been wrong for lack of accurate open information that was dismissed for being open, but also harmful to the democratic fabric, in that they tended to lead to conspiracy theories and other forms of public distancing from the federal government. He concludes: "The central fact is that we live today in an Information Age. Open sources give us the vast majority of what we need to know in order to make intelligent decisions. Decisions made by people at ease with disagreement and ambiguity and tentativeness. Decisions made by those who understand how to exploit the wealth and diversity of publicly available information, who no longer simply assume that clandestine collection—that is, 'stealing secrets'—equals greater intelligence. *Analysis*, far more than secrecy, is the key to security....Secrecy is for losers."

Treverton, Gregory F., *Reshaping Intelligence for an Age of Information* (Cambridge, 2000)

Greg, both a distinguished academic and the former Vice Chairman of the National Intelligence Council, has given us a thoughtful examination of both the premises and objectives of national intelligence. As Greg puts it, "Then, the world was one of a single predominant target, the Soviet Union, of too little information, most of which -- spy reports and satellite photos -- was both "owned" by intelligence and regarded as reliable. Now, intelligence has many targets, not one, many customers -- including foreign governments and private citizens -- not few, and and too much information, not too little, but of widely varying reliablility. Collecting information used to be the

394

problem; now selecting and validating it is the task. U.S. intelligence used to think it was in the secrets business, but now it is in the information business. It needs to be decentralized and opened; it used to wall itself off in compartments lest secrets seep out, but now it needs to be opened—to think-tanks, NGOs, academics and Wall Street—lest the information that is out there in the world not seep in."

Turner, Stansfield, *Secrecy and Democracy: The CIA in Transition* (Harper & Row, 1985).

Stansfield Turner was a Rhodes scholar and naval officer who rose to command of a carrier task group, a fleet, NATO's southern flank, and the Navy's most prestigious intellectual institution, the Naval War College. He served from 1977-1981 as Director of Central Intelligence under President Jimmy Carter, and his book in my mind was the first serious contribution—perhaps even a catalyst—to the growing debate over whether and how much reform is required if the U.S. Intelligence Community is to be effective in the 21st Century. His eleven-point agenda for reform is of lasting value, as are his ideas for intelligence support to those responsible for natural disaster relief and other non-military challenges.

Zegart, Amy B., *Flawed By Design: The Evolution of the CIA, JCS, and NSC* (Stanford, 1999).

This is a very worthy and thoughtful book. It breaks new ground in understanding the bureaucratic and political realities that surrounded the emergence of the National Security Council, the Joint Chiefs of Staff, and the Central Intelligence Agency. The CIA was weak by design, strongly opposed by the military services from the beginning. Its covert activities emerged as a Presidential prerogative, unopposed by others in part because it kept CIA from being effective at coordinated analysis, for which it had neither the power nor the talent. Most usefully, the book presents a new institutionalist theory of bureaucracy that gives full weight to the original design, the political players including the bureaucrats themselves, and external events. Unlike domestic agencies that have strong interest groups, open information, legislative domain, and unconnected bureaucracies, the author finds that national security agencies, being characterized by weak interest groups, secrecy, executive domain, and connected bureaucracies, evolve differently from other bureaucracies, and are much harder to reform. On balance, the author finds that intelligence *per se*, in contrast to defense or domestic issues, is simply not worth the time and Presidential political capital needed to fix *but* that if reform is in the air, the President should either pound on the table and put the full weight of their office behind a substantive reform proposal, or walk away from any reform at all—the middle road will not successful.

Management, Acquisition

I'm not going to review these books, simply because this is not my area of expertise and I want to use them as passing examples of what may be the single most important area where intelligence, properly done, and management, properly exercised, could save up to $50 billion or more a year—perhaps as much as $100 billion across the entire government.

Fishner, Stanley, *A Report on Government Procurement Practices: What's Needed to Reverse the Trend* (Camelot Publishers, 1989).

Fox, J. Ronald, *The Defense Management Challenge: Weapons Acquisition* ((Harvard, 1988).

Mullins, James P., *The Defense Matrix: National Preparedness and the Military-Industrial Complex* (Avant, 1986).

Stewart, Rod and Annie, *Managing Millions: An Inside Look at High-Tech Government Spending* (John Wiley, 1988).

Tolchin, Martin and Susan J., *Selling Our Security: The Erosion of America's Assets* (Alfred A. Knopf, 1992).

Weiner, Tim, *Blank Check: The Pentagon's Black Budget* (Warner, 1990).

Management, Future

Abshire, David M., *Preventing World War III: A Realistic Grand Strategy* (Harper & Row, 1988).

This book, apart from being the world's longest job description (for a Counselor to the President for Grand Strategy), remains a vibrant and provocative discussion relevant to guiding the Nation into the 21st Century. Part I discusses the "world theater" and Part II discusses in turn a grand strategy and then political, public, deterrence, negotiating, resources, technology, Third World, and economic strategies. The book ends with thoughts on organizing for strategy that should, because of who wrote them and how good they are, be required reading, in their twelve-page entirety, for the President and his entire Cabinet team.

396

Friedman, George and Meredith, *The Future of War: Power, Technology and American World Dominance in the Twenty-First Century* (St. Martin's, 1996).

The authors begin by noting that there is "a deep chasm between the advent of technology and its full implementation in doctrine and strategy." In their history of failure they note how conventional wisdom always seems to appreciate the systems that won the past wars, and observes that in the U.S. military there is a long history of transferring power from the political and military leadership to the technical and acquisition managers, all of whom have no real understanding of the current and future needs of the men who will actually fight. They address America's vulnerability in both U.S. based logistics and in overseas transport means—"Destroying even a portion of American supply vessels could so disrupt the tempo of a logistical build-up as to delay offensive operations indefinitely." They have a marvelous section on the weaknesses of U.S. data gathering tools, noting for example that satellites provide only a *static* picture of one very small portion of the battlefield, rather that the wide-area and dynamic "situational awareness" that everyone agrees is necessary. They go on to gore other sacred oxes, including the Navy's giant ships such as the carrier (and implicitly the new LPH for Marines as well as the ill-conceived arsenal ship) and the largest of the aircraft proposed by the Air Force. They ultimately conclude that the future of war demands manned space stations that are able to integrate total views of the world with control of intercontinental precision systems, combined with a complete restructuring of the ground forces (most of which will be employed at the squad level) and a substantial restructuring of our navel force to provide for many small fast platforms able to swarm into coastal areas.

Modis, Theodore, *Predictions: Society's Telltale Signature Reveals the Past and Forecasts the Future* (Simon & Schuster, 1992).

Or, everything you ever wanted to know about the S-curve and why it all makes sense in the end. This book is about creativity, competition, and the natural order of things. Mutants are most important during times of violent change (the end of a paradigm) when they offer substantial variation from the non-workable past and hence improve the shift toward survival by being more fit for the new circumstances. Interestingly, each successive transport infrastructure (canals to rails to roads to airways) provides an order of magnitude improvement in productivity. One could consider the personal computer and modem a way station on this trend, with networking and true global collaborative work tools as the next node. In the life spiral of change 1996 is the center of a "charging" period with new order and new technology, and will lead to tension and grow in the 2000-2010 period followed by a discharge boom and then relaxation and recession in the 2010-2020 period. Pollution is the next "global war" that needs to be fought, and we will not have a global village until we can reduce the travel time between any two points anywhere to 70 minutes and a cumulative cost for a year of such travel to 15% of the average global income.

Petersen, John L., *Out of the Blue: Wild Cards and Other Big Future Surprises* (Arlington Institute, 1997).

John lays out 78 "wild card" scenarios in this book that are, literally, "earth-shaking." For me the book was a litmus test for the relevance and structure of national intelligence and the answer is not pretty. By and large, across every single major issue of fundamental importance to national security and prosperity, from the collapse of world fisheries to epidemic disease jumping from Africa to Europe to the USA to developments in energy, religion, migration, and climate, the U.S. Intelligence Community is neither ready nor relevant. This is something we have to change.

Scales, Robert H. Jr., *Firepower in Limited War* (Presidio, 1995).

Major General Bob Scales may well be the Army's brightest light and this generation's successor to General Don Starry and Dan Morelli (who inspired the Toffler's book on *War and Anti-War*). First published by the National Defense University Press in 1990, this book reflects deeply on the limitations of firepower in limited war situations, and the conclusion is a telling indictment of our national intelligence community and our joint military intelligence community, neither of which is willing to break out of their little boxes to find a proper response to this statement: "The common theme in all five case studies presented here is the recurring inability of the side with the firepower advantage to find the enemy with sufficient timeliness and accuracy to exploit that advantage fully and efficiently."

Scales, Robert H. Jr., *Future Warfare: Anthology* (U.S. Army War College, April 1999).

This book is a compendium of his thinking on the future of war, and I will summarize just one train of thought that he presents: it places great emphasis on "global scouts" as the foundation for everything, followed by forward-deployed forces, pre-emption forces, and projection forces based in the US. Trust, not technology, sustains coalitions and wins wars. I would add the observation that trust comes from shared intelligence, not from shared technology.

Simpkin, Richard E., *Race to the Swift: Thoughts on Twenty-First Century Warfare* (Brassey's UK, 1988).

First published in 1985, Brigadier Simpkin's book has a forward from General Donn Starry and another from MajGen Perry Smith, USAF (Ret.) and one of our best strategic thinkers. It is the best book I have found to date with which to begin any discussion about the future of warfare. This was the book that inspired my conceptualization of the four warrior classes and also deepened my understanding of the relationships between mobility, accuracy, intelligence, tempo, mass, politics, and cost.

Toffler, Alvin and Heidi, *War and Anti-War: Survival at the Dawn of the 21*st *Century* (Little Brown, 1993).

900 copies of this book were handed out at OSS '94 when the Tofflers were our keynote speakers, and it's hard to do anything other than praise a book with a chapter on "The Future of the Spy" built around OSS and my vision. With that disclosure, I will offer the observation that this book, which has gotten enormous attention within the U.S. military, is an excellent companion to Brigadier Simpkin's book, and the two, perhaps with General Scale's book, could be used to drive any graduate-level course on structuring a future warfighting *and peacekeeping* force.

Management, Leadership

Gardner, Howard, *Leading Minds: An Anatomy of Leadership* (HarperCollins, 1995).

I bought this book sometime after concluding that national intelligence leadership needed to inspire and appeal to the citizens of the USA at large, rather than being so narrowly focused on staying out of trouble with Congress while collecting secrets. This book reviews leadership of both domains and nations, with case studies on Margaret Mead (Culture), J. Robert Oppenheimer (Physics), Robert Maynard Hutchins (Education), Alfred P. Sloan, Jr. (Business), George C. Marshall (Military), Pope John XXII (Religion), Eleanor Roosevelt (Ordinariness and Extraordinariness), Martin Luther King (Minority) and Margaret Thatcher (National). The best leaders that emerge are those who are willing to confront authority and take risk, while also creating networks of contacts that number in the hundreds or thousands rather than tens. Most tellingly, aleader in a discipline (e.g. intelligence) only emerges as a long-term leader if he finally realizes that "he is more likely to achieve his personal goals or to satisfy his community if he addresses a wider audience than if he remains completely within a specific domain." The six constants of leadership are the story, the audience (beginning with a message for the unschooled mind), the organization, the embodiment, a choice between direct (more practical) and indirect (more reflective and often more enduring) leadership, and a paradox—the direct leaders often lack knowledge while the indirect leaders often have greater knowledge, and transferring knowledge from the indirect leader to the direct leader may be one of the central challenges and opportunities of the 21st Century.

Burns, James McGregor, *LEADERSHIP* (Harper, 1978).

This is an exhaustive examination of leadership beginning with its psychological, social, and political origins and then going on into reviews of transforming leadership (intellectual, reformist, revolutionary, and ideological) and transactions leadership (opinion, group, party, legislative, and executive). He concludes that leadership is a poorly-understood concept and that there is both demand and room to grow for future leaders. Leadership is collective, dissensual, causitive, morally purposeful, and elevating. At the end of the day, he has three rules: 1) don't assume your opponents, even Presidents, are too powerful to beat—in all probability they have feet of clay; and 2) integrate the views and needs of those to be led, or change will not occur; and 3) persist, and focus on the particular, and you will eventually prevail.

Management, Organizational

Drucker, Peter F., *Innovation and Entrepreneurship: Practice and Principles* (Harper & Row, 1985).

Drucker has a remarkable ability to deflate any self-styled entrepreneur and "innovator." His book discusses the sources of innovation, concluding rather significantly that knowledge-based innovation is rarely successful—that innovation generally works best when all the factors are known and put into new combinations that work exceedingly well—and that successful innovations start small, focus on the simplest element that can be understood by any half-wit, don't cost a lot, and are never grandiose.

Drucker, Peter F., *Post-Capitalist Society* (Harper, 1993).

Drucker and Toffler agree on one important idea: fiscal and monetary policy is no longer the real driver for national prosperity. At best it is a place-holder, a means of keeping the economy stable. There is a strong element of accountability throughout the book, first with respect to the managers of governments and corporations, and finally with the managers of schools that must ultimately be held accountable for producing students who are competent at both learning and sharing knowledge. For Drucker, the organization of the post-capitalist society must commit itself to being a *destabilizer* able to change constantly. "It must be organized for systematic abandonment of the established, the customary, the familiar, the comfortable—whether products, services, processes, human and social relationships, skills, or organizations themselves. It is the very nature of knowledge that it changes fast and that today's certainties will be tomorrow's absurdities." So speaketh Drucker of the U.S. Intelligence Community....

Farrell, Larry C., *Searching for the Spirit of Enterprise: Dismantling the Twentieth Century Corporation: Lessons from Asian, European, and American Entrepreneurs* (Dutton, 1993).

400

Excellent airplane book. Articulates concerns about business schools that disdain real business, for managers that count money instead of making it, and for governments that are complacent about the lack of an entrepreneurial culture within their business ranks. His general approach is to deconstruct companies into smaller units where the management can be close to the actual value-creation, there are simpler more honest relationships, and there is a combined sense of pride and urgency that increases the momentum and productivity of the group.

Hammer, Michael and James Champy, *Reengineering the Corporation: A Manifesto for Business Revolution* (HarperCollins, 1993).

This was the original "reengineering" book and rather than summarize the components of his process I will just name the one big "no no" that the current leadership of the U.S. Intelligence Community is passively pursuing...the most frequently committed error: "Try to fix a process instead of changing it."

Kantor, Rosabeth Moss, *The Change Masters: Innovation & Entrepreneurship in the American Corporation* (Simon & Schuster, 1983).

This book was meaningful to me because it documents the relationship between an open organizational environment, individual employee productivity, and innovation.

Kantor, Rosabeth Moss, *World Class: Thriving Locally in the Global Economy* (Simon & Schuster, 1995).

This book sparked my understanding of "community intelligence" and the need for an integrated network of civic leaders, corporate leaders, academic leaders, and social or non-profit leaders all sharing the same "intelligence" on what the threat to the local community is in terms of losing jobs and remaining attractive as an investment. The author boils it down to each community deciding if it is a thinker, a maker, or a trader community, and then setting out to ensure that everything about the community supports that specific kind of business at a "world-class" level.

Osborne, David and Peter Plastrik, *Banishing Bureaucracy: The Five Strategies for Reinventing Government* (Addison-Wesley, 1991).

Well, the Vice President loved it and the President bought into it, but it did not make a difference. As I document in Chapter 12, the National Performance Review identified a number of substantive objectives for intelligence reform, and the intelligence bureaucracy was successful in ignoring the White House. I suspect it has something to do with one of the fundamentals: "Unleash—but Harness—the Pioneers." The U.S. Intelligence Community can't stand pioneers unless they are spending billions of dollars on something really, really secret that has a high probability of failure. Reinvention boils down to uncoupling or deconstructing a whole bunch of stuff, and then allowing the pieces to compete. It requires managers that can "let go" and employees that can "take hold." Above all, it requires openness and accountability....

Pinchot, Gifford & Elizabeth, *The End of Bureaucracy & The Rise of the Intelligent Organization* (Berrey-Koehler, 1993).

The seven essentials of organizational intelligence include widespread truth and rights; freedom of enterprise, liberated teams, equality and diversity, *voluntary learning networks*, democratic self-rule, and limited corporate government. It was this book, and the very strong applause that the author received from all those attending OSS '96, that caused me to realize that the U.S. Intelligence Community is just chock full of very good people that *want* to change, but are not being *allowed* to change by the organizational circumstances within which they are trapped—frozen in time and budget.

Senge, Peter M., *The Fifth Discipline: The Art & Practice of The Learning Organization* (Doubleday, 1990).

Without a shared vision there can be no shifting of minds, no team leaning, no local initiatives consistent with the shared vision, and so on. The U.S. Intelligence Community is confounded by its new circumstances, where commercial technology is better than spy technology, commercial sources are better (in the aggregate) than spy sources, and there is a real question as to whether anyone really cares whether the U.S. Intelligence Community exists or not. We need a vision for national intelligence that imparts two distinct values to each intelligence professional: first, a value as a member of a larger global community of experts, each of whom is dedicating to protecting the people and improving their lot; and second, a value as a member of an exclusive elite group of intelligence professionals dedicated to the dangerous and difficult profession of espionage. These are not contradictory values. We need a Director-General for National Intelligence (DGNI) able to impart this vision, not only to the employees across all the agencies, but to the President and Congress as well as the public.

Treacy, Michael & Fred Wiersema, *The Discipline of Market Leaders: Choose Your Customers, Narrow Your Focus, Dominate Your Market* (Addison-Wesley, 1995).

There are three disciplines discussed in this book: operational excellence, product leadership, and customer intimacy. The most important is customer intimacy. "For customer-intimate companies, the toughest challenge is to let go of current solutions and to move themselves and their clients to the next paradigm."

Open Source Intelligence Conference Proceedings

This section is in table format so that it can be used to sort papers by author, year, and topic. The downloadable electronic version of this section is at www.oss.net/Papers/white/index.doc. Each volume can be obtained individually for $50.00 ($60.00 outside USA) inclusive of Priority/Air Mail shipping. Roughly half of the presentations listed are available free online at <www.oss.net>, just use the Search Engine to list items by author.

AAA: Keynotes BUS: Business GEN: General GOV: Government LEA: Law Enforcement MIL: Military NAT: National SEC: Security	The first column identifies the year and the volume number or location for the following two general citations: 92-93: *Proceedings of the Annual International Conference on "National Security & National Competitiveness: Open Source Solutions"* 93-99: *Proceedings of the Annual International Conference on "Global Security & Global Competitiveness: Open Source Solutions"* E=EuroIntel, P=PacIntel, G=Global

92-II	Dedijer, Stevan	AAA	Privatization of Intelligence & Development of Human Intelligence
92-II	Gage, John	AAA	Information, Global Realignments, and our National Infrastructure
92-II	Kahn, Robert	AAA	Outline of a Global Knowledge Architecture: Visions and Possibilities for the Future
97-IV	Pinchot, Gifford III	AAA	Beyond Bureaucracy: The Rise of the Intelligence Organization
95-II	Prusak, Larry	AAA	Seven Myths of the Information Age
96-II	Strassmann, Paul	AAA	U.S. Knowledge Assets: The Choice Target for Information Crime
92-II	Studeman, Bill	AAA	Teaching the Giant to Dance: Contradictions and Opportunities in Open Source Exploitation within the Intelligence Community
93-II	Toffler, Alvin & Heidi	AAA	National Knowledge Strategies, National Intelligence Restructuring, and Global Economic Competitiveness
96-II	Zuckerman, Mortimer	AAA	The Central Importance of Economic and Financial Intelligence to Political Stability and Prosperity

403

98-E	Bauemelin, Yves	BUS	From Black to White to Gray: The Realities of the International Investigative Marketplace
98-G	Bianco, Gene del	BUS	Reuters Methods for Obtaining Open Source Intelligence
98-E	Borry, Marc	BUS	Electronic Sources and Methods: A Belgian Business Perspective
93-II	Caldwell, Paul A.	BUS	The International Investigative Market: Sources, Methods, and Products
96-II	Call, Melissa	BUS	Day to Day Realities and Myths Regarding Financial Research Using Open Sources
98-E	Clerc, Philippe	BUS	Economic Intelligence
99-E	Collier, Harry	BUS	Overview of New Horizons in Business Intelligence Sources, Software, and Services
98-E	Feiler, Gil	BUS	Open and Personal: Economic Intelligence Methods for the Middle East
98-G	Feiler, Gil	BUS	Economic Intelligence Methods for the Middle East
92-I	Harvard JFK	BUS	National Intelligence and the American Enterprise: Exploring the Possibilities
93-I	Hedin, Hans	BUS	Europe's To BI (Business Intelligence) or Not to BI: Inventory of a New Business Innovation
93-I	Herring, Jan	BUS	Business Intelligence: Some Companies Have It, Some Don't—How Do They Know?
93-I	Herring, Jan	BUS	The Role of Intelligence in Formulating Strategy
95-II	Herring, Jan	BUS	Using the Intelligence Process to Create Competitive Advantage for Global Companies
95-II	Herring, Jan	BUS	Intelligence to Enhance American Companies' Competitiveness
95-II	Herring, Jan	BUS	Business Intelligence in Japan and Sweden: Lessons for the US
93-II	Himelfarb, Daniel	BUS	Intelligence Requirements for Executives
94-II	Himelfarb, Daniel	BUS	An Introduction to Competitive and Business Intelligence
92-II	Hlava, Marjorie	BUS	Key Organizations and Personalities in the International Information Business
96-II	Kolb, Guy	BUS	The Society of Competitive Intelligence Professionals
94-II	Marcinko, Randall	BUS	Association of Information Dissemination Centers
92-II	Meyer, Herb	BUS	Intelligence at the Cutting Edge: How Multinational Have Jumped Ahead with Open

			Source Systems
96-II	Nachmanoff, Arnie	BUS	Economic Intelligence Services for the Private Sector: Integrating Online, In-House, and Global Experts
92-II	Nobel, Erika	BUS	From A to Z: What We've Done with Open Sources
99-G	Robinson, Mark	BUS	Open Sources and Services Used by a Fortune 500 Sleuth
96-II	Ruh, William	BUS	Optimizing Corporate Capital Through Information Technology
92-I	Shaker, Steven M	BUS	Intelligence Support to U.S. Business
94-I	Shaker, Steven M.	BUS	Beating the Competition: From War Room to Board Room
94-II	Shaker, Steven M.	BUS	Beating the Competition: From War Room to Board Room (Presentation)
94-II	Sharp, Seena	BUS	Head Them Off At the Pass: How to Identify the Changes that Threaten Your Business or Activity
96-II	Sibbit, Dan	BUS	Emerging Business Models for Commercial Remote Sensing
95-II	Simon, Neil	BUS	Emerging Issues in Competitive Intelligence
94-II	Stanat, Ruth	BUS	Making the Business Case for Business Intelligence: What You Don't Know *Can* Hurt You
98-G	Stara, Michael	BUS	Valuing Competitive Intelligence
93-I	Steele, Robert D.	BUS	Corporate Role in National Competitiveness: Good People + Good Tools + Information = Profit
97-IV	Suggs, Susan	BUS	International Trade and Commerce: Search Strategies for Intelligence Production
94-II	Weiner, Michael	BUS	Constructive Contributions to Business Intelligence Capabilities from Government Information Technology Programs
92-II	Allen, Kenneth	GEN	Data Pathologies, Standards, and other Obstacles of Common Concern to Government and the Private Sector
92-II	Anderson, James	GEN	Information Validation & Auditing
92-II	Andriole, Stephen	GEN	Multi-Media Analysis Methodologies
93-I	Anonymous	GEN	Illustrative Extracts from Alternative Press Index
93-I	Anonymous	GEN	Illustrative Extracts from Alternative Press Review

93-I	Anonymous	GEN	The Definitive Guide to the Zine Revolution
98-E	Arnold, Stephen	GEN	New Trends in Automated Intelligence Gathering Software
98-G	Arnold, Stephen	GEN	The Future of Online
97-IV	Arnold, Steve	GEN	Technology Vectors: 1998 and Beyond
94-II	Basch, Reva	GEN	On-line Searching for Competitive Advantage: How to Do It for Best Results at Least Cost
96-II	Bates, Mary Ellen	GEN	Recent and Emerging Trends in Information Brokering
93-I	Bermudez, Joseph	GEN	Letter from a Source
98-E	Bernard, Christian	GEN	European-Based Imagery Assets and Their Application to Military and Business Intelligence
94-II	Bernhardt, Douglas	GEN	Primary Sources and the End-Game
97-IV	Blejer, Hattie	GEN	Intelligent Information Systems
98-E	Boyer, Nate	GEN	U.S. One Meter Imagery, Canadian Radar Imagery, and Other Considerations for European National and Business Intelligence
98-G	Boyer, Nate	GEN	Commercial Imagery Support Options: Trade-Offs and Value-Added
93-I	Brenner, Anita Susan	GEN	Don't Call it Cyberlaw™: Recent Developments in Law and Policy of Telecommunications and Computer Database Networks
98-E	Brenton, Mike	GEN	Applying Existing Commercial Technologies to Optimize Acquisition and Exploitation of Multiple Sources of Information
93-I	Brodwin, David	GEN	Information Overload
98-G	Brueckner, Annette	GEN	Information and Knowledge Management in Intelligence Situations
98-G	Burwell, Helen	GEN	Commercial Online Source Validation Methods
99-G	Caputo, Anne	GEN	The Internet Search-Off: Traditional Search Services Challenge the Web
94-II	Carroll, Bonnie	GEN	Harsh Realities: Science & Technology Acquisition Costs, Obstacles, and Results
92-I	Castagna, Michael	GEN	Book Report: Alvin Toffler's *PowerShift: Knowledge, Wealth, and Violence at the Edge of the 21ˢᵗ Century*
93-II	Christian, Eliot	GEN	Wide Area Information Servers (WAIS) and Global Change Research
95-II	Clagan, Don	GEN	Tailored News Alerts for a Competitive Edge
94-II	Collier, Harry	GEN	Overview of the Global Information Industry

98-G	Collier, Harry	GEN	The Pricing of Electronic Information
97-IV	Dolan, Kate	GEN	Meta-Data and Systems Issues
92-II	Driver, Robert K.	GEN	N-STAR: An Automated Tool for Open Source Data
98-G	Dunn, Ronald	GEN	Confronting the Future: Bracing for the Brave New World
99-E	Dunnink, Jan	GEN	A User-Centric Approach to the Use of Modern Tools for Database Visualisation & Image Processing
96-II	Eiblum, Paula	GEN	HARD COPY: Freedom of Information, Free Information, and Fishing for Information with GILS (Government Information Locator Service)
93-II	Elias, Arthur	GEN	An Overview of the Information Industry
94-I	Englebart, Douglas	GEN	Toward High Performance Organizations: A Strategic Role for Groupware
95-II	Farwell, Lawrence	GEN	Brain Fingerprinting
97-IV	Franco, Tanny	GEN	Do We Still Need Cataloging Standards?
98-G	Geanakos, Jim	GEN	Making Data Pay Dividends: Real-time News Meets Knowledge Management
92-I	Hlava, Marjorie	GEN	Selected Professional/Trade Associations in Information
93-I	Horowitz, Richard	GEN	Understanding Sources: The Real Challenge
97-IV	Hunter, Cheryl	GEN	HELP! The Impact of the Internet on Customer Service
98-G	Hunter, Mike	GEN	Creating Intelligence Automatically
99-P	*Information Today*	GEN	The Year the Information Industry Hit Bottom
97-IV	Jacobs, Paul	GEN	Software for Managing Information Overload
93-I	Jacso, Peter	GEN	The Linear File
92-II	Kahin, Brian	GEN	New Legal Paradigms for Multi-Media Information in Cyberspace
96-II	Kahin, Brian	GEN	What Is Intellectual Property?
92-II	Kees, Terry	GEN	Advanced Information Processing & Analysis
92-I	Kovaly, Kenneth	GEN	Unique Wire Service Provides Early Intelligence on World's Technical Developments
94-I	Liddy, Elizabeth	GEN	Information Retrieval via Natural Language Processing
97-IV	Mani, Inderjeet	GEN	Extending Access: A Study of Search Engine Technologies
97-IV	Maybury, Mark	GEN	Knowledge Management
98-G	Maybury, Mark	GEN	Tools for the Knowledge Analyst: An

			Information Superiority
92-II	McIntyre, Pamela	GEN	Competitive Advantage: The Power of Online Systems
98-E	Mulschlegel, Frans	GEN	Internet Search Tools and Search Techniques from a User Point of View
94-I	Ogdin, Carol Ann	GEN	Cyberglut and What To Do About It
92-II	Ogdin, Carol Anne	GEN	Words Are Not Enough
96-I	OSS Inc.	GEN	Open Source Intelligence Handbook
97-I	OSS Inc.	GEN	Open Source Intelligence Handbook
97-II	OSS Inc.	GEN	Open Source Intelligence Reader
97-III	OSS Inc.	GEN	Open Source Intelligence Strategy
93-II	Pedtke, Thomas	GEN	Putting Functionality into the Open Source Network
92-II	Pincus, Mike	GEN	Metamorph: Theoretical Background and Operational Functionality
98-E	Rathmell, Andrew	GEN	The Revolution in Space-Based Imagery
97-IV	Rodrigues, Ron	GEN	Targeted Decision Support from Commercial Online Services versus the Internet
92-II	Ruh, William	GEN	Multi-Media Open Source Exploitation: Report on an Internal Research & Development Project
92-I	Sacks, Risa	GEN	Using the Telephone as a Research Tool
92-II	Sibbet, Daniel	GEN	Commercial Remote Sensing: Open Source Imagery Intelligence
92-I	Steele, Robert D.	GEN	Book Report: Paul Strassmann's *Information PayOff: The Transformation of Work in the Electronic Age*
92-I	Steele, Robert D.	GEN	Information Concepts & Doctrine for the Future
94-I	Steele, Robert D.	GEN	DATA MINING: Don't Buy or Build Your Shovel Until You Know What You Are Digging Into
95-II	Steele, Robert D.	GEN	OSS '95 Executive Summary of Remarks by Congressman Larry Combest, Dr. Jeffrey Eisenach, and The Honorable William Colby
98-E	Steele, Robert D.	GEN	Recommended Approach to Creating an Open Source Capability
96-II	Stein, William	GEN	Mapping, Charting, and Geodetic Needs for Remote Sensing Data
99-G	Straub, John	GEN	Adding Value to Open Source Information in an Information Rich World
92-II	Thompson, Paul	GEN	Ranked Retrieval and Extraction of Open

			Source Intelligence
92-II	Tow, Rob	GEN	Painting the Future: Some Remarks Following the INTERVAL RESEARCH Brainstorming Session of 7 May 1992
94-II	Vajta-Williams, Tish	GEN	Commercial Imagery and You
92-II	Whitney-Smith, Elin	GEN	Information Revolution and the End of History
97-IV	Wiegand, Jack	GEN	Reducing Risk in Forecasting Through Practical Sources and Methods
97-IV	Wilson, Stephen	GEN	CORE Software Technology: Business Plan Summary
92-II	Wood, Norman	GEN	Pre-Reception Remarks
98-G	Yankeelov, Dawn	GEN	High-Ticket Research and the Human Hire: Pushing the Assets of Time and Talent
97-IV	Bauldock, Barbara	GOV	Overview of the CENDI Information Exchange Process
97-IV	Carroll, Bonnie	GOV	The CENDI Information Managers' Group
92-II	Cotter, Gladys	GOV	National Aeronautics and Space Administration Requirements
98-G	Dearth, Douglas	GOV	The Government and the Information Marketplace
97-IV	Hodge, Gail	GOV	Separate Agencies, Common Challenges: The CENDI Approach to Information Awareness Issues
98-G	Hughes, Kenneth	GOV	FBIS 1995-1998: Transition and Transformation
92-II	Johnson, Don	GOV	National Technical Information Service Requirements
97-IV	Johnson, Donald	GOV	The National Technical Information Service
92-II	Molholm, Kurt	GOV	The CENDI Program: How Some Federal Managers Have Organized to Improve Science & Technology Information Use
97-IV	Molholm, Kurt	GOV	Building a Virtual Knowledge Warehouse
92-II	Mortimer, Louis	GOV	Federal Research Division Requirements & Capabilities
97-IV	Pedtke, Thomas	GOV	Overview of Existing Scientific & Technical Capabilities
92-II	Pedtke, Thomas	GOV	Open Source Activities, Foreign Aerospace Science & Technology Center
97-IV	Robideau, Rob	GOV	Technical Information Management Program in the Office of Scientific and Technical

			Information (DOE)
92-II	Tenney, Glenn	GOV	Government Information Wants to be Free
99-E	Baeumlin, Yves	LEA	Espionage versus Business Intelligence: Shades of Gray
92-I	Bodansky, Yossef	LEA	The GOP Terrorism Task Force: Research Techniques & Philosophy
95-II	Campen, Tim	LEA	Information Collection and Analysis at the National Drug Intelligence Center
96-II	Campen, Tim	LEA	Open Source Collection and Processing in Support of Law Enforcement Operations Against Strategic Drug Organizations
96-II	Cascallar, Marijke	LEA	Foreign Language Operational and Training Issues in Law Enforcement
98-E	Cucuzza, Osvaldo	LEA	Globalization of Crime: Consequences and Risks
96-II	Dixon, Albert	LEA	Online Public Records and Criminal Investigations: Missing Links
99-E	Edwards, Steve	LEA	Open Source Intelligence at Scotland Yard
98-E	Fry, Alan	LEA	Open Sources and Law Enforcement— Learning Curves and Pain Barriers
98-G	Fry, Alan	LEA	Learning Curves and Pain Barriers in Using Open Sources to Fight Transnational Crime
95-II	Heibel, Robert	LEA	The Mercyhurst College Research/Intelligence Analyst Program in Support of Law Enforcement
92-II	Holden-Rhodes, James	LEA	Devining Secrets: Open Source Intelligence in the War on Drugs
99-E	IALEIA	LEA	Intelligence-Led Policing (Eight Articles)
96-II	Krattenmaker, Jeff	LEA	LEXMAP Demonstration and Discussion
99-E	Lejeune, Philippe	LEA	Open Source Intelligence: The Interpol Experience
96-II	Lodge, Scott	LEA	OSINT Measures Against Financial Crime Targets
95-II	Oehler, Gordon	LEA	Intelligence Support to Transnational and Domestic Law Enforcement with Respect to Counter-Proliferation
99-E	OSS Inc.	LEA	Listing of Transnational Crime-Related Internet Sites
97-IV	Peterson, Marilyn	LEA	Obstacles and Emerging Solutions in Using Open Sources Against Transnational Crime
98-E	Rodriguez, Ruben Jr.	LEA	The Internet and Missing Children: Video Summary

96-II	Roger, Paul	LEA	Open Source Strategies for Law Enforcement
95-II	Schneider, Stephen	LEA	The Criminal Intelligence Function
95-II	Schnittker, Lori	LEA	Use of Open Sources in the Criminal Intelligence Program of the Royal Canadian Mounted Police
99-E	Schnittker, Lori	LEA	The Royal Canadian Mounted Police Open Source Analysis Unit
95-II	Smith, Ivian	LEA	Open Source Intelligence Support to Transnational and Domestic Law Enforcement
99-G	Storbeck, Jurgen	LEA	Open Source Intelligence: A Foundation for Regional Cooperation in Fighting Crime and Establishing a Regional Intelligence Community
99-P	Barrows, Walt	MIL	Information Sharing in Humanitarian Disasters (the DIA Perspective)
99-P	Beavers, Garry	MIL	Operationalizing Information Operations in Bosnia-Herzegovina
96-II	Bermudez, Joseph	MIL	OSINT and the North Korean Chemical Program
99-G	Bernstein, Adam	MIL	Keeping an Eye on the Islands: Remote Monitoring in the South China Seas
98-G	Bjore, Mats	MIL	Open Sources—Military Lessons Learned
95-II	Bjore, Mats	MIL	Six Years of Open Source Information: Swedish Military Lessons Learned
99-P	Boyer, Nate	MIL	High Resolution Commercial Imagery
94-I	Brooks, Randy	MIL	Split-Based Intelligence Operations During Desert Storm: A Glimpse of the Future Digital Army
97-IV	Clark, James	MIL	EAGLE VISION: National Eagle, Joint Eagle (C-130 Transportable Ground Link for Receiving Both Commercial and National Imagery in Real and Near Real Time)
92-II	Clift, Dennis	MIL	Military Open Source Requirements, Capabilities, and Contracting Directions
99-P	Connors, Sean	MIL	Joint Vision 2010 Initiative: Virtual Information Center
95-II	Dandar, Ed	MIL	Army Intelligence Strategy for the 21st Century
99-P	Dearth, Douglas	MIL	Peacekeeping in the Information Age
94-II	Fuchs, Peter	MIL	Information Handling in Humanitarian Actions within Armed Conflicts: The International Committee of the Red Cross Approach
99-E	Fuchs, Peter	MIL	Handling Information in Humanitarian

			Operations within Armed Conflict: The International Committee of the Red Cross Approach
95-II	Garfield, Andrew	MIL	The UK MOD OSIF Centre
98-G	Glabus, Edmund	MIL	Metaphors and Modern Threats: Biological, Computer, and Cognitive Viruses
97-IV	Gupta, Vipin	MIL	Open Sources and Indian Nuclear Testing: A Case Study
93-II	Hall, Robert	MIL	Jane's Approach to the New Threat Environment
92-II	Hutchinson, Robert	MIL	RUMOR OF WAR: An Information Vendor's View of the Role of Open Source Data in an Unstable World
96-II	Hutchinson, Robert	MIL	The Secret Parts of Fortune: The Role of Confidential Sources in Open Source Intelligence
99-P	Lee, Kent	MIL	New Developments in Access to Russian Military Mapping
99-P	Lee, Kent	MIL	Summary of Available Geospatial Information on Iran
99-P	Lee, Kent	MIL	Letter to HPSCI on Commercial Mapping Technologies
99-E	Lepingwell, John	MIL	Center for Proliferation Studies Activities with Open Source Collection
98-G	Metz, Steven	MIL	Transnational Enemies
98-E	Molander, Peter	MIL	Open Sources and Methods for the Military
94-II	Munro, Neil	MIL	INFORMATION WARFARE: Snake Eaters Meet Net Heads
95-II	Nanz, Ted	MIL	Commercial Imagery and Military Requirements
96-II	Nanz, Ted	MIL	Remarks on Commercial Imagery Applications for the Military
97-IV	Necoba, Barbara	MIL	The Marine Corps Approach to Open Source Intelligence
97-IV	Oehler, Gordon	MIL	The Acquisition of Technology Relating to Weapons of Mass Destruction and Advanced Conventional Munitions
94-I	Pedtke, Thomas R.	MIL	The National Air Intelligence Center and the Intelligence Community Open Source Architecture
92-I	Periscope	MIL	Commercial Open Source Provides Multi-Media Periscope for Military Analysts

95-I	Peters, Ralph	MIL	After the Revolution
92-I	Petersen, John L.	MIL	Staying in the National Security Business: New Roles for the U.S. Military
95-II	Ricardelli, Richard	MIL	OSINT and Military Operations in Haiti
99-E	Sanz, Timothy	MIL	Nuclear Terrorism Bibliography
96-II	Smith, Doug	MIL	Defense Mapping Agency and the Commercial Sector
99-P	Smith, Hugh	MIL	Intelligence and UN Peacekeeping
99-P	Sovereign, Michael	MIL	Information Superiority for the Lower End of the Spectrum
92-I	Steele, Robert D.	MIL	Defense Intelligence Productivity in the 1990's: Executive Outline
92-I	Steele, Robert D.	MIL	Open Source Intelligence Clarifies Global Threats
95-I	Steele, Robert D.	MIL	Open Source Intelligence: What Is It? Why Is It Important to the Military?
96-II	Steele, Robert D.	MIL	Information Peacekeeping: Open Source Intelligence as a Policy Option and Operational Alternative
98-G	Steele, Robert D.	MIL	Open Source Intelligence: Private Sector Capabilities to Support DoD Policy, Acquisitions, and Operations
98-G	Steele, Robert D.	MIL	Takedown: The Asymmetric Threat to the Nation
98-G	Steele, Robert D.	MIL	Takedown: Targets, Tools, & Technocracy
98-G	Steele, Robert D.	MIL	Information Peacekeeping: The Purest Form of War
99-G	Steele, Robert D.	MIL	Post-Mortem on Bombing the Chinese Embassy: Budget
99-P	Steele, Robert D.	MIL	Setting the Stage for Information-Sharing in the 21st Century: Three Issues of Common Concern to DoD and the Rest of the World
99-P	Steele, Robert D.	MIL	Intelligence Lessons Learned from Recent Expeditionary Operations
99-P	Steele, Robert D.	MIL	Intelligence Preparation of the Battlefield: The Marine Corps Viewpoint
92-II	Strassmann, Paul	MIL	Forcing Innovation, Cutting Costs, and Increasing Defense Productivity: Open Source Solutions
97-IV	Tyrrell, Patrick	MIL	Proposal for the Development of an Open Source Programme to Support NATO and Partners for Peace Activities

98-E	Tyrrell, Patrick	MIL	Open Source Intelligence—The Challenge for NATO
99-P	U.S. Air Force	MIL	Background Paper on EAGLE Vision
99-P	U.S. Air Force	MIL	Frontier Missions: Peacespace Dominance (Air Force 2025)
99-E	Various	MIL	Defending the United States Against Weapons of Mass Destruction
97-IV	Vesely, David	MIL	Striking a Balance: One Warfighter's View of the Need to Balance National, Commercial, and Tactical Source Acquisition
94-II	Whitney-Smith, Elin	MIL	Refugees as an Offensive Weapon, Information as a Defensive Option
92-II	Williams, James	MIL	Utilization of Open Source Information to Create Intelligence in a Commercial Environment
99-P	Wirtz, James	MIL	Bridging the Gap: Open Source Intelligence and the Tet Offensive
93-I	Ackerman, Robert	NAT	Intelligence Aim Veers to Amassing Overt Information
99-G	Allen, Charlie	NAT	The Role of Open Sources as the Foundation for All-Source Collection Strategies
97-IV	Andrew, Christopher	NAT	Presidents, Secret Intelligence, and Open Sources: Past Experience and Future Priorities
99-P	Anonymous	NAT	Global Disaster Information Network (GDIN)
99-P	Anonymous	NAT	Background on Meeting of International Disaster Relief Experts
98-G	Arnold, Stephen	NAT	The Changing Intelligence Environment
92-II	Barlow, John Perry	NAT	The Electronic Frontier Foundation and the National Public Network
93-II	Baumard, Philippe	NAT	Learned Nations: Seeking National Competitive Advantages Through Knowledge Strategies
93-I	Baumard, Philippe	NAT	A Think-Tank to Anticipate and Regulate Economic Intelligence Issues
95-II	Bender, David	NAT	The Information Highway: Will Librarians be Left by the Side of the Road?
93-I	Bonthous, Jean-Marie	NAT	Culture: The Missing Intelligence Variable
97-IV	Botbol, Maurice	NAT	The Open Source Revolution: Early Failures and Future Prospects
98-E	Cailloux, Danielle	NAT	Belgian Observations on Intelligence Oversight and Strategic Opportunities for Change

93-I	Castagna, Michael	NAT	Book Report: Robert Reich, *The Work of Nations: Preparing Ourselves for 21st Century Capitalism*
93-II	Chantler, Nicholas	NAT	To Demonstrate the Need for Australia to Develop a Strategic Policy on Open Source Information (OSI) Which Capitalizes on Emerging Trends
94-II	Chantler, Nicholas	NAT	Indicators of Change and the Need for an Australian Open Source Information Strategy
93-I	Civille, Richard	NAT	The Spirit of Access: Equity, NREN, and the NII
96-II	Clerc, Philippe	NAT	Economic and Financial Intelligence: The French Model
99-P	Coile, Russell	NAT	Preparing for and Coping with Local Disasters: An Information Overlay
95-I	COSPO	NAT	Community Open Source Intelligence Program Strategic Plan
99-P	CSIS (Canada)	NAT	Exploiting the New High Resolution Imagery: Darwinian Imperatives
99-P	CSIS (Canada)	NAT	Islamic Unrest in Xinjang Uighur Autonomous Region
99-P	Dearth, Douglas	NAT	Intelligence in the 21st Century: Re-focusing Intelligence to Shape the Strategic Environment
93-I	Dedijer, Stevan	NAT	The State of the National Intelligence and Security Community in Sweden
92-II	Donahue, Arnold	NAT	There Is Plenty of Money for Open Source Intelligence
98-E	Donahue, Arnold	NAT	Balancing Spending Between Spies, Satellites, and Schoolboys
93-II	Etheredge, Lloyd	NAT	National Knowledge Strategies, the Intelligence Community, and the Library of the Future
95-II	Farmer, Michael	NAT	The Department of Energy Open Source Intelligence Program
93-I	Fedanzo, Anthony	NAT	A Genetic View of National Intelligence
93-I	Fedanzo, Anthony	NAT	Implementing Open Source Intelligence Through a Distributed Contribution Model
97-IV	Felsher, Murray	NAT	Viability and Survivability of U.S. Remote Sensing Industry as a Function of U.S. Policy
93-II	Fraumann, Roger	NAT	2025, Fisher & Paykel, and Geelong District Water Board... What Do They Have in

			Common? – or "Business is War"
93-I	Greenwald, Jeff	NAT	The Unrepresented Nations and Peoples Organizations: Diplomacy's Cutting Edge
97-IV	Haakon, Chris	NAT	Commercial Imagery Options and Trade-Offs
93-II	Halberstadt, Mitchell	NAT	High Tech and Low Life: Power and Communications in the Information Age
99-E	Heidenrich, John	NAT	Early Warning of Genocide: The Utility of Open Sources and Methods
97-IV	Herman, Michael	NAT	Has the Community a Future?
93-II	Hughes, David	NAT	Communication to Mike Nelson on Estimated Costs of Networking Nation's Public Schools
99-G	Hulst, S. J. van	NAT	Open Source Intelligence: the *Lingua Franca* for Regional Intelligence Co-Ordination and Information Sharing
93-II	Ishii, Hiroshi	NAT	Cross-Cultural Communication and Computer-Supported Cooperative Work
94-II	Kahin, Brian	NAT	Establishing New Laws for Government and Business Operations in Cyberspace
96-II	Kalil, Thomas	NAT	National Economic Council and Cyberspace
93-I	Karraker, Roger	NAT	Highways of the Mind
94-II	Kelly, Maureen	NAT	Association of Information and Dissemination Centers Contributions to National Competitiveness
97-IV	Kerr, Richard	NAT	Remarks on the Intelligence Community Today and "Well, What Should We Do?"
92-II	Keyworth, Jay	NAT	Changing Definitions: Technology, Intelligence, Security, and National Competitiveness
93-II	Kumon, Shumpei	NAT	From Wealth to Wisdom: A Change in the Social Paradigm
93-II	Kumon, Shumpei	NAT	Toward Co-Emulation: Japan and the United States in the Information Age
99-G	Lee, Kent	NAT	New Developments in Access to Russian Military Mapping
93-II	Leijonhielm, Jan	NAT	The Critical Role of Open Sources and Products in Economic Intelligence Cooperation Between Government and Industry: A Swedish Example
93-I	Love, James	NAT	Comments on the Clinton Administration "Vision" Statement for the National Information Infrastructure
96-II	Lucas, Jim	NAT	The Community Open Source Information

			System
99-G	Madison, Earl III	NAT	The Future of All-Source Analysis: What Analysis, Who Does the Analysis?
93-I	Magee, Charlie	NAT	The Age of Imagination: Coming Soon to a Civilization Near You
95-II	Markowitz, Joseph	NAT	The Community Open Source Intelligence Program
92-II	McConnell, Bruce	NAT	Planned Revisions to A-130 Regulation on Information
93-II	McGill, Mert	NAT	The Private Sector Role in Collecting, Processing, and Disseminating Intelligence
97-IV	Meyer-Kress, Gottfried	NAT	The World Brain
93-I	Monaco, Sal	NAT	Economic Intelligence and Open Source Information
98-G	Mti, Linda (Mr.)	NAT	Open Source Intelligence, The African Renaissance, and Sustainable Development: The Emerging National Intelligence Model for South Africa
99-E	OSS Inc.	NAT	Listing of Genocide-Related Sites
95-I	*OSS NOTICES*	NAT	Extract: Intelligence Building Blocks
95-I	*OSS NOTICES*	NAT	Extract: Mapping, Charting, & Geodesy Deficiencies
95-I	*OSS NOTICES*	NAT	Extract: House Appropriations Committee Survey
95-I	*OSS NOTICES*	NAT	Extract: Lip Service, Great Pretenders, and OSINT
95-I	*OSS NOTICES*	NAT	Extract: Commercial Imagery
97-IV	Ostle, Robin	NAT	Special Intelligence: A Case Study of Islam and the West
99-E	Ostle, Robin	NAT	Special Intelligence: Islam and the West as Seen Through the Eyes of History
95-II	Peters, Ralph	NAT	Inadequate Answers: Bureaucracy, Wealth, and the Mediocrity of U.S. Intelligence Analysis
93-I	Petersen, John	NAT	A New Twenty-First Century Role for the Intelligence Community
92-II	Rheingold, Howard	NAT	Tools for Thinking & Virtual Reality: How Our Information Eco-System is Changing
92-II	Riddle, Niles	NAT	Foreign Broadcast Information Service Requirements & Capabilities
99-P	Roeder, Larry	NAT	Peace Wing: An Experiment Merging Politics and Technology

95-II	Rolington, Alfred	NAT	A Theory of Open Source Information
98-E	Schlickmann, Theo	NAT	Ensuring Trust and Security in Electronic Communications
93-II	Schmidt, Olivier	NAT	A History of Failure, a Future of Opportunity: Reinventions and Déjà vu
94-I	Schmidt, Olivier	NAT	The State of Intelligence
92-I	Shepard, Andrew	NAT	Intelligence Analysis in the Year 2002: A Concept of Operations
93-II	Shima, Keiji	NAT	Overview of Japanese Media & Information Systems
93-I	Splitt, Frank G.	NAT	The U.S. Information Industry: Creating the 21st Century
92-I	Steele, Robert D.	NAT	Applying the "New Paradigm: How to Avoid Strategic Intelligence Failures in the Future
92-I	Steele, Robert D.	NAT	E3I: Ethics, Ecology, Evolution, and Intelligence
92-I	Steele, Robert D.	NAT	Intelligence in the 1990's: Recasting National Security in a Changing World
92-II	Steele, Robert D.	NAT	Consumer Needs, Data Changes, Technology Changes, Organizational Changes: Future Visions & Issues
93-I	Steele, Robert D.	NAT	NAT A Critical Evaluation of U.S. National Intelligence Capabilities
93-I	Steele, Robert D.	NAT	ACCESS: Theory and Practice of Intelligence in the Age of Information
93-I	Steele, Robert D.	NAT	Notes on Information Peacekeeping
93-I	Steele, Robert D.	NAT	Talking Points for the Director of Central Intelligence
93-I	Steele, Robert D.	NAT	Testimony and Comments on Executive Order 12356, "National Security Information"
93-I	Steele, Robert D.	NAT	The Intelligence Community as a New Market
93-I	Steele, Robert D.	NAT	The Role of Gray Literature and Non-Traditional Agencies in Informing Policy Makers and Improving National Competitiveness
93-II	Steele, Robert D.	NAT	Reinventing Intelligence: The Advantages of Open Source Intelligence (OSINT)
94-I	Steele, Robert D.	NAT	Talking Points for the Public Interest Summit
94-I	Steele, Robert D.	NAT	National Security Act of 1994
94-I	Steele, Robert D.	NAT	TEAM O: Expansion of Aspin/Brown Commission Questions
94-I	Steele, Robert D.	NAT	Private Enterprise Intelligence: Its Potential

			Contribution to National Security
95-I	Steele, Robert D.	NAT	National Intelligence: The Community Tomorrow?
95-II	Steele, Robert D.	NAT	Creating a Smart Nation
97-IV	Steele, Robert D.	NAT	OSS '97: Opening Presentation
98-E	Steele, Robert D.	NAT	Strategic Issues in National and Regional Intelligence and Electronic Security
99-E	Steele, Robert D.	NAT	Reinventing Intelligence: The Vision and the Strategy
99-E	Steele, Robert D.	NAT	Intelligence Strategique aux Estas-Unis: Mythe ou Realite?
95-II	Straub, Chris	NAT	The Congressional Perspective on OSINT
99-P	Various	NAT	Proposal for a Coordinated Flexible Approach to Increase the Amount and Quality of Essential Information Posted on ReliefWeb
93-II	Wallner, Paul	NAT	Overview of the U.S. Intelligence Community's Open Source Requirements and Capabilities
99-P	White House	NAT	The Clinton Administration's Policy on Managing Complex Contingency Operations: Presidential Decision Directive 56 (May 1997)
93-I	Whitney-Smith, Elin	NAT	Analysis for Information Revolutions: Dynamic Analogy Analysis
93-I	Whitney-Smith, Elin	NAT	Toward an Epistemology of Peace
99-P	Wing, Ian	NAT	Optimising Open Source Information Sharing in Australia: Report and Policy Prescription
93-II	Wood, Norman	NAT	The Intelligence Community and the Open Source Information Challenge
99-P	Xiao, Xing	NAT	Chinese Red Cross Information Practices in Relation to National Disasters
99-P	Xiao, Xing	NAT	Presentation on Chinese Red Cross Information Practices
97-IV	Alger, John	SEC	Building the Knowledge Base of Emerging Information Warfare Technologies
96-II	Ayers, Robert	SEC	Vulnerabilities and Opportunities in the Open Source System: Protecting the Civilian Infrastructure as an Aspect of Information Warfare
94-I	Devost, Matthew	SEC	The Digital Threat: United States National Security and Computers
97-IV	Fialka, John	SEC	War by Other Means: Economic Espionage in America

98-E	Horowitz, Richard	SEC	Economic Espionage and Open Sources: Legal and Security Implications for Planning
96-II	Keuhl, Daniel	SEC	National Defense, Information Warfare Threat, and Strategy
96-II	O'Malley, Edward	SEC	Countering the Business Intelligence Threat
98-E	Rathmell, Andrew	SEC	Assessing the Information Warfare Threat from Sub-State Groups
93-II	Schwartau, Winn	SEC	Computer Warfare, Computer Terrorism
97-IV	Schwartau, Winn	SEC	Information Warfare: The Weapons of Intelligence and Conflict in the Information Age
94-I	Steele, Robert D.	SEC	National and Corporate Security in the Age of Information
94-I	Steele, Robert D.	SEC	Testimony to the National Information Infrastructure Security Committee
97-IV	Tenney, Glenn	SEC	Cyber-Law and Cyber-Theft: Spamming Methods and Costs
97-IV	Tsuruoka, Doug	SEC	Asian Perceptions of What Is and Is Not Legal in Economic Intelligence Collection
96-II	Winkler, Ira	SEC	Electronic Industrial Espionage: Defining Ground Zero

Personal Publications

"Intelligence and Counterintelligence: Memorandum for the President", forthcoming in *International Journal of Intelligence and Counterintelligence* (Winter 2000), working draft at www.oss.net/Papers/white/PresidentialIntelligence.doc

"Muddy Waters, Rusting Buckets: A Skeptical Assessment of U.S. Naval Effectiveness in the 21st Century", accepted for publication by the U.S. Naval Institute *Proceedings*, withdrawn and published at www.defensedaily.com/reports/gonavy.htm (17 November 1999)

"Presidential Leadership and National Security Policymaking", funded paper for the 10th Army Strategy Conference, April 1999, published at www.defensedaily.com/reports/securpolicy1099.htm (17 Nov 1999)

"Relevant Information and All-Source Analysis: The Emerging Revolution" in *American Intelligence Journal* (Spring 1999), available at www.oss.net/Papers/white/AIJ-RelInfo.doc

"First to Fight but Not Fighting Smart: A Skeptical Assessment of U.S. Marine Corps Effectiveness in the 21st Century", *Marine Corps Gazette* (May 1999), available at www.oss.net/Papers/white/EE21.doc

"TOUGH LOVE: An External Perspective on the Future of the IC", presented to the members of the Security Affairs Support Association at their Fall 1999 Top Secret/SI/TK session, 16 September 1999. Published at www.oss.net/Papers/white/TOUGHLOVE.ppt

"Relevant Information: A New Approach to Collecting, Sharing and Analyzing Information", at www.defensedaily.com/reports/isdoctrine.htm

"Virtual Intelligence: Conflict Avoidance and Resolution through Information Peacekeeping", *Journal of Conflict Resolution* (Spring 1999), author's draft at www.oss.net/VIRTUAL

"TAKEDOWN: The Asymmetric Threat to the Nation," *Defense Daily Network* at www.defensedaily.com/reports/takedown.htm. and JFQ

"INFORMATION PEACEKEEPING: The Purest Form of War," in Douglas Dearth and Alan Campen, *CYBERWAR: Myths, Mysteries, and Realities* (AFCEA Press, June 1998) at www.oss.net/InfoPeace

"TAKEDOWN: Targets, Tools, & Technocracy," funded research and presentation for the Ninth Annual Strategy Conference, U.S. Army War College, "Challenging the United States Symmetrically and Asymmetrically: Can America be Defeated," 31 March-2 April 1998 at www.oss.net/TAKEDOWN

"Open Source Intelligence: Private Sector Capabilities to Support DoD Policy, Acquisitions, and Operations," *Defense Daily Network* (Special Reports, March 1998), at www.defensedaily.com/reports/osint.htm

"Concept for Creating a 'Bare Bones' Capability for Open Source Support to Defense Intelligence Analysts," funded paper for the Defense Intelligence Agency, subsequently published in *Open Source Intelligence: Strategy* (OSS Inc., September 1997), at http://www.oss.net/DIAReport

"Eyes Wide Shut," *WIRED Magazine* (August 1997)

INTERVIEW "Intelligence Strategique aux Etats-Unis: Mythe ou Realite?" *Revue Francaise de Geoeconomie* (Spring 1997)

Intelligence and Counterintelligence: Proposed Program for the 21ˢᵗ Century (OSS White Paper, April 1997), at http://www.oss.net/OSS21

"Open Sources and Cyberlaw," *Fringeware* (#11, April 1997)

"The Military Perspective on Information Warfare: Apocalypse Now," *Enjeux Atlantiques* (#14, February 1997)

"Creating a Smart Nation: Information Strategy, Virtual Intelligence, and Information Warfare," in Alan D. Campen, Douglas H. Dearth, and R. Thomas Goodden (contributing editors), *CYBERWAR: Security, Strategy, and Conflict in the Information Age* (AFCEA, 1996)

"Creating a Smart Nation: Strategy, Policy, Intelligence, and Information," *Government Information Quarterly* (Summer 1996)

"Reinventing Intelligence: The Vision and the Strategy," *International Defense & Technologies* (December 1995), bilingual in French and English

"Private Enterprise Intelligence: Its Potential Contribution to National Security," paper presented to the Canadian Intelligence Community Conference on "Intelligence Analysis and Assessment," 29 October 1994. Reprinted in *Intelligence and National Security* (Special Issue, October 1995), and also in a book by the same name, 1996

"Reinventing Intelligence: Holy Grail or Mission Impossible?" *International Journal of Intelligence and Counterintelligence* (Summer 1994)

"ACCESS: The Theory and Practice of Competitor Intelligence," Keynote Speech to Chief Executive Officers and strategic planners at the 1994 Annual Conference of the Association for Global Strategic Information, Heidelberg, 14 June 1994, reprinted in *Journal of the Association for Global Strategic Information* (July 1994)

"Corporate Role in National Competitiveness: Smart People + Good Tools + Information = Profit", *Proceedings*, Society of Photo-Optical Engineers (Spring 1994)

"A Critical Evaluation of U.S. National Intelligence Capabilities," *International Journal of Intelligence and Counterintelligence* (Summer 1993)

"Information Concepts & Doctrine for the Future" (Personal Memorandum for the Deputy Assistant Secretary of Defense for Intelligence, 1 December 1992)

"E3I: Ethics, Ecology, Evolution, and Intelligence: An Alternative Paradigm for National Intelligence," *Whole Earth Review* (Fall 1992)

"Intelligence Lessons Learned from Recent Expeditionary Operations" (C4I Department, Headquarters, U.S. Marine Corps, 3 August 1992)

"Intelligence Preparation of the Battlefield: The Marine Corps Viewpoint" (C4I Department, Headquarters, U.S. Marine Corps, 10 July 1992)

"C4I: The New Linchpin," *Proceedings* (U.S. Naval Institute, July 1992)

"Corporate Information Management and Future War—Actionable Considerations" (Memorandum for the Director of Defense Information, 14 March 1992)

"National Intelligence and the American Enterprise: Exploring the Possibilities" (Working paper for Intelligence Policy Seminar, Harvard, 14 December 1991)

"Applying the 'New Paradigm': How to Avoid Strategic Intelligence Failures in the Future," *American Intelligence Journal* (Autumn 1991)

"Defense Intelligence Productivity in the 1990's: Executive Outline" (Official contribution to Assistant Secretary of Defense for C3I Working Group on Intelligence Restructuring, 18 May 1991)

"Intelligence in the 1990's: Recasting National Security in a Changing World," *American Intelligence Journal* (Summer/Fall 1990)

"Intelligence Support to Expeditionary Planners," *Marine Corps Gazette* (September 1991)

Abbreviations

ADCI	Assistant Director of Central Intelligence
ADCI	Assistant Director of *Classified* Intelligence
API	Application Program Interfaces
B	Billion (dollars)
C3I	Command, control, communications, and intelligence
C4I	Command, control, communications, computers, intelligence
CATALYST	Computer Aided Tools for the Analysis of S&T
CENDI	Commerce, Energy, NASA, Defense, Interior
CEO	Chief Executive Officer
CEOS	Center for the Exploitation of Open Sources
CI	Competitive Intelligence (business community)
CI	Counterintelligence (government)
CIA	Central Intelligence Agency
CIM	Corporate Information Management
CINC	Commander-in-Chief (of a military theater of operations)
CINCSOC	Commander-in-Chief U.S. Special Operations Command
CIO	Chief Information Officer
CMS	Community Management Staff
CNN	Cable News Network
COSPO	Community Open Source Program Office (largely defunct)
COTR	Contracting Officer's Technical Representative
COTS	Commercial Off-the-Shelf Software
CRS	Congressional Research Service
CSA	Clandestine Service Agency
DA	Directorate of Administration (CIA)
DARO	Defense Advanced Reconnaissance Office (defunct)
DARPA	Defense Advanced Research Projects Agency
DAS	Defense Attaché Service
DCI	Director of Central Intelligence
DCI	Director of *Classified* Intelligence
DEA	Drug Enforcement Administration
DGIS	Defense Gateway Information System
DGNI	Director-General of National Intelligence

DI	Directorate of Intelligence (CIA)
DIA	Defense Intelligence Agency
DMA	Defense Mapping Agency (absorbed into NIMA)
DMP	Digital Marshall Plan
DNI	Director of National Intelligence
DO	Directorate of Operations (CIA)
DoD	Department of Defense
DOE	Department of Energy
DS&T	Directorate of Science & Technology (CIA)
DTIC	Defense Technical Information Center
E3i	Ethics, Ecology, Evolution, and intelligence
ECON CI	Economic Counterintelligence
FAC	Forward Analysis Center
FBI	Federal Bureau of Investigation
FBIS	Foreign Broadcast Information System
FCIE	Future Collaborative Information Environment (USACOM)
FFRDC	Federally-Funded Research & Development Center
FIRCAP	Foreign Intelligence Requirements & Capabilities Plan
FIRCAP	Foreign Intelligence Requirements & Capabilities Plan
FOIA	Freedom of Information Act
FRD	Federal Research Division (of the Library of Congress)
GDIN	Global Disaster Relief Network
GIC	Global Intelligence Council
GIM	Global Information Management
GIO	Global Intelligence Organization
GKF	Global Knowledge Foundation
GPS	Global Positioning System
GS	Global Strategy Staff
HIC	High Intensity Conflict
HPSCI	House Permanent Select Committee on Intelligence
HUMINT	Human Intelligence (generally clandestine)
I&W	Indications & Warning
IC	Intelligence Community (U.S.)
IC21	Intelligence Community in the 21st Century (HPSCI Study)
ICRC	International Committee of the Red Cross
IMINT	Imagery Intelligence
INR	Intelligence and Research Bureau (Department of State)

IO	Information Operations (DoD)
IO	International Organizations (international)
IT	Information Technology
IW	Information Warfare
JCS	Joint Chiefs of Staff
JMIP	Joint Military Intelligence Program
JPRS	Joint Publications Research Service (defunct)
LEA	Law Enforcement Agencies
LIC	Low Intensity Conflict
LLB	Bachelor of Laws
M	Million (dollars)
MASINT	Measurements & Signatures Intelligence
MCIA	Marine Corps Intelligence Activity
MPF	Maritime Pre-Positioned Force
MRC	Major Regional Conflict
NASA	National Aeronautics and Space Administration
NATO	North Atlantic Treaty Organization
NCD	National Collection Division
NEC	National Economic Council
NFAIS	National Federation of Abstracting and Indexing Services
NFIP	National Foreign Intelligence Program
NGO	Non-governmental Organizations
NI	National Intelligence Staff
NIA	National Intelligence Agency
NIC	National Intelligence Council
NIF	National Intelligence Forum
NIMA	National Imagery and Mapping Agency
NLM	National Library of Medicine
NP	National Policy Staff
NPIC	National Photographic Interpretation Center (NIMA)
NPR	National Performance Review
NR	National Research Staff
NRO	National Reconnaissance Office
NSA	National Security Agency
NSC	National Security Council
NTIS	National Technical Information Service
OBE	Order of the British Empire

OIA	Office of Imagery Analysis (NIA)
OIC2	Office for Intelligence Communications and Computing
OIPMB	Office for Intelligence Personnel, Management, and Budget
OIR	Office of Information Resources (CIA/DDI)
OIRD	Office for Intelligence Research & Development
OMA	Office of Measurements & Signatures Analysis (NIA)
OMB	Office of Management and Budget
OPSEC	Operational Security
OR	Operations Research
OSA	Office of Signals Analysis (NIA)
OSIF	Open Source Information
OSINT	Open Source Intelligence
OSPRI	Open Source Processing Research Initiative
OSS	Office of Open Sources (NIA)
OSS	Office of Strategic Services
OSS	OPEN SOURCE SOLUTIONS Inc.
OSWR	Office of Scientific & Weapons Research (CIA)
PDD	Presidential Decision Directive
PFIAB	President's Foreign Intelligence Advisory Board
PfP	Partners for Peace
PIAB	Public Intelligence Advisory Board
PIAC	President's Intelligence Advisory Council
PPBS	Planning, Programming, and Budgeting System
RN	Royal Navy
ROC	Required Operational Capability
ROI	Return on Investment
RSO	Regional Security Office (Department of State)
S&T	Science & Technology
SAP	Special Access Program
SCI	Sensitive Compartmented Information
SCIF	Sensitive Compartmented Information Facility
SDO	Support to Diplomatic Operations
SI/TK	Sensitive Information/TK Control
SIG	Senior Inter-Agency Group
SIGINT	Signals Intelligence
SIG-NC	Senior Inter-Agency Group—National Competitiveness

SIG-NS	Senior Inter-Agency Group—National Security
SMO	Support to Military Operations
SOLIC	Special Operations/Low Intensity Conflict
SSCI	Senate Select Committee on Intelligence
STAR	System Technical Assessment Report
TCA	Technical Collection Agency
TIARA	Tactical Intelligence and Related Activities
UN	United Nations
USACOM	U.S. Atlantic Command
USG	United States Government
USIA	United States Information Agency
USIP	United States Intelligence Program
USMC	United States Marine Corps
USN	United States Navy
USPACOM	U.S. Pacific Command
VIC	Virtual Information Center (USPACOM)

About the Author

Robert David Steele was born in New York in 1952. The son of a petroleum engineer, he spent most of his life in Latin America and Asia, including four years in Viet-Nam (1964-1967). Married to Kathy Lynette Steele, he is the father of Patrick James, Matthew Brian, and Sean Joseph. The family lives and votes in Virginia.

Steele, twice named to the *Microtimes* 100: Industry leaders and unsung heroes...who created the future, has been featured in the chapter on the "The Future of the Spy" in Alvin and Heidi Toffler's book, *War and Anti-War: Survival at the Dawn of the 21st Century*, among other publications, and was the first recipient of the "Sages of the Ages" intelligence award from *SOURCES eJournal*.

Steele has been a Marine Corps infantry officer serving in a variety of command & staff positions, a military intelligence officer with responsibility for the tactical exploitation of national capabilities, and the senior civilian responsible for creating and managing the USMC Intelligence Center, our Nation's newest intelligence production facility. He has also been a spy, serving three-back-to-back tours as a clandestine case officer, one of them in a combat environment. Unusually for a case officer, he has served in three of the four Directorates of the Central Intelligence Agency, with Washington-based roles in determining future intelligence collection requirements and capabilities; the application of advanced information technology to global operations; and global counterintelligence operations against a denied area country.

Steele is a graduate of Muhlenberg College in Allentown, Pennsylvania, where he earned an AB in Political Science with a thesis on multinational corporations and home-host country issues pertaining to capital and technology transfers. He earned his first graduate degree, a Masters in International Politics, from Lehigh University, with a thesis on predicting revolution; and his second graduate degree, a Masters in Public Administration, from the University of Oklahoma, with a thesis on strategic and tactical information management for national security. He is a distinguished graduate of the Naval War College, and completed the Harvard Executive Seminar in Intelligence Policy.

431

Index

435

451

461